Days of Hope

- ask Stan
  about Puttins
  thesis

Patricia Sullivan

Days of Hope

RACE AND DEMOCRACY IN THE NEW DEAL ERA

The
University
of North
Carolina
Press

Chapel Hill
and London

Manufactured in the
United States of America

The paper in this book
meets the guidelines for
permanence and durability
of the Committee on Pro-
duction Guidelines for
Book Longevity of the
Council on Library
Resources.

Library of Congress
Cataloging-in-Publication
Data
Sullivan, Patricia.
Days of hope: race and
democracy in the New Deal
era / Patricia
Sullivan.   p.   cm.
Includes bibliographical
references (p.   ) and index.
ISBN 0-8078-2260-4
(cloth: alk. paper).
ISBN 0-8078-4564-7
(pbk.: alk. paper)
1. Afro-Americans—
Southern States—Politics
and government.
2. Southern States—
Politics and government—
1865–1950. I. Title.
E185.61.S93   1996
975'.00496073—dc20
95-365   CIP

00 99 98 97 96
5 4 3 2 1

Publication of this volume was aided by a generous
grant from the Z. Smith Reynolds Foundation.

For my parents,
Thomas and Doris Sullivan,
and in memory of
Palmer Weber

Contents

Illustrations

Acknowledgments

When I first met Palmer Weber in the summer of 1978, our visit was a postscript of sorts. Several months earlier I had completed a graduate seminar paper on the 1948 southern campaign of Progressive Party presidential candidate Henry Wallace. I was curious to meet the man who had helped orchestrate Wallace's southern effort.

"Seminar paper!" he exclaimed. "Why, you're just getting started. You have a dissertation here. A book even." So our meeting began. Palmer spouted a litany of names, places, and events that had shaped the political landscape of the 1930s and 1940s for him and many of his contemporaries. Charlie Houston, Mary McLeod Bethune, Osceola McKaine, Cliff and Virginia Durr, Bob Weaver, Mojeska Simkins, A. T. Walden, Louis Burnham, Clark Foreman, Beanie Baldwin, Sidney Hillman . . . the Scottsboro case, efforts to gain the admission of black students to the University of Virginia, the poll tax fight, FEPC, wartime voter-registration drives. . . . Some of it was familiar, some was not. But Palmer's way of remembering gave an intriguing coherence to an ocean of seemingly random facts. He invited new questions and further investigation. My interest was sparked.

As I pursued my study of the New Deal era, Palmer became a mentor and more. We worked together to document the history of the early decades of the southern movement, particularly through oral history interviews. He introduced me to a wide circle of his friends and associates from organizing days in the South and in Washington, D.C. There were visits to southern places that had been sites of earlier struggles. And endless discussions about the workings of the democratic process in a society steeped in the politics of racial difference and inequality. The ideas that shaped this book grew from our collaborative pursuit.

Oral history interviews have been essential to the research and writing of the book. I am deeply grateful to all who have shared their recollections and insights; their names appear in the bibliography and throughout the text. As a result of these interviews, several people shared personal papers, introduced me to other sources, and helped in a variety of ways.

Virginia Durr has been an inexhaustible source of inspiration and information over the years, as has her dog-eared address book. Virginia engages the past as a drama of human triumph and tragedy, a story without end. Her steady stream of insights and questions, punctuated by a keen sense of the absurd, ensured that this project sustained its vitality. Her generous spirit and bountiful friendship are beyond compare.

Mairi Fraser Foreman has supported this project from its earliest inception and has contributed in countless ways to its successful completion. She provided me with full access to Clark Foreman's personal papers while sharing the splendor of the mountaintop home she and her late husband built in Adjuntas, Puerto Rico. Mairi also spent many hours answering my queries and offering her own recollections of the events and personalities described here.

Several long interviews with John H. McCray in Talladega, Alabama, deepened my understanding of southern politics during this period. McCray's personal history as a newspaper publisher, NAACP organizer, voting-rights activist, and cofounder of the Progressive Democratic Party embodies the political struggles of many of his contemporaries and invites further study. This work has also benefited from the support and encouragement of Robert C. Weaver, who generously shared his time, his library, and his vast store of experience and insight. Others who have been especially helpful include Dorothy Burnham, John Henry Faulk, Marge Frantz, Tex and Wicky Goldschmidt, Rob and Micky Hall, Dan and Rachael Powell, Arthur Raper, and Junius Scales.

I am deeply grateful to Tony Badger, Adam Fairclough, and John Simon. Each read drafts of the entire manuscript, provided detailed critiques, and offered suggestions about the book's organization. Dan Carter supported this work through its earliest stages as a dissertation topic. Ray Gavins shared insights from his own extensive work on southern black protest; his frequent reminders to "keep running and keep writing" became a mantra. Julian Bond, Reginald Butler, Kathleen Cleaver, Virginia Durr, Peter Lau, August Meier, Bob Moses, Richard Newman, Gail Shirley-Warren, and Robert Weaver have read parts of the manuscript in various forms, offered suggestions, and helped me work through some of the major themes.

Other friends and colleagues have helped in lots of different ways over the long haul. Special thanks to Donna Bohanan, Andrew Buni, Bill Elwood, Shelagh Foreman, Joanne Grant, Winston Lane, Anna Laszlo, Mel Leffler, Leon Litwack, Chuck McDew, Catherine Macklin, Waldo Martin, Ron and Patricia Rapaport, Mary Rose, George Sims, and Lara Smith.

Lewis Bateman expressed interest in this project when it was barely a gleam in my eye. His unflagging support and prodding over the years have been nothing short of remarkable. I am fortunate to be among the authors who have benefited from Lewis's exemplary talents as executive editor at the University of North Carolina Press. Moreover, he wins the John Henry

Faulk distinction of "foul-weather friend," one of those folks who can always be counted on.

Pamela Upton of the University of North Carolina Press guided the book through the final stages of preparation with good cheer and endless patience. Teddy Diggs copyedited the manuscript with care and skill.

Many librarians and archivists have provided assistance. I am grateful to all, especially Robert McCown and Earl Rogers at the University Libraries, University of Iowa; Herb Hartsook, Tom Johnson, Allen Stokes, and Elizabeth Vildebeck of the South Caroliniana Library, University of South Carolina; Linda Matthews of the Robert Woodruff Library, Emory University; and Lee Alexander, former archivist of the Trevor Arnett Library, Atlanta University.

A research grant from the Eleanor Roosevelt Institute and fellowships from the Carter G. Woodson Institute at the University of Virginia and the Virginia Foundation for the Humanities provided support for this project at various stages. I completed the book at the W. E. B. Du Bois Institute for Afro-American Research at Harvard University, with the generous support of the Institute and its director, Henry Louis Gates Jr.

Finally, I thank my family, especially my parents, Thomas and Doris Sullivan, and my grandparents, Michael and Catherine Sullivan and John and Johanna Archer. They nurtured my curiosity about the past, taught me about fairness and justice, and have helped in ways that are impossible to measure.

Days of Hope

Introduction

Shortly after James Agee's famous sojourn in rural Alabama, chronicled in
Let Us Now Praise Famous Men, Henry Wallace began his first journey
through the Deep South. The forty-eight-year-old secretary of agriculture
traveled by automobile over the back roads of the Mississippi Delta, over
"two thousand miles of tobacco road," according to the lone reporter who
accompanied Wallace on the two-week trip in the fall of 1936. Will Alexander, the newly named director of the Resettlement Administration, and
his assistant, C. B. Baldwin, completed the foursome.[1]

Wallace went south to observe the work of the Resettlement Administration, a New Deal program established earlier in the year to aid sharecroppers

and tenant farmers, landless tillers of the soil who made up half of the region's farmers. The trip quickly became a sobering introduction to life in the rural South. Wallace, a farmer, scientist, and avid student of agrarian life, often slipped off alone and visited with black and white sharecropper families in their homes. He found people living in "tumble down cabins," some with neither doors nor windows; sleeping on the floor, the sharecroppers used the only blankets they owned to cover newly picked tobacco. They lived on corn bread, fatback, and molasses; fresh garden foods composed less than 10 percent of the diet of those who worked the most productive land in the South. Pellagra, hookworm, and rickets, diseases resulting from dietary deficiencies, were common. Referring to Arthur Raper's newly published *Preface to Peasantry*, Wallace incredulously commented that to call them peasants "really offends the peasantry of Europe." Raper himself referred to the 8.5 million landless tenants as subpeasants. "Schooled in dependency," they had no property, no self-direction; their prospects did not match those of a feudal serf.[2]

The defeating culture of poverty that Wallace observed had deep southern roots. But the depression, which hastened the demise of the region's plantation economy, exposed its pervasive legacies. Federal fieldworkers and photographers, writers and reporters, "discovered" a South that had been beyond national consciousness or concern. During the 1920s, the South had been popularized by H. L. Mencken and others as a land of fundamentalism, night-riding, lynchings, and "hog-wallow politics." The social realism and political ferment of the depression decade challenged observers to look beneath the veneer of intellectual and cultural destitution and consider the human face of the region's poverty and its implications for the nation's economic recovery.

The sharecropper served as a metaphor for a region caught in a web of dependency and exploitation. Raper described the Black Belt as "the seed bed of the South's people and culture." A plantation economy, resting on a cheap and abundant labor supply, had endured into the twentieth century. Although the South experienced accelerated rates of industrial growth in the decades following the Civil War, the growth was static and adaptive and was not accompanied by rapid urbanization. The spread of tenancy in the late nineteenth and the early twentieth centuries created an elastic labor supply of unskilled workers suited to the growth of low-wage, labor-intensive industries, best epitomized by the textile industry. Whereas the idea of a "colonial economy" might describe the relationship between outside capital and southern industry in certain instances, it is not a sufficient explanation of the South's economic plight so evident in the 1930s. Regional factors, particularly the nature of the labor market, were equally significant in determining the South's economic development.[3]

The South's economic structure was buttressed by a political order established with the final triumph of conservative Democrats at the turn of the century. The codification of white supremacy and widespread disfranchisement secured a closed, one-party system dominated by Black Belt elites and New South entrepreneurs. Dedicated to minimalist government in the social welfare sphere, they were joined in their determination to maintain a dependent, poorly educated, and racially divided labor force. "After 1900 only external pressures could threaten the rule of conservative Democrats," observed one historian. An unquestioning commitment to states' rights prevailed among white southerners joined together by their allegiance to a caste system.[4]

The severity of the depression and its seeming intractability overwhelmed the South's long-held aversion to federal intervention. By 1932, southerners led the chorus of voices insisting on government action, and they were among Franklin D. Roosevelt's most enthusiastic supporters. New Deal programs were a transfusion for the South. The Agricultural Adjustment Act, which created the Agricultural Adjustment Administration (AAA), boosted the sagging fortunes of landowners and introduced rationality and planning to halt the spiraling plunge of prices.

As the primary recipients of federal dollars going to the South, southern landowners and their business associates controlled the administration of New Deal programs. Indeed, the success of the AAA's voluntary crop-reduction program depended on their cooperation. Thus, as many historians have pointed out, the New Deal bolstered the power of Black Belt planters, the bulwark of the solid, segregationist South. It is not surprising that during the first year of the Roosevelt administration, they were full of praise for the president. A field investigator from Washington, D.C., traveling through the Deep South in 1934, reported that prominent citizens hailed Roosevelt as the first president since the "War between the States" who made them feel "really a part of the United States."[5]

At the same time, New Deal programs and legislation stirred the stagnant economic and political relationships that had persisted in the South, unchanged and largely unchallenged, since the dawn of the century. Federal work relief and credit, along with the legalization of labor unions, implicitly threatened the culture of dependency that had secured an abundant, cheap labor supply. Early in 1934, a South Carolina peach grower complained that black women would not work in the fields so long as their husbands had jobs with the Civil Works Administration.[6] In Arkansas, sharecroppers organized the Southern Tenant Farmers Union (STFU) to demand federal enforcement of guarantees provided by the AAA. That same year, black citizens in Georgia and South Carolina made an organized effort to vote in the all-white Democratic primary election. Such developments, though isolated and sporadic, attracted the attention of a new generation of southerners, black and white, who had come of age during the depression and were attentive to the new possibilities created by the New Deal.

White southerners were among the young policymakers, lawyers, and social workers who flocked to Washington to, as one put it, "help right the wrongs that had befallen the country." They included Clark Foreman, the son of a prominent Atlanta family, who had served as director of the Georgia Commission of Interracial Cooperation; Aubrey Williams, a social worker from Birmingham, Alabama; C. B. Baldwin, a small businessman from Radford, Virginia; Clifford Durr, a lawyer and former Rhodes scholar from Birmingham; and Virginia Foster Durr, vice-president of the Birmingham Junior League, who had helped distribute relief in that city. The young New Dealers embraced Roosevelt's experimenting, forward-looking vision, which elevated the federal government to a leading role in securing the economic welfare of the nation. Viewing their region from a national perspective, southerners were particularly sensitive to its unique problems and to the critical role of government in advancing the South's economic and political modernization.

As an arena for redefining the role of government and politics in modern life, Washington became the focus of groups long on the margins of national politics—industrial workers, sharecroppers, and African Americans of all classes—who found sympathetic allies among the young recruits of the New Deal. Henry Wallace's trip south in 1936 was occasioned by the ability of the STFU and its supporters within the Agriculture Department to compel federal action on behalf of tenant farmers after landlords had denied them the benefits afforded by New Deal programs. The brutal repression of unionizing efforts among Arkansas tenant farmers won national attention. Largely as a result of the publicity surrounding the STFU, the Resettlement Administration was established, and Senator Robert La Follette convened a congressional committee to investigate antilabor violence in the South and other parts of the nation.

By the end of 1936, seasoned southern Democrats feared that the New Deal was reeling beyond their control. The industrial unionism of the Congress of Industrial Organizations (CIO), established in 1935 with the support of New Deal legislation, threatened to undermine the region's tradition of low-wage, nonunion industries. Moreover, the new industrial unions and northern black voters were major components of Roosevelt's landslide victory in 1936. As part of a "New Deal coalition," both groups secured a pivotal role in national politics and eclipsed the singular dominance of old-line southerners in the Democratic Party. The president's failed attempt to pack the Supreme Court early in his second term provided the occasion for southern Democrats to join with Republicans in opposing the excesses of the New Deal and blocking further reform legislation.

In 1938 the line dividing southern Democratic Party leaders and the active contingent of southern New Dealers was clearly drawn when Roosevelt attempted to defeat prominent New Deal opponents in the primary elections that summer. Senator Walter George of Georgia, among those targeted, called Roosevelt's action "a second march through Georgia." Yet southerners, confident that the New Deal had the support of the majority of the region's people, led in orchestrating the president's effort. Clark Foreman and several of his associates compiled the *Report on the Economic Conditions of the South*, the primary campaign document that supported Roosevelt's charge that the South was "the nation's number one economic problem." Drawing on the work of the South's leading social scientists, it highlighted the consequences of the region's economic underdevelopment in all areas of southern life and demonstrated the critical role of federal assistance in facilitating the development of the South's bountiful resources.[7]

A less noted but equally significant challenge to the political status quo in the South occurred in 1938. In December of that year, the National Association for the Advancement of Colored People (NAACP) won its first major Supreme Court victory in the nascent legal assault on segregation when the Court ordered Missouri's all-white law school to admit Lloyd Gaines. The NAACP's campaign, under the direction of Charles Houston and his assistant Thurgood Marshall, engaged black southerners in an organized movement to secure the full rights of citizenship. Houston and his team of lawyers were particularly sensitive to the fact that the response of African Americans to the New Deal and to the racial liberalism of Franklin and Eleanor Roosevelt provided fertile ground for realizing the promise of the constitutional amendments enacted during Reconstruction. Moreover, the interracial unionism of the CIO created new possibilities for a biracial movement to advance economic and political democracy in the South, a critical element in the movement that Houston and other young black leaders envisioned.

Thus, although Roosevelt failed in his attempt to unseat his southern opponents, the related events of 1938, combined with the changing composition of the national Democratic Party, opened the way for a new political alignment in the South. With the support of Franklin and Eleanor Roosevelt, the authors of the southern report and several of the CIO's southern organizers convened a mass meeting to address the issues raised by the report. More than one thousand people crowded into Birmingham over Thanksgiving weekend. It was, participant Arthur Raper recalled, "one of the most exaggerated expressions of change in the South. . . . Everyone was represented, high and low, black and white, labor and management."[8] The occasion lent itself to the free mixing of the predominantly white group in plenary sessions and discussion groups. When Police Commissioner Eugene "Bull" Connor insisted on enforcing segregated seating, the newly established Southern Conference for Human Welfare (SCHW) resolved never again to meet at a place where racial segregation could be enforced. From the start, then, opponents dubbed the SCHW a racial egalitarian organization— an overstatement in 1938 but a characterization that the organization grew into as it sought to enfranchise the New Deal's constituencies in the South.

Even though 1938 marked the end of the legislative phase of the New Deal, the struggle over its political consequences was just beginning. From 1938 to 1946 a heated contest over the future of the New Deal and the political realignment it invited was waged among southerners in Washington and throughout the region. The SCHW organized the National Committee to Abolish the Poll Tax (NCAPT), a national coalition of labor, civil rights, and civil liberties groups. Since the poll tax affected blacks and whites, the effort to eliminate it created an opportunity for building a biracial effort to restore voting rights in the South. It also succeeded in drawing national attention to the widespread curtailment of the right to vote in all southern states. The NCAPT successfully lobbied Congress to introduce a federal anti-poll-tax bill, allowing for the first congressional debate on voting rights since the 1890s.

One of the unifying themes of this book is the changing nature of the relationship between the federal government, the Democratic Party, and the South during the 1930s and 1940s. The introduction of anti-poll-tax legislation marked the culmination of the Washington-centered phase of what had become a loosely jointed movement to expand political democracy in the South. By then, war mobilization fully occupied the concern of the president and further secured the ascendancy of southern conservatives in Congress. Whereas successive anti-poll-tax bills passed in the House, southern-led filibusters prevented a vote in the Senate. The energy for expanding voting rights shifted to the South during the war years and was carried forward by locally and regionally based organizations.

The last half of this study charts the course of these developments through the war years and the immediate postwar period. During this time, black southerners emerged as the "generating force" of the emerging voting-rights movement. The war, as numerous studies have demonstrated, saw an acceleration of black civil rights activism under the umbrella of the "Double V" campaign. A. Philip Randolph's well-known "March on Washington" movement compelled a reluctant Roosevelt to establish the Fair Employment Practices Committee (FEPC) in 1941 and made civil rights a national issue. In the South, however, a deeper and more subtle transformation was under way. The NAACP's southern membership and branch affiliates multiplied in the early 1940s, and the organization won several important victories in the area of education and voting rights. Ruling on *Smith v. Allwright* in 1944, the Supreme Court outlawed the all-white primary, eliminating what had been the greatest legal obstacle to black political participation and opening the way for a dramatic increase in efforts by African Americans to vote.

These changes, along with the social and economic upheaval caused by the war, occurred in a highly segregated world, taut with racial tension and suspicion. The SCHW, individual CIO unions, and Highlander Folk School, which served as a training center for union organizers, responded directly to white racial fears and hostilities and attempted to build on the tentative inroads made during the 1930s. They sponsored interracial gatherings and organizing workshops and experimented with various methods of political education. These groups, which often worked in conjunction with NAACP branches, the Southern Negro Youth Congress (SNYC), and other community-based organizations, attempted to build a biracial movement around issues of economic and political democracy.

But conservative politicians easily traded on the growth of black political activity to revive white solidarity as a unifying force in southern politics. They portrayed New Deal reformers and labor activists as part of a sinister effort to overturn white supremacy. The *Smith v. Allwright* decision, following on the heels of FEPC hearings in Birmingham, gave easy credence to such charges. State defiance of *Smith v. Allwright* invited widespread electoral fraud and an escalating campaign of antiblack violence and set the stage for the politics of massive resistance.

By 1944, the South and the national Democratic Party stood at a crossroads. Racial polarization during the war years had taxed the capacity of the national party to, in the words of one contemporary, "carry water on both shoulders with regard to Negro voting."[9] How could the Democratic Party maintain the newly won allegiance of northern black voters while tolerating the official exclusion of black voters from Democratic Party elections in the South? How could the Democratic Party be a liberal party so long as it accommodated a southern wing that enforced a caste system? Race was at the core of the party realignment that Roosevelt sought, yet he did not confront it directly. During the war, however, others did, most notably Vice-President Henry Wallace, who maintained that the future of New Deal reform depended on it. Southern conservatives had already declared their independence from the New Deal. A core group of New Deal loyalists argued that the southern wing of the party should no longer be accommodated at the expense of black voters, who had proven to be the most steadfast supporters of progressive reform.

The 1944 Democratic national convention marked the opening round of the postwar struggle to determine the future of New Deal liberalism and its role in defining the Democratic Party. Several southern delegations verged on open revolt. When Texas Democrats nominated an anti-Roosevelt slate of delegates, Roosevelt loyalists sent a competing delegation. The Credentials Committee admitted both and split the delegate count between them. Black Carolinians sent a delegation representing the newly organized South Carolina Progressive Democratic Party (PDP). The PDP challenged the seating of the South Carolina "Regulars," who continued to bar black voters from the Democratic primary in defiance of *Smith v. Allwright*; the Credentials Committee disqualified the PDP on a technicality. All of this was played out against the larger drama surrounding the vice-presidential nomination.

Vice-President Henry Wallace, who had the near unanimous support of the newly formed CIO Political Action Committee (CIO-PAC), the NAACP, the black press, and progressive New Dealers, faced the united opposition of southern conservatives, urban machine bosses, White House "insiders," and a vacillating president. In the end, party machinations clinched the nomination for Harry Truman, but just narrowly. Wallace's strong showing, despite the powerful opposition, encouraged labor and progressive New Dealers to work toward expanding the New Deal and advancing the liberal realignment of the Democratic Party. They took FDR's 1944 "Economic Bill of Rights" as their platform and engineered an ambitious voter-registration campaign under the umbrella of the CIO-PAC.

From 1944 to 1946, the CIO-PAC, the NAACP, the SCHW, and the SNYC coordinated a drive throughout the South as part of a national effort to elect liberal representatives in 1946. Fieldworkers from each organization, together with local and state groups, orchestrated a highly successful campaign for voter education and registration. The number of black voters multiplied, showing the most impressive gains in Georgia and South Carolina, despite a campaign of terrorism that included the murder of several World War II veterans who dared to register. At the same time, racial animus dovetailed with anticommunism, strengthening conservative unionists and wearing away at the fragile bonds of interracial unionism so critical to advancing economic and political democracy in the South. Fraud prevailed in numerous primary races. But, despite it all, progressive candidates scored important victories in several key southern races in 1946.

Nationally, the results of the 1946 midterm elections were less ambiguous. A Republican sweep elevated the electoral appeal of anticommunism. President Harry Truman, who had served in Roosevelt's shadow since his death in April 1945, emerged from the 1946 debacle projecting a new decisiveness. The enactment of the Truman Doctrine and the federal loyalty program in March 1947 made anticommunism a core issue in Democratic Party politics in the post-Roosevelt era. The bipartisan embrace of a domestic cold war hastened the breakup of the CIO and contributed to a weakening of popular confidence in the democratic process and in the federal government, a confidence that was fundamental to the southern movement to expand political democracy. The implementation of Truman's civil rights program, announced later that year, was compromised by the prerequisites of his domestic cold war.

In an effort to resist the closing circle of Democratic Party politics, key architects of the southern movement endorsed the third party candidacy of Henry Wallace in 1948. This, in effect, marked the end of the New Deal–inspired phase of the movement. The epilogue of this book highlights Wallace's Progressive Party campaign in the South. Building on the decade-long struggle to expand political participation in the South, the Wallace campaign employed strategies that anticipated the civil rights movement of the 1960s.

Days of Hope is the study of a generation. It draws on the stories of more than a hundred women and men who helped create the political possibilities of the 1930s and 1940s. They represent a broad range of experiences— student radicals, CIO organizers, civil rights litigators, national policymakers, congressional lobbyists, voting-rights activists—traversing the regional, racial, and political boundaries that frequently define studies of this period. Joined by their vision of a new social possibility, they acted toward its realization even while compelled to live within the constraints of a segregated society. The nature of their struggle and the consequences of their efforts illustrate the ways in which racial realities shaped the democratic movements of the New Deal era.

The [Democratic Party] platform is a model of force, brevity and sincerity. . . . Declaring that the "only hope for improving present conditions . . . lies in a drastic change in economic and government policies," it urges that the nation turn back to the fundamental democratic doctrine of "Equal rights to all, special privileges to none."

Atlanta Constitution, 1 July 1932

In this very state of confused despair and bitter disillusionment lay the seeds of a new racial attitude and leadership.

LESTER GRANGER, *Opportunity*, July 1934

1

On the Eve of the New Deal

In 1932, as the nation sank deeper into the depression, an official of the Hoover administration told Congress, "My sober and considered judgement is that . . . federal aid would be a disservice to the unemployed."[1] The promotion of self-reliance rang hollow, however, as the number of farm foreclosures multiplied and as people from all levels of society fattened the ranks of the unemployed. Even southern Democrats abandoned what had been an uncompromising opposition to federal intervention in southern affairs, the cardinal principle of post-Reconstruction state governments. As the presidential campaign approached, they pressed for government action and rallied behind the candidacy of the governor of New York, Franklin D. Roosevelt.

The South's retreat from a dogmatic adherence to states' rights showed the region's desperation. The *Atlanta Constitution*'s confident promotion of the Democratic Party as the guardian of "equal rights," however, reflected the extent to which national and regional sensibilities regarding race and citizenship were one. Except for the Reconstruction period, the federal courts and the nation's political institutions had accommodated the white supremacist order in the South. Woodrow Wilson, the last Democrat in the White House, had extended racial segregation to include all federal facilities in the nation's capital.

Yet, as Lester Granger and other young black leaders anticipated, the political upheaval spawned by the depression created new opportunities for African Americans to assert their citizenship. Black voters in northern cities, fed by the wave of war-induced migration from the South, earned strategic positions among the urban coalitions that transformed the national political landscape during the 1930s. The great majority of black Americans, however, remained in the South, where they were barred from politics. But even there, the nationalizing trends and democratic activism surrounding the New Deal stirred efforts among the disfranchised to find a way out of what one contemporary called the "economic and political wilderness."[2]

On the eve of the New Deal, Horace Mann Bond, a young black scholar and educator, explored the schizophrenic contours of southern life in an essay for *Harper's* magazine. He began by noting the widely popular "cult of the South." Here, "The white man is the Southerner, the Negro—well, a Negro." Drawing on family memory and on his extensive travels throughout the region, Bond looked beneath this veneer and inquired into the nature of the South as a "geographical portion, a psychological entity." He wove a textured portrait of black and white life and of the transparent boundaries of the caste system. "Customs, politics, society, all of the deeper and more extensive ramifications of culture," Bond observed, "bear the imprint of those of us who, being Southerners, are also Negroes."[3]

Regional identity, however, often failed to embrace the richness and complexity of southern life and culture. Bond explained that for whites and many blacks, the idea of the South was corrupted by the habitual celebration of a "white" South in which the Negro was a mere shadow "deepen[ing] the effect of the leading silhouette." It was this South that captured the national imagination. Although it had no basis in material reality, it reflected a political reality whereby "the accolade of Southern citizenship, of participation in the fate of the region," had been "appropriated by white persons." When Bond wrote in 1931, amid widespread economic despair, the South's deeply racialized civic life appeared to be unyielding, thus obstructing his effort to articulate a vision of the region's future.[4]

Black exclusion was emblematic of the political order established at the turn of the century with the final triumph of the Democratic Party. In a relentless campaign of fraud and violence, Democrats had navigated the tumultuous electoral contests of the late nineteenth century under the mantra of white liberty and home rule, appealing to the white South's abiding mistrust of politics and government. The contentious politics of the era crested with the Populist challenge of the 1890s, along with a growing movement to restrict the franchise. Democrats adroitly manipulated the economic unrest and anxieties that fed the Populist movement, pinning the region's woes on the newly enfranchised black voters and promising their complete removal from public life. By the first decade of the twentieth century, suffrage restrictions were in place in all southern states, segregation laws penetrated every facet of southern life, and Democratic Party hegemony—or what North Carolina newspaperman Josephus Daniels hailed as "permanent good government by the Party of the white man"—had been secured.[5]

The South's new order, which virtually nullified the constitutional amendments enacted during Reconstruction, won the approval of the Supreme Court and the sympathetic support of northern white sentiment. Reconciliation of northern and southern whites advanced on the battlefield of the Spanish-American War in 1898, a war that reinforced white racial arrogance. Meanwhile, the widely popular tenets of social Darwinism, offering "scientific" validation of Anglo-Saxon superiority, seasoned the politics of the Progressive Era. In the north, reformers blamed immigrants for labor turmoil and the corruption of urban politics and supported suffrage restrictions as essential to the smooth functioning of democracy. The history of Reconstruction, as it was written early in the twentieth century, offered a powerful lesson in the perils of enfranchising the ignorant and socially inferior. William A. Dunning and his graduate students at Columbia University provided scholarly legitimacy for the white South's indictment of Reconstruction as a horrific time, a fatally flawed experiment. D. W. Griffith further popularized this view in his 1915 celluloid testimonial to sectional reconciliation and white supremacy, *The Birth of a Nation*.[6]

Having prevailed as the party of white solidarity and regional self-determination, the Democratic Party offered the South "a politics of balance, inertia and drift." Disfranchisement barred many whites as well as virtually all blacks from the electoral process. The party represented a diverse range of potentially conflicting economic interests, from Black Belt planters to New South boosters, with all kinds of state variations. A type of negative politics, committed to maintaining the fundamental principles of the racial and economic status quo, provided some coherence. As historian Michael Perman has explained, in the state constitutional and legislative battles to "redeem" the South, the Democrats "saddled the region with a constricted governmental apparatus and a repressive system of land and labor" that doomed the region to decades of static and adaptive economic development.[7]

Federal endorsement of white hegemony had robbed black southerners of their last defenses against the usurpation of their civil and political rights. But traditions of freedom and citizenship, born in the crucible of Reconstruction, sustained communities of resistance. Black southerners developed an expansive vision of democracy in their efforts to secure the fruits of emancipation. The black church, as Elsa Barkley Brown has explained, was the site of mass meetings where the newly freed "enacted their understanding of democratic political discourse." During the tumultuous decades of the 1880s and 1890s, black men and women met white terrorism at the polls with a group presence on election day. As an organized and articulate body of citizens, black communities throughout the region took an active part in Republican Party politics and explored alliances with independent groups such as the Farmers' Alliance and the Populist Party. Indeed, the persistence and endurance of African Americans in an increasingly hostile political environment was used by proponents of disfranchisement to rally white support.[8]

By the dawn of the new century, government and politics had become "inaccessible and unaccountable to Americans who happened to be black." African Americans continued to develop strategies for social and political development within a separate public sphere. This was dominated, in large part, by the church but also included fraternal organizations, the black press, and other institutions. Churches often focused the mobilization of community resources to provide educational and social welfare services, leadership training, and organizational networks. The church, notes Evelyn Brooks Higginbotham, served as a vehicle of collective identity and empowerment and provided a place "to critique and contest America's racial domination."[9]

While the rudiments of citizenship expired, formative developments shaped possibilities for future change. Resistance to new laws segregating streetcars erupted in locally organized boycotts in at least twenty-five southern cities from 1900 to 1906. These failed to stem the tide of segregation, however, demonstrating the futility of such actions. Black leaders and intellectuals continued to debate a broad range of political thought and strategies, framed by the accommodationism of Booker T. Washington, the civil rights protests of Ida B. Wells, W. E. B. Du Bois, and others, and the legal activism of the National Association for the Advancement of Colored People (NAACP), founded in 1909. Ideological divisions and tactical differences were enhanced by the daunting nature of the struggle, namely to sustain black communities amid the crushing environment of white racism while envisioning a way forward.[10]

Black migration, confined largely within the South, had been a vehicle of freedom, self-determination, and survival since the earliest days of emancipation. Starting in 1914, however, the "Great Migration" of the World War I era stimulated a steady and ultimately transforming movement of black southerners to the North. Black migration continued even after wartime demands ceased and jobs became scarce. The boll weevil and growing pressures of surplus labor pushed increasing numbers of blacks off the land during the twenties. Nearly one and a half million southern blacks went north from 1915 to 1929, an internal migration of vast proportions and significance. (At emancipation in 1863, the total population of freed blacks in the South has been estimated at four million.)[11]

The North hardly resembled "the promised land." During the "Red summer" of 1919 racial violence erupted in riots in northern urban centers as well as in the South; the worst outbreak was in Chicago. But discrimination and segregation in northern cities lacked the relentless brutality seen in the southern system. In the North, blacks responded to white violence with a militancy that was refracted in the "New Negro" movement of the twenties, while the Garvey movement stirred mass demonstrations of racial pride. During the twenties, black communities in the North nurtured the outpouring of cultural, literary, and musical creativity that flowered in the Harlem Renaissance. And, in the North, black citizens had free access to the ballot. As their numbers increased, black participation in northern urban politics gradually became a factor of national consequence.[12]

For the great majority of blacks remaining in the South, however, industrialization and urbanization extended the grip of segregation. During the war and postwar years, mechanization and upward pressure on unskilled wage earners sharpened racial dualism within the southern labor market. Black jobs and white jobs, with few exceptions, became increasingly noncompeting. Black men and women continued to dominate the tobacco industry, but white employees worked the machine-tended jobs in separate buildings. A similar trend of racial distinction emerged in the iron and steel industry, also dominated by blacks, who held both skilled and semiskilled positions. The textile industry had excluded blacks from the start; by the

During the 1930s, writers and government investigators "discovered" a South that had been largely beyond national consciousness. Images of the region's impoverishment were captured by photographers for the New Deal's Resettlement Administration/ Farm Security Administration.

Above. Two women and a child standing in front of a shack and behind barbed wire, Alabama, 1936. (Photograph © Dorothea Lange Collection, Oakland Museum, City of Oakland; gift of Paul S. Taylor)

Facing page, top. Children being schooled at home in Transylvania, Louisiana, 1939. (Photograph by Russell Lee; courtesy of the Louisiana Collection, State Library of Louisiana, Baton Rouge)

Facing page, bottom. Drought refugees from Oklahoma in Blythe, California, 1936. (Photograph by Dorothea Lange; courtesy of the Library of Congress)

"Damned if we'll work for what they pay folks here-abouts." Migrants on the road, Crittendon County, Arkansas, 1936. (Photograph by Carl Mydans; courtesy of the Library of Congress)

1920s, its white workers were paid well above black wage earners. Unionization of skilled crafts increased during the 1920s, and these unions, such as the building trades, were among the most racially exclusive. In seeking to explain these developments, some historians have suggested that by the 1920s, black and white southerners were entering the work force with increasingly dissimilar educational backgrounds. But for most industrial jobs in the South, education bore little relevance to the job requirements. As historian Gavin Wright has explained, job classifications became primarily a function of caste and were "symptoms of the larger process of creating a segregated society."[13]

Southern industrialists proudly presided over an abundant supply of "native" white labor—"thrifty, industrious, and one hundred percent American." They advertised a cheap and inexhaustible supply of nonunion labor as the region's greatest resource. A flurry of union activity among segments of the textile, mining, and tobacco industries met severe postwar wage cutbacks in 1919, but it quickly dissipated. Ten years later, worker opposition to the stretch-out system in the textile industry erupted in a series of strikes and unionization activities in the Carolinas. The most notorious and least typical confrontation came in Gastonia, where the Communist Party embarked on its preliminary effort to promote class struggle in the South. But Gastonia provided a lightning rod for antiunion sentiment. All efforts toward unionization ultimately yielded to combinations of employer intimidation, police force, and deep-rooted community hostility toward unions and "outsiders." Yet the most effective deterrent to unionization remained the vast pool of cheap white labor, desperate for work, and the army of black labor at the extreme margins of subsistence.[14]

Black southerners were the first to absorb the economic downturn of the 1920s. The ravages of the boll weevil and the post–World War I economic slump stimulated a mass exodus of people "fleeing from hunger and exposure" in the countryside. African Americans dominated the rural movement to southern cities during 1922–24. In the latter part of the decade, whites began to follow in growing numbers. Rural refugees crowded into growing slums, where work was often irregular or nonexistent. As the economic squeeze tightened, white workers steadily took away what had been traditionally black jobs. Some towns passed municipal ordinances restricting black employment. But in most cases, intimidation and appeals to racial loyalty were most effective in securing jobs for whites.

In several cities, white terrorist organizations mobilized the frustration and helplessness of unemployed whites into sporadic drives to claim jobs held by blacks. In 1930, the Black Shirts marched up Peachtree Street in Atlanta with banners demanding, "Niggers, back to the cotton fields—city jobs are for white folks." They forced Atlanta hotels to replace black bellhops with whites and pressured for the employment of white domestics, street cleaners, and garbage collectors. Future Governor Eugene Talmadge and the Georgia commissioner of agriculture were among the prominent members of the association. Although such extremist organizations were short-lived, black displacement by whites was widespread. In 1932, a New Orleans city ordinance that would have reserved jobs on publicly owned docks for "eligible electors," costing thousands of black dockworkers their jobs, was blocked by the U.S. Court of Appeals. By then, however, the unemployment rate for black males in New Orleans, Atlanta, and Birmingham was twice the rate for whites.[15]

By 1930, economic desperation enveloped the entire society. The depression issued the final, devastating blow to the plantation economy and unhinged its commercial and industrial dependencies. Thousands of landowners who had participated in the brief cotton boom of the mid-1920s through land speculation and increased production now faced foreclosures when the price of cotton plummeted. Between 1929 and 1930 farm income was cut in half. The urban boosterism of Atlanta, Birmingham, and other oases of New South prosperity fizzled with the collapse of the agrarian economy. Manufacturing dropped by a third nationally during the depression, but the South fared even worse. Total manufacturing dropped by 50 percent in Atlanta and New Orleans from 1929 to 1933; Birmingham, hailed as the "Pittsburgh of the South" in the early twenties, saw manufacturing plummet by more than 70 percent. Jobless rates in southern cities also surpassed the national average, which in 1932 was estimated at 25 percent. Among the hardest-hit urban areas, southern cities lacked the funds to provide emergency relief for the masses of unemployed. Birmingham, the only city that had a Department of Public Welfare, abandoned it in 1924.[16]

The depression stood as the worst crisis the United States had endured since the Civil War. The dilemma was unprecedented: growing poverty and unemployment in the midst of the abundance produced by modern methods of agriculture and industry. But during 1930 and 1931, local, state, and national political leaders relied on traditional remedies, assuming and hoping that the cycle would run its course. Herbert Hoover's blend of progressive conservatism, with its emphasis on volunteerism and a limited role for the federal government, framed the government's initial response to national economic collapse. The failure of Hoover's efforts to stem the rapid downward plunge stiffened his resolve against more aggressive measures. This only compounded the fatalism and desperation that gripped the country and prepared the ground for a dramatic departure from old certainties and values.[17]

The limited vision in Washington was matched at the state level. Political leaders relied on the old formulas of retrenchment, a balanced budget, and regressive taxation. During 1930 and 1931, southern politicians and businessmen reiterated the sanctity of states' rights, along with their opposition to federal intervention and any suggestion of a national dole. At the same time, localities proved increasingly unable to meet the mushrooming demand for unemployment relief and often engaged in futile efforts to shift the burden to black men and women and, in some cases, to white women. From 1929 to 1932, white men replaced white women in six thousand manufacturing positions in Memphis. Several states established emergency welfare commissions, but these were dominated by businessmen and distributed no funds to the cities. Commenting on the performance of the Georgia legislature, historian James Patterson concluded that no other legislature could "compare in stupidity, selfishness, and lack of purpose with the body which twiddled its thumbs while the fires of hope died to ashes in the hearts of its citizens."[18]

By 1932, the failure of these limited measures forced a sobering confrontation with the destitution and despair that blanketed the nation. "A creeping paralysis had taken hold of the people," an Alabamian observed, "and everything was falling apart." Individual self-reliance, a cultural bedrock, proved to be completely ineffectual in countering personal misfortune. "People were losing homes like ripe fruit falling from a tree; farmers were being foreclosed off their lands and homes by the thousands." The transient populations had multiplied; tens of thousands of people wandered "aimlessly, hopelessly over the country," noted one observer. They included members of every class: "businessmen, salesmen, lawyers, doctors, . . . and ex-convicts." A New Orleans businessman cautioned: "The whole white collar class . . . [is] taking an awful beating. . . . They're whipped, that's all. And it's bad."[19]

Edward O'Neal, a northern Alabama planter and chairman of the conservative American Farm Bureau Federation, was among the chorus of voices demanding aggressive and imaginative action by the federal government. Late in 1932 he warned, "Unless something is done for the American farmer, we will have revolution in the countryside in less than twelve months." In their enthusiastic embrace of Franklin D. Roosevelt and his amorphous plan for a New Deal, the South's political leaders could not know that Roosevelt's reforms would invite a bold new challenge to the South's economic and political order.[20] *key*

Franklin Roosevelt's boundless confidence, his infectious good cheer, and his commitment to positive action revived the national mood almost instantly. The collapse of the nation's banking system on the eve of his inauguration did not break his stride. Rather, it served to level the playing field bequeathed by his predecessor, leaving no question that "the bottom had dropped out of everything." The outworn economic verities of the 1920s were spent, and the way was clear for the thorough restructuring that Roosevelt was prepared to orchestrate. Political action and leadership, long thought to be the handmaidens of "natural" economic forces, moved to center stage. "Public discussion, public criticism and public agitation" fueled the collective enterprise of the New Deal.[21]

There was no master plan, no promised panacea. Roosevelt was the "Great Experimenter," "Master of Ceremonies," "Chief Croupier" of the New Deal. He energized the political process, giving full play to a wide range of ideas, personalities, and interests. Ever eager for information, Roosevelt "cast a net as wide as possible." His cabinet included fiscal conservatives, progressive agrarians, and social welfare liberals, Democrats, Republicans, and Independents, and with the appointment of Frances Perkins as secretary of labor, the first woman cabinet chief. New Deal agencies were staffed with professors, financiers, labor leaders, social workers, and politicos and included an unprecedented number of black professional appointments. From the beginning, Roosevelt included the American people in the New Deal through his radio "fireside" chats. "The wildest radical in America can win a hearing for his idea just as well as the most powerful banker," a contemporary observed. In addition to oiling the wheels of the country's political machinery, Roosevelt was engaged in "sinking tap roots into the whole American experience."[22]

Although the rhetoric and dazzling momentum of the Roosevelt team heralded a new departure, historians have emphasized the basic conservatism of the early New Deal recovery program. The National Recovery Industrial Act and the Agricultural Adjustment Act stood as the crowning achievements of the whirl of legislation that marked the first hundred days. Both were tailored to the traditional constituent interests of industry and large farmers and easily enjoyed the support of conservative southern Democrats, with several notable exceptions. Senators Harry Byrd and Carter Glass of Virginia and Senator Josiah Bailey of North Carolina clung stubbornly to their belief in the unhampered workings of the free enterprise system and opposed federally sponsored price supports and minimum wages as a dangerous intrusion. According to Senator Bailey, "The accepted doctrine for one hundred and fifty years is that fundamental economic laws are natural laws, having the same source as physical laws."[23]

But from the beginning of the Roosevelt administration, there was a deep, abiding awareness that a sea change in American politics was under way. Byrd, Glass, and Bailey possibly sensed it and tried to nip it in the bud. Secretary of Agriculture Henry Wallace was among those who welcomed and nurtured the potential inherent in the New Deal. "We are children of the transition," he told a group in 1934. "We have left Egypt, but we have not yet arrived in the promised land." After the depression had eroded old confidences, Roosevelt's election stirred the expectations of people and constituencies who had never completely secured representation in the national political arena. The pragmatic, open spirit of the New Deal, along with Roosevelt's promotion of government as a vehicle for advancing human betterment, provided a focus for the political currents released by the depression.[24]

Will Alexander, founder and director of the Atlanta-based Commission on Interracial Cooperation (CIC), sensed that the Roosevelt administration would have a profound effect on the southern United States. "I had a hunch," Alexander later recalled, "that Washington was going to become the center of the country and that perhaps the next stage of race relations in this country . . . would center around what happened in Washington." Alexander wanted someone in Washington who could monitor national initiatives for their effects on American race relations and who could make federal officials aware of the special problems faced by black Americans. Alexander and Edwin Embree, director of the Rosenwald Fund, went to Washington early in 1933 to lobby for the creation of such a position, to be subsidized by the Rosenwald Fund. After contacting the White House and several government agencies, they arranged for a "Special Adviser on the Economic Status of Negroes" to serve under Harold Ickes, secretary of the interior. Ickes selected Clark Foreman, a Georgian and one of Alexander's young protégés.[25]

The appointment of a white man from Georgia to the newly created post drew a storm of opposition from the black press, the NAACP, and other black leaders. The protest was not directed against Foreman personally but against "the idea of a white advisor for Negroes." Foreman agreed and advised Ickes to fill the post with a black person. Ickes insisted, however, that a white person be appointed, at least initially, whether or not Foreman took the job. He approved Foreman's suggestion that Robert Weaver, a young black economist and Harvard Ph.D. candidate, be hired as Foreman's assistant and potential successor in the post.

Clark Foreman was part of a new generation of white southern liberals who passed under the tutelage of Will Alexander and the CIC but who had outgrown the constraints of that pioneering organization. Foreman demonstrated an impatience with southern racial mores, an impatience that even Alexander considered unwise. When Alexander had submitted a list of names for Ickes to consider for the position of special adviser, he had added Foreman's name as an afterthought, with qualifications. Foreman was "a man of highest motives," Alexander told Ickes, "but he leaned over backwards to be on the liberal side and had a feeling that the way you got things done was to get at the billy-goat—just butt right into them and keep butting until you're through." He was "a young man of great charm, a very keen mind, but a very impatient lad who didn't pick any counsel of caution but went straight ahead into anything he chose." Alexander later recalled Ickes's response. Foreman was just the kind of person he wanted, "the only one who [could] do any good in a job like this."[26]

Clark Howell Foreman was born to privilege in Atlanta, Georgia, at the turn of the century. His worldview was shaped by an inherited sense of noblesse oblige and energized by a strong dose of Wilsonian idealism. On graduating from the University of Georgia in 1921, Foreman embarked on a wide-ranging pursuit of education and experience, searching for a way to participate in advancing "the good of humanity." Cambridge, Massachusetts, Europe, the southern United States, New York, and the Soviet Union were home to Foreman for stretches of time between 1921 and 1933. His abiding interest in America's racial mores evolved as he experienced the dynamic intellectual and political ferment in postwar Europe and the new Union of Soviet Socialist Republics. By the late 1920s, Foreman had become keenly aware of the ways the caste system dominated all of southern life and enforced a sterile conformity even among its most "enlightened" white citizens. Not until the New Deal, however, was he able to envision a way to challenge the seemingly intractable color line.

Foreman's ancestry was rooted in the pre-Revolutionary South, marrying slaveholding aristocracy to sturdy yeoman stock. His immediate family were among the leading citizens of Atlanta. His mother's father, Evan P. Howell, purchased the *Atlanta Constitution* in 1876 and made it the leading promoter of a "New South" under the editorship of Henry Grady. Clark Howell, the son of Evan P., succeeded Grady as managing editor in 1889, a position he held until his death in 1936. The *Constitution* reflected Howell's paternalistic views toward blacks, but his views contrasted with the more virulent racism of the time, such as that promoted by the former Populist leader Tom Watson. Clark Howell ran unsuccessfully against Hoke Smith, who had the enthusiastic support of Watson, in the 1906 gubernatorial campaign that led to the notorious Atlanta race riot.

Robert Foreman, Clark's father, was a successful businessman who tended to be more of a progressive liberal than a New South booster. He had, Clark later recalled, "a great sense of justice" and was a fiercely independent individual, who taught his four sons "not to bend [a] knee to any man." Robert and Effie Howell Foreman held no organizational religious affiliation. They encouraged their sons to think freely and develop their own ideas about religion, but they imbued Clark with a deeply felt obligation "to leave the world a better place for having lived." All of the Foreman brothers pursued college and postgraduate study, acting on their father's counsel to train their minds "for the duties and possibilities of life."[27]

In the fall of 1917, Clark Foreman entered the University of Georgia at the age of sixteen. He pursued a classical course of study and engaged contemporary issues and ideas through participation on the debating team and in speaking contests. The Great War stimulated much discussion on the pastoral Athens campus and caused the university to eliminate German from the curriculum. It did not challenge the personal expectations of Clark and his contemporaries, nor intrude on the carefree spirit that dominated student life at Georgia. For Clark, another event shook the sense of security and privilege that he shared with most of his classmates. In February 1921 a black man was lynched in Athens, one of Georgia's "oldest and most en-lightened communities."[28]

Clark wrote to his parents describing the day's events in great detail. Talk about an alleged rape and murder of a pregnant white woman by a black man spread among the students, along with rumors that a lynch mob was gathering. Clark and other students looked on as a crowd collected outside the "mob-proof" courthouse in Athens from early afternoon on. An esti-mated three thousand people had assembled by early evening when several men forced their way into the courthouse with sledgehammers and blow-torches. Two county sheriffs and their deputies were in another part of the courthouse at the time but later said they were unaware of the mob's visit. The group crowded into the jail on the fifth floor and "burned and ham-mered their way" into the cell where John Lee Eberhardt was confined. They chained and dragged Eberhardt from the jail, put him in one of the auto-mobiles, and led the mob back to the scene of the crime five miles outside of the city. Clark jumped onto the running board of an automobile and followed along to see what was going on. In the letter to his parents, he described what happened next:

The negro was carried to the place of the murder. He was shown the lady he was supposed to have murdered in the hopes that he would confess. The lady was about 23, fair and beautiful. She had a baby eighteen months old and was expecting another in June. The negro would not confess. He was brought out in the yard and tied to a pine tree, about a hundred yards from the house. The crowd of about three thousand people gathered around the tree in a large circle. A leader made a speech forbidding any shooting on account of the danger of onlookers. Strict order was preserved. Everyone was made to sit down, so that the ones behind them might see with ease the ghastly spectacle that was about to take place. A fire was built about the negro's feet and lit. Neither gasoline nor kerosene was used, in order that the job might not be done too fast. The family was brought to the center of the ring so that the negro might have one more chance to confess. He pleaded to God to testify his innocence. More wood was thrown on the fire. The negro yelled for mercy.

The fire leaps up and seems to burn him too fast. Some hardened onlooker smolders it so that the negro might suffer longer. He tries to choke himself, his hands tied behind him. Finally with a monster effort he bends over far enough to swallow some flame. He dies amid the jeers of the crowd.

The people . . . grab souvenirs from the branches of the guilty tree. Even the dead negro is not spared. Fingers and toes are pulled from the scorched corpse to remind the participants of the deed. At this juncture a woman comes forth with a pistol and asks to be allowed to shoot the negro. The request is granted. More wood is piled on, and the funeral pyre flares up and lights the faces of the watchers. The mob disperses each to his home, with an air of conquest and satisfaction rather than horror and condemnation.[29]

This "sadistic orgy," Foreman later recalled, brought him "face to face with the barbarism" underlying race relations in the South" and made an "indelible impression" on his mind. But he was not yet capable of connecting it to the core issue of racial discrimination in the South. "About that," he reflected, "I was still almost completely ignorant." He was a young man of nineteen, and his framework still reflected the racial liberalism and paternalism of his father. Robert Foreman was repulsed by the barbaric nature of the mob action and shamed by the duplicity of law enforcement officials. Such a complete breakdown of law and civility reflected on the entire society. In the valedictorian address to his graduating class, Clark echoed these sensibilities in an appeal to his classmates. "It is our solemn duty to uphold the laws of our state and see that they are enforced fearlessly by the constituted authorities, and not by cowardly mobs of night-riding ruffians—an unspeakable example of which was recently perpetrated at the very doors of this University."[30]

Following a family tradition, Clark took a year of study at Harvard after his graduation from Georgia. The Harvard experience inaugurated a personal odyssey that took Clark far from his southern moorings. Living among northerners for the first time, he was a proud and sometimes chauvinistic ambassador for his region and frequently sought refuge at the Southern Club, where he met Virginia Foster of Birmingham, Alabama, then a student at Wellesley. (Foreman's friendship with Virginia Foster Durr blossomed in Washington more than a decade later.) But he delighted in the collection of companions he quickly became associated with, which included several young men from New York and Boston. Gradually, he became more questioning about the South. Foreman's first break from southern tradition came when he joined a group of students for dinner with W. E. B. Du Bois before a talk Du Bois delivered to the Liberal Club. Foreman had planned to attend the talk but did not know that a dinner was involved. At first he refused to go. He had never sat down to a meal with a black person before and said he could not do it. But his friends and roommates argued with him "until [he] had no rational defense."[31]

When Clark went off to Harvard, he assumed that he would ultimately make his living as a banker. His family thought he had "a knack for finance." However, a steady diet of Leo Tolstoy, Ivan Turgenev, and other great novelists, digested in constant conversation and debate with his new Cambridge friends, revealed ways of thinking Clark had never considered. The idea of confining himself to a career at this point quickly dissolved. He realized that his education was just beginning. In an essay on Pyotr Kropotkin's *Memoirs of a Revolutionist* he wrote: "I have decided that he is what my mind requires a great man to be. A person with the highest ideals and the knowledge and fight that it took to carry them out despite all the obstacles and difficulties that made his path a briar patch, such a man was Kropotkin." By the end of the year, Clark announced that, for the present, he had lost "all desire for money and material pleasures" and was prepared to dedicate his life to social reform and advancement. But he added, "If I only knew how!"[32]

Robert and Effie Foreman indulged their son's thirst for a broader education with a trip to Europe, which his two older brothers had also enjoyed as their parents' final investment. H. G. Wells's massive tome *Outline of His-*

tory, a gift from his mother, was Clark's companion during the sea crossing. Wells's analysis and prescription gave concrete form to Clark's sense of expectation and adventure.

"We are in the dawn of a great constructive effort," Wells announced, in concluding his review of the evolution of world civilization through World War I. The final chapter of the book offered an eloquent plea for collective and "conscious struggle to establish an international political community." Cooperative effort in behalf of the "common good," he explained, would not compromise diversity but would, rather, enhance tolerance and promote social justice, "countering the almost universal bad manners of the present age," manners that had made "race intolerable to race." Universal education was essential to advancing Wells's hopeful plan. It would tap into the vast reservoirs of human potential throughout the world and make a democratic world government possible. Wells did not doubt that mankind had the creative capacity to establish human institutions that could initiate and maintain such an ambitious enterprise. The successful harnessing of the energies of the material world in behalf of scientific and industrial advancement during the eighteenth and nineteenth centuries, he suggested, offered proof of that. Whether humankind would create a different type of world, one in which men would "not hate so much, fear so much, cheat so desperately," remained a question of collective will and sustained effort.[33]

On arriving in London, Foreman immediately set out to meet H. G. Wells and seek the author's advice about how he might make himself useful in establishing the new international order. Clark later recalled that he told Wells he had come to Wells as a patient to a doctor. Wells responded that since he did not know "the patient" well, he was reluctant to prescribe a specific career or life's work. After engaging Clark in a thirty-minute conversation, Wells recommended several books and suggested that Clark visit Germany and France, study their languages, and conclude with a course of study at the London School of Economics. During the next year, Clark traveled through most of Europe, staying in Young Men's Christian Association (YMCA) lodgings and living as cheaply as possible to stretch his budget of one thousand dollars. He spent an extended period studying in Germany and volunteered as a teacher at an experimental school in Dresden. That was followed with a term at the London School of Economics. Along the way, he read Wells and George Bernard Shaw continuously and embraced a socialism of the utopian variety.

Clark's tour was interrupted when he visited his uncle, Clark Howell, who was then the publisher of the *Atlanta Constitution* and was staying in Paris. It was, he later wrote, a startling contrast, which revealed to him how far he had traveled since he had left Atlanta. He was uncomfortable with the opulent lifestyle and reported that they spent "at one meal enough to keep [him] in Europe for a month." What struck him more than the extravagant living was how conventional his uncle's thinking appeared to be. Friction between Clark and his uncle poured over into correspondence with his parents. "I am now sure," he told them, "that I shall never work in a bank, certainly not in the South. Uncle Clark said I was the only southerner he had ever heard say that the South was the most backward part of the United States. I believe it is, and I think the only remedy is in the recognition of the fact." His correspondence also confronted the hypocrisy of southern race relations, noting that one of his uncle's young associates from Atlanta had argued that no black person was "good enough to sit at a table with him" but that this same person had boasted that he would have sexual intercourse with a black prostitute "to change his luck."[34]

Robert and Effie Foreman commented on the critical tone of their son's letter. His mother advised him not to become "one-sided and unable to enter into the lives of your natural companions." His father assumed that Wells had been filling Clark's head with radical ideas about race. He conceded that although Wells might know more about most things, Wells could learn something from Robert Foreman about the southern Negro. Clark assured his father that no man was his infallible guide and that he did disagree with Wells on points, but he added, "They are the ones on which I am even more radical." He challenged his parents' tendency to dismiss people by calling them "dreamers and idealists." He wrote: "The dreamers are the ones which tend to progress and the other people just carry out the dreams. The idealist to me is the best thing to be." Clark then went on to explain his thoughts on "the Negro question":

Now the negro question: In the spring when I was with you I felt as you do now—and that is an uncommonly broad attitude for a Southerner. Since then I have read and thought a good deal. I have been able to get away for a time from the present filthy details of the question and look at it as a whole from a distance. My discovery is not startling nor is it an idea based on new convictions. I have simply applied the principles I have always held to a question which I had before accepted as a necessary evil.

I have always thought it was wrong for one man to assume superiority over another and to force a weaker one to obey him. That a man should get all he pays for, has been one of my cardinal principles. When we take advantage of our probably temporary superiority in education to the negro and force him to do things that he does not want to do, and do not allow him to vote or to have the schools and libraries which his tax should bring to him, I say we are wrong.

. . . My position about eating with them is this: If a negro is in every way equal to a white man, no discrimination should be made against him on account of his color. . . . The color of the skin is no argument against him. . . . This is not an extreme or radical idea and I hope you will be able to see my way of looking at it.[35]

In her response, Effie Foreman affirmed her opposition to "social equality." But she reassured her son, "I am glad for you to think it all out for yourself." Concerned that Clark was becoming "one of those lost Americans in Europe," she urged her son to return to Atlanta. Then he could study these questions from "a practical standpoint" and work to bring more changes about. She added, "There is much more to be done." The letters appealing for Clark to return home, and fulfill his responsibility to the people of the South, became more frequent during his year at the London School of Economics (LSE).[36]

During the 1923–24 academic year, Clark studied economics and the "Psychology of Political Theory" at LSE, immersed himself in British politics, and began undergoing psychoanalysis with Dr. M. E. Eber. He developed friendships with young men and women from the Soviet Union, Japan, and Germany and with several black American students, including Ruth Anne Fisher, who introduced Clark to Lawrence Brown, who was then studying piano in London and who later became Paul Robeson's primary accompanist. The British political scene fascinated Foreman. He met Susan Lawrence, the first woman elected to Parliament on the Labour Party ticket, at the home of the noted socialist writers Beatrice and Sidney Webb, and he worked on her successful campaign. "If politics were an honorable profession in America," Foreman wrote, he would choose that as his mode for advancing social reform. Education, he concluded, offered the best possibility for a worthwhile career, being "the most immediate need of the world and more especially America." But his plans for the future remained vague, as evidenced by his new motto, paraphrasing Abraham Lincoln: "My work is to prepare myself so that I shall be able to help when I am needed."[37]

Such an opportunity appeared quite unexpectedly. Early in the spring term Foreman reviewed *Christianity and the Race Problem* by James Oldham for a school magazine. Here, for the first time, Foreman learned of the work of the five-year-old, Atlanta-based Commission on Interracial Cooperation. "As soon as I read about it," he recalled, "I knew that it offered me the solution I was looking for; an interesting job at home."[38] The CIC's work applied the philosophy of social development that Foreman had been studying under Professor L. T. Hobhouse, author of *The Rational Good*. As soon as the term ended in July 1924, he boarded a freighter, in great anticipation of the possibilities awaiting him in Atlanta. Within weeks of his return home, he was working as the secretary of the Georgia Committee of the CIC.

The CIC was a bold departure in the field of southern race relations. Founded in the wake of the racial violence and rioting that rocked the country in 1919, it aimed to provide an organizational structure to promote dialogue and interaction among black and white community leaders as the essential first step to constructive race relations. Will Alexander, a former Methodist minister who had worked with the YMCA during World War I, was the guiding force behind the CIC and attracted the interest and financial backing of major philanthropic organizations. Although Alexander himself was deeply sensitive to the injustices embedded in the segregation system, he understood that it was necessary to proceed cautiously. White supremacy was firmly entrenched in the South, and white southerners spurned any reform effort that, however indirectly, challenged the racial status quo. Moreover, the CIC was isolated in the America of the 1920s. Its efforts received little recognition or encouragement from the national liberal community and were ignored by both major political parties. The group avoided all discussion of ultimate goals; its primary aim was to move beyond mutual ignorance.[39]

The CIC provided fertile ground for Foreman and enabled him to become acquainted with the racial situation in Atlanta and around the state. He witnessed, firsthand, the inequities that compelled black people to struggle mightily in order to make a living, stay healthy, and gain even a rudimentary education. The general ignorance and indifference with which "respectable" white people accepted this situation was also a revelation. In Augusta, Foreman succeeded in convening a group of prominent black and white citizens, after representatives of both races assured him that a chapter of the CIC was not needed in Augusta because race relations were fine. During the first meeting, the white participants appeared genuinely shocked to learn that municipal services and paved roads did not extend into the black sections of town. They petitioned city hall and succeeded in getting funds apportioned for a few improvements. But even this encouraging result, Foreman concluded, would be temporary in nature, since it would be "difficult to keep a group functioning on a basis of pure philanthropy and dependent entirely on their powers of persuasion."[40]

His efforts in Atlanta with the white medical community proved even less satisfactory. Segregated and dependent on the poorest segment of the community, black doctors in the city labored under blatant disadvantages. They were barred from practicing or training in the municipal hospitals, which thus restricted the care that black doctors could offer black patients. Many white doctors gladly treated black patients who paid in advance, and they exploited their privileged position over their black counterparts. Anxious to help relieve the situation, Foreman supported the efforts of black doctors to find ways to keep themselves informed of new developments in science and medicine. On their behalf, he gained a hearing before the Fulton County Medical Society and proposed that the society's monthly lectures on current developments be open to black physicians. The majority voted against black participation in the monthly meetings, even on a segregated basis. As Foreman recalled, they argued "that the Negro doctors would have to hang their hats on the same racks that the white doctors used, and that would be an insufferable indignity." Several who voted for the proposal said that the primary motive of the opponents was to maintain their advantage with black patients.[41]

Foreman's exposure to black communities in Georgia, and his expanding network of black acquaintances, composed the most rewarding aspect of his work with the CIC. Clark was in frequent contact with Morehouse College President John Hope and his wife, Lugenia Burns Hope, and with the sociologist E. Franklin Frazier. His work took him to Tuskegee, where he became acquainted with Robert R. Moton, president of Tuskegee Institute, with the noted black scientist George Washington Carver, and with Henry Lee Moon, a young instructor. At a YMCA summer camp in Blue Ridge, North Carolina, he first met and heard "the very eloquent" and inspiring educator Mary McLeod Bethune, with whom he developed a deep and abiding friendship. David Jones, his colleague at the CIC, was his "first Negro friend," the first black person with whom Foreman was on a first-name basis.

In 1926, Jones and Foreman organized a "welcome home" concert for the Georgia-born and internationally celebrated singer Roland Hayes. Hayes, who refused to perform in concert halls that discriminated against blacks, had never performed in his native state. Enlisting the support of leaders in both the black and the white communities and the press, Jones and Foreman developed a plan for "equal seating." The five-thousand-seat City Auditorium was divided vertically, with blacks to the front on one side and whites on the other. It was the first time black people were not restricted to the balcony. Clark's Aunt Cornelia proudly announced that she had bought tickets for herself and her black chauffeur, but she worried over his using the traditionally white-only entrance to the auditorium. The sold-out event was widely hailed as a great step forward. Will Alexander commented, "[It] was the first time I ever saw segregation that did not seem to discriminate." But one observer recalled that John Hope was unimpressed. He "didn't care anything much about what happened when they [black people] were allowed to sit up to the front on one side and look across at their white friends. . . . He'd just as soon be segregated front to back as sideways."[42]

Foreman felt increasingly isolated in Atlanta's white community and frustrated with his work at the CIC. His family and friends tolerated his concern with racial issues but showed no genuine interest in what he was doing. His circle of friends included future "Nashville Agrarian" John Donald Wade and authors Frances Newman and Margaret Mitchell. Not one of his "natural companions," as his mother called them, shared any "sympathetic understanding" of his position on the race question. "The general opinion," Foreman recalled, "was that I was just a little 'nutty' on the subject of Negroes." By 1926, he concluded that the CIC did little to challenge the ignorance and apathy that marked white Atlanta's attitude toward the injustice and brutality pervading race relations. Although the CIC was making a change, "it was so pitifully small and ineffectual compared to the total job that had to be done," Foreman observed. "We were treating symptoms on the assumption that eventually the disease would be cured." There was no discussion "of the fundamental cause of the problem." After two years, the twenty-four-year-old Foreman felt the need to get away once again and develop a fuller perspective on the problems confronting the South.[43]

Foreman had confronted the intractability of the color line and the apparent inability of the white community to initiate meaningful change. But the encouragement and support he received from black Atlantans shaped Foreman's understanding of the problem and sustained his efforts. When Foreman left the CIC, Rutherford Butler Sr. wrote:

Sometimes, to me it looks so dark ahead I hardly know whether to forge ahead or turn back. I have tried so hard over a span of more than fifty years to trust God and have faith in white humanity, and if it were not for a few souls like yourself, Bishop Reese, Mr. W. W. Alexander, Rev. Wilmer and Rev. Ashby Jones and others, I would give up the fight and go to some foreign country and become a Mohamedan priest and bring that faith back to my people; Christianity has made such a mockery that it seems only a "sounding brass and tinkling cymbal." I need your prayers that I may keep the FAITH. May God go with you and bless you in your every effort to serve Him and Humanity.[44]

Will Alexander sympathized with his young protégé's desire to cast a wider net and recommended Foreman to several key associates in the philanthropic world. During the next five years, Foreman pursued graduate work at Columbia University while working for the Phelps-Stokes Foundation and later the Rosenwald Fund. His primary interests were ethics and the racial situation in the South.

Foreman's evolving views on race relations had outgrown the paternalistic mode that characterized white racial liberalism in the 1920s. His challenge to the assumptions that underlay white beneficence met with a cool response from Phelps-Stokes director Thomas Jesse Jones. When Foreman suggested that equal access to the vote was essential if blacks were to achieve a fair deal in American society, Jones, he recalled, dismissed this as "a very radical position." Jones insisted that all emphasis should be placed on training black people for jobs. But, Foreman countered, few economic opportunities would be available to blacks unless their influence on elections was greatly increased. Jones remained, Foreman recalled, "unpushable" on the subject.

During the summer of 1927, Foreman helped establish the Highlands Museum of Natural History near his family's summer home in Highlands, North Carolina; the museum grew to become a regional center for the study of biology. Otherwise, he concentrated his attention on completing his master's degree and his thesis on "The Development of Interracial Cooperation in the South."

In the course of his studies, and through continuing work on interracial concerns, Foreman consulted with Charles S. Johnson, editor of *Opportunity* magazine and benefactor of the Harlem Renaissance. Foreman assisted Johnson with a major interracial conference, held in Washington, D.C., in the fall of 1928. This was his first introduction to segregation in the nation's capital. As the person responsible for local arrangements, Foreman confronted a policy that prohibited American blacks from staying in Washington hotels but that welcomed "colored people" from other countries. After much persistence, Foreman persuaded several hotels, including the Willard Hotel, to make an exception and to admit black American guests. But the change was only temporary.

The Julius F. Rosenwald Fund provided Foreman with an ideal opportunity for pursuing his doctoral research on "Environmental Factors in Negro Education." Established in 1917 by the founder of Sears & Roebuck, the Rosenwald Fund was the major patron of black education in the South. When Edwin Embree, the fund's director, hired Foreman late in 1928, the stock market was cresting, and the foundation was earning money faster than it could spend it. Julius Rosenwald had stipulated that the foundation should not be perpetual, requiring that the endowment be spent within twenty-five years. As associate for the Southern Program, Foreman's job was to travel throughout the South and devise more ways for quickly distributing the Rosenwald money.[45]

Working out of the fund's Nashville office, Foreman developed a plan for supporting public libraries in the South. At a time when no southern county had a library that served all of the people, the Rosenwald Fund offered generous assistance to counties that would extend library services to all of its citizens—black and white, rural and urban. The fund supported programs in eleven counties in seven southern states. This project broke from the Rosenwald Fund's almost exclusive concern with black schools and health programs. Foreman found that several board members were hostile toward providing any assistance for southern whites, reflecting a common northern attitude that "the white people of the South were really all slaveholders at heart."[46] The project, however, had Embree's enthusiastic support. It was supplemented by an infusion of money into library schools in the South to support the training of black and white librarians. Tommie Dora Barker, of Atlanta, worked with Foreman as the primary coordinator of this program, which was later continued with support from the Carnegie Foundation.

With the collapse of the stock market in October 1929, the Rosenwald Fund adopted a conservative approach to spending its shrinking resources in the South, enabling Foreman to devote most of his time to his dissertation research. Foreman worked with Horace Mann Bond in pursuing a study of "Environmental Factors in Negro Education." Bond, then an instructor at Fisk University, had taken his Ph.D. at the University of Chicago under Robert E. Park and had written his dissertation on black education in Alabama. Bond and Foreman developed and implemented a research design to measure the ways in which environmental factors influenced the achievement of black students in the South, documenting a high correlation between expenditures and achievement. They worked from a representative sample drawn from North Carolina, Alabama, and Louisiana.

From October 1929 to May 1931, the team visited 569 schools and administered the new Sanford Achievement Test to ten thousand students in the third and sixth grades. In each place, they examined the wide range of factors shaping a child's educational environment: school facilities, the presence or absence of textbooks, term length, teacher qualifications and salaries, health and community organizations, and the local school superintendent. Since blacks had no political influence in any of the counties tested, the attitude of the local school superintendent proved to be an important factor in determining the quality of black education. Of the schools visited, they found 61 percent of them to be "unsatisfactory for school purposes." Their report noted: "If the schoolhouse is bad enough it can almost completely stop the educational process, as may be illustrated by one very small and dilapidated shack without windows, in which the investigators on opening the door found the school in absolute darkness and the teacher and pupils asleep. The teacher [who] faced the alternative of light and cold air through the open door and darkness and relative warmth with the door closed, chose the latter despite the soporific effect."[47]

Fieldwork with Horace Mann Bond in the South introduced Foreman to the daily indignities and insults endured by black people, regardless of their class or achievement. The two men worked closely throughout the course of the study. Foreman recalled, "The difficulties in the way of our working together were so great that it made me appreciate more than ever the conditions which Negroes have to face in this country." When Foreman tried to ride with Bond in the Jim Crow coach on the train, the conductor forced him to move. When they traveled together by automobile, "there was always a great problem as to where he could find food and lodging." In many of the small southern communities they visited, the accommodations for white people were often far from comfortable. "But I always knew," Foreman recalled, "that Mr. Bond was having to put up with much worse."[48]

Foreman's travels throughout the South during 1929–31 also confirmed his belief that southern whites were incapable of providing a solution to the racial injustice that permeated southern society. He was "greatly depressed" by the static, repressed condition of southern intellectuals. The Nashville Agrarians were reigning over the only intellectual movement of note, in the wake of the publication of their manifesto, *I'll Take My Stand*, in 1930. With the possible exception of Robert Penn Warren, Foreman concluded that these so-called fugitives were leading the retreat from reality, pining for an agrarian utopia that was built on the backs of a cheap, inexhaustible supply of black labor. He dubbed them "Neo-Confederates."

Liberal and humane sympathies were isolated or repressed in the South. An unspoken code of self-censorship seemed to prevail at private and public colleges; it was clearly understood that any questioning of the racial status quo would probably bring dismissal. Foreman admired the efforts of southern liberal journalists like Josephus Daniels, Mark Ethridge, and Julian Harris and found them to be enthusiastic supporters of the Rosenwald Fund. But none of them publicly endorsed fair treatment for black people, and it seemed unlikely that they would. After Julia Collier Harris and Julian Harris, editors of the *Columbus Enquirer-Sun*, won a Pulitzer Prize for their courageous campaign against the Ku Klux Klan, local opposition to the pair was so great that they finally left Columbus.

Foreman returned to Columbia University in the fall of 1931, wiser about the ways of the South but uncertain how to find a path forward. As the country sank deeper into the depression, the Rosenwald Fund continued to pay his salary while he completed his dissertation. He was awarded a Ph.D. in the spring of 1932. Since Foreman had no job prospects, Embree decided to keep him on for another year. The Rosenwald Fund sent him to Europe to broaden his education and suggested that he study rural organization in preparation for further work in the South. While visiting with his family in Highlands, North Carolina, before his departure, Clark listened to Franklin Roosevelt accept the Democratic Party's nomination in Chicago, pledging a "new deal."

Clark was most interested in observing the great socialist experiment firsthand, and he spent seven months of his year abroad in the Soviet Union. He felt more at home in Russia than he had in any other European country, remarking that the friendly, easygoing Russian people bore similarities to southerners. He developed a network of friends through his LSE connections. During the first part of his stay he lived in Moscow and devoted his time to studying the language and reading Karl Marx and Vladimir Lenin. There were ongoing discussions and arguments with friends as Clark sought to gain a fuller understanding of the Soviet state. He was impressed by the apparent ability of the new government to keep everyone employed. At a time when unemployment was crippling Western societies, the Soviet Union implemented a concept of "work therapy," providing jobs and training for institutionalized people. But contradictions abounded. After a hot political debate with his friends about the new egalitarian society, Clark would return to his hostel, where the domestic who looked after his room would insist on kissing his hand. Freda Utley, who was part of Clark's circle in Moscow, later wrote: "Clark . . . was one of the very few foreign visitors to learn something of the realities of Soviet life. . . . [He] studied it all with admirable objectivity. . . . He had staunch views concerning the need for a planned society, but no illusions concerning the Soviet Union or the foreign communists."[49]

Overall, his impressions of the people and of their socialist experiment were positive. Russian views on "the Negro question" varied. Misinformation on the racial situation in the United States was not uncommon. In discussing the discrimination suffered by blacks in the United States, one critic charged that blacks were not allowed to speak their own language. But Soviet policy barring discrimination against minorities and nationalities was widely publicized and acted on. A black American told him about an incident on a bus in Moscow. When one of the passengers made an anti-

Semitic remark, the other passengers protested and apologized to the black man for the ignorance and prejudice of the man who had made the remark. Then they took the offending citizen to the nearest policeman. "Such an incident means more to a victim of discrimination than any number of speeches," Foreman commented. Foreman was also favorably impressed by the efforts of the Soviet government to grant women full equality.[50]

After several months in Moscow, Foreman spent two months traveling around the countryside, mostly by himself. The vast countryside of the Soviet Union revealed the poverty and backwardness of this largely peasant society. Clark noted similarities to the rural southern United States. In his travels through the Ukraine and the Crimea, Foreman observed widespread hardship and near starvation, conditions that people endured as the cost of the rapid industrialization of a society besieged by hostile external forces. The Ukraine exported grain in exchange for machinery while people went hungry. Communities worked the collective farms in the Crimea, often under brutal conditions. "But the people were struggling with the conviction that they were all equally a part of a great new society," Foreman wrote, "and that whatever sacrifices were made would result in the benefit of all fairly."[51] Although he heard many complaints about the rigors of the regime, and witnessed individual misfortunes, he discovered that people generally supported their government. The Soviet Union marked a new and hopeful departure from Russia's tsarist past. But given the vast internal struggle to modernize, and the demonstrated determination of the Western powers to undermine the Bolshevik revolution, Foreman concluded that Soviet aspirations to lead an international socialist movement had been reduced to mere rhetoric.

If the Soviet experiment would not reach beyond its borders, the question remained: What sorts of national and international economic arrangements would emerge in the aftermath of worldwide depression? Foreman arrived in London early in June 1933, just as the World Economic Conference was about to begin. "I felt I could see the international capitalist economy, on the basis of which England had dominated the trade of the world for so long, crumbling before my eyes," he later recalled. Foreman observed the emergence of a new synthesis, which combined national planned economies and intergovernmental trade. He felt guardedly hopeful about Roosevelt's break with conventional economics. During the summer of 1933 he wrote:

America is approaching by peaceful means the road which in Russia, Italy, Turkey and Germany was adopted only as the result of violent revolutions. To a certain extent, it is true, the severity of the economic crisis in

America, and its appalling effects in a country which, unlike England, makes no provisions for the millions of unemployed, coupled with the distinctly revolutionary attitude of impoverished farmers, threatened with expropriation, were acute and menacing enough to compel a change from above without waiting for an upheaval from below. The fact that Roosevelt has obtained dictatorial powers from the Congress constitutionally does not render less revolutionary the application of those powers.[52]

Early in July, Clark received a cablegram from Embree urging that he return home immediately. Foreman was able to stall Embree long enough to keep his date to meet Mairi Fraser's train when it arrived in Paris on 20 July. Clark had met the young reporter for the *Toronto Daily Star* when he had sailed to Europe the previous year. They were hastily married in Geneva and sailed to New York, where Embree was waiting. The next day, Foreman was on the train to Washington to talk with Harold Ickes about the job of "Special Adviser on the Economic Status of Negroes." That was a Thursday. When he agreed to take the job, he told Ickes that he would like a little time to travel to Canada to meet the family of his new wife. Ickes responded with an air of magnanimity, "All right then, start Monday." The opportunity for which the thirty-one-year-old Georgian had been preparing himself had arrived.

To maintain a democracy of effort requires a vast amount of patience in dealing with differing methods, a vast amount of humility. But out of the confusion of many voices rises an understanding of dominant public need. Then political leadership can voice common ideals and aid in their realization.

FRANKLIN D. ROOSEVELT, Inaugural Address, 1937

... the greatest chance which has come to the Negro in America since the World War. The chance to swing upward under the shout and echo of the New Deal.

LAWRENCE D. REDDICK, *Opportunity*, July 1934

2

Challenge to the Solid South

THE POLITICS OF NEW DEAL REFORM, 1933–1938

"The New Deal was so abruptly different it was startling," recalled a reporter who had been covering national politics since the presidency of Calvin Coolidge. "Suddenly Washington was alive."[1] The feverish activity of the first one hundred days transformed the nation's capital. New agencies sprang up, and old departments were made over; the rash of New Deal programs gave Washington a grip on every phase of the nation's economic life.

If the legislative whirlwind that produced the early New Deal was embedded with contradictions and crosscurrents, there was no question that a fundamental reordering of government was under way. Process prevailed over form. Franklin Roosevelt's endorsement of government as a tool to advance economic security and human betterment promised to stretch the parameters of government and politics. This national experiment implicitly challenged the static and insular political culture that had prevailed in the South since the turn of the century.

The urgency of the depression combined with the innovative and confident milieu of New Deal Washington to create "a freedom of experimentation that was unexampled."[2] Roosevelt orchestrated a new concept of government through the constellation of policymakers he convened. Among the boldest strategists were Relief Administrator Harry Hopkins and the cabinet secretaries Harold Ickes, Henry Wallace, and Frances Perkins. Each had apprenticed in the progressive reform politics of the late 1910s and the 1920s, working toward local and state-based reforms in the areas of social welfare, labor, and farm policy and, in Wallace's case, toward federal legislation to protect farmers from the vicissitudes of a free market economy.

The New Deal provided the opportunity to join progressive ideas, in all their regional variations, to a national plan of action. In navigating this unchartered course, the Roosevelt administration enlisted the talents and enterprising spirit of the legion of young lawyers, social workers, and economists who flocked to Washington to "help right the wrongs that had befallen the country."[3]

"It was a glorious time for obscure people, because the big names themselves were in a quandary," Paul Freund, one of the young New Deal lawyers, recalled. "The field was open for young people with new ideas."[4] The New Deal nurtured a new generation of policymakers and political activists who played a pivotal role in initiating and implementing Roosevelt's reforms. Clark Foreman, who never anticipated a career in government or politics, was, in many ways, typical of this group. He also represented a very different kind of southerner on the national scene, one who offered a stark contrast to those southern statesmen who had risen through the ranks of the Democratic Party to powerful positions on Capitol Hill.

In addition to Foreman were Will Alexander, C. B. "Beanie" Baldwin, Clifford Durr, Aubrey Williams, Mary McLeod Bethune, Arthur "Tex" Goldschmidt, Oscar Chapman, and others. Brilliant, young black professionals, such as Robert C. Weaver and William Hastie, were also drawn to the potential for social engineering inherent in the New Deal. As policymakers, lobbyists, and activists, these individuals endorsed and helped to create new forms of political participation and alliances that gave voice to constituencies long disfranchised by law and custom in the South. They also played a pivotal role in drawing national attention to the poverty that pervaded southern life and that thwarted the recovery effort.

As Anthony Badger's history of the New Deal demonstrates, the depression created constraints as well as opportunities. The experimental and "refreshingly self-critical" spirit that animated the New Deal was contained by persistent political realities that "sharply limited the room of . . . policymakers to maneuver." The predominantly conservative southern bloc in Congress, coupled with the traditional emphasis on localism and volunteerism in the region, stood as the greatest obstacle to the New Deal aspirations toward a new, more equitable social order. As has been amply documented, the National Industrial Recovery Act (NIRA) and the Agricultural Adjustment Act, the cornerstones of the early New Deal, were easily tailored by local southern elites and their powerful representatives in Congress to fit the prevailing economic and political arrangements in the region.[5]

But the persistence of old forms and old allegiances masked subtle shifts in the expectations and political consciousness of people who responded directly to the emergence of the federal government as a dominant force in the economic life of the nation. The unfair and racially inequitable administration of federal programs in the South became a focus of protest, an occasion for organized action. In August 1933 twelve hundred black Atlantans gathered in a mass meeting to denounce the discriminatory administration of the National Recovery Administration (NRA) wage codes. The assembly petitioned the Roosevelt administration to ensure that the benefits of the New Deal "be accorded to all citizens alike, irrespective of race." In 1934, black and white tenant farmers in Arkansas formed the Southern Tenant Farmers Union (STFU) to protest the rampant inequities in the New Deal farm program. For groups such as these, the New Deal offered a way to create "an avenue out of the political and economic wilderness."[6]

Rather than try to diffuse such protests, many New Deal reformers encouraged them. White southern progressives and black New Deal administrators sought out and supported new constituencies stirred by federal initiatives, viewing them as essential to the vitality of the New Deal as a political process. As their efforts to secure fundamental reforms from within the Roosevelt administration met with frustration, they became more deliberate in their support and encouragement of political action and organization among traditionally disfranchised groups. They acted as catalysts in a long-term effort to institutionalize the democratic aspirations of Roosevelt's recovery program by appealing to the expectations of groups long on the margins of southern politics. Their efforts prepared the way for Roosevelt's 1938 attack on the unyielding dominance of conservative white southerners in the political life of the region and the nation.

The creation of a position to ensure the participation of black Americans in the recovery effort was emblematic of the new departure heralded by the New Deal. Commenting on Clark Foreman's appointment as "Special Adviser on the Economic Status of Negroes," the New Republic called it "an experiment . . . worth watching." The editorial observed that wage differentials based on race were the major contributing factor in "the appalling plight of the Negro, particularly in the South." Yet, the editorial explained, enforcement of an equal wage often led to the replacement of black workers by whites. "Of course," it was assumed that no government official could "compel employers to end this discrimination." Foreman could be most useful, the New Republic predicted, by helping to "create conditions under which the Negroes [could] organize and fight for their own rights."[7]

The potentially disruptive nature of New Deal reform was most readily apparent in the implementation of the NIRA, which aimed to apply national standards to industry and labor. Southern manufacturers, desperate for regulation, swallowed their initial objections to this unwieldy piece of legislation. Clearly, however, NIRA provisions for an industry-wide minimum wage and NIRA protection of the right of labor to organize implicitly threatened the maintenance of a low-wage, nonunion labor force. Federal work relief and credit also challenged the culture of dependency that had secured an abundant, cheap labor supply. The principle of an equal wage for white and black workers under the NRA codes, and in government-funded work projects, struck at the very basis of the southern system. Efforts of industrialists and their southern political representatives to secure and maintain a racial wage differential inaugurated the first major contest over the New Deal in the South.[8]

"Aside from the damage to the Negroes, prejudice complicates the working of our whole economic machinery, as was clearly evident when the NRA started the making of codes," Clark Foreman explained in a New York Times article. The National Industrial Recovery Act was primarily an enabling act that relied on the voluntary cooperation of business to set industry-wide codes that could stimulate recovery by providing for fair competition and a restoration of purchasing power. The codes, which regulated prices and set maximum hours and minimum wages, had federal sanction. Commenting on the implementation of the NIRA, black sociologist Ira DeA. Reid wryly observed, "One may safely give long odds that when the Economic Fathers set out to establish the present machinery for industrial recovery they had not the slightest idea that they would meet such a problem as that of a wage differential based on race." The obvious question concerning southern practices, however, quickly became apparent. Would southern workers, and most specifically black workers, be treated fairly and equitably under the New Deal, or would federal programs bend to the power of southern Democrats and reinforce the caste system?[9]

Southern manufacturers, joined by the unmatched power of southern conservatives in Congress, were determined to maintain a racial differential under the NRA codes. Ira Reid reported that members of the Labor Advisory Board of the NRA "found themselves facing a most complicated array of statistics, inferences and assumptions of southern industrialists," data proving that it was "both necessary and expedient to permit a differential wage for Negro workers." Although no reputable labor-efficiency studies based on race were available, employers insisted that because of the inefficiency of black workers, they could not afford to pay black workers an equal wage. Furthermore, they warned that if such a policy was enforced, black workers would lose their jobs, and many of the affected businesses would shut down, thus undercutting the NRA's goal of stimulating production. Southern employers used this apparently grim fact in their effort to persuade southern black leaders to endorse a lower minimum wage, compelling them to weigh the short-term consequences of swelling the ranks of the black unemployed against the less-pressing but equally troublesome choice of sanctioning a federal endorsement of the southern caste system.[10]

The code-making process, though technically democratic, reflected existing political realities in the nation's capital. All groups to be affected by a proposed code had a right to speak at public NRA code hearings in Washington. To streamline the procedure, however, NRA officials attempted to resolve major issues at prehearing conferences between representatives of the affected industry and the affiliated, all-white, trade unions. Foreman reported to Harold Ickes that his efforts to convince NRA officials of the need for special attention to the status of black workers were fruitless. Their ignorance of the racial dimension of economic dislocation was compounded by the political pressure exerted by southern manufacturing interests "determined to keep Negro labor cheap and amenable."[11]

The swift convening of a system of NRA code hearings for nearly six hundred industries taxed the capacity of the established civil rights organizations like the National Association for the Advancement of Colored People (NAACP) and the National Urban League to respond quickly and effectively. Neither organization had a permanent representative in Washington, and the challenges and opportunities inherent in the inauguration of the New Deal were beyond the tactics and strategies perfected in the struggles of an earlier time. The negative program of protest that had served the NAACP well since its founding was inadequate to the vast social reordering spurred by economic collapse and national intervention. The implementation of a national recovery program would have immediate and long-term consequences for black Americans, the great majority of whom were disfranchised and denied basic citizenship rights. On resigning from the NAACP in 1934, W. E. B. Du Bois chided his associates: "We are called to formulate a positive program of construction and inspiration. We have been thus far unable to comply."[12]

During the summer of 1933, Robert C. Weaver and John Preston Davis returned to their hometown of Washington determined to obtain a hearing for black workers. Weaver, a doctoral candidate in economics at Harvard, and Davis, a recent graduate of Harvard Law School, were deeply concerned that none of the major national black organizations appeared to be addressing the issue of black participation in the New Deal. With the assistance of Robert Pelham, a retired government worker who ran an independent news release operation, Weaver and Davis established themselves as the Negro Industrial League (NIL). Pelham provided them with free office space, a typewriter, and supplies. From this base, the two monitored the daily flow of NRA announcements, wrote testimonies, and became regular attendees at code hearings, where they lobbied for fair treatment of black workers and testified on the adverse effects of specific codes. They were, Weaver later recalled, "something of an oddity." He added, "No one expected us, we were literate and we were contentious."[13]

Weaver and Davis had been part of a small group of young black intellectuals whose personal strivings and social concerns were galvanized by the devastating impact of the depression on black communities. Their close associates at Harvard included William Hastie and Ralph Bunche, and they were in frequent contact with the slightly older Charles Hamilton Houston, then vice-dean of the Howard University Law School. These young men brought a fresh perspective to the challenges presented by the federal initiatives of the New Deal and a willingness to act on their understanding of the inherent opportunities afforded by the expansion of federal power. Throughout the New Deal period, they worked collectively through the federal government, the NAACP, the labor movement, and other organizations, helping to build an effective political movement to advance racial and economic justice.

Weaver, Davis, Hastie, and Houston had grown up in Washington, D.C. During Weaver's youthful years, President Woodrow Wilson extended the racial mores of this southern city to the federal government, decreeing the segregation of lunchrooms and rest rooms in government buildings.

Weaver's father had worked for the U.S. Post Office at the time, and Weaver remembered his deep resentment. "In fact, he wouldn't go to the lunch room [any more]. He carried his lunch to work with him." By the eve of the New Deal, a local NAACP committee reported that Washington was so thoroughly segregated that "a colored man [could] escape insult . . . only by locking himself in his room or associating only with his own people."[14]

Educational opportunities for Washington's black middle class formed one area that provided a reprieve from the pervasive constraints of the segregation system. The Paul Laurence Dunbar High School was the only segregated school in the country in which black teachers were paid salaries equal to those of their white counterparts. Offering higher salaries than those at any of the black colleges, Dunbar easily attracted outstanding black graduates of the nation's premier northeastern colleges and universities. "There were Phi Beta Kappa keys all over the place," Weaver recalled. Rigorous scholastic training included an in-depth study of black history under Nevall H. Thomas, who was also president of the Washington branch of the NAACP. Thomas's students became fully acquainted with the history of the Reconstruction period. The sense of racial pride and self-confidence that Dunbar inspired, Weaver explained, only reinforced family values. Parents instilled in their children an aspiration "to fix our wagon to a star, but it had to be a star of progress, rather than a perpetuation of the status quo, as far as your opportunities were concerned."[15]

A letter from a teacher at Dunbar was sufficient to win students a place at the college of their choice. Houston and Hastie attended Amherst College, Davis went to Bates College, and Weaver enrolled in Harvard College, where he was one of two black students in his class. While Weaver, the youngest in the group, was in college, Hastie and Davis both enrolled in Harvard Law School. In addition to providing an atmosphere free of the psychological and physical constraints of segregation, there was, Weaver recalled, a remarkable nucleus of black students at Harvard in the late 1920s, mostly in the graduate and professional schools. There were occasional gatherings that included most of these students, among them Rayford Logan, William Dean, and Percy Julian. But Weaver, Davis, Hastie, and Ralph Bunche, who was a graduate student in political science, got together more frequently for poker games and "bull sessions."

A frequent topic of discussion among these young men concerned the limitations facing black students who had excelled at institutions like Harvard. Unless they took a low-paying job at a black college, it was unlikely that they would have an opportunity to apply their education toward a career. Through the early 1930s, public service and politics in the black community were a function of a tightly controlled patronage system. "All of us were completely disgusted with and critical of the so-called Republican Negro leaders," Weaver recalled. The leaders' primary function was to make speeches for the Republican Party and provide jobs for their friends and relatives while "not doing anything for the mass of black people." Black Republicans, with their ties to the fraternal organizations and churches, were "a great impediment" for those "interested in public service."[16]

With the depression, the abysmal social conditions of black Americans emerged in sharp relief and completely engaged the intellectual ferment of the young men in Cambridge. "The impact of unemployment and dislocation . . . especially in the South" was "unbelievable," Weaver recalled. The depression had exposed "just how tenuous the economic base of blacks in America was. In fact, it wasn't even a base. It was a moving target down." The men sought out social science literature that might shed some light on this vast problem, finding little available. Discussions on how to meet the emergency and the deep structural problems it exposed dominated mealtime conversations and frequent discussion sessions in Cambridge and sometimes at Howard Law School with Charles Houston. "As we tried to look at what could be done," said Weaver, "it became crystal clear to Bill [Hastie], John Davis, Ralph [Bunche] and myself that the precedents were in the Reconstruction period and that you had to look to the federal government. This was the only way you were going to get meaningful activity because, of course, by this time all the states in the South had completely disfranchised blacks." The New Deal provided a new opportunity to get federal action that could counter the dual system that had brutally proscribed the opportunities of black Americans.[17]

Davis and Weaver were moved by the potential inherent in the new administration's initiatives and by the expectations generated by these initiatives. But during the summer of 1933 they were driven more by a sense of urgency that was shared by other young black intellectuals. If the interests of black workers were not quickly and effectively represented in the national arena, in all likelihood federal policy would sanction existing arrangements. Lester Granger voiced a widely shared concern when he charged in *Opportunity*, the magazine of the National Urban League, that the depth of the economic crisis was aggravated by the "bankruptcy of effective leadership among American Negroes." He explained, "Few of the old line Negro 'intellectuals' have taken pains during the past decade to keep abreast of the increasingly intricate industrial problems which involve the fate of America's black working masses." Economic collapse had exposed the "rapidly widening gulf of misunderstanding between the masses of Negroes and that educated group who would be their spokesmen." But Granger predicted that the deep discontent simmering among the laboring classes, black and white, would seek and find a solution to their desperate plight, as evidenced in the appeal of Communist Party and other left-wing groups. "In this very state of confused despair and bitter disillusionment lay the seeds of a new racial attitude and leadership," he predicted.[18]

Weaver and Davis typified the new political leadership that emerged from the dual impact of the depression and the federal initiatives of the New Deal. Dynamic and improvisational, they were guided by their determination to secure a voice in the process surrounding the development and implementation of the New Deal. Their effort to defeat the wage differential was joined to a broader and more far-reaching goal, which was to help facilitate the full and active participation of black Americans in the recovery effort. This included New Deal–sponsored programs and the newly invigorated labor movement, which, for the first time, enjoyed federal protection. Weaver, Davis, and their political associates acted on the assumption that, in addition to aiding those who had suffered the greatest economic hardships, such a policy was essential to the success of New Deal reforms. The maintenance of a substandard wage for one group inhibited the possibility of building a viable labor movement and would ensure that the South remained an economic backwater. Thus, in an effort to join black efforts to a larger political coalition, they sought out and joined with those individuals in the labor movement and from the South who recognized that racial discrimination and exclusion thwarted any effort to secure fundamental economic and political reform.

The NIL succeeded not only in focusing attention on the issue of racial discrimination in the administration of NRA codes but also in establishing a national organizational structure for representing the special economic conditions and concerns of black Americans. By September 1933 the NAACP, the National Urban League, and thirteen other black organizations had joined with the NIL to form the Joint Committee on Economic Recovery, with John Davis as executive secretary and Robert Weaver as director of research. Financial assistance from the NAACP and a small grant from the Rosenwald Fund provided for a five-thousand-dollar annual operating budget, which included a modest salary for Davis; the limited funding required Weaver to return, reluctantly, to a teaching position at A&T College in Greensboro. "My heart was in what was going on in Washington," he recalled.[19]

Although it never approached the power of the better-organized, and well-funded, business groups and trade unions, the Joint Committee served multiple purposes. Largely as a result of its efforts, the NRA decided against providing federal sanction to lower wage and hour standards for black workers. In each case, requests by southern businessmen for racial differentials were denied. Nevertheless, discrimination against black workers under NRA codes was widespread. The Joint Committee opened the way for effective protest and political action by keeping the issue of racial discrimination in the national recovery effort before the public. The committee became a clearinghouse for hundreds of individual reports of code violations; Davis conducted numerous surveys and made several investigative tours through parts of the South. His published findings in the NAACP's *Crisis* magazine attracted the interest and concern of Eleanor Roosevelt, who passed his article, "NRA Codifies Wage Slavery," along to Donald Richberg, assistant to the administrator of the NRA.[20]

Southern businessmen did succeed in writing a regional wage differential into NRA codes. Through regional codes and widespread local subterfuge, they were often able to achieve a racial wage differential in practice. Regional codes were applied to nearly one hundred industries, which employed more than half a million black workers. The code for the laundry trade, for example, contained six different wages based on geography, with the lowest, at fourteen cents an hour, in states where black women composed the great majority of laundry workers. In many cases, employers changed the job classification of black workers so that they would not be covered by the code; in other cases, employers simply ignored the code provisions.

At the Maid-Well Garment Company in Forrest City, Arkansas, 200 of the 450 women employed were black. The company was required to pay the workers $12 a week under the cotton code but persisted in paying the black women $6.16, with ten cents deducted for a doctor's fee. A complaint filed with the Labor Department by one of the black workers was referred to the Joint Committee on Economic Recovery. After further investigation, John Davis filed a complaint with the NRA on 13 January 1934. On 30 January Maid-Well dismissed all of its black employees. Davis's efforts to secure restitution of back wages for the women were frustrated by "constant malingering on the part of both local and national compliance officials entrusted with the enforcement of the National Industrial Recovery Act."[21]

A similar case developed in Montgomery County, Alabama. The case of Southland Manufacturing Company won much attention when Robert R. Moton, president of Tuskegee Institute, petitioned the NRA to allow the company to maintain a substandard wage. Southland, owned by the Reliance Manufacturing Company of Chicago, was one of the few textile plants that employed black workers. When Reliance lost its appeal to the NRA for an exemption from the code minimum wage of $12 a week for its Southland branch, it shut the plant down, throwing three hundred black employees out of work. Reliance appealed to the NRA a second time, with the support of Moton and other Tuskegee officials. In a hearing before the NRA Industrial Appeals Board in the fall of 1934, G. Lake Imes, secretary of Tuskegee Institute, testified on behalf of Southland's former employees. Imes appealed to the board to permit Southland to pay blacks below the code minimum until the company was able to "bring up the efficiency of the workers . . . to the point where . . . the workers themselves" could earn "the equivalent of the minimum requirements of the code." He added that a dual code might be the only practical way to keep thousands of black workers from joining the army of the unemployed, which included 80 percent of the black population of Montgomery County. Herbert Mayer, president of Reliance Manufacturing Company, maintained that the company could not afford to operate Southland at a higher wage. When asked why Southland was not operating at a profit, Mayer replied, "It must be on account of the characteristics of the people who have not had the experience and the background, and their racial characteristics."[22]

Clark Foreman, the white Georgian assistant to Harold Ickes, testified before the board on behalf of the Department of the Interior. Foreman argued that it was "very important for the federal government not to place any stigma on Negro labor," for it would have consequences for every black worker in the country. He urged that the case was not one of the NRA versus three hundred black workers in Montgomery. It was necessary to think of these three hundred workers as part of two groups: as part of the workers in the country and as part of the Negro race. Whatever action the federal government took in this case would affect both groups. The argument that black workers were less efficient was a specious one. "If the federal government makes an exemption for Negro workers because of their lack of skill or background, due to a lack of proper educational facilities in Montgomery County, there is very little hope of solving the problem because the worst school system in the country for Negroes is in Montgomery County." Moreover, Foreman noted, if the workers were not satisfactory, why was it that, according to company records, Reliance had not dismissed one single person, especially considering that there was an enormous pool of unemployed workers in Montgomery County? Secretary of Labor Frances Perkins endorsed Foreman's position: "To grant such a petition, in my opinion, would be contrary to the ends that are being sought through the National Recovery Act." The NRA board denied Reliance's appeal. The plant remained closed.[23]

As sociologist Ira DeA. Reid observed, the politics of NRA code-making underscored one of the defining issues of the New Deal in the South. "The current question is, in view of the fact that all of the southern states sanction a lower wage for Negro workers such as school teachers and other public employees, should this differential be given the legal sanction and approval of the recovery machinery of the Federal Government?" The threat of job displacement and of the further elimination of job opportunities was a real one, as Southland and other cases illustrated. This was, Weaver recalled, "a very tough issue." But he, Davis, Reid, and others started from the premise that there should be no discrimination, especially when public funds were involved. "Wherever the Federal government touches interracial life it should stand for the policy of interracial cooperation instead of separation," Davis argued. "Any measure that will place Negroes on a lower, segregated status should be opposed." This position was widely endorsed in the black press and in journals of black opinion, such as *Crisis* and *Opportunity*. The initiatives of the Joint Committee invited the exploration of tactics and strategies to secure a no-discrimination policy.[24]

The struggle surrounding the NRA codes and wage differentials highlighted the racial stratification of the South's labor market, providing a focus for the thorough examination of the South's economic problems that had been sparked by the depression. Davis and Weaver's efforts won the support of sympathetic members of the Roosevelt administration and of a number of liberal white southerners who were prepared to look beyond the racial divide in their search for structural solutions to the region's impoverishment. The NRA's rejection of racial wage differentials established an important precedent. "For once," Will Alexander proclaimed, "the federal government has acted on the assumption that Negro laborers are American laborers." The government thus created new opportunities for black workers and the American labor movement to move beyond the debilitating tradition of racial exclusion and discrimination. Among black activists, southern progressives, and a new generation of labor organizers, there was a growing consensus that such a policy was essential not only to the security of black workers but also to the success of the newly revitalized labor movement. This opinion was informed by the work of young social scientists and economists such as Horace Cayton and George Mitchell, who, with the assistance of Foreman, secured employment with the Interior Department, where they conducted research for their book *Black Workers and the New Unions*.[25]

New Deal Washington was a seedbed for new political alliances and strategies. With free rein to define and implement his assignment as "Special Adviser on the Economic Status of Negroes," Foreman worked to expand channels of access between the New Deal and its black constituencies. Complementing Harold Ickes's aggressive efforts to promote the hiring of black professionals, Foreman staffed his small office with black employees, including Lucia Pitts, one of the few black women to be employed as a secretary in the federal government. He became acquainted with the people who were politically active in the black community, people such as Robert Weaver and John Davis, whom he met during the code hearings, and William Hastie and Charles Houston, who were coordinating the NAACP's legal campaign against unequal education in the South. In November 1933, Foreman easily persuaded Weaver to resign from his position at A&T College and to join Ickes's staff as "Associate Adviser on the Economic Status of Negroes." Hastie joined the Interior Department that same month as assistant solicitor. One of the first things Weaver and Hastie did was to desegregate the lunchroom at Interior, initiating a reversal of the segregation policies Woodrow Wilson had enacted some twenty years earlier.[26]

Weaver was intrigued by the New Deal and eager to be a part of it. When he joined Ickes's staff late in 1933, there was no way of knowing the specifics of what he could do or would do in his position. It was new; there were no precedents. He was also under attack from established black leaders, who charged that he was too young, lacked experience, and had no reputation in race relations. Feeling "out there" by himself, Weaver was nevertheless enthusiastic about the possibilities before him. He was confident that much could be accomplished with the racially progressive Ickes. He also joined the staff knowing that he would soon be fully responsible for the Office of Negro Affairs. From the start, Foreman informed Weaver that he intended "to work himself out of a job." In the interim year, they worked together as equal partners. Foreman was the first of a handful of "emancipated white Southerners" whom Weaver encountered in the New Deal. The progressive development of New Deal policies, and the political will demonstrated by his growing network of associates within the Roosevelt administration, encouraged Weaver's hopes that elemental reform was possible if it was joined to an expanding process of political participation on the part of black Americans.[27]

Foreman and Weaver liberally defined the scope and mandate of their office. Confident of Ickes's full support, they moved freely throughout the executive branch in an effort to ensure black participation in the various recovery programs. Early in 1934 they convened an "Interdepartmental Group Concerned with the Special Problems of Negroes," drawing together black and white representatives from a broad cross section of government agencies. The Interdepartmental Group produced several studies on how black people were faring under the various New Deal programs. Bureaucratic jealousies, negative political pressures, and ingrained racial attitudes ultimately inhibited the effective functioning of this group, which disbanded after four meetings. An appeal to Harry Hopkins for permission to investigate reports that black people were being denied relief in Alabama and were on the verge of starvation met with an indignant response. Hopkins said that he could not have people outside his department telling him what to do. Foreman surmised that Hopkins's hostility was probably due in part to his ongoing bureaucratic feud with Ickes. But Will Alexander suggested that Hopkins's ambitions for a presidential candidacy in 1940 encouraged him to avoid tangling with southern politicians on the race issue. A later effort by Foreman to obtain equal wages for black teachers in Louisiana, under the Civil Works Administration (cwa) program, was also nixed by Hopkins.[28]

Among FDR's major appointments, Ickes was exceptional in his willingness to act unequivocally in behalf of racial fairness and inclusion, providing Foreman and Weaver with an important wedge for stretching the limits of an often inflexible bureaucratic structure. Foreman's success in cracking the Civilian Conservation Corps (ccc) policy of barring blacks from supervisory positions offers a useful example. The ccc, which provided employment for young men under army supervision, maintained segregated camps. All of the officers and supervisory personnel, however, were white. Foreman's appeals to the army to hire black supervisors for the black camps were rebuffed. Since the Interior Department had authority over the camps located in the national parks, Foreman obtained an order from Ickes requiring that a black person be hired to fill the next supervisory position available in a black camp on park land.

When an opening for an archaeologist occurred for a project restoring the Civil War battlefields in Gettysburg, Foreman and Weaver located Dr. Louis King of West Virginia to fill the position. A delegation from the National Park Service protested the appointment and warned that there was no place for King to eat and that white people in Gettysburg were not used to associating with black people. King's very presence could easily provoke violence and bloodshed. Their grim warnings made Foreman fearful for King's safety, but he did not retreat. King took the job and got along very well. His appointment was an incremental change, which failed to secure any fundamental reform in hiring policies. But beyond the singular victory, Foreman later recalled that the experience afforded a useful lesson. "I became convinced that fear was the tool of reaction and that a person who wanted to fight for decent conditions for all human beings had to make up his mind that he would not be frightened away from a position he knew to be correct."[29]

The $3.3 billion Public Works Administration (PWA), administered by Ickes, provided an unprecedented opportunity to develop a mechanism for defining and enforcing a no-discrimination policy on federally funded work projects. Ickes's initial order that a no-discrimination clause be included in all PWA contracts met with cautious enthusiasm from black spokesmen. A black newspaperman warned that a previous federal no-discrimination order, enacted by Secretary of the Treasury Ogden Mills in 1932, had been easily ignored, since no criteria existed to measure discrimination. Ickes referred the matter to the Office of Negro Affairs. In preparation for the establishment of the Housing Division of the PWA, he advised Foreman and Weaver to devise an affirmative policy to ensure the full participation of black labor in federally funded projects.

Weaver was primarily responsible for developing the new policy. Working closely with William Hastie, he devised a procedure whereby PWA contract recipients were required to employ a minimum percentage of black skilled labor, based on the percentage of skilled black laborers in the local population according to the 1930 occupational census. Meeting this minimum requirement would serve as prima facie evidence that contract recipients were complying with the no-discrimination policy. Implementation of the new policy was complicated by the exclusion of blacks from the building trade unions and from the licensing procedures for plumbers and electricians in northern and southern cities. In these cases, the Department of Labor was able to negotiate agreements with local union officials. By 1936, the policy had been implemented in twenty-nine cities, including Birmingham, Atlanta, Columbia, and Memphis. The Housing Program, under Weaver's supervision, proved to be the most racially inclusive New Deal initiative, securing black participation in all phases of the slum-clearance and low-rent housing programs.[30]

The PWA's quota system was not devised to open new job opportunities for black workers. Developed in a time of depression and unemployment, it served as a holding action, ensuring that black workers retained past occupational advantages. New Deal policy efforts in behalf of racial and economic reform were piecemeal and limited. Although opponents had blocked official racial wage differentials, regional wage differentials and local subterfuge maintained racial-based wages. In the short term, progressives in the Roosevelt administration had to accommodate conservative southerners, whose support was deemed essential to the president's overall program. Foreman later reflected, "Almost all of the work I was doing seemed to be patchwork, getting a man here, protesting there, but not solving anything fundamental."[31]

Nevertheless, the process surrounding the New Deal offered a unique opportunity to test strategies, establish new precedents, and stretch the boundaries of participation. As they engaged the social forces released by the depression and the New Deal, Foreman, Weaver, and other young progressives were participating in a broader movement. "More important than the factual representation of New Deal programs," Weaver advised the annual convention of the NAACP in 1937, "is the interpretive analysis of results and the evolution of techniques for the future. . . . Unless a group like ours is constantly developing, consciously or unconsciously, such techniques, it will not only fail to advance, but must rapidly lose ground."[32]

The political struggle unleashed by the implementation of the New Deal farm program fed the process that Weaver described. The success of southern planters in tailoring the Agricultural Adjustment Act to their interests sparked a reaction that drew national attention to the problem of chronic rural poverty in the South. When the Arkansas-based STFU entered the debate over the New Deal farm program, it created an opportunity for liberal and progressive New Dealers to publicly explore the economic and political underpinnings of the South's impoverishment. The plight of the rural poor, black and white, stood as compelling testimony to the inadequacy of "recovery" measures and documented the need for far-reaching, federally sponsored reforms. It was an issue that informed the debate surrounding the 1936 presidential campaign and the shifting political alignments that led Franklin Roosevelt to identify the South as "the nation's number one economic problem."[33]

Henry Wallace's Department of Agriculture, probably more than any other New Deal agency, reflected the eclectic mixture of policymakers that composed the Roosevelt administration. Veterans of the decade-long struggle to secure federal price-support policies for agricultural products rubbed shoulders with energetic young reformers whom the director of the Agricultural Adjustment Administration (AAA), George Peek, cryptically described as "an entirely new species." Lodged primarily in the general counsel's office under Jerome Frank, the young reformers were among the most brilliant legal minds of the New Deal, including Alger Hiss, Thurman Arnold, Telford Taylor, Lee Pressman, and John Abt, along with Gardiner Jackson, who worked in the consumer counsel's office. These young urban lawyers arrived in Washington imbued with the confidence and hope of the early New Deal days but with little firsthand knowledge about agriculture. "The spirit was rather as though we were going to fight for the country," Hiss recalled. "We were like a militia in mufti and we had enlisted for the duration."[34]

Conflicting interpretations of the authority and objectives of the farm program quickly divided the representatives of large agricultural interests and the lawyers in the general counsel's office, who were concerned about the full implications of the farm program for all who made their living from the land. Tensions were briefly obscured by the economic emergency and institutional political factors that guided the implementation of the Agricultural Adjustment Act, the centerpiece of the recovery effort. Described as "the greatest single experiment in economic planning under capitalist conditions . . . in a time of peace," the act provided for a voluntary program of acreage reduction, supported by government payments, to decrease production and raise prices. Southern planters, working through established networks of the Extension Service and the American Farm Bureau, easily controlled the implementation of the act in the region. John P. Davis, sent to the South by the NAACP in 1934 to interview black tenant farmers, and Socialist Party leader Norman Thomas were among those who reported on the devastating consequences. By pouring millions of dollars into southern agriculture without addressing the evils of the plantation system, critics charged, the federal government shored up the old system and aggravated the desperate plight of tenant farmers and sharecroppers, who composed more than 45 percent of the South's farming population.[35]

AAA policy required landowners to pay a portion of the government payment for crop reduction to their tenants, but there was no adequate enforcement mechanism. Widespread cheating by landowners precipitated the organization of the STFU in Tyronza, Arkansas, in July 1934. An organizer of the interracial union recalled: "The sharecroppers wanted their share of the government money. It was that simple. That's why they organized."[36] The STFU, which enjoyed the support of the young liberals in the AAA, mounted a vigorous critique of New Deal farm policy, charging that it intensified the displacement of tenant farmers and denied them any representation in the local administrative structure of the AAA. When Hiram Norcross, chairman of the local AAA committee, evicted twenty-seven STFU members from his plantation, the union sued Norcross in court. The plaintiffs argued that the widely disputed section seven of the cotton contract required that landlords participating in the AAA program keep the same tenants, not simply the same number of tenants.

Emboldened by the STFU's action, AAA General Counsel Jerome Frank issued an interpretation of the cotton contract. He endorsed the STFU's position, arguing that it was essential to protect the rights of sharecroppers and tenants. Frank's ruling challenged the autonomy of southern landowners and contested the political clout of cotton growers, political power that was lodged securely with the Democratic leadership in the Senate, including Majority Leader Joseph Robinson of Arkansas. Henry Wallace conceded that Frank and his associates had acted on the highest of motives but that their interpretation of section seven was indefensible in view of the political realities and the larger agricultural picture. The ruling would result in the collapse of the entire cotton program. Thus, in the well-known "purge" of 1935, Wallace dismissed Frank and several of his top assistants.[37]

Assistant Secretary of Agriculture Rexford Tugwell persuaded C. B. "Beanie" Baldwin, his young protégé from Virginia, not to resign from Secretary Wallace's staff in the wake of Frank's expulsion, advising him that "the fight was only beginning" and that he should save himself for another day. The failure of Frank's blunt strike on behalf of the rural poor did not slow the political momentum gathering behind the cause of tenant farmers and sharecroppers. Early in 1935, Will Alexander, Edwin Embree, and Charles Johnson published the findings of a year-long study of cotton tenancy. Funded by the Rockefeller Foundation and the Rosenwald Fund, the study documented how the government, under the AAA, had assumed "many of the risks of the landowners and thrown them on the tenants." The STFU continued to organize and protest, growing to thirty thousand members in six states by 1937, one-third of whom were black. Their efforts met with evictions and a widely publicized reign of terror. "There can be no doubt of the reversion to slave law, mob violence and fascist methods in Arkansas," editorialized the *New York Post*. Growing pressure from national organizations and liberal groups, along with the populist challenge of Huey Long, convinced Roosevelt of the need to establish a separate organization to redress the plight of the rural poor. In April 1935, he authorized Tugwell's plan for such an agency. Tugwell organized the Resettlement Administration, with Will Alexander as deputy administrator and C. B. Baldwin as assistant administrator.[38]

The STFU, in conjunction with its sympathetic supporters in the Roosevelt administration, succeeded in broadening the debate over federal farm policy and compelling the government to address the issues of rural poverty and displacement. The process focused national attention on the South and put a human face on the economic misery that plagued the region. Tugwell's Resettlement Administration undertook an ambitious campaign of public information, which "harnessed the creative abilities of writers, journalists, and scholars to the purpose of educating the country about impoverished land and people." The Photographic Section of the Resettlement Administration (which continued under its successor organization, the Farm Security Administration) employed the nation's most creative young photographers, whose visual rendering of rural poverty was unsurpassed. Late in 1936, at Tugwell's urging, Secretary of Agriculture Henry Wallace traveled through the Deep South with Will Alexander and C. B. Baldwin to examine conditions firsthand. Wallace, who carried Arthur Raper's newly published *Preface to Peasantry* with him, was visibly shocked by what he found. He became increasingly attentive to the South and its peculiar relationship to the politics of the New Deal. As a region, it was most desperately in need of federally sponsored economic reforms to break the cycle of poverty that drained the region's human and natural resources. Yet the South's elected representatives became the leading opponents to the more reformist course of the Roosevelt administration, heralded by the 1936 election.[39]

The "discovery" of rural poverty in the South was played out against growing polarization in Washington over the course of the New Deal. In a series of decisions during 1935 and 1936, the Supreme Court struck at the heart of the New Deal when it overturned the National Industrial Recovery Act, the Agricultural Adjustment Act, the Railroad Retirement Act, and a New York State minimum-wage law. These rulings severely restricted "the government's right to regulate the economy under the commerce clause, to tax and spend for the general welfare, and to interfere with the freedom of contract." Roosevelt blasted the Court for creating a constitutional "no-man's land" where neither federal nor state government could function. The judicial revolt reinforced increasingly vocal attacks by conservatives, wed to a strict laissez-faire ideology, compelling Roosevelt to take the offensive. During the summer and fall of 1935, the president embarked on the legislative battle of the second hundred days. Under intense lobbying from the White House, Congress passed the Wagner Act, the Social Security Act, a holding company bill curbing the power of giant utilities, and a new tax law that increased rates for higher incomes and corporations. Countering the Supreme Court's assault on the New Deal, Roosevelt told a group of young Democrats, "My friends, the period of social pioneering is just beginning."[40]

"We will win easily next year," Roosevelt told his cabinet late in 1935, "but we are going to make it a crusade." Roosevelt had presided over a dramatic upsurge in the economy and a multibillion-dollar program of jobs, credit, and relief that touched the lives of a broad cross section of the citizenry. Allowing for its deficiencies and inequities, the New Deal marked a decisive break with the past. New Deal legislation fundamentally altered the relationship between the government and the individual citizen and invested the newly revived labor movement with strength and confidence. Roosevelt made the 1936 election a referendum on the role of government in a modern society. Campaigning against those "economic royalists" who had come to see government "as a mere appendage of their own affairs," Roosevelt pledged an activist federal government, committed to the "establishment of a democracy of opportunity for all the people." He proclaimed, "Freedom is no half and half affair." Whereas his opponents would concede "that political freedom was the business of Government," they "maintained that economic slavery" was "nobody's business." Protection of political rights, Roosevelt insisted, must be joined by protection of "the citizen in his right to work and his right to live."[41]

The 1936 election transformed the nation's political landscape. The unprecedented popular plurality of votes that Roosevelt commanded weakened old regional and state allegiances and created a new majority defined along class, rural-urban, and ethnic lines. The Roosevelt sweep embraced "ideologically compatible progressive Republicans or independents and converted Socialists." Rooted in its old base of urban machines and southern and border states, the Democratic Party emerged as a national party, incorporating new constituencies that had been drawn to the programs and party of Franklin Roosevelt. The base of Roosevelt's vote spread to 81 percent among the lowest income groups. A commentator observed, "He had waged his campaign against the minority at the top and the rest responded."[42]

Secure in his electoral mandate, Roosevelt pressed ahead in his effort to redefine and sharpen the tools for sustaining an expansion of New Deal reform. Woven through his inaugural address was a litany describing the poverty and despair that continued to proscribe the opportunities of millions of citizens. He ended with the immortal refrain, "I see one-third of a nation ill-housed, ill-clad, ill-nourished." He reminded the nation of the vision guiding the collective experiment that had begun four years earlier, in the darkest days of the depression, "a vision—to speed the time when there would be for all the people that security and peace essential to the pursuit of happiness." In the intervening years, the president noted, the country had come to recognize "a deeper need—the need to find through government the instrument of our united purpose to solve for the individual the ever-rising problems of a complex civilization. . . . Attempts at their solution without the aid of government left us baffled and bewildered." Only through government was it possible "to create those moral controls over the services of science which are necessary to make science a useful servant instead of a ruthless master of mankind. To do this we knew we must find practical controls over blind economic forces and blindly selfish men." He continued, "The essential democracy of our Nation . . . depends not on the absence of power, but upon lodging it with those whom the people can change or continue . . . through an honest and free system of elections."[43]

In initiating his second term, Roosevelt predictably turned his attention to the Supreme Court, which stood in bold defiance to his expansive view of government. With the Wagner Act and the Social Security Act awaiting the Court's review, the conservative judiciary threatened to completely dismantle the New Deal. However, the ensuing battle over the president's bill to increase the number of justices by up to six emboldened a more formidable adversary. Roosevelt's effort to wield his popular mandate to force Congress into line behind his Court-reform plan failed; it aggravated deep divisions within his own party, planting the seeds for open revolt. Breaking ranks in significant numbers for the first time, southern conservative Democrats led the bipartisan opposition to defeat the president's Court-packing plan. Meanwhile, the Court had reversed its course when it upheld the Wagner Act and the Social Security Act in the spring of 1937. Soon thereafter a succession of retirements enabled the president to secure a majority of justices sympathetic to the philosophy of the New Deal. But by then Congress had emerged as the primary battleground over the future of New Deal reform.

As Roosevelt pushed to expand the New Deal during 1937, southern Democrats steadily joined the ranks of the opposition. The Fair Labor Standards Act, which, along with a revived labor movement, promised to further erode regional wage differentials, met strong opposition from key southern congressmen, including Finance Committee Chairman Byron "Pat" Robinson of Mississippi. In the wake of the fall recession in 1937, a number of Republican and Democratic senators who had joined forces in the Court fight met in November at the instigation of Senator Josiah Bailey of North Carolina. Their "Conservative Manifesto" claimed that a restoration of business confidence was essential to economic recovery. Toward this end, they recommended the reduction of taxes, the primacy of a balanced budget, a restoration of states' rights, and the strict observation of private property rights and the rights of capital. Facing an increasingly recalcitrant southern bloc, Roosevelt prepared to take the battle for the New Deal directly to the southern people.[44]

The South, more than any other region, offered a striking dichotomy between mass popular support for New Deal initiatives and a stiffening opposition among its elected representatives in Congress. Indeed, the South was the one region where, according to a Gallup poll, a majority of the people backed the Court-packing plan. Lyndon Johnson's vigorous support of the president's plan won him a Texas congressional seat in 1937. Even though there were a notable number of young, southern supporters of the New Deal in the House and the Senate, supporters like Lyndon Johnson and

Claude Pepper, seasoned representatives of the South's landowners and industrialists had emerged as key opponents.

In February 1938, Lucy Randolph Mason, the southern director of public relations for the Congress of Industrial Organizations (CIO), reported to Eleanor Roosevelt on the precarious political situation in the region. She warned of a growing opposition to the Roosevelt administration "among the power holding group," regardless of the "lip service" they might be giving it. If a vote was taken among this group, she was confident the president would lose. "The only hope for progressive democracy in the South," she observed, "lies in the lower economic groups, particularly the wage earner." They adored Roosevelt. Yet most of these people did not vote. Mason advised that the poll tax be abolished and that a deliberate campaign be waged to enfranchise the great majority of nonvoting southerners, "a hope more likely filled if the mass production industries" could be organized to give the unions "real strength." Robert Weaver recalled that for people in Washington who were concerned with the situation in the South, one fact had become increasingly evident: "If you were going to make real basic changes, you had to do something about the electorate."[45]

On 23 March 1938, Roosevelt brought his campaign for an expanded New Deal into the heart of Dixie. Sharing a platform in Gainesville, Georgia, with Senator Walter George, who had voted against the Court-reform plan, the president appealed to the citizens of "Georgia and the lower South." Wages and purchasing power in the South were still much too low, he said, limiting the establishment and growth of new industries in the region. The maintenance of a low-wage economy stifled the recovery effort in the South and continued to deprive the region's people of the benefits of economic growth—"better schools, better health, better hospitals, better highways." Yet a selfish minority in Congress, more concerned with a balanced budget, consistently voted against legislation aimed at alleviating the economic imbalance that plagued the South. These legislators were content to maintain "a feudal economic system" in the South. Roosevelt charged: "There is little difference between the feudal system and the fascist system. If you believe in one you lean on the other." Looking toward the upcoming midterm elections, the president predicted, "The people of the United States and in every section of the United States are going to say 'we are sorry, but we want people to represent us whose minds are cast in the 1938 mold and not in the 1898 mold.'"[46]

In preparing for an expanded challenge to his southern opponents that summer, Roosevelt was aided by the new generation of southern policy-makers and elected officials who had cohered around the initiatives of the

New Deal. Starting with informal weekly discussions at Hall's Restaurant in Washington, young southerners, many of them new to Washington, had established themselves as the Southern Policy Committee (SPC) in 1935. The SPC, which established local committees in several southern cities, was an affiliate of Francis Pickens Miller's National Policy Committee. Miller, a Virginian who had worked with the Young Men's Christian Association (YMCA) and the World Student Christian Federation, aimed to provide an independent forum for policymakers and citizens to study policy issues in preparation for legislative and political action. Clark Foreman, Hugo Black, Clifford Durr, and Lister Hill were among the prime movers of the SPC in Washington, which claimed about forty members from the executive and legislative branches.

The SPC provided a forum for addressing the peculiar problems of the region in order to help inform New Deal policies and legislation. SPC meetings were particularly useful, Foreman recalled, "because they brought the more liberal southerners together and gave them opportunities of knowing each other better." Brooks Hays, who went on to a distinguished career as a congressman from Arkansas, recalled that his experience with the SPC was "the most fascinating part of [his] history." He explained: "It threw me into some of the real divisiveness of the South; folks attached to the old ways and those of us who thought that change had to come. We had plenty of drama and plenty of fun because with all of the bruises we got, the resistance we met from the gentry, still there was great vision in that group."[47]

Jerome Frank accompanied Foreman to an SPC dinner at Hall's Restaurant early in 1938. Inspired by the efforts of the group, he advised that they distribute a pamphlet that would enable other people to better understand the situation in the region. Foreman later recalled Frank's explanation: "Most people were very ignorant about the South and just attributed the problems of the region to the cussedness of the people." Enthusiastic about the idea, Foreman and Frank spoke with White House Assistant Tom Corcoran. Shortly thereafter, Foreman received a call from the White House inviting him to meet with the president.[48]

Roosevelt sought Foreman's advice about several possible candidates who might run against Walter George in the Georgia Democratic primary. Foreman, who was then director of the Power Division of the PWA, had no particular candidate to recommend, though he supported the president's plan to challenge George in the primary. However, he advised that for the president to mobilize support for the New Deal in the South, it was essential that the people of the South understand what the New Deal meant to them. Neither the politicians nor the press in the South, Foreman observed, had provided the people with any real understanding of what the president was trying to do. Roosevelt and Foreman agreed that a pamphlet on this subject could be useful during the summer primaries by illustrating how the South had benefited from the New Deal and by describing the serious economic problems that remained. Roosevelt authorized Foreman to implement the project under the aegis of Lowell Mellett, executive director of the National Emergency Council (NEC).

Early in the summer of 1938 Foreman convened a small group of southerners working in the Roosevelt administration to draft the report anonymously. The report was then reviewed and endorsed by an advisory committee of prominent southerners. Many people throughout the government provided assistance, but the core group consisted of Clifford Durr of Alabama, who was a lawyer for the Reconstruction Finance Corporation, John Fisher of Oklahoma, who worked for the Farm Security Administration, and Arthur "Tex" Goldschmidt of Texas, who had been instrumental in establishing the Works Progress Administration (WPA) and was then working for the Consumer's Counsel of the Bituminous Coal Administration and serving as vice-president of the Federal Workers Union. Foreman consulted frequently with southern representatives during the preparation of the draft. On the recommendation of Senator Lister Hill of Alabama, the group limited their discussion of the fifteen subjects covered in the report to four pages each so that individual sections could be easily reproduced and widely distributed as pamphlets and campaign literature. The topics ranged from "Soil," "Water," and "Ownership and Use of Land" to "Health," "Education," and "Women and Children." The concise style and the simple, straightforward language were aimed to ensure a wide audience. When Goldschmidt's sister, marveling at the scope and depth of the report, compared it to Howard Odum's *Southern Regions*, Goldschmidt was indignant. "I blew my top," he recalled. "That can't be used the way this can. The report was for the little guy."[49]

The advisory committee convened in the auditorium of the Labor Department on 5 July to review the draft and make final recommendations. Headed by University of North Carolina President Frank Graham, the committee consisted of twenty-two members, representing the states of the former Confederacy, plus Kentucky and Oklahoma. All of the committee members were white. Lowell Mellett felt that the political impact of the report among white southerners was dependent on such an arrangement. The committee included Carl Bailey, governor of Arkansas; John C. Persons, president of the First National Bank of Birmingham; H. L. Mitchell, secretary-treasurer of the STFU; Barry Bingham, publisher of the *Louisville Courier-Journal*;

L. O. Crosby, a lumberman from Picayune, Mississippi; and Lucy Randolph Mason. Lyndon Johnson, Lister Hill, and John Sparkman were among the congressmen who "hovered around," along with other interested parties. The meeting lasted all day as the committee discussed each of the fifteen sections, making only minor changes. Clark Foreman edited the final copy, and on 25 July Mellett transmitted the *Report on the Economic Conditions of the South* to the president.[50]

The president announced the publication of the NEC report during a speech in Barnesville, Georgia, where he shared the platform with Senator Walter George, former Governor Eugene Talmadge, and U.S. Attorney Lawrence Camp. Explaining how sectional imbalance drained the potential for southern development, Roosevelt declared that the South was "the nation's number one economic problem." Discriminatory freight rates, depressed wages, and purchasing power that fell well below the national average not only were problems for the region but contributed to an economic imbalance in the nation as a whole and required national solutions. The Rural Electrification Administration (REA), which the president dedicated that day, was a "symbol of the progress" being made. The REA aimed to bring electricity "to every village, every home and every farm in every part of the United States" and promised to be especially beneficial to the South.

The support of Congress was essential if New Deal initiatives like the REA were to continue. It was for this reason, Roosevelt explained, that he felt compelled to intervene in the 1938 primary elections on behalf of liberal candidates who shared his commitment to a broad program of economic and social reform. He closed his speech by endorsing U.S. Attorney Lawrence Camp over incumbent Walter George for the U.S. Senate. The president traveled on to Greenville, South Carolina, where he endorsed Governor Olin Johnston in a bid for "Cotton" Ed Smith's seat in the U.S. Senate. Roosevelt also endorsed William Dodd Jr.'s challenge to Congressman Howard Worth Smith of Virginia, the powerful chairman of the House Rules Committee.[51]

Walter George called the president's Barnesville speech "a second march through Georgia." He reminded his fellow Georgians, "We answered this question before when federal bayonets stood guard over the ballot box . . . honest men cast honest ballots for the Redemption of this State." Generally, the southern press, southern public figures, and many southern liberals outside of the New Deal shared George's sentiments and resented the president's interference in state political contests. Commenting on the reaction to Roosevelt's challenge to George, *New York Herald Tribune* columnist Mark Sullivan observed that just below the surface was the issue of states' rights, namely the right to control elections. The principal use the South had for this right, Sullivan explained, was to exclude blacks from voting in Democratic Party primaries. Half of Senator "Cotton" Ed Smith's final speech before the primary election was a strident defense of white supremacy. For six years, Sullivan continued, the Democratic Party had been trying to "carry water on both shoulders with regard to Negro voting." The "practical" politicians succeeded in quietly winning the black vote in the North away from the Republicans, in many cases a crucial vote providing the balance of power. Meanwhile, the "idealists" in the party were turning their attention to securing the vote for southern blacks.[52]

In the South, the poll tax and other restrictions kept most blacks and a majority of low-income whites from voting. This was the constituency of the New Deal, and the great majority of them did not participate in the 1938 primary elections. In Georgia, for example, Tom Stokes observed that four-fifths of the fifty-three thousand WPA workers in the state were black. They were legally excluded from voting in the Democratic primary. In addition, voter registration was low among white WPA workers in the state. Thus, Roosevelt's attempt to purge conservative southern Democrats seemed destined to fail in the short term, and it did. But it marked the opening battle in a growing movement to open up the political process in the South.[53]

The significance of the NEC report reached beyond the 1938 primary season. It turned a national spotlight on the South and on the economic and political significance of the region. Front-page headlines in the *New York Times* announced the publication of the report, and the paper reprinted the report in full. The report was widely noted and excerpted in the nation's other major newspapers, and highlights were carried in most newspapers throughout the South. The report and the president's aggressive participation in the 1938 primary season dramatized the national consequences of the region's insular economic and political culture. Political analysts interpreted Roosevelt's "new attack on reactionary Southern Democrats" as central to his effort to hurry along the liberal realignment of the Democratic Party, an alignment that had crested in the 1936 election. Indeed, conservative southern Democrats complained that the president was trying "to woo southern labor and tenant farmers into the camp of his new liberalism with a promise of a New Deal to southern specifications."[54]

The NEC report became "a kind of Bible" for southern New Dealers, anti-poll-tax activist Virginia Durr recalled. Jonathan Daniels, then the editor of the *Raleigh News and Observer*, wrote enthusiastically to Lowell Mellett: "I am amazed at the amount of fact and intelligence you have packed into so brief a space. If the President acts in aid [sic] with the direction of your report, we shall begin to get somewhere." Daniels advised that the president pay little mind to those southerners who resented his description of the South as the nation's number-one economic problem. These critics, he confided, were the "same old Daughters of the Confederacy—though some in pants—who in all the long years" had been "a more destructive crop than cotton." He added: "They are not talking for the thoughtful men and women in every class in the South. . . . We know we are in a hell of a fix even when we sit in the shade and we are grateful for his help out of the hole."[55]

Later that fall, Mellett sent a memo to the president analyzing the impact of the report. The timing had been perfect, he said. "It brought into focus and into summarized and understandable form a great movement already underway in the South. For years there has been a lot of good thinking among liberal educators and political people in the South about the section's own peculiar problems and about the South's place in the national scheme." Herein lay the hope for change. Mellett cautioned that correction of the conditions described in the report could come only in small part from Washington; change also demanded "southern pressure." The great value of the NEC report was that it "was lending itself to that pressure."[56]

Clark Foreman and other members of the SPC joined with labor representatives Joseph Gelders and Lucy Randolph Mason in organizing a southern-wide conference in response to FDR's challenge. Over Thanksgiving weekend in 1938 more than twelve hundred people—"representing all classes and conditions," black and white, from each of the southern states—met in Birmingham to consider the subject matter of the NEC report and to establish a permanent organization that would work toward some solution of the problems it described. The result was the Southern Conference for Human Welfare (SCHW). According to Frank Graham, president of the newly formed SCHW, the organization had grown from a combination of influences and forces. He cited Howard Odum's monumental study *Southern Regions of the United States*, Charles S. Johnson's *Wasted Land*, Jonathan Daniels's *A Southerner Discovers the South*, and the pioneering work of the SPC. But the SCHW reached beyond these earlier efforts and deliberations and provided a forum for all people of the South, "regardless of party, religion or race," to prepare for political action. Arthur Raper, a founding member of the SCHW, believed that the time was ripe for such an organization. The depression and the New Deal had shaken the foundations of the "Solid South." He noted: "A lot of folks were standing up on their feet and talking and expecting things that they had never expected before. . . . Here was a ferment, a very basic, vital ferment, and people needed to respond to it in some way."[57]

[With the depression and the New Deal] there came unemployment and relief ... [and] a direct connection between politics and
industry, between government and work, between voting and
wages, such as the South was born believing was absolutely impossible and fundamentally wrong.

W. E. B. Du Bois, 1941

3

Southern Seeds of
Change, 1931–1938

"At the heart of the dark labyrinth of America's complex
problems is the crisis in the South," wrote University of Virginia student
Palmer Weber in 1938. Weber commended Franklin Roosevelt's successful
effort to focus national attention on the region with the widely noted *Report
on the Economic Conditions of the South*. Southerners themselves had finally
become conscious "of the inherited shackles of tenancy, disease and illit-
eracy." Such general social problems, he noted, had become "accepted subjects of discussion," and this was a significant development. "But," Weber
continued, "the black thread in the crisis ridden pattern of [the region's]

social culture has not yet been examined. Neither Mr. Roosevelt nor the Southern New Dealers have publicly considered the social significance of the Southern Negro."[1]

As illustrated by Lowell Mellett's decision to exclude blacks from participating in the report of the National Emergency Council (NEC), the Roosevelt administration carefully avoided any suggestion that it aimed to upset the racial status quo in the South. But Roosevelt's attempt to purge southern obstructionists in the 1938 primary elections and bring the South into line with the national Democratic Party implicitly challenged the political foundation of white supremacy. Roosevelt's ill-fated intervention supported the political aspirations of disfranchised groups who had mobilized in response to the depression and the New Deal. It resulted in the founding of the Southern Conference for Human Welfare (SCHW), a biracial coalition dedicated to ending voter restrictions in the South and completing the liberal realignment of the Democratic Party.

By 1938 a loose political network had developed around the labor movement, local branches of the National Association for the Advancement of Colored People (NAACP), voter leagues, Communist Party initiatives, and New Deal programs. During the 1930s a small number of individuals from widely different backgrounds gave form and direction to the democratic activism that developed outside of the insular structure of southern politics. Palmer Weber, Charles Houston, and Lucy Randolph Mason serve as useful examples of the range of leadership that emerged. Palmer Weber, a native of Smithfield, Virginia, was a radical student organizer at the University of Virginia before joining southern New Dealers in Washington in 1940 and the SCHW's legislative fight to abolish the poll tax. Charles Hamilton Houston, a brilliant legal mind and strategist, traveled tens of thousands of miles throughout the South, building the NAACP's southern-based campaign to equalize education and secure voting rights. Lucy Randolph Mason, whose Virginia lineage stretched back to George Mason, a signer of the Declaration of Independence, became the leading public representative of the Congress of Industrial Organizations (CIO) in the South and worked as a union publicist and voting-rights proponent.

The political development of Palmer Weber during the depression years suggests the eclectic nature of the evolving democratic movement. A student of Karl Marx and Thomas Jefferson, Weber participated in the Communist Party during the 1930s, as well as the student movement, labor-organizing activities, and the NAACP's pioneering challenge to racial discrimination in public education. Weber was a self-described free radical, confined by neither orthodoxy nor organizations. Like many others of his generation, he was convinced that the depression had exposed the bankruptcy of capitalism as an economic and political system and had opened the way for a complete reconstruction. Marxist analysis informed Weber's understanding of the causes of the depression and his belief that class consciousness and struggle were essential vehicles both for securing economic justice and for realizing the democratic process "in its full and rich sense." Jeffersonian ideals and the U.S. Constitution provided the political and legal basis for acting. Socialism, as Weber understood it, complemented Jefferson's vision of a dynamic democratic society, which held that nothing was unchangeable or inalienable except the natural rights of man. "The original impulse in socialism," Weber observed, "was how do you arrange social institutions so that social injustice is eliminated. . . . It's not an end in itself. The end . . . is the development of mankind."[2]

When Weber arrived at the University of Virginia in the fall of 1931, he was well-grounded in the social values and philosophical framework that shaped his political development. The small tidewater community of Smithfield, Virginia, where Weber had spent his first twelve years, was nurturing and secure, "a marvelous place to grow up," he later recalled. Across the James River from Jamestown, Smithfield was steeped in the traditions of the Old Dominion. It was a graceful river town that wore the prosperity of an earlier age. Weber, who lived with his mother, brother, and maternal grandparents, described his family as "poor, honest white people." They "went by water": Grandfather William Pittman, known locally as Captain Billy, was an oysterman. All members of the family were expected to work and contribute to the welfare of the household. One of Weber's earliest memories was of his grandfather "putting a one and a half pound hatchet in my hand . . . because I had to learn to make kindling wood . . . my brother and I had the responsibility to keep the wood boxes full." The centrality of work also encouraged an enterprising spirit driven by the "opportunity to make a nickel." As a young boy, Weber took advantage of everything within his reach to earn spending money: he collected scrap iron, shined shoes, sold newspapers, picked cotton, helped on the oyster boats, and after receiving a bicycle for Christmas, became a delivery boy for the dry goods store and the post office.

Weber's social activism was rooted in the church, which was central to community life in Smithfield. Every Sunday his family attended the Baptist Church for morning and evening services; each year he won a medal for perfect Sunday school attendance. The primary lesson that informed Weber's social values was the idea of stewardship: the idea "that your life is not your own, that your life is in effect a trust—you are a trustee of a life that has been given to you by something greater than yourself." There was something larger than personal well-being, something "that demanded your attention and allegiance." He embraced a fundamental belief in the brotherhood of all mankind, the basis for his later response to the issue of racial discrimination. As a child, he grew up in a segregated world. But he recalled: "Racism never took hold of me. I never absorbed it in the way some southerners did." He attributed this to his family's basic decency and lack of racial hostility, as well as his Christian values.

Diagnosed with glandular tuberculosis at the age of twelve, Palmer left the insular world of Smithfield and traveled 150 miles to the Blue Ridge Sanitarium, which sits in the shadow of Thomas Jefferson's Monticello. His five years at the sanitarium provided a formative educational and intellectual experience. In his eagerness to make himself useful and earn money to enlarge his stamp collection, Weber took on a number of jobs that brought him into daily contact with the patients in the adult ward of the sanitarium. Here was, he remembered, "a whole collection of people in the midst of dying and getting well, all of whom were concerned with the state of the human soul, the state of economics and politics." It was "a magic mountain type of experience where you had a continual dialogue going on." A Greek immigrant and a railroad worker from Richmond engaged the young Weber in his first discussion of socialism, based on the debate between Harold Laski and Sumner Schlecter in *Current History*. Francis Franklin, a recent graduate of the University of Richmond and a student of Samuel Chiles Mitchell, introduced Weber to the Buddhist sutras and Mohandas Gandhi's *Young India*. He also read Gandhi's correspondence with Leo Tolstoy on nonviolent civil disobedience. Plato's *Dialogues*, the *Communist Manifesto*, and current issues of *Foreign Affairs* were shared by others and discussed. And Weber, who became superintendent of the sanitarium's Sunday school, pursued a thorough study of the Old and New Testaments. When he enrolled in the University of Virginia at the age of seventeen, Weber was a committed student of philosophy. "I wanted to understand the answers to the meaning of life, why people did this, why they did that, what things they held of value. I wanted to study ethics. I wanted to study politics."

While the state of Virginia was slipping deeper into the depression in the fall of 1931, the University of Virginia maintained its reputation as one of the country club colleges of America, a place where students took great pains to dress well and master the etiquette of play. Palmer Weber did not have the time, the resources, or the inclination for either. A $100 gift from Dr. William Brown, the superintendent of the sanitarium, plus $100 from his mother and a $100 scholarship covered Weber's first year of study. He "worked like a sledgehammer" to stay at the head of his class, a goal that was necessary to maintain scholarship assistance. And he succeeded. Virginius Dabney, historian of the University of Virginia, described Weber as probably the most brilliant student at the university during the 1930s. He completed his bachelor's degree in three years, graduating Phi Beta Kappa, and continued for a Ph.D. in philosophy. During his time in Charlottesville, only his deepening involvement in political activity would compete with his rigorous academic schedule. Often, politics took precedence over academics.[3]

"You could describe me as a Gandhi socialist, Christian socialist, a Marxist socialist, any kind of variation where it was a questioning of authority or where an effort was made to bring justice," Weber recalled. Justice was central, very much as in Plato's *Republic*. Weber compared Plato's famous statement "giving each man what is his own" to Marx's "from each according to his ability, to each according to his need." There was one guiding question, according to Weber: "How do you carry out justice? What is your responsibility . . . as a citizen to see that the body politic embodies justice?" Thus, the study of philosophy, of social institutions, of economic history, was essential but not sufficient. Paraphrasing Marx, Weber explained, "The philosophers have interpreted the world in various ways; the point, however, is to change it." Weber "did anything that was within reach . . . that represented in practice trying to bring some justice into [the] local community, in race relations, in student discussion, whatever."[4]

Palmer Weber was the primary catalyst of a small but vocal student movement, which interacted with a national student movement that grew up around campus unrest during the early years of the depression. The Virginia movement had its origins in a Marxist study group of roughly twenty-five students, organized by Weber in 1932 as a spin-off of a reading group directed by Rev. William Kyle Smith, secretary of the local Young Men's Christian Association (YMCA). Later in 1932, Francis Franklin enrolled in the graduate program of philosophy at the University of Virginia. Through his connections with the state Communist Party headquarters in Richmond, he, Weber, and three or four other students joined the party, an affiliation that was openly acknowledged.

As a Marxist organization in the South, the Communist Party had a special appeal as an action-oriented organization, as demonstrated by its efforts in behalf of the unemployed and disfranchised workers and its bold defense of nine young black men in the widely publicized Scottsboro trials. Moreover, by 1932, students were stretching beyond the narrow sectarianism that dominated national party policy. The Communist-led National Student League (NSL), founded in 1931, provided an organizational framework

Walter White, executive
secretary of the NAACP,
with defense attorneys at
George Crawford's 1933
murder trial in Leesburg,
Virginia. *Left to right:* Wal-
ter White, Charles
Houston, James G. Tyson,
Leon Ranson, and Edward
Lovett. (Photograph from
the *Richmond Times-
Dispatch*; courtesy of
Moorland-Spingarn Re-
search Center, Howard
University)

75

Above. Mary McLeod Bethune speaking at a testimonial dinner in her honor at Bethune-Cookman College, Daytona Beach, Florida; at right is Eleanor Roosevelt. Bethune was "a one-woman employment agency trying to get black professional people placed in every bureau of the federal government," remembered Palmer Weber. She also exhorted African Americans throughout the nation to take full advantage of political openings created by the New Deal. (Photograph from Big Four News Service; courtesy of Bethune Museum and Archives)

Facing page, top. Virginia Foster Durr, executive secretary of the National Committee to Abolish the Poll Tax. Through her efforts to organize support for anti-poll-tax legislation, Durr helped put together a national biracial coalition committed to extending federal protection of voting rights in the South. (Photograph courtesy of the Progressive Party Collection, University of Iowa Libraries)

Facing page, bottom. Palmer Weber (*lifting glass*) and Senator Claude Pepper. Weber described his arrival in Washington in 1940 as "a fabulous piece of luck." He joined the ranks of southern New Dealers as they sought to counter the wartime ascendancy of conservative southern Democrats. Pepper inscribed the photo to Weber: "To my friend and fellow conspirator." (Photograph courtesy of Palmer Weber)

To My friend and fellow conspirator Palmer Weber
nov. 10-1962. [signature]

for student protest and linked it to scattered movements on the labor, civil rights, and civil liberties fronts. In addition to marking a departure from the tradition of campus radicalism, the NSL broke from the orthodoxy of the Third Party period that ruled the students' adult counterparts in the Communist Party.

Following a tour of college campuses in the spring of 1931, Paul Porter, a student member of the Socialist League for Industrial Democracy (LID), reported: "The pot of social thinking is boiling briskly these days. I know of no time in recent years when so many liberals and radicals have emerged on the college campus with a keen and sustained interest in diverse fields of social change."⁵ Founded in 1921 as an outgrowth of Upton Sinclair's Intercollegiate Socialist Society, the LID stressed education for a new social order. As the lonely voice of campus radicalism during the 1920s, student affiliates of the adult-run LID functioned primarily as study groups. National leaders like Norman Thomas approached their student protégés more like teachers than political organizers.

In December 1931, a small group of students from various New York City colleges, some members of the Young Communist League and some sympathetic to the Communist approach, responded to the new mood of political interest and urgency by establishing the National Student League. The NSL, which proposed to mobilize students for political action, marked a major breakthrough for the American student Left. The NSL built an autonomous movement, responsive to the concerns of students. It also provided a vehicle for realizing and acting on the connections between the economic troubles facing America's youth and the deeper social crisis generated by the depression.⁶

In implementing its founding pledge to build a mass movement among the nation's college students, the NSL pioneered Popular Front techniques and strategies in direct contradiction to the militant sectarianism of official Communist Party policy. The NSL endured occasional criticism from the Communist Party leadership, but the party hierarchy evidenced no interest in controlling "the seemingly unimportant world of student organizing." NSL founders included Joseph Starobin, Max Gordon, Joseph Clark, and Robert F. "Rob" Hall. They represented a new generation of radical activists, and their ideas about socialism and politics would help shape the course of the party during its heyday. The students were adherents of the American Communist Party's militant anticapitalism and looked to the Soviet Union as "the world's only worker-run, depression proof country." Organizing, however, took precedence over orthodoxy. Rob Hall's membership in the party represented a direct outgrowth of the economic and political concerns that had led this native Alabamian to Columbia University in 1929 to study agricultural economics under Rex Tugwell. Hall recalled that he "grew into" the party. "This was what you believed. These were the people you worked with." Citing Marx's prediction that the peaceful development of socialism could be realized in England and the United States, Hall looked toward political organization and action as prelude to the democratic realization of a socialist state in America.[7]

The NSL-led expedition to aid striking miners in Harlan County, Kentucky, in March 1932 signified the political baptism of the student movement. Socialists and unaffiliated students, as well as Communist Party members, were among two busloads of students carrying relief to the miners. Hall, the group's organizer, emphasized the nonconfrontational nature of the trip; students were advised to forgo proletarian fashion, such as leather jackets, for dresses and suits and to avoid revolutionary rhetoric. The purpose of the trip was to investigate conditions in the coalfields and provide humanitarian assistance. However, the hostile reception awaiting the students in Kentucky ensured that the students would draw national attention to the desperate conditions of the striking miners and on the routine civil liberties violations encountered by unionization efforts and prolabor supporters. Stopped at gunpoint on the highway and hauled into court, the students were harassed by the local prosecutor as "Russian-born Jewish Communists" and then carried to the state line and forced to leave. The delegation continued on to Washington to appeal for federal protection of the constitutional rights of the striking miners. Hall's testimony before a subcommittee of the U.S. Senate Committee on Manufactures aided liberal senators in their battle for a congressional investigation of the coal strike.[8]

The Harlan expedition, recalled LID leader Joseph Lash, demonstrated that a unified student movement, transcending ideological boundaries, was possible and necessary "to fight . . . fascism."[9] Political action joined to Marxist analysis initiated a process of questioning and radicalization that shaped a new student culture in the 1930s. The NSL's aggressive efforts pushed the student LID groups to adopt a more activist program; cooperation between the two organizations around a common agenda culminated in their merger into the American Student Union (ASU) in 1935. Student organizers mobilized youth around campus-based problems such as cuts in student assistance, fraternity control of student government, the establishment of book cooperatives, free speech for political dissidents, and antiwar protest and linked student activism to the broader social movements of the depression decade. In the process, this activism supported and created opportunities for interracial associations and political action.

The student movement at the University of Virginia carved out multiple areas of activism. With the exception of the strike for peace in 1935, however, student protest at Virginia never engaged more than several dozen young men. Yet these students spearheaded a successful challenge to fraternity control of student government, organized a cooperative bookstore, and mobilized one thousand students and faculty members as part of the nationwide student strike for peace in April 1935. Working through the Liberal Discussion Group and a local chapter of the NSL, they succeeded in publicizing social and racial issues that had never been raised on white college campuses in the South. They sponsored a series of interracial lectures; speakers included Ronald Ely, president of the student union at Virginia Union University, a black college in Richmond, and leading Communist Party figures such as J. B. Matthews and Earl Browder. When the university refused to let Richard B. Moore, a black Communist, speak on campus grounds, Palmer Weber asked, "What manner of small-minded men have inherited Mr. Jefferson's University?" His column blasted the university administration for violating "the ancient and revered traditions of free speech and free thought . . . in the futile endeavor to support social mores," mores that could "no longer be justified." The controversy won attention in the northeastern press; it was the last time such a restriction was imposed.[10]

Weber's politics and organizing skills were tested by the peculiarities of southern politics and race relations and were forged in the changing contours of national politics. He served as a student representative on the Virginia State Committee of the Communist Party, was the first president of the Virginia chapter of the NSL, and joined the national board of the NSL in 1935. When Earl Browder visited Charlottesville in 1936 to discuss the upcoming presidential election, Weber told Browder that he was ready to engage in full-time organizing work either for the party or with a labor union. Browder advised Weber to stay at the university and complete his Ph.D.; the party needed competent people.

On 1 May 1934, in the first of a series of columns he published intermittently over the next four years in *College Topics*, the student paper at Virginia, the twenty-year-old Weber, writing as a strident Marxist, appealed to his readers: "The future of youth lies in the rising tides of the industrial proletariat, may we grasp their hands in unity and struggle with them this May day." But as he acted on this challenge, participating in local efforts to organize the unemployed and workers at a local textile plant, Weber's political understanding increasingly reflected the social and economic realities of Virginia and the South in general. Commenting on his organizing efforts among the unemployed of Charlottesville, Weber recalled: "There was no community leadership. . . . It was just as though you had people released from slavery." If there were two hundred jobs in the textile mill, there were three thousand people waiting to be hired for any available opening. There was one brief, unsuccessful strike at the Ix textile mill on the outskirts of Charlottesville, where Weber and several others were arrested for distributing leaflets. Desperate conditions and police repression of union activity seemed to defy the most resourceful organizers.[11]

Race became a dominant factor in Weber's analysis of the South's economic and political structure and a defining element in his development as an activist and organizer. More than any other issue, lynching exposed the routine lawlessness and antidemocratic ideology that permeated southern society in the guise of white supremacy and states' rights. In a series of columns urging the passage of federal antilynching legislation, Weber argued: "Let it be repeated that those people who keep hollering about States Rights and the American form of government are the very people who violate the American constitution. They are the people who have limited the franchise in the South to the point where not one third of the Southern people vote. They are the people who never mention the decades long violation of the thirteenth, fourteenth and fifteenth amendments to the constitution. Rather, keeping their foot firmly in the Negro's face, violating his every human and legal right, they spend their effort hollering about States' Rights."[12]

Supported by a series of studies published in the early 1930s, Weber debunked the charge that lynch victims had been accused of rape; only 16 percent in the previous fifty years had been so accused. "Negroes have been lynched in the South," Weber explained, "for asking [for] a written receipt for a bill paid, or a written contract for tenancy, or for slapping a white man, or for talking back, or a hundred other reasons that reflect the struggles of the Negro people to obtain a better living for themselves." Lynching was "outright terror used in the South to keep Negro tenants and workers in an inferior economic position . . . to beat down their protests . . . to [deny] them simple civil liberties." Such brutal, state-sanctioned suppression of citizenship rights was a national problem, Weber argued, and required federal action.[13]

Weber's racial concerns complemented an emerging movement among southern black activists to challenge the legal and political foundation of white supremacy. Acting decisively on its commitment to fight racial discrimination, the NSL provided a forum for black and white students, one that went beyond the formal interracial "get-togethers" that had characterized groups like the Commission on Interracial Cooperation (CIC), the Young

Women's Christian Association (YWCA), and other tentative engagements. Contrasting the NSL's 1933 "Student Conference on Negro Student Problems" with these efforts, a Howard student observed, "The sugary spirit was absent; instead there was a common resolve to go back to the South and, for that matter, many areas of the North and tackle shoulder to shoulder the problems of discrimination." The NSL brought black and white southern colleges into the national student movement and linked the small handful of student activists on southern campuses around common programs of action. James Jackson, a Virginia Union University delegate to the NSL conference, recalled that the NSL provided "the foundation and the basis" for organizing students at black colleges, where conservative administrations often exceeded white colleges in their repression of student protest.

In the summer of 1935, students from several colleges in Virginia, including William and Mary and the University of Virginia, met at Virginia Union University in Richmond. The group drafted a model bill calling for increased expenditures on education, equal allocation of state funds among black and white students, and an end to segregation.[14] At the end of the conference, an interracial delegation of students went to the State House to present the bill. James Jackson recalled:

> Palmer was mister finger-in-your-chest, an aggressive type. With him in the lead we all marched from the conference to the state capitol in Richmond, under the arrogant glare of Stonewall Jackson, sneering down on us. Palmer just opened the door to the State Assembly and said, "Gentlemen, we have business," and we all marched up to the front. He said "Mr. Speaker, here is Mr. Jackson. He has a proposal to present to this house." And so with no further ado, I read the draft of this bill to abolish segregation. Towards the end of my reading—I didn't get to the last chapter—the Speaker banged the gavel on his desk. He said this session is over, and we'll give you boys ten seconds to get out.[15]

Virginia, like all other southern states, did not provide access to graduate education or professional schools for black students. In the fall of 1935, Alice Jackson, the sister of James Jackson, applied for admission to the graduate school at the University of Virginia. Jackson's application was part of the NAACP's initial legal challenge to racial discrimination in public education, a challenge that would culminate with the *Brown v. Board of Education* ruling two decades later. The University of Virginia chapter of the NSL supported Jackson's application and invited a representative of the NAACP to address an NSL-sponsored student forum on the case. Despite efforts to inform student opinion, Jackson's application garnered little support among the university's student body. Weber estimated that a scant 5 percent favored Jackson's admission to the graduate school.

The university refused Jackson's application on the grounds that "the education of white and colored persons in the same school" was "contrary to the long established and fixed policy of the Commonwealth of Virginia." Student supporters of Jackson's admission protested the university's action with a statement that won notice in the *New York Times*. "We ask whether a long established policy is never to be changed; we ask whether in the present time of general political reaction and antagonism against racial minorities it is not necessary to assert the right of equal opportunity for all people regardless of color or creed. In short, we criticize the Board's stand because it simply implies the desirability of continuing education inequality. We are confident that every liberal, radical and Christian thinker will concur with us in this protest." The state of Virginia met the challenge posed by Jackson's application by hastily establishing an out-of-state scholarship program for black students seeking graduate and professional education.[16]

Palmer Weber's political interests and activities extended beyond the student movement into Charlottesville's black community. Most black people in Charlottesville were dependent on the University of Virginia for their livelihood, and few were willing to engage in overt protest activity. But Weber found allies in the black community who were open to the possibilities of collective action. He collaborated with Randolph White, a black technician at the University of Virginia hospital, in a successful effort to organize hospital workers to secure an eight-hour day and increased wages and to get black patients "out of the basement," the location of the segregated ward. Weber met frequently with White and his associates to plan strategies and to lobby state officials to improve conditions at the hospital. White and Weber often traveled to Staunton, Virginia, to aid organizing efforts among black workers at Mary Baldwin College. Attempting to explain Weber's enlightened racial views and political activism, White observed: "Palmer was a po' boy. He had a rough time. He was in the same boat." And, White recalled, they shared a mutual understanding of the importance of organizing. The established economic and political powers "didn't care nothin' about the individual." White added: "Whether you're white or black, they'll just cut you down, like mowin' hay. But when people band together, you can do a whole lot."[17]

By the end of 1938, Weber had drifted beyond the orbit of the Communist Party; he found it, as an organization, to be increasingly irrelevant to the political changes that were happening in the South. The Democratic Party had become the most promising arena for realizing a biracial political coalition capable of securing social and economic change in the South. With the large-scale crossover of black voters to the party of Roosevelt in the 1936 election, northern Democrats were speaking more boldly for equal rights. In an article titled "The Negro Vote in the South, " Weber reported on a less noted but equally significant development in the South, where there was a growing movement among black southerners to vote in the all-white Democratic primary. Racial unity was, he explained, something to be achieved, for it existed only "in part in scattered organizations and localities." Its full realization, he predicted, depended on the growth of black and white unity "in labor organizations, among tenant farmers, and in the Democratic primary."[18]

Charles Hamilton Houston also navigated the possibilities created by the economic dislocation and shifting political alliances of the depression years. As chief legal counsel for the NAACP, he was uniquely able to recognize openings in the South's caste-bound society. Starting in 1934, Houston began traveling extensively in the South, observing and documenting conditions in black communities, becoming familiar with local leadership and organizations, and encouraging the renewed political interest and activism evident in the early 1930s. Although Houston's personal experiences were very different from Palmer Weber's, both acted on a common set of beliefs about the central role of race and region in the economic and political contests that were reshaping the nation. "The work of the next decade," Houston wrote NAACP Executive Secretary Walter White in 1934, "will have to be concentrated in the South."[19]

Charles Houston was slightly older than the New Deal generation of black activists. He was born in Washington, D.C., in 1895 and, like Robert Weaver, was part of Washington's black middle class. The grandson of runaway slaves, Houston inherited a strong sense of racial pride and benefited from William and Katherine Houston's commitment to provide their only son with the best education possible. From Dunbar High School, he went on to Amherst College, where, during his first year, he was the only person of African descent at the college. "The alienation born of racism," wrote biographer Genna Rae McNeil, became a "catalyst for Charles's . . . personal self-reliance."[20] He graduated Phi Beta Kappa in 1915 and delivered a commencement address on the life of Paul Laurence Dunbar, despite protests from faculty members unfamiliar with the subject.

Formal education was interrupted by service in World War I, an experience that fundamentally shaped Houston's personal expectations and goals. The daily indignities heaped on black soldiers in the segregated armed forces were compounded by his experience as a judge-advocate, during which he witnessed the blatant disregard of fairness and justice when black soldiers were the subjects of prosecution. Houston wrote, "I made up my mind that I would never get caught again without knowing something about my rights; that if luck was with me, and I got through this war, I would study law and use my time fighting for men who could not strike back." In the fall of 1919, Houston enrolled in Harvard Law School and became the first person of his race elected to the editorial board of the *Harvard Law Review*. During his second year, he organized a student luncheon at Harvard for Marcus Garvey, who, Houston later explained, "made a permanent contribution in teaching the simple dignity of being black." After obtaining an LL.B. and a doctorate in law from Harvard, he received a Harvard-sponsored scholarship to support a year of study in comparative law at the University of Madrid. Spain afforded Houston an experience of racial egalitarianism that "colored [his] entire life on the race question."[21]

With the normal channels of political participation closed to black Americans, Charles Houston envisioned a unique and critical role for black lawyers. As early as 1922, Houston proposed that there must be a black lawyer in every community, preferably trained at black institutions by black teachers. Applying the innovative theory of social jurisprudence advanced at Harvard by Roscoe Pound, Felix Frankfurter, and others, Houston explained that through the creative exploration and application of the Constitution, the black lawyer could achieve reforms that were unattainable through traditional political channels. Houston applied his vision as a member of the Howard University Law School faculty (1924–35), where he was appointed vice-dean in 1929. He transformed the school from a nonaccredited night school into a full-time, accredited program and created a laboratory for the development of civil rights law. The rigorous course he implemented reflected his conception of social engineering and the responsibilities of black leadership. The black lawyer, Houston maintained, should "be trained as a social engineer and group interpreter." He added, "Due to the Negro's social and political condition . . . the Negro lawyer must be prepared to anticipate, guide and interpret his group's advancement." Houston educated a generation of black civil rights lawyers, many from the South, who would implement the NAACP's protracted assault on the legal foundation of white supremacy.[22]

By enhancing the power of the federal government, the economic crisis of the depression and the advent of the New Deal reinforced Houston's emphasis on national citizenship. He was alert to the vastly expanded range of possibilities for political education and action, possibilities created by the social dislocation and government experimentation of the 1930s. Houston investigated the racial application of New Deal programs and publicized cases of discrimination, lobbied the Roosevelt administration for fair treatment, testified before Congress on the racial implications of a wide array of legislation, and played a leading role in the fight for antilynching legislation.

The development of racially progressive political views among white liberals won Houston's attention. Speaking to groups like the Virginia Commission on Interracial Cooperation and the YWCA, he cautioned them not to act "out of any sentimental interest in the Negro." It was in the self-interest of white liberals to confront the race problem, which, he warned, could "yet be the decisive factor in the success or failure of the New Deal." Their goal, Houston advised, should be to "free white America from the senseless phobias and contemptuous arrogance towards all peoples of the non-nordic stock." He acknowledged the magnitude of the task but suggested that they strive to make their "own generation open its eyes" and realize when it was "cutting off its nose to spite its face." He noted, "The South is doing [this] when it squeezes Negro wages and as a consequence cuts down his consuming power in the community." And he urged them to "save young America from the blight of race prejudice."[23]

Houston publicized promising legal developments that might offer new tools for advancing the movement. Judge James A. Lowell's ruling in the case of George Crawford was one example. In 1933 the Boston judge refused to extradite Crawford, a black man accused of murder, to Virginia on the grounds that the state excluded blacks from serving on juries in that state. Houston anticipated the "opening up of a new underground railroad for Negroes in the South" if Lowell's ruling was upheld. The principle, Houston explained, was simply that Virginia, which was making the request for extradition, could not "invoke the United States Constitution on the one hand for the purpose of obtaining extradition and on the other hand kick the United States Constitution by denying the Negroes the right to serve on juries." Further attention was drawn to the matter when Virginia Congressman Howard W. Smith introduced a bill calling for Judge Lowell's impeachment. George Crawford was finally returned to Virginia and tried for murder. He was represented by an all-black defense team led by Charles Houston for the NAACP.[24]

The early years of the New Deal coincided with Houston's deepening involvement in the NAACP. As the association's legal counsel and trusted adviser to Executive Secretary Walter White, Houston played a critical role in the NAACP's development during these years. By the early 1930s, the NAACP was in the process of completing a major transition, at least at the national level, away from the predominantly white-led organization founded in 1909 and toward an expanding role for black leadership and a greater reliance on black membership. But the New York–based organization continued to maintain a narrow legal focus, tended to rely on prominent white constitutional lawyers for its major cases, and remained remote from the lives and experiences of the majority of black Americans, especially those living in the South. The brief flurry of branch activity in the South after World War I failed to reach much beyond the professional classes and receded by the late 1920s. The NAACP meeting in Oklahoma in 1934 marked the first time a national convention had been held in the South since the Atlanta meeting of 1921. Speaking to the national convention in 1933 and 1934, Houston joined a chorus of voices in urging a major revision of association policy and priorities to meet the crisis of the depression. "Take the Association home to the people in 1934," he implored the Oklahoma gathering.[25]

A case in the 1930s exposed the inadequacy of the NAACP's approach to the South. When news of the arrest of nine young black men charged with raping two white women near Scottsboro, Alabama, reached New York in the spring of 1931, Walter White had no local contacts to call on for a direct report. The nearest NAACP branch, in Chattanooga, had collapsed in 1930. White followed the case in the press, which relied primarily on southern newspapers, and the NAACP remained aloof. Meanwhile, when Charles Dirba, assistant secretary of the International Labor Defense (ILD) and a member of the Communist Party's Central Committee, read about the arrest, he telegraphed Lowell Wakefield, a party organizer in Birmingham, whom he urged to conduct a careful investigation of the case. Wakefield and Douglas McKenzie, a black organizer for the League of Struggle for Negro Rights, attended the trials in Scottsboro. Dependent on a weak and ineffectual team of defense lawyers, the young men were quickly tried and sentenced to death, amid a mob atmosphere. The ILD immediately acted to secure representation for the appeal of the case and publicized the "legal lynching" of the Scottsboro defendants. The ILD won the acclaim of much of the black press and its readership, which chided the NAACP's belated efforts to wrest control of the case from a group that had acted boldly and decisively.[26]

The unfolding of the Scottsboro case, recalled Robert Weaver, was comparable to the dramatic impact of Bull Connor turning the hoses and dogs on young black protesters in Birmingham some thirty years later. "It was a great shock to a large number of people, and made many people face up to a situation which they would have not faced up to before." The ILD's fight on behalf of the defendants would not be confined to the courtroom, though it did win a major case before the U.S. Supreme Court with *Powell v. Alabama*

(1932), which extended the rights of criminal defendants. Through mass demonstrations, the ILD brought the case and the larger racial and economic reality it represented before the nation and won international attention. By contrast, the cautious, legalistic approach of the NAACP, which sought to secure a measure of justice by appealing to the goodwill of white southern moderates, fell flat. In 1934, Charles Houston predicted that the Scottsboro case would one day be acknowledged as a "milestone" in American history.[27]

The Scottsboro case challenged the NAACP to broaden the focus of its campaign against lynching. As Houston viewed it, "relief from physical terrorism" was at the basis of all black progress. He agreed that it was the essential prerequisite to all other struggles for equal rights and "necessary in order to get people to go into court." Though Houston campaigned for federal antilynching legislation, he questioned the tendency of the NAACP to focus on the passage of the bill as the sole cure for lynching in the South. Observing that local elected officials permitted lynchings, Houston argued, "You give nine million Negroes the ballot and they will settle the question of lynching." Scottsboro, he explained, was a judicial lynching with the same social effect "as though a mob had taken them and strung them on a telephone pole." Houston predicted that the "extra-judicial" mob lynchings would turn into "judicial and official lynchings unless the drive of the liberal forces" was "carried way beyond a federal anti-lynching law to complete justice in the courts and to true universal suffrage."[28]

Throughout the 1930s, Charles Houston referred to the Scottsboro case as a pivotal event in the development of black protest. The ILD's "uncompromising resistance to southern prejudice," he explained, "set a new standard for agitation for equality." As a symbol of "the whole position of oppression of the Negro people in America," the Scottsboro case "fused all the elements of the Negro people into a common resistance more than any other issue within a generation." Whereas most black people had tended to "stay away" from black people in trouble—"with the idea of not letting trouble spread to themselves"—they joined in the fight for the "Scottsboro Boys" because they "were made to feel that even without the ordinary weapons of democracy . . . [they] still had the force . . . with which they themselves could bring to bear pressures and affect the result of the trial and arbitrations." Furthermore, he explained, "The Communists have made it impossible for any aspirant to Negro leadership to advocate less than full economic, political and social equality and expect to retain the respect and confidence of the group."[29]

For Houston, ideological disputes about Communist Party assumptions and goals were of little consequence. What mattered were the patterns of interaction that developed between Communist Party organizers and black people in Alabama. Unlike traditional civil rights and interracial groups, which maintained a paternalistic approach to the "masses," Communists worked among the sharecroppers and unemployed, "offering them full and complete brotherhood, without regard to race, creed or previous condition of servitude." Consequently, they were "the first to fire the masses with a sense of their raw, potential power, and the first to openly preach the doctrine of mass resistance and mass struggle: Unite and Fight!" Through their organizing efforts, Communists turned the attention of blacks to the issue of class and emphasized its relation to racial oppression.[30]

Although Houston concentrated his organizing efforts within the black community, he viewed this as part of a broader effort to build class-based alliances among southern blacks and whites. "The white and black miners in the Birmingham district have presented the ultimate solution," he observed in 1934, "by forming together in one common union to fight shoulder to shoulder for their common interest." That same year, Houston told the annual convention of the NAACP that permanent black progress against injustice and discrimination in the South would depend on whether or not blacks could form an alliance with poor whites, because the separation of the two races was impeding the progress of both. "Together they can win against the forces which are seeking to exploit them and keep them down. Separately they will lose and the other fellow will continue to win."[31]

Houston never doubted that the NAACP had a unique role to play as potentially the most effective black organization in the country, but the role would require a major reorganization and reorientation of the association's program. By the time Houston assumed responsibility for the NAACP's legal campaign against racial discrimination in education in 1934, he was prepared to mediate between the national office and its potential southern constituency. Houston was an astute student of the region and its people, having traveled through the South extensively, always on multipurpose trips. A month-long trip late in 1934 was typical. He visited eleven towns in Georgia, the Carolinas, and Virginia, several of them more than once. He spoke at thirteen black colleges, recruited applicants for Howard University Law School, consulted with black lawyers in each state, spoke in churches, attended the district conference of the African Methodist Episcopal (AME) Zion Church in Rock Hill, South Carolina, and met with teachers groups, NAACP branches, and the North Carolina statewide conference of the Tobacco Workers Union. On the same trip, he investigated school facilities, rural conditions, and the administration of federal relief and jobs and, with the assistance of Edward Lovett, began to document his findings with photographs and films. All the while, he deliberately cultivated support for the NAACP's program and sought out individuals "of force, vision . . . [and] keenness" who had the capacity to "be effective on the race issue in the South."[32]

Houston's efforts to expand the base of NAACP activity in the South were equaled by his steady drive to place the southern situation at the center of national NAACP deliberations. He pressed for a reorganization of the association's structure so that the southern membership could participate in defining the national program. In supporting the nomination of Roscoe Dunjee, editor of the *Oklahoma Black Dispatch*, to the NAACP national board, Houston advised White: "Dunjee is a man of the people, and knows the Southwest situation." Certainly, he added, White needed someone on the board who could vocalize "the aspirations of that section."[33]

A critique of the proposed program for the NAACP annual conference in 1935 contrasts Houston's vision with the conventional leadership that dominated the national office. Houston wrote Assistant Secretary Roy Wilkins that the program emphasis on appealing to white southern goodwill and on pursuing "nationally known names" was irrelevant to the economic and political crisis facing the great majority of black Americans. Commenting on the preview of White's speech on the antilynching fight, Houston said: "Walter can tell all he wants about the change in white southern sentiment. We don't want to waste an evening listening to it. [He] should tie up lynching with all the evils we suffer from; show how it perpetuates political disfranchisement, what that means; how it keeps down labor organizing, etc.; how it keeps down protest against intolerable relief conditions, etc., etc."[34]

Houston compared the proposed program for the annual convention with the Conference on the Economic Status of the Negro, organized by John P. Davis and Ralph Bunche and sponsored by the Joint Committee on National Recovery and the Social Science Division of Howard University earlier that year. "The presence of workers gave this conference an impact of reality wholly different from the usual gab-fest conference," Houston advised Wilkins. The NAACP, he insisted, must concentrate on the vital problems of unemployment and relief. He volunteered to bring some relief workers up from the South, and he suggested that his films on relief in Alabama, education facilities in South Carolina, and NAACP-organized picketing be shown. Houston wanted workers, sharecroppers, and victims of relief discrimination to participate in the various panels. "They may not make grammatical speeches," he told Wilkins, "but their very presence is more eloquent than all the prepared speeches you could present." And it would indicate that the association was "getting away from being paternalistic and becoming frater-nalistic with the masses of Negroes."[35]

Under Houston's direction, the NAACP's legal campaign against racial dis-crimination in education stimulated the revival and expansion of NAACP branch activity. Beginning with a protracted challenge to the most blatant inequities in public education, namely the denial of graduate and profes-sional educational opportunities to black students and the racial basis of teachers' salaries, Houston and his associates crafted a strategy that steadily eroded the legal foundations of segregation. Houston's insistence on work-ing with all-black counsel had particular resonance in southern courtrooms. Here, often for the first time, black people witnessed one of their race func-tioning in a context of total equality, calling white state officials to account in full public view. Such trial scenes were reenacted in pool halls and bar-bershops. By 1938, Houston noted, hopefully, that the fight for graduate and professional education was "generating spontaneously out of the group itself"; every case had "been fought by Negro lawyers who practically do-nated their services."[36]

Houston's efforts in the South, an associate recalled, were fueled by his confidence in the capacity "within the black community and the Negro race to bring about change." The legal campaign was a slow and deliberate pro-cess, which sought to establish roots in local communities. In endless rounds of meetings with small and large groups throughout the South, Houston and Thurgood Marshall, his protégé and former student, explained the me-chanics of the legal fight, its political significance, and its relationship to broader community concerns. They routinely encouraged people to pay their poll tax, persist in the effort to register and vote, and organize political clubs, explaining that legal victories must be backed up by organized pres-sure and support. Often they found people fearful of initiating litigation or political action and, in some cases, apathetic about the need for struggle. "This means we have to . . . slow down," Houston would say, "until we have developed a sustaining mass interest behind the programs. . . . The social and public factors must be developed at least along with and if possible before the actual litigation commences."[37]

Yet subtle signs of change abounded. Houston reported on organized attempts by black citizens in South Carolina, Alabama, and Texas to gain admission to the all-white Democratic primary elections in 1934. Voting clubs increasingly appeared in black communities throughout the region. Based on extensive fieldwork during the later 1930s, Ralph Bunche reported that in a number of southern cities, blacks elected "bronze" mayors in mock election campaigns that followed a regular campaign with posters and meetings. Bunche and his team of investigators also found a growing movement among black southerners at least to attempt to register and vote in the face of legal restrictions and potential reprisals. Bunche noted, "Despite the hardships frequently imposed by registrars . . . increasing numbers of Negroes in the South are demonstrating an amazing amount of patience, perseverance and determination . . . and keep returning after rejections until they get their names on the registration books." In 1937 Arthur Shores, the only practicing black attorney in the state of Alabama, filed suit against the Board of Registrar in Bessemer, Alabama, on behalf of eight schoolteachers who had been disqualified by the board. The board reversed itself and issued registration certificates, beginning the long struggle to break down discriminatory registration procedures in Alabama.[38]

Bunche and others documented direct links between New Deal initiatives and growing black political participation. Peter Epps, a Works Progress Administration (WPA) worker in Columbia, South Carolina, was typical. When asked whether blacks on a local farm ever talked politics, Epps replied: "They's talked more politics since Mistuh Roosevelt been in than ever befo'. I been here twenty years, but since WPA, the Negro sho' has started talkin' 'bout politics." A 1938 WPA directive served as an inadvertent spur to black political participation. In an effort to defuse conservative charges that the agency fraudulently sought to influence the votes of its beneficiaries, WPA administrator Elizabeth Wickenden prepared a notice to accompany every WPA check and to advise the recipients that they were free to vote for whomever they pleased. Wickenden was inundated with reports of black southerners showing up at the courthouse with a notice from the WPA endorsing their right to vote.[39]

The 1936 election gave form to the sea change in political attitudes and aspirations that had been shaped, in large part, by the rhetoric and initiatives of the early New Deal. Roosevelt's embrace of class-based politics absorbed much of the energy generated by nascent independent movements on the Left. The campaign also marked the political debut of the new industrial unions of the CIO. Working through the Labor NonPartisan League (LNPL), CIO unions organized local get-out-the-vote campaigns in nearly every state, among white and black workers, with no pretense to being "nonpartisan." The LNPL was unabashedly a part of the Roosevelt reelection machinery and was key to the president's historic landslide at the polls. Commenting on "the tremendous proportions of the victory based on labor, farmer, and lower middle class voters," Palmer Weber pointed to the parallels in American history, most recently the capture of the Democratic Party by the Populists in 1896. "This grand American tradition of an alliance," he observed, had sharpened class antagonisms in the past and, he predicted, would do so once again. And, because the election had been fought and won on the basis of class politics, Roosevelt would not be able to contain the consequences.[40]

The election also marked the culmination of a three-year effort on the part of the Roosevelt administration to fully engage the tentative allegiance of black voters, who had been steadily drifting away from the party of Lincoln. The battle for the northern black vote emerged as a major feature of the 1936 campaign. For the first time, the black vote was a part of the political reporting in the national press, and both parties pursued an aggressive advertising campaign in the black press. Although the Roosevelt administration failed to endorse any racially sensitive policies, such as antilynching legislation, it presided over a national convention that, for the first time, opened its doors to the equal participation of black reporters and the handful of black delegates in attendance, drawing a howl of protest from Senator E. D. Smith and the South Carolina delegation. Mary McLeod Bethune and other members of the "Black Cabinet" took part in a sophisticated campaign aimed at black voters; the campaign included an extravagant, multicity celebration of the seventy-third anniversary of the Emancipation Proclamation. These appeals only reinforced the bonds woven by New Deal relief and jobs, ensuring Roosevelt's sweep of the black vote. "The amazing switch of this great group of voters," wrote political analyst Frank R. Kent, "is the real political sensation of the time."[41]

The successful wooing of the northern black vote dominated the rhetoric of southern conservatives as they swelled the ranks of the anti–New Deal coalition. "Acceptance of the Negro on terms of political equality," stormed Senator Smith, had "humiliated the South."[42] But the black vote was still tightly confined by law and custom in the South. It was the new labor movement, working in tandem with the Roosevelt administration and congressional supporters, that immediately threatened to penetrate the "Solid South" and undermine the economic and racial status quo. During 1937 and 1938, the CIO sponsored its first southern organizing drive, providing critical reinforcement to efforts that had taken root among industrial workers and sharecroppers earlier in the decade and generating a reaction that further exposed the police repression, violence, and political disfranchisement that pervaded southern society.

Established in the fall of 1935, the CIO was a product of the psychological change sparked by the rhetoric of the early New Deal and of the formal acknowledgment of the right of labor to organize as provided for by Section 7a of the National Industrial Recovery Act (NIRA). Clark Foreman hailed

Section 7a as "a second emancipation proclamation for southern workers." The fact that the provision lacked adequate enforcement procedures mattered little. Political propaganda about a new deal, about shorter hours and higher pay, had changed the outlook of thousands of workers. With scant backing from the Roosevelt administration, the United Mine Workers of America (UMW), the Amalgamated Clothing Workers of America (ACWA), and several other industrial unions scored spectacular gains in 1933 and 1934. The enactment of the National Labor Relations Act (Wagner Act) in the spring of 1935, providing for the enforcement of collective bargaining through the National Labor Relations Board (NLRB), put the Roosevelt administration squarely behind a new industrial democracy. The organization of the industrial unions into the CIO, led by the UMW's John Lewis and ACWA leader Sidney Hillman, provided a political structure for the insurgency that reshaped the national labor scene in the immediate aftermath of the 1936 electoral landslide. As one historian has explained, the CIO "was nourished by and in turn fed the fusing elements of the second New Deal."[43]

The industrial unionism of the CIO marked a dramatic departure from the racially and culturally exclusive world of the craft-oriented American Federation of Labor (AFL) and its commitment to "pure and simple unionism." The CIO's constituency of semiskilled workers represented a newer, more fluid, and ethnically diverse segment of the laboring class. Rapid technological changes in industrial production combined with the leavening influence of an emerging mass culture to loosen ethnic and racial stratifications during the 1920s and 1930s. Simultaneously, the collective experience of the depression and the social welfare initiatives of the New Deal forged a new labor consciousness, which, through the deliberate efforts of the CIO, became a defining component of Roosevelt's Democratic coalition. Assessing the unique potential inherent in the initiatives of the CIO toward a "more wholesome economic democracy," black sociologist Charles S. Johnson observed that it was "easier to incorporate Negroes into a new movement before racial distinctions [could] become traditional and fixed than to find a secure place in the old order," even after theories supporting the old order had undergone modification. This, Johnson concluded, was "a social fact of great importance" in affecting the participation of black workers in the ranks of organized labor.[44]

A wave of nationwide strikes and massive union sign-ups fueled the growth of the CIO as a mass movement in the months following the 1936 election. The CIO energized the scattered progressive movements in the South and broadened the possibilities for interracial association. Sidney Hillman, whose artful orchestration gave form to the militant insurgency, was attentive to the unique opportunities and challenges presented by the South. The region was a stronghold of antiunion sentiment, and its powerful congressional representatives defied the political winds of change that swept the country in 1936, threatening to undermine the progressive realignment of the Democratic Party and defuse the potential of a national labor movement.

Hillman responded with a three-pronged strategy. First, the national CIO provided direct support for the fledgling union movement in the South and affiliated movements to broaden political participation in the region. Second, the CIO lobbied for and promoted a more aggressive role on the part of the federal government in extending and protecting basic citizenship rights, which were routinely violated by local and state police powers throughout the region. Working closely with the NLRB and the La Follette Committee on Civil Liberties, which had been established in response to the repression of the Southern Tenant Farmers Union (STFU), the CIO brought national attention to antilabor violence and to police violations of union organizers' civil liberties. Meanwhile, the NLRB expanded its efforts to enforce collective bargaining agreements. Finally, Hillman and the CIO were the primary lobbyists in behalf of the Fair Labor Standards Act, national wage and hour legislation that promised to break down the regional differentials continuing to depress labor in the South, to the detriment of a national labor movement. As part of this effort, Georgia-born journalist Thomas L. Stokes's syndicated newspaper series on the sweatshops of the South was issued by Hillman's ACWA as a pamphlet, "Carpetbaggers of Industry," and was distributed to members of Congress and to governors.[45]

The CIO tapped into the generation of southerners who had emerged from the student movement, the YWCA and YMCA, and earlier labor-organizing efforts. Of the 112 organizers initially employed by the CIO to work in the South, most were southern-born and many were women. James Jackson, the former student organizer for the NSL and founding member of the Southern Negro Youth Congress (SNYC) in 1937, worked as an organizer for the CIO among black tobacco workers in Richmond, where more than five thousand workers signed up and seven union contracts were secured. The CIO provided an infusion for Highlander Folk School in Tennessee, which had struggled since 1931, with little success, to nurture trade union leadership among industrial workers and farmers. In 1937, Highlander became the CIO's primary vehicle for training southern organizers. In Birmingham, Alabama, the CIO's Steel Workers Organizing Committee (SWOC) launched a drive in the summer of 1936, invigorating the Popular Front movement that had grown up around earlier Communist-led efforts among the unemployed, sharecroppers, and industrial workers. Under the CIO umbrella, these diverse and widely scattered movements created a southern network and a spur to more effective political action and organizing.[46]

The popular image of union activists as northern troublemakers with foreign ideas met its most effective challenge in the person of Lucy Randolph Mason, the CIO's primary publicist in the South. She was a Virginian of prominent lineage, the great-great-granddaughter of George Mason, a signer of the Declaration of Independence and author of the Virginia Bill of Rights. "People could place her," a contemporary recalled. A slight woman with white hair, she was the quintessential southern lady. "When Miss Lucy entered a union meeting, the men instinctively got to their feet."[47]

Lucy Randolph Mason was born in 1882. Her family lived in West Virginia and Georgia before finally settling in Richmond in 1891, where Mason's father, an Episcopal minister, served as rector of Grace Church. From her parents, Mason imbibed religious values informed by the Social Gospel, with its commitment to community service and social reform. Her political development was further shaped by her exposure to factory life in Richmond at the turn of the century; she was particularly sensitive to the plight of working-class women. Mason endorsed the union movement and the expansion of suffrage as essential to the advancement of social justice, and she devoted her efforts to both. She was a leading force in the woman's suffrage movement in Richmond and in 1914 became the first industrial secretary of the YWCA in the South. Mason served as general secretary of the Richmond YWCA during the 1920s and honed her skills as a lobbyist and publicist for legislation regulating working conditions for women and children. A wide-ranging community activist, Mason did not avoid the implications of racial discrimination; she publicly acknowledged that it inhibited any real progress toward economic and social justice. In 1929 she was the only white reformer to oppose a Richmond City Council measure requiring residential segregation.[48]

In September 1932, Mason became general secretary of the National Consumer's League (NCL), which provided a national focus for her efforts to secure protective labor legislation in the South. Almost immediately, the New Deal sparked the revival of the flagging, forty-year-old feminist organization and created possibilities for reaching beyond the state-based focus of the NCL's program. In April 1933, Mason wrote that she felt "a curious lift and thrill, as if some great adventure were just around the corner." Mason was part of the network of women in the wave of new talent that populated New Deal Washington and that helped shape legislation and policy. She represented the NCL at the National Recovery Administration (NRA) hearings on wage and hour codes, where she joined the opposition to the racial wage differential, and she consulted with New Deal legislative strategist Ben Cohen and others on the drafting of minimum-wage legislation. Her lobbying efforts in Washington brought her into contact with labor leaders such as Sidney Hillman and David Dubinsky and with Eleanor Roosevelt, who became a friend and confidante. Played out against the futile efforts to secure state legislation regulating working conditions in the South, her experience also convinced her of the necessity of federal initiatives and support to secure fundamental reform. By the time Mason joined the CIO in July 1937, it was clear to her that the future of New Deal reforms would depend largely on what happened in the South. A strong labor movement, she believed, was essential to translating Roosevelt's regional support into a politically effective constituency.[49]

Mason worked primarily with the Textile Workers Organizing Committee (TWOC); the effort to organize the South's major industry was at the core of the CIO's drive. Her confidence that the labor movement could advance economic and political reform in the South was quickly tested by the unbridled power of local authorities to defy federal law and basic constitutional protections. "When I came South I had no idea of the frequent attacks on people peacefully pursuing legitimate purposes," she reported to President Roosevelt in August 1937. "I am appalled at the disregard of the most common civil rights and dangers to bodily harm to which organizers are often exposed." As the CIO's bold offensive rallied progressive forces in the South, it also helped to galvanize powerful anti–New Deal and antilabor forces in the South and in Congress. Mason wrote to Eleanor Roosevelt that organizing efforts met a solid bloc of resistance from "civil authorities, the press and all other agencies," while company spies infiltrated the ranks of the union movement and while the Ku Klux Klan and other vigilante groups terrorized and assaulted union members and labor organizers. Nineteen southern organizers were murdered between 1936 and 1939. By the end of 1937, early signs of progress had dissipated.[50]

During a textile strike in Tupelo, Mississippi, late in the spring of 1938, Mason met with Joseph Gelders, who suggested a southwide conference on civil rights to organize an effective opposition to the wave of terror and repression. Gelders—a Birmingham native, a former University of Alabama professor, and the southern representative of the National Committee for the Defense of Political Prisoners—had been the subject of widely publicized hearings early in 1937 before the La Follette Committee on antilabor violence in the South. Because of his activities on behalf of Jack Barton, he had been beaten and left for dead by guards employed by the Tennessee Coal and

Iron Company. Barton, a longtime member of the International Union of Mine, Mill, and Smelter Workers in Bessemer, Alabama, had joined the Communist Party in 1933 and had been arrested under an antisedition law. After being denied legal representation and a jury trial, Barton was fined and sentenced to hard labor; court officials refused to accept bail from the ILD. Gelders was abducted during his investigation of the case. Though publicly known, his attackers were never brought to trial. In an examination of the circumstances surrounding Barton's arrest and trial and Gelders's beating, the La Follette hearings exposed how industry and local government conspired to suppress labor organizing and political activity in the South.[51]

Gelders's discussion with Mason coincided with the preparation of the *Report on the Economic Conditions of the South*. Mason arranged for Gelders to meet with Eleanor Roosevelt to discuss his plan, and this was followed by a meeting between Gelders and the president at Hyde Park in June 1938, on the eve of the summer primary elections. Both Eleanor Roosevelt and the president endorsed Gelders's idea but advised that the scope of the conference be broadened to address the entire range of problems confronting the South, as put forward in the report. And the president specifically urged that the conference act on the issue of voting rights, beginning with an expansion of the campaign to abolish the poll tax.[52]

Immediately following his session with the president, Gelders convened a small group in Birmingham to plan for a regional conference late in the fall. One of the first people Gelders contacted was H. C. Nixon, chairman of the Southern Policy Committee (SPC), who played a major role in organizing the conference. The Birmingham committee also included Rob Hall, a founder of the NSL, who had returned to his native Alabama in 1934 and was district organizer for the Communist Party. Birmingham Congressman Luther Patrick, Judge Louise Charlton, a member of the Alabama Democratic Committee, and William Mitch, director of the Alabama CIO, also aided in organizing and local arrangements. They coordinated their plans with the president's advisory committee on southern economic problems. Late in July, Gelders and Judge Charleton met with Lucy Randolph Mason and Clark Foreman in Atlanta, where Foreman was managing Lawrence Camp's challenge to Senator Walter George in the Democratic primary. The conference aimed to provide southerners with a collective way to address the *Report on the Economic Conditions of the South*.[53]

While conference planners built on the pioneering work of Howard Odum's cadre of social scientists at Chapel Hill and the deliberations of the SPC, they acknowledged the limitations of both approaches. Lucy Mason expressed the sentiment best: "The South cannot be saved by middle class liberals alone—they must make common cause with labor, the dispossessed on the land and the Negro. . . . Some may find it too shocking to have the other three so articulate about their needs. But this is the basis for progress in democracy, economic justice and social values in the South." Organizers drew from the networks that had grown up around the New Deal, labor-organizing efforts, and local reform movements, and they succeeded in bringing together what was arguably the most diverse meeting of south-erners to occur up to that time.[54]

Business executives, labor organizers, WPA workers, state and federal gov-ernment officials, members of Congress, sharecroppers, newspaper editors, and college professors and students were among the twelve hundred people who gathered at Birmingham Municipal Auditorium over Thanksgiving weekend in 1938. Roughly 20 percent of the delegates were black, and they sat and mixed freely with the white participants. Arthur Raper remembered it as "one of the most exaggerated expressions of change in the South . . . here was a revival, a bush-shaking, something that just jumped up." For Virginia Durr, "[It was] a wonderful sort of love feast because it was the first time that all of these various elements from the South had gotten together. And we were not segregated." In a more sober, but still hopeful assessment, black poet Sterling Brown said that the conference was a sign that the South was "on the move." He added, "The hind wheel may be off and the axle dragging, but the old cart is hovering along."[55]

For three days the participants met in small groups to discuss sections of the NEC report; Eleanor Roosevelt, Supreme Court Justice Hugo Black, and University of North Carolina President Frank Graham addressed the ple-nary sessions. The conference adopted a number of proposals, which called for state and federal action to redress the economic imbalances that had stifled the development of the region's people and its resources. The con-ference endorsed federal antilynching legislation and equal salaries for black and white teachers. John P. Davis, Clark Foreman, and Mary McLeod Be-thune were among those elected as officers of a permanent organization, further indicating a new departure for southern reform. In establishing itself as a permanent organization, the SCHW embarked on the challenging if vaguely defined task of creating and organizing a political movement capa-ble of advancing its resolves. Whereas the matters of strategy and organiza-tion were left for future deliberation, the group was unexpectedly compelled to confront the issue of racial custom, something that white southern lib-erals instinctively avoided.[56]

Conference leaders had not intended to make an issue out of segregation;

nonsegregated meetings had been held before in the municipal auditorium. But halfway through the second day the Birmingham police, led by Eugene "Bull" Connor, informed conference organizers that a municipal ordinance requiring segregation in the auditorium would be enforced. Under threats of arrest, and with limited options available, participants decided to comply with the ordinance so that the meeting might continue. Whites sat on one side of the auditorium, blacks on the other. Further attention was drawn to the matter when Eleanor Roosevelt, arriving late for the afternoon session, sat among the black participants. A policeman immediately informed her that she would have to move. Roosevelt did not move to the white side. She took her chair and put it on top of the line set down to divide the two sides. "That was a glorious moment," recalled Rob Hall. Later that evening, when questioned about the incident, Roosevelt avoided outright condemnation of legalized segregation. "I do not believe that is a question for me to answer," she said. "In the section of the country where I come from it is a procedure that is not followed. But I would not presume to tell the people of Alabama what they should do." Her explanation hardly dulled the symbolic import of Roosevelt's action. The *Afro-American* observed, "If the [white] people of the South do not grasp this gesture, we must. Sometimes actions speak louder than words."[57]

Bull Connor's intrusion placed the issue of segregation squarely before the new organization. After several hours of discussion and debate, conference organizers voted that the SCHW would never again hold a segregated meeting. Although this resolution hardly justified the claims of critics that the SCHW was a "racial equality" organization, the group's response marked an important departure from the customary caution of white southern liberals who shrank from any overt challenge to racial segregation. Several prominent politicians in attendance, including John Bankhead, Lister Hill, and Luther Patrick, avoided further association with the group. The episode, and its consequences, made it easier for the SCHW to move beyond traditional white southern liberalism and work with the movement that was developing around the NAACP's legal campaign to end voting restrictions and racial discrimination in the South.[58]

The end of 1938 found the New Deal in retreat on Capitol Hill, with southern conservative Democrats leading the charge. That same year, the Supreme Court, now dominated by Roosevelt appointees, ruled that Lloyd L. Gaines be admitted to the University of Missouri Law School, giving the NAACP its first major legal victory in the campaign for equal education. Pauli Murray, whose application to the University of North Carolina had been rejected solely on racial grounds, observed that *Gaines* was the "first major breach in the solid wall of segregated education since *Plessy*." It was "the beginning of the end."[59] Black southerners, in increasing numbers, continued to petition state Democratic parties for admission to the primary elections; the NAACP would soon prepare to take another challenge to the Supreme Court in its twenty-year legal battle against the all-white primary. In 1939, the SCHW launched a movement to abolish the poll tax. Its lobbying campaign for federal anti-poll-tax legislation made the right to vote a national issue.

Although the legislative phase of the New Deal may have ended by 1938, its political consequences for the South, for African Americans, and for the Democratic Party were just beginning to be realized. Palmer Weber and Charles Houston were among those who maintained that the fate of New Deal reform would depend largely on what happened in the South. "The economic wage slavery and social suppression cursing the South today stood between the progressive forces of the New Deal and the recovery and reform they sought," observed Houston. Weber concurred. Perhaps, he wrote hopefully in November 1938, "as the tides of liberalism run deeper, the value of racial cooperation will come to be understood—even in the far South."[60]

The whole Southern bloc is blocking us at every turn. They realize it is the beginning of their end. Thank God for that happy day.

VIRGINIA DURR, Executive Secretary, National Committee to
Abolish the Poll Tax, to Eleanor Roosevelt, 30 September 1941

The Dixie octopus strangling the rest of the country must be
shaken off.

Crisis, January 1944

4

Whose South?

WARTIME BATTLES ON CAPITOL HILL

Palmer Weber arrived in Washington in the fall of 1940
to take a staff position with the Tolan Committee on Interstate Migration.
The New Deal may have been in retreat, but wartime mobilization created
new opportunities for social engineering and economic experimentation,
opportunities that Weber aggressively pursued. As the committee's associate staff director, he helped shift its focus away from the migration of
destitute people and toward the movement of labor to the centers of defense
industries. In nationwide hearings on federal sponsorship of wartime production, the committee pressed for the full and efficient use of labor and

exposed racial discrimination and substandard facilities for migrant workers as a deterrent to the war effort. The Tolan Committee was the predecessor to several wartime Senate committees established to oversee full mobilization of labor and production facilities. Weber helped to organize and became staff director of one of these, Claude Pepper's Subcommittee on Health and Education.

Weber described his arrival in Washington as "a fabulous piece of luck." His plans to teach philosophy had fizzled when his professors refused to recommend him for a position. A chance meeting at a party led the unemployed Ph.D. to a job with the Tolan Committee. Washington provided Weber with a vastly expanded arena for pursuing his political concerns. "I had a running license over the whole Senate and the whole Congress," Weber recalled. He became well acquainted with numerous members of Congress, as well as with the leadership of the labor movement, black New Deal officials and activists, and "the big group of Southerners" who had been there since 1933. Weber helped to energize the ranks of southern New Dealers as they sought to counter the emergent anti–New Deal coalition led by conservative southern Democrats.[1]

While World War II heightened the democratic aspirations and movements inspired by the New Deal, it also secured the conservative ascendancy in Washington as anti–New Deal southern Democrats wielded the balance of power. Republican gains in the 1938 midterm elections, along with Roosevelt's unsuccessful effort to purge conservative Democrats, marked the end of the legislative phase of the New Deal. Republicans remained twenty-three seats shy of a majority in the Senate and fifty seats short in the House, but they found allies among Democrats who shared their opposition to the reformist and largely urban agenda of the New Deal and to the aggressive new labor movement it spawned. By the late 1930s, one-half of the southerners in the Senate consistently voted against the president; in the House, southern opposition ranged from twenty to as many as seventy. The power of a bipartisan anti–New Deal coalition was quickly demonstrated in the new Congress. Republicans and southern Democrats slashed relief spending and scaled down appropriations for public works and housing projects. Clifton Woodrum and Howard Smith of Virginia launched investigations of the Works Progress Administration (WPA) and the National Labor Relations Board. In 1939 the House increased appropriations fourfold for the Special Committee on UnAmerican Activities, headed by Texas Democrat Martin Dies, thus sanctioning Dies's widely publicized search for Communists in the government and in the Congress of Industrial Organizations (CIO).[2]

A widely shared concern over the consequences of the New Deal fractured party ranks. With the worst of the depression over, and with tobacco and cotton prices stabilized, southern representatives were anxious to contain the broader implications of New Deal reform. Although southern critics of the New Deal railed against the expansion of federally sponsored welfare dependency, their greatest concern was that the New Deal threatened the traditional patterns of dependency that had long defined economic and political relations in the region. Minimum-wage legislation, CIO organizing drives, rural poverty programs, and the expressions of political awareness and interest among traditionally disfranchised groups were slowly undermining the political and economic hegemony maintained by industrialists and Black Belt landowners. The emergence of northern black voters as a major constituency within the Democratic Party was a particular cause for alarm among southern conservatives and was a factor they emphasized in their campaign to discredit the New Deal and its supporters.

War mobilization supported the conservative resurgence in Washington. The social engineering of the 1930s was eclipsed by a proliferation of wartime agencies staffed by corporate executives and production experts. From their leading positions on the most powerful committees of Congress, southern conservatives led in rolling back New Deal initiatives and countering the assumptions and policies that had transformed the government during the 1930s. They portrayed New Deal programs as wasteful, excessive, and possibly subversive, amplifying the charges routinely paraded by the Dies Committee. While Roosevelt remained occupied with defense preparations, New Deal administrators and lobbyists waged a defensive battle on Capitol Hill. In the process, two divergent streams of southern thought and politics engaged each other in the national arena. Southern New Dealers prepared to challenge their conservative counterparts by focusing on the basis of their power—a constricted southern electorate.

The ascendancy of an anti–New Deal southern vanguard in Washington sharpened divisions within the Democratic Party and focused national attention on the workings of southern politics. The inordinate power enjoyed by southern members of Congress was dependent on a small electorate restricted by race and class. Eugene Cox, acting chairman of the powerful Rules Committee, offered a typical example. In 1938 he won reelection with 5,137 votes; the population of his Georgia district was 263,606. The implications of widespread disfranchisement in the region became increasingly apparent to the new generation of labor leaders and progressive New Dealers as Cox, Howard W. Smith of Virginia, Tom Connolly and Martin Dies of Texas, and others led the assault on New Deal programs and introduced a host of antilabor legislation. The National Association for the Advancement of Colored People (NAACP) magazine, *Crisis*, observed, "Belatedly, the rest of the country has come to realize that Senators and Congressmen from poll tax states menace the democratic process everywhere because they enjoy a power in Washington which they could not wield if the elections were free."[3]

In 1939, when the Southern Conference for Human Welfare (SCHW) launched its campaign for federal legislation to repeal the poll tax, it appealed to a broad coalition of support. The poll tax became a potent symbol nationally of the undemocratic political structure that supported the most powerful members of Congress. Moreover, since the poll tax discriminated against poor whites and poor blacks, the fight for its repeal created an arena for interracial cooperation and action. Southern New Dealers were ever-mindful of the squandered potential of the Populist movement. C. Vann Woodward's biography of the Populist leader Tom Watson, published in 1938, was widely read and discussed by the organizers of the anti-poll-tax fight. Woodward's history of Watson and the politics of the 1890s retrieved a moment in history intimately linked to the challenges they faced.[4]

The poll tax was a defining element in the antidemocratic movement that swept through the South in the late nineteenth century. While waving the banner of white solidarity, the "Redeemers" sought to defuse the remnants of Populism by disfranchising underprivileged whites as well as blacks. The poll tax, which had been adopted in every southern state by 1908, served this purpose well. Voter turnout for the 1936 presidential election in the remaining eight poll-tax states stood as testimony to its effectiveness. Less than one in four of the voting-age population in those states cast a ballot in that hotly contested election, compared with nearly three in four in the rest of the United States. A 1937 survey sponsored by the U.S. Department of Labor demonstrated that many workers, farmers, and tenants were prevented from voting because of their inability to pay the poll tax, a restriction that was felt with increasing severity after the onset of the depression. In 1939 the *Louisville Courier-Journal* reported, "As many as 64% of the white adult voters have been disfranchised in the poll tax states, and in every one of those states, more whites than Negroes are barred from the ballot box by the tax." The all-white Democratic primary, racially discriminatory voter-registration procedures, and intimidation often combined to take precedence over the poll tax in blocking black voter participation.[5]

The efficiency of the poll tax as a disfranchisement tool was based on the cost and the method of collection, and the patterns varied from state to state. The tax ranged from $1.00 to $2.00. In Mississippi and Virginia the tax was cumulative for two and three years, respectively; in Georgia it was cumulative from the age of twenty-one, and Alabama's $1.50 tax was cumulative up to $36.00. Labor organizers attempting to increase voter participation among their constituents reported that in Alabama, people over thirty were beyond reach, since their accumulated taxes would be prohibitive. And when a family was able and willing to make the financial sacrifice that voting often required, most often the husband was the one who exercised the privilege, contributing to even lower voter turnout among women (except in South Carolina, where the tax applied only to men). In addition to the cost, the fact that the tax had to be paid far in advance of election day, and usually during the winter when cash was scarce in rural areas, also served as a deterrent. Commenting on the fact that poll taxes were due in Texas by 1 February, one observer wrote that it was "like buying a ticket to a show nine months ahead of time, and before you know who's playing, or really what the thing is all about."[6]

Beyond restricting voting privileges, the poll tax easily lent itself to vote-buying and was widely recognized as a source of fraud and corruption. Electoral reform movements to repeal the poll tax gained momentum around the South during the 1930s. Senator Huey Long's forces led a successful effort in Louisiana in 1934, and Claude Pepper's supporters eliminated the poll tax in Florida in 1936; North Carolina had repealed its poll tax in 1920. In each case, the subsequent increase in voter participation was notable: in North Carolina voter turnout climbed by 70 percent, Louisiana's voting rolls grew by 90 percent, and Florida reported an increase of 140 percent. But Ralph Bunche, a chief investigator for the Myrdal-Carnegie study, reported that the obstacles to the repeal of the poll tax in the eight remaining poll-tax states were "virtually insurmountable." Powerful state legislators and their constituents benefited from a political system that kept the vote small and easily manipulated. The enfranchisement of thousands of new voters, particularly during the politically volatile decade of the 1930s, was something to be avoided. Opponents to the repeal movement deflected attention from the fact that the poll tax was most effective in disfranchising whites by raising the specter of another Reconstruction. George C. Stoney, Ralph Bunche's white research assistant, found widespread fears that any tampering with voting restrictions, including the poll tax, would open the floodgates to black political participation.[7]

Short on funds and dependent largely on volunteer efforts, the executive council of the newly established SCHW voted to concentrate the scant resources of the organization on the poll-tax issue. In February 1939 it established a Committee on Civil Rights, chaired by Maury Maverick and administered by Joseph Gelders, SCHW executive secretary, to initiate a campaign to abolish the poll tax. Gelders's plan included support for a legal challenge by Henry Pirtle of Tennessee, who intended to contest the use of the poll tax as a qualification for voting in federal elections. Just two years earlier, however, the Supreme Court had upheld the constitutionality of the poll tax in *Breedlove v. Suttles*. Not surprisingly, the Pirtle case stalled after being rejected through the court of appeals. Gelders's committee used a grant it obtained from the William C. Whitney Fund for a study of the poll tax; directed by Eleanor Bonteacou, the study supplemented the efforts of Bunche and his investigation of southern voting practices. Finally, Gelders and Virginia Durr, who had been elected to chair the anti-poll-tax committee at the Birmingham meeting, organized a lobbying effort on Capitol Hill for legislation to prohibit a poll-tax requirement in federal elections.[8]

The campaign for anti-poll-tax legislation initiated the nearly three-decade struggle to extend federal protection of voting rights to the South. It also linked southern-based efforts to expand voting rights with the political vitality of New Deal Washington. Gelders's experience as a labor organizer in Alabama was complemented by Virginia Durr, who joined him in navigating Capitol Hill and plotting how to get a bill introduced in Congress. Durr was a unique product of the Washington circle of southern New Dealers and emerged as probably the most effective organizer in behalf of the national anti-poll-tax effort.

"Until I got to Washington [in 1933] and began getting education, everything was personal," Durr recalled. "I was almost completely apolitical. I didn't have any framework for the way I felt." Virginia Durr was thirty years old when she and her husband, Clifford Durr, and their young daughter left Birmingham for Washington, where Clifford joined the legal staff of the Reconstruction Finance Corporation (RFC). The Durrs were immediately drawn to other young southerners who were part of the New Deal experiment, including Alabama Senator Hugo Black, who was married to Virginia's sister Josephine, and Clark Foreman, whom Virginia had known during her college days in Boston. Virginia's enthusiasm for Roosevelt and the New Deal was initially motivated by the confidence that Roosevelt's leadership inspired. But as the political struggle around the New Deal sharpened, her attention was drawn to the South, compelling a complete re-evaluation of assumptions she had inherited. Her ideas about race, politics, and economic reform developed during this period.[9]

Virginia Foster Durr was born in 1903 in Birmingham, where her father, Sterling Foster, was parson for the South Highland Presbyterian Church. She was raised on the aristocratic traditions of the Old South and experienced the contradictions and constraints that the society imposed. Her mother, Anne Patterson Foster, was the daughter of Josiah Patterson, a celebrated Confederate hero who fought under Nathan Bedford Forrest. Patterson served in Congress after the war and spent his last days as custodian of Shiloh, the Confederate cemetery outside of Memphis. Virginia's paternal grandfather, Sterling Foster, was the proprietor of a thirty-five-thousand-acre plantation in Union Springs, Alabama. He opposed the Civil War and bought a substitute to fight in his place. Foster's failure to enlist in the Confederate cause shamed the family, but his foresight in investing his money abroad during the war ensured their continued prosperity while others were left destitute with the collapse of the Confederacy. Among Virginia's most vivid childhood memories were of summers on the Foster plantation in Union Springs, where the benevolence and servitude of the pre–Civil War South prevailed. Former slaves still worked for Grandmother Foster and lived in old cabins out back.

When Virginia was ten years old, some members of the South Highland Presbyterian Church accused her father of heresy. In the proceedings that followed, a tribunal asked Dr. Foster whether he believed in a literal interpretation of the Bible, specifically whether Jonah was swallowed by the whale and spewed up whole three days later. Virginia remembered that her father paced for days, while her mother wept, as he anguished over how he should respond. Although he knew what the consequences would be, he could not conform to a fundamentalist interpretation of the Bible. His efforts to explain the importance of Jonah and the whale as a parable were futile. The Southern Presbyterian Church expelled Sterling Foster as a heretic. At barely forty years of age, he lost his parsonage and attempted to make a living selling insurance to black people. Her parents, Virginia recalled, never fully recovered from the reversals that this event precipitated.

From then on, there was "always a sense of insecurity, not knowing what was going to happen next." Their share of the Foster plantation enabled the family to "keep the best foot forward" and maintain their status in the upper segment of the community. They lived on the fashionable southside of Birmingham, belonged to the country club, and had an automobile. Virginia was a curious child, full of questions, and an avid reader; her father worried that his "bookish" daughter might never marry. But she accepted the contradictions that surrounded her, later explaining that there was an answer for everything. Society was firmly stratified, and "the important thing was to stay where you were or get to the higher rung." Virginia had a year of Miss Finch's finishing school in New York, attended the Cathedral School in Washington, and then in 1921 enrolled in Wellesley College, the academically prestigious women's institution outside of Boston.

Although she attended Wellesley for only two years, it was a formative experience intellectually and socially. Discussions about economics, religion, and the roles of women in society stretched her provincial attitudes. Several of her professors, whom she admired greatly, demonstrated that women could lead fulfilled lives without marrying. At Wellesley she experienced the first affront to her racial mores. On learning that her dining table included a black student, she recalled: "I nearly fell over dead. . . . I promptly got up [and] marched out of the room." The head of the hall told Virginia that she could either accept her seating assignment or withdraw from the college. Realizing that her greatest fear was what her father would say, she resolved not to tell him, and she stayed. Although the experience did not spark a reevaluation of her racial attitudes, it planted a doubt. At around the same time she met Clark Foreman, who was then enrolled at Harvard, and they established a friendship that they renewed later in Washington. Her time at Wellesley was cut short, however, at the end of her second year. As she explained, "The boll weevil ate up my education." The boll weevil infestation of the early 1920s, along with the falling price of cotton, forced her father to gradually sell off his share of the Foster plantation at a drastically deflated price, leaving the family coffers nearly empty.

Her family's economic losses during the 1920s, combined with the widespread devastation of the depression, intensified the contradictions and insecurities Virginia had grown up with. Her mother, unable to withstand the shock of losing everything, went into a deep depression. Economic difficulties were compounded as the trappings of status receded. To help the family meet its bills, Virginia took a job as a librarian for the county bar association. Such a necessity was a source of humiliation for her parents. Durr recalled: "[Until then] I had been a conformist, a southern snob. I actually thought the only people who amounted to anything was the very small group which I belonged to. The fact that my family wasn't as well off as those girls I went with—I was vice president of the Junior League—made me value even more the idea of being well born. . . . What I learned during the depression changed all that."

In 1926, Virginia married Clifford Durr, a bright, successful young lawyer working for the premier corporate law firm in Birmingham. While Cliff's career prospered, Virginia enlisted as a Junior League volunteer to aid the Red Cross in its investigation of families in the steel mill villages applying for relief. "All of a sudden," she recalled, "Birmingham broke on me and I just couldn't believe it. I had never been in these mill villages before. It was absolutely horrible." People were starving. "[They] were cold, they were sick, and so many children had rickets which I thought was a form of cerebral palsy. . . . They couldn't walk simply because they didn't have any milk." The poverty and accumulated misery that had long been invisible gave Durr her "first and ineradicable lesson on the injustice and inequalities of . . . society." This experience, along with the hardship and uncertainty her own family suffered, led her to probe contemporary economic and political theory in search of a way to understand the economic disintegration that surrounded her.

As Birmingham sank deeper into the depression, Virginia and Clifford Durr began to examine the social and economic factors that had caused the collapse. The development of their thought during these years was influenced by their close association with Virginia's brother-in-law Hugo Black, who won election to the U.S. Senate from Alabama in 1926. Black, a vigorous defender of labor unions, was a controversial figure among the Birmingham elite. Before long, Clifford Durr came to a parting of the ways with the partners in his law firm. While Cliff had continued to prosper at the firm, having been made partner in 1927, junior staff people had borne the brunt of bad times. Early in 1933, a number of people were arbitrarily fired at a time when scarce relief money had dried up. Durr protested the firings and suggested that the senior members of the firm take a pay cut in order to avoid further dismissals. The partners rejected this idea, leading to Durr's departure from the firm. Clifford, Virginia, and their young daughter, Ann, retreated to a small fishing cabin they owned while Cliff contemplated the prospect of opening his own law office. It was there that they received word from Hugo Black about a job with the new administration in Washington. Cliff left immediately for Washington in May 1933, followed shortly by Virginia and six-year-old Ann.[10]

Arriving in New Deal Washington from Birmingham, Alabama, "was just like light after darkness," Virginia remembered. Clifford Durr was at the center of the recovery effort, working day and night on the reorganization and recapitalization of the banks as an attorney with the RFC. In October 1933 he wrote his mother, "I get a 'kick' out of feeling that I have a very definite part in the big experiment." The Durrs' circle of friends included other newcomers to Washington, such as Clark and Mairi Foreman, Aubrey and Anita Williams, and Tex and Wicki Goldschmidt. Clark Foreman, in particular, had a tremendous effect on both Virginia's and Clifford's political development. "He was so enthusiastic and absolutely believing," Virginia recalled. And there were many others. "Some [were] more radical than others, but all shared the same feeling that the New Deal was a great event. . . . It got to be a community. Friendships formed. Children grew up and married each other. It was just a marvelous time to be in Washington."[11]

The Durrs settled in an old farmhouse on Seminary Hill in Alexandria. Clifford Jr. was born in September 1935, followed sixteen months later by Lucy. While running the household and looking after her young family, Virginia also became one of the more popular hostesses in New Deal Washington. Jessica Mitford, a long-term houseguest, recalled that Virginia "adored entertaining and had an insatiable appetite for meeting new people, seeing old friends. . . . The kaleidoscopic mix of people who came to visit included judicial dignitaries, southern legislators . . . New Deal functionaries, earnest young radicals." Virginia absorbed the energy and optimism of the New Deal and shared the general feeling that Roosevelt had "saved the country." In her desire to be a part of it all she joined the Women's Division of the Democratic National Committee as a volunteer.[12]

Virginia's economic and political education began in earnest during Wisconsin Senator Robert La Follette's investigation of antilabor violence. The committee's investigation early in 1937 of Joseph Gelders's brutal beating by Tennessee Coal and Iron Company police outside of Birmingham initially captured her attention and personalized the political upheaval surrounding the New Deal. The testimony on "Bloody" Harlan County was most gripping and dramatic, but it was the committee's investigation of the Tennessee Coal and Iron Company that had a profound impact on Virginia. As labor organizers described their efforts to establish unions among the destitute people she had encountered during her work with the Red Cross, she began to understand the nature of economic relationships and politics in places like Birmingham and Bessemer. Witnesses testified that antilabor violence and the wholesale repression of labor activity were supported by the leading citizens of Birmingham, some of whom Virginia had known since childhood. She wrote to several of these men, seeking an explanation, but rather than refute their actions, they justified their deeds. They dismissed the charges against them as propaganda and explained that they had done all they could to assist the people who worked for them. They were merely trying to protect their workers from "outside agitators." Having seen the miserable conditions in the mill villages firsthand, Virginia realized that these men were unwilling to take any responsibility for the welfare of their workers.

Eager to learn more about Gelders and labor-organizing efforts in Alabama, Virginia sought out Gelders during a visit to Birmingham. "We found all kinds of common ground immediately," Durr recalled. Although their backgrounds and personalities were quite different, they had Birmingham in common, as well as their enthusiasm for the New Deal and the labor movement. Gelders's fortitude inspired Durr. He reminded her of a Jewish prophet, tall and slender with an ascetic face, undeterred by the terrible beating he had survived. The two quickly became devoted friends. Durr was one of the first people Gelders contacted after his meeting with the Roosevelts in Hyde Park, seeking her assistance in planning the Birmingham meeting. She put him in touch with the work of the Southern Policy Committee (SPC) through Clifford Durr and Clark Foreman. And Virginia agreed to prepare a report for the meeting to document the distortion and misinformation that characterized the southern press coverage of the La Follette Committee hearings.[13]

The founding meeting of the SCHW completed Virginia Durr's separation from the confines of her past. The coming together of all of the various groups from around the South, black and white, embodied the spirit of the New Deal as she had experienced it during the previous five years and filled her with joyful optimism. But her mood was tempered by the response from her closest friends in Birmingham. They were vehemently opposed to Roosevelt. The disturbance over segregation at the meeting confirmed their fears that racial equality was a central component of the New Deal agenda. Virginia's efforts to defend the New Deal were ignored. People she had known since childhood accused her of being "an outright traitor, an outlaw," she recalled. "It was painful for me to see all of my friends against me so badly, but I never had a moment's doubt where I stood."

Durr attended the 1938 meeting as a representative of the Women's Division of the Democratic National Committee. The Women's Division had been working to repeal the poll tax for white women in the South, a cause in which Durr took an active interest. Eleanor Roosevelt frequently participated in their discussions about the poll tax. Mary McLeod Bethune, the noted educator and most prominent black New Deal official, occasionally accompanied Roosevelt to these meetings. Bethune advised the group that their efforts would be futile unless they joined forces with black civil rights activists who had long been working for the repeal of the poll tax, along with other voting reforms. When Durr expressed interest in Bethune's suggestion, Bethune introduced her to William Hastie, who provided entrée to the core group of black New Dealers, NAACP legal strategists, and Howard University social scientists.[14]

In an effort to avoid the united southern opposition that routinely met antilynching legislation, Gelders and Durr had hoped to find a southern congressman to introduce a bill. Luther Patrick, congressman from Birmingham, initially agreed to sponsor a bill but then changed his mind. As an early supporter recalled, although the impetus for the abolition of the poll tax came from southerners, "the political ability to do it" required "Senators and Congressmen outside the South to introduce the legislation." Durr and Gelders finally found a supporter in California Congressman Lee Geyer, representative from Los Angeles, who, in addition to introducing legislation, provided Gelders and Durr with office space. The legislation Geyer put forward did not challenge the constitutionality of the poll tax, since the Supreme Court had sanctioned the qualification two years earlier. Rather, Geyer proposed that Congress eliminate the tax in order to protect federal elections from the influence of corrupt politicians who commonly bought and sold poll-tax receipts.[15]

The poll-tax bill widened the rift between the southern bloc and the Democratic majority. It became a core issue among the New Deal coalition. Northern and urban members of Congress, representing large black constituencies, touted their support of legislation that, they claimed, would aid in the enfranchisement of southern blacks. Labor unions embraced the repeal of the poll tax as essential to opening up the political process to southern labor and unseating labor's most powerful opponent in the Congress. But a majority of southern members of Congress viewed it as the first attempt since the 1890s on the part of the federal government to control the election machinery of the South. With a handful of exceptions, they formed a solid block of opposition and brought their considerable political weight to bear on the White House as well as in the Congress. Durr recalled that "all hell broke loose" when Geyer introduced the bill. James Farley insisted that the Women's Division of the Democratic National Committee stop all work relating to the poll tax, leading to Durr's departure from the group. From then on, Durr worked out of Geyer's office while Gelders divided his time between Washington and fieldwork in the South, until enlisting in the army in 1941.[16]

Geyer introduced the first anti-poll-tax bill in October 1939; it died after extensive hearings in the House Judiciary Committee. Early in the next session of Congress, Geyer introduced a similar bill, this time cosponsored by Claude Pepper, the junior senator from Florida. Since Pepper was a southern senator, his sponsorship of the bill was especially valuable. Yet he was under steady attack from the southern bloc in Congress, especially Tom Connally and Sam Rayburn of Texas. Durr complained about Rayburn, "[He] scares off everybody we think we've got hitched." In an effort to counter these pressures, Durr asked Eleanor Roosevelt if she would convene a meeting of southerners who supported the poll-tax fight and who could give Pepper a real sense of political support—people like Nelson Poynter, editor of the *Petersburg Times*, or like Aubrey Williams, Will Alexander, and Frank Graham. Roosevelt did; she also personally praised Pepper for his efforts and pledged her full support. Eleanor Roosevelt's accessibility and her willingness to serve as an intermediary in support of the anti-poll-tax cause were vital to Durr's efforts. She observed that it was Mrs. Roosevelt who plowed the ground while Mr. Roosevelt tried to placate the southern wing of the Democratic Party.[17]

Geyer established the National Committee to Abolish the Poll Tax (NCAPT) in 1941 as an umbrella organization for all of the various groups and individuals that enlisted in the anti-poll-tax cause. It replaced the SCHW's earlier Civil Rights Committee and served as a clearinghouse and center for anti-poll-tax activity. The NCAPT brought together a notable group of national sponsors. Prominent among them was the NAACP, which had waged a long legal campaign to eliminate voter restrictions and which lent legal talent, lobbying support, and publicity to the anti-poll-tax campaign. Other cosponsors included the American Federation of Labor (AFL), the CIO, the Railway Unions, the National Farmers Union (NFU), the Young Women's Christian Association (YWCA), the League of Women Voters, and the National Negro Congress (NNC). Eleanor Roosevelt, Frank Graham, Mary McLeod Bethune, A. Philip Randolph, Howard University President Mordecai Johnson, Philip Murray, NFU President James Patton, and Kathryn Lewis, daughter of CIO President John L. Lewis, were among those who served on the NCAPT's national board. Geyer chaired the NCAPT, and Virginia Durr, serving as vice-chairman, was responsible for running the organization.[18]

Although the NCAPT enjoyed broad support, finances remained tight. As the organization's sole staff member, Durr found the task before her to be overwhelming. "I was totally untutored in the very basics. I couldn't even type [and] I had no idea of how Congress worked." Then, unexpectedly, a "horde of young men" from the Tolan Committee office descended on the NCAPT office one afternoon "dying to do something" and volunteering their services. Their leader was Palmer Weber. Weber had a brilliant ability, Durr recalled, "to take hold of something, organize it and set it in motion." He became a regular, spending several hours at the NCAPT office each day. Weber and his staffers began publishing a newsletter, "The Poll Tax Repealer," and fed press releases to newspapers around the country in an effort to mobilize public opinion behind the bill. Virginia was free to lobby members of Congress for their support of the bill and to cultivate outside sponsors and financial supporters. Meanwhile the NCAPT office continued to attract all kinds of volunteer support. Aliene Austin Cohen was among the students who helped stuff envelopes and lick stamps. The poll-tax fight was *the* issue among the politically active students she knew then; it represented "the crying inconsistency in the country. . . . it was just natural for Antioch students in Washington to go to the poll tax office."[19]

While the Geyer-Pepper bill made its way through committee hearings and a vote in the House toward a final showdown on the Senate floor, the United States entered World War II. The proponents of electoral reform scored a significant victory with the Soldiers Vote Bill of 1942, which aimed to provide absentee ballots for federal elections to men and women serving in the armed forces. It was "the most volatile measure dropped in the hopper since Pearl Harbor," reported the *New York Times*; the debate on the bill "turned into a dog-fight, with far-flung ramifications." John Rankin of Mississippi led the opposition in the House, charging that any federal regulation of election procedures violated the rights of the sovereign state. Tennessee Representative Estes Kefauver's proposed amendment, to suspend poll-tax requirements for soldiers, threatened to provoke full-scale revolt and was swiftly disposed of by the House, but the bill passed.[20]

When the bill came before the Senate in August, administration forces, including Senate Majority Leader Alben Barkley, hoped to avoid any divisive amendments in order to secure timely passage of the legislation. Failing to follow Barkley's instructions, Senator Pepper and Senator C. Wayland Brooks of Illinois added an amendment to the bill to suspend poll-tax requirements for all members of the armed services for the duration of the war. The Senate endorsed the amendment by 33 to 20, and another amendment was added to provide for absentee ballots for primary elections as well. Senator Tom Connolly of Texas and Lister Hill of Alabama charged that the Senate had voted to "rupture constitutional processes" by invading the rights of the states. Walter George threatened to filibuster. But no one was willing to take the lead in denying soldiers easy access to the ballot. There was no filibuster. The final bill, with wartime suspension of the poll tax for soldiers, was signed by the president in mid-September.[21]

Passed only six weeks before the general election, the bill did not spur widespread voter participation among those serving in the armed forces. But for proponents and opponents of the legislation, that was a secondary matter. Both sides saw it as the first step toward complete repeal of the poll tax in federal elections. In addition, the racial implications of the bill, which theoretically provided free and equal access to the ballot for the roughly four hundred thousand black men and women from southern states serving in the armed forces, were widely addressed. Edgar G. Brown of the National Negro Council hailed the adoption of the Brooks-Pepper amendment as "comparable to the thirteenth, fourteenth and fifteenth amendments to the

Constitution so far as equal rights and franchisement regardless of race, creed and color is concerned." John Rankin warned that the bill was "part of a long-range communistic program to . . . take the control of our elections out of the hands of white Americans." Commenting on the impact of the bill in Birmingham, Virginia Durr's father wrote and warned, "All white people in Alabama are buying pistols and other ammunition in preparation for the race war that is coming."[22]

Less than a month after the enactment of the Soldiers Vote Bill, a discharge petition forced the release of the Geyer-Pepper bill from the House Judiciary Committee, where it had been bottled up by the committee's chairman, Hatton Sumners of Texas, for nearly three years. Palmer Weber played a key role in getting the bill to the floor of Congress for a vote. Weber persuaded George Bender, congressman from Ohio, who served on the Tolan Committee, to take the lead in support of the bill. Bender was horrified to realize that more people voted in his congressional district than in the whole state of Mississippi. Weber and Bender lobbied members of Congress for the 218 signatures needed to get the poll-tax bill discharged from the House Judiciary Committee. According to Weber, Tom Corcoran, former White House staffer, predicted that they would never be able to get the bill discharged. "It hasn't happened in fifty years," he said. Weber asked Corcoran if he would give the NCAPT one thousand dollars if they succeeded. Corcoran agreed, and Weber happily collected the sum when the Geyer-Pepper bill made it to the floor of the House in the summer of 1942.[23]

The Geyer-Pepper bill initiated the first full-scale congressional debate over federal protection of voting rights in the southern states since the defeat of the Lodge elections bill in 1890. Southern members of Congress led the opposition, based on the constitutionally guaranteed rights of the states to establish voter qualifications. The issue, they warned, was not the poll tax but the creeping power of the federal government, which threatened to undermine the sovereignty of the states. William Colmer of Mississippi predicted: "The direct object of this movement is to enfranchise the Negro in the South. If Congress can remove the poll tax requirements it can also remove educational requirements and registration itself."[24]

A handful of southern members of Congress vigorously supported the bill. Luther Patrick charged that "the reactionary political and economic interests" wanted "to keep the South in a semifeudal condition" and were using the race issue as an excuse. The poll tax leveled a "hardship . . . on good white people." Its abolition would not interfere with the South's ability "to handle any race proposition that may arise." Estes Kefauver of Tennessee favored repeal of the poll tax as a way to defeat the corrupt political machine of Boss Ed Crump of Memphis. Race and the northern black vote, however, played an important part in lining urban Democrats solidly up behind the bill. When it came to a vote on 13 October in the House, 254 representatives prevailed over 84 who voted against repeal, giving the anti-poll-tax forces a stunning victory.[25]

As Claude Pepper predicted, Senate opponents of the Soldiers Vote Bill "saved their powder" for the Geyer-Pepper bill. The Geyer-Pepper bill went beyond the House version and directly addressed the issue of the poll tax as a voter qualification, holding that it was not a reasonable qualification and therefore improperly interfered with federal elections. Senate opponents of the legislation dug in their heels with an eight-day filibuster, ensuring that the bill would never come to a vote. During those eight days proponents of the measure focused national attention on voting procedures in the South, explored the meaning of national citizenship, and indirectly endorsed the wartime "Double V" campaign being waged among black Americans for democracy at home and abroad. For southern opponents of the bill, the filibuster provided a platform for their ongoing campaign against the excesses of the New Deal, which they linked to extremist groups such as the CIO, the NAACP, and the Communist Party.

George Norris (Nebraska) and Senate Majority Leader Alben Barkley (Kentucky) joined Pepper in presenting a carefully reasoned defense of the bill. Central to their argument was that the ability to pay a poll tax was not a reasonable qualification for voting. It was arbitrary and class-based, excluding people simply because they were poor. Thus, whereas the states clearly maintained the constitutionally guaranteed right to establish voter qualifications, they did not have the authority to disqualify a voter otherwise qualified to vote. It was within the jurisdiction of the federal government to protect this fundamental right of citizenship, the right to vote, from such infringement by the state. Pepper explained that a recent Supreme Court ruling, in the *Edwards* case, spoke directly to the principle involved. In that case the Court had overturned a California statute that held that no indigent person could be brought into the state. The Court ruled that citizenship was national and that a state could not bar entry to a citizen of the United States simply because he or she was indigent.

That the poll-tax statutes aimed to discriminate, Norris explained, was evident in the proceedings of the constitutional conventions that had enacted them at the turn of the century. He used Virginia as an example. At the beginning of Virginia's constitutional convention in 1901, Carter Glass announced: "The chief purpose of this convention is to amend the suffrage law. . . . We were sent here to make distinctions. We expect to make distinctions. We will make distinctions." Glass betrayed the racial motivations of the convention when, after a poll-tax and other suffrage requirements had been adopted, he proclaimed to great applause, "No body of Virginia gentlemen could frame a constitution so obnoxious to my sense of right and morality to submit its fate to 146,000 ignorant Negro voters whose capacity for self-government we have been challenging for thirty years." But the poll-tax requirement satisfied the requirements of the Fifteenth Amendment, by not being race-specific and by excluding *all* people who were poor and unable to pay. Norris, however, maintained that it was in clear violation of the terms under which Virginia and other southern states had been readmitted to the Union. The congressional act that had readmitted Virginia to the union in 1870 stated, "The Constitution of Virginia shall never be so amended or changed as to deprive any citizen or class of citizens of the United States of the right to vote, who are entitled to vote by the constitution herein recognized."

Supporters of the bill maintained that the issue of voting rights was not the exclusive purview of the federal courts. Although the Supreme Court had upheld the poll tax as a voting requirement in the *Breedlove* case, it had not ruled on the right of Congress to legislate the repeal of the poll tax in federal elections. Now that issue was before Congress. In response to critics who charged that the poll-tax bill was divisive and deterred from the war effort, Pepper and Barkley reminded Congress what the war was about. "Has not the surge of the wave of democracy touched our own shores?," asked Pepper. In a firm endorsement of the "Double V" effort, Barkley asserted, "I know of no more opportune time to try to spread democracy in our country than at a time when we are trying to spread it in other countries and throughout the world." It was not a racial issue, or a geographical issue, but one that involved "the very basis of democracy and freedom," government by the consent of the governed.

Opponents, ignoring the primary arguments put forward by supporters of the bill, started from the premise that voting was a privilege and not a right. As one of Senator John H. Bankhead's constituents stated, "I do not believe in that theory . . . that every Tom, Dick and Harry should vote." The opposition crafted a narrow and closely argued interpretation of constitutional rights and spiced it with suspicions about the motives of supporters of the bill. Lister Hill emphasized the central theme of the opposition when he warned that the poll-tax bill struck "at the very foundation of our dual system of government." The right of the states to fix voting qualifications was the core issue involved, and this was the "last existing cornerstone of states rights and local self-government." Hill predicted, "Once we start abolishing the poll tax we must admit that the federal government and the Congress have the power to get into the whole field of qualifications."

The "floodgate" theory was developed further by Senator Theodore Bilbo of Mississippi. "If they can have this bill," he warned, the Supreme Court would uphold it even though it was "unconstitutional." He added, "Then the flood gates will be open." Bilbo reminded his colleagues of the Soldiers Vote Bill and how it quickly evolved beyond the initial intentions of the bill as senators tacked on various amendments. The Mississippi senator supported state repeal of the poll tax; what mattered was the final result once the federal government began tinkering with voting procedures. "The next step will be an effort to remove registration qualifications, the educational qualification of negroes. If that is done we will have no way of preventing Negroes from voting."[26]

The anti–New Deal ideology that had come to dominate the politics of southern conservatives informed the tone of much of the discussion. "A few smart, keen manipulators and dreamers" in Washington were trying to take advantage of the war situation to take hold of the entire government and do away with the Constitution. Tom Connolly of Texas suggested that this bill set the ideals of the Founding Fathers against the likes of the Communist Earl Browder, who had announced to the world that he was "the real leader of this campaign for federal control of elections," and "the masses who assail[ed] the Senators on their way to their offices or from the galleries." Bilbo charged that it was "the Negroes, the C.I.O, the American Federation of Labor, the Railroad Brotherhoods, the Communist Party and Mr. Browder" who were not satisfied with the constitutional method and were willing to subvert it. In an affront to Senator Norris, Bilbo asked how a man from a state with only twelve thousand blacks out of a population of over two million could dare "to come here and tell the southern states [with] three-fourths of all the Negroes in the United States within their borders, how they should treat, control, handle and solve the race problem, governmentally, economically and socially." Senator Norris commented on the "very ungentlemanly and discourteous and offensive treatment on the part of some Senators" who so impugned the motives of the bill sponsors and who referred to the bill "almost disrespectfully."[27]

Southerners in Congress scored another victory in their effort to contain the changes stirred by the New Deal when cloture was voted down, tabling the Geyer-Pepper bill of 1942. Roosevelt's refusal to comment on the legislation and its temporary defeat was a measure of the political climate in wartime Washington. But the groundwork had been laid for expanding the

legislative battle, and the war provided supporters with a powerful rationale ✓
for protecting the right to vote.

While the poll-tax campaign moved haltingly forward, the contest between southern conservatives and southern New Dealers was being waged ✓
in other arenas. Clark Foreman and C. B. Baldwin continued to act on the
progressive impulses of the New Deal, ensuring a head-on confrontation
with southerners in Congress. Their fate reflected the shifting alliances in
wartime Washington and underscored the essential importance of electoral
reform in the South if New Deal reforms were to be secured.

Clark Foreman remained at the center of innovative and controversial
New Deal policy. After a year as "Special Adviser on the Economic Status of
Negroes," Foreman served as special adviser to Harold Ickes and in 1935 became director of the newly established Division of Public Power of the Public Works Administration (PWA). The agency was Foreman's idea. It aimed to
accelerate the processing of grants and loans to municipalities so that they
could expand public access to the cheap electricity available through the
Tennessee Valley Authority (TVA) and other government-built dams around
the country. Up until then, private utility companies had succeeded in stall-
ing the application procedure in the courts, warning against the socialization
of the power industry. When Foreman began approving backlogged applications, Duke Power Company and Alabama Power obtained federal injunctions to halt PWA-approved projects and joined with other major power
companies to challenge the constitutionality of the PWA. After three years of
litigation, Foreman and his general counsel, Jerome Frank, prevailed when
the Supreme Court unanimously ruled that the private power companies
had no legal standing to question the validity of PWA loans and grants to
municipalities even if there was a resulting destruction of private enterprise
from the construction of municipally owned plants. The injunctions that
had held up sixty-one public power projects in twenty-three states were
removed, and the projects went forward. Although the private utilities lost
their battle to halt the New Deal drive to expand power distribution, they
proved to be among the major beneficiaries of the dramatic increase in
consumption spurred by federal policies.[28]

In 1940, Foreman became director of the newly established Division of
Defense Housing, which was part of the Federal Works Administration
(FWA). The FWA, under the Lanham Act, was charged with developing and
managing housing for individuals engaged in national defense. Foreman
assisted and advised John Carmody, administrator of the FWA, in the construction of more than thirty-seven thousand units. Late in 1941 a contro-

versy arose over the planned Sojourner Truth housing project for black defense workers in Detroit, leading to Foreman's departure from the Roosevelt administration.

The Sojourner Truth housing project heightened an already tense racial situation in wartime Detroit. Severely constricted by residential segregation, overcrowded black neighborhoods could not accommodate the influx of black defense workers. As Foreman pointed out in congressional testimony, the site for additional black housing would inevitably be an area where blacks did not already live. Sojourner Truth was located near a predominantly Polish neighborhood that had a few black residents. A middle-class black community, Conant Gardens, was located four blocks away. Black homeowners, fearful that temporary housing would jeopardize their investments, initially protested, along with whites, against the site. They dropped their protest when they learned that the units would be permanent and when they also realized that the issue had become racial. White realty interests and the neighborhood improvement agency organized local protests and sent several delegations to Washington, demanding that the project be redesignated for white occupancy. When Foreman refused to accommodate the petitioners, their congressman, Rudolph Tenerowicz, appealed directly to the House Committee on Public Buildings and Grounds, which appropriated funds to federal housing authorities. On 15 January 1942, housing officials did an about-face and announced that Sojourner Truth would be for white occupancy. That same day the acting administrator of the FWA requested Foreman's resignation. Several months later, blacks in Detroit, in alliance with the United Automobile Workers, succeeded in reversing the decision, and black defense workers finally moved into the completed project.[29]

The Sojourner Truth housing controversy provided Foreman's opponents with the opportunity rather than the motive to secure his resignation. Frank Boykin of Alabama, ranking Democrat on the Committee on Public Buildings and Grounds, led the fight against Foreman. The roots of Boykin's hostility toward Foreman went back to the days when Foreman had served as head of the PWA's Power Division and had defeated Alabama Power's challenge to the public power program. Alabama Power was one of Boykins's major supporters. According to Foreman, there was a personal grudge as well. Boykin had asked Foreman to appoint his brother as project manager for a housing project near Mobile. A report on the man's background revealed that he would not have made "a reliable night watchman, much less a project manager," Foreman recalled. Foreman refused to make the appointment. The Sojourner Truth controversy provided Boykin with an opportunity to settle past scores. In alliance with Congressman Tenerowicz, he effectively appealed to the racial animus of southern members of the committee. The committee demanded Foreman's resignation before it would appropriate any additional funds to the Division of Defense Housing.[30]

Foreman's ouster came a month after the attack on Pearl Harbor. The war, Foreman noted, strengthened the position of Boykin and other southern conservatives, whose support was essential to defense mobilization. " 'Dr. New Deal' . . . had been supplanted by 'Dr. Win the War' and nothing was to get in [the president's] way."[31] Civil rights leaders and New Deal supporters were concerned about Foreman's treatment and wondered about its larger significance. Speaking for several other black leaders, Walter White, head of the NAACP, Mary McLeod Bethune of the National Youth Administration (NYA), and Channing Tobias, head of the Colored Young Men's Christian Association (YMCA), reminded the president of Foreman's commitment to evenhanded racial justice, which was "notable in any person" but was "particularly effective because of his Southern background." Despite strong pressure, Foreman stood firm in his position that black citizens were equally entitled "to enjoy the benefits of housing made possible by the taxing of all people." Consequently he lost his position, but that was not all. The controversy over the Sojourner Truth Project unleashed "an organized and determined campaign to drive him from government because of the stand which he took on behalf of the Negro." White, Bethune, and Tobias urged Roosevelt to investigate the situation and do whatever was necessary "to prevent the crucifixion of a man because he had the courage to practice as well as talk about democracy."[32]

Senator George Norris confided in the president that he and "a great many of our best friends" were very disturbed about Foreman's dismissal. He bemoaned the fact that "such trustworthy and competent officials" were being cast aside and usually replaced by "reactionary persons" who were not "friends of yours or of the progressive cause." Lucy Randolph Mason expressed similar concerns in a letter to Eleanor Roosevelt: "Honest, earnest and capable Democrats . . . are now being penalized because the reactionary Democrats do not like them." She was hopeful that something could be done to keep Foreman in public service. "Clark is a grand, courageous, honest man and we need him." Mason advised Roosevelt that Foreman would have the backing of labor groups, and she wrote CIO President Phil Murray to ensure CIO support.[33]

Eleanor Roosevelt passed Lucy Randolph Mason's letters on to the president and began lobbying from within the administration to find Foreman a position. Foreman was recommended by Senator William Smathers of New

Jersey and others for the executive position on the War Manpower Board. Eleanor Roosevelt sent a memo to the president requesting that he ask Paul McNutt to appoint Foreman to the War Manpower Board. She added that if this was not possible, some other place should be found for him. Roosevelt explored the possible opportunities for Foreman with Frances Perkins. However, no firm offers were forthcoming. In the meantime, Foreman accepted a position in the Navy Department as a specialist in operational research. He wrote Eleanor Roosevelt that his technical qualifications rather than his political beliefs had won him the appointment and that he was "delighted to be once more actively in the fight." Foreman's job with the navy took him to London for eight months, and in 1943 he accepted an assistant professorship at Black Mountain College in North Carolina.[34]

Foreman's ouster in 1941 coincided with the beginning of a prolonged congressional assault on the Farm Security Administration (FSA) and its director, C. B. "Beanie" Baldwin. The effort lasted for two years and has been described as "one of the most bitter domestic issues during World War II."[35] In the end, the FSA was stripped down to a shell, and Baldwin was forced to resign. The short history of the FSA and of Baldwin's role in shaping the agency, along with the powerful opposition both attracted, illustrates the changing constellation of economic and political relationships in Washington and in the South.

From the time they accompanied Henry Wallace on his 1936 tour of the Mississippi Delta, Will Alexander and Beanie Baldwin were responsible for planning and implementing the New Deal rural poverty programs, first through the Resettlement Administration and then through its successor organization, the FSA, established in 1937. Baldwin served as Alexander's deputy administrator and succeeded him as FSA director in 1940. Like Clark Foreman, Beanie Baldwin was a young protégé of Alexander's who moved beyond the more temperate style of the seasoned reformer in ways that enhanced the partnership. Alexander said Baldwin was nearly indispensable. Baldwin oversaw the financial and personnel management of the FSA and negotiated political difficulties, causing Alexander to marvel at the ease with which Baldwin "acquired an understanding of the mechanical processes of government." But his quick mind and keen political instincts were tempered by a personal integrity that Alexander found remarkable. Alexander recalled that Baldwin had said that he had to watch himself to "keep from doing unfair things to people—taking advantage of them . . . getting them to commit themselves to things when they don't see what it's all about, how it's going to work out."[36]

Baldwin had traveled far beyond his days as a hardware store proprietor in Radford, Virginia. Growing up in the foothills of the Blue Ridge Mountains, he inherited the political sensibilities of his father, a reform-minded flour miller who detested the machine politics that ran Virginia. But his horizons were limited. He left Virginia Polytechnic Institute before earning a degree, married, went to work for the railroad, and then established a small hardware business. In 1926 the Iowa-born newspaper publisher Paul Appleby bought Radford's two newspapers and opened a print shop next to Baldwin's store. The two became inseparable friends, with Appleby serving as a mentor of sorts. Alexander commented on the relationship between the two men: "Beanie began to realize what he had missed intellectually and Paul began to furnish a great deal of that for him." Called to Washington by his friend Henry Wallace, Appleby urged Baldwin to join him as an administrative assistant to the secretary of agriculture. Baldwin went, reluctantly. He felt out of place among the Ph.D.'s and Ivy League lawyers assembled in the secretary's office by Assistant Secretary Rex Tugwell. John Abt later confided that he and the other young lawyers in the office were all "very suspicious" of this "southern boy." Secretary Wallace commented approvingly, "We've been looking for someone with a southern accent in this office." Baldwin thrived and became a key operative for the members of the reformist group in the Agriculture Department. He wanted to quit when they were purged in 1935. But Tugwell, noting that the fight had just begun, persuaded Baldwin to stay.[37]

The FSA applied the social vision and creative energy of the New Deal to the problems of rural poverty, aiming to tackle them at their source. FSA administrators were sensitive to the interconnections of rural poverty, social isolation, racial discrimination, ignorance, and the political impotence of the masses of southern people. Through a variety of programs, the FSA aided more than eight hundred thousand families, 20 percent of whom were black, and pursued a liberal interpretation of its congressional mandate. In addition to providing loans and grants, the FSA promoted economic and social interaction among its client families through cooperative associations, collective farming techniques, and neighborhood action groups; it cooperated with the Southern Tenant Farmers Union (STFU), the CIO, and other progressive groups toward this end. Blacks and union members served on local FSA committees. The tenant improvement program tried to institute written tenure agreements and educate tenants regarding their rights, especially in the South, where oral agreements were common. Ever mindful of the fact that the agency's constituency, though large, was generally unorganized and politically inarticulate, FSA workers hoped to change that. One official remarked: "If out of our work there does not . . . arise a leadership which can take over and carry on where our 'management' leaves off, our new white houses are destined to become tombstones for a great idea."[38]

Migrant farm workers, whose ranks had swollen in the 1930s, were also beneficiaries of FSA programs. "These were really the poorest people in the country," noted Baldwin, "subject to all the hazards of the worst part of our system." The FSA attempted to improve the living conditions of migrant families by establishing camps with sanitary and recreational facilities and a special medical program. By the early 1940s there were ninety-five FSA camps accommodating seventy-five thousand people. While focusing on the immediate needs of adequate shelter, FSA leaders looked forward to helping these families secure "greater permanent economic and social security and stronger bargaining power." The author John Steinbeck became particularly interested in the FSA's migrant worker program. With the idea of writing a book on migrant workers, Steinbeck contacted the FSA and expressed his desire "to live this thing for a while." Baldwin offered full cooperation on the part of the FSA. Arrangements were made for Steinbeck to meet with Tom Collins, a migrant worker from northern Virginia who had finally ended up in the pea fields of California. Collins had been selected by the FSA to manage one of their camps. Steinbeck worked full-time in the fields, alongside Collins, and was paid a salary. Collins was later hired to serve as technical director for the film version of Steinbeck's book *The Grapes of Wrath*.[39]

Steinbeck's dramatic portrayal of the plight of the migrant worker in *The Grapes of Wrath* proved to be helpful politically for the FSA. Senator John Bankhead of Alabama, though a friend to the FSA, had been an opponent of the migrant worker program. After viewing the movie, he expressed his amazement to Baldwin that people actually lived in such desperate conditions. He promised support for the migrant program in the future. Senator Richard Russell of Georgia had supported the FSA's more traditional programs, such as rural rehabilitation, which lent money to farmers with the understanding that it would be paid back, but he was against many of the other projects the FSA undertook, including the migrant worker program. During hearings he questioned Baldwin about *The Grapes of Wrath* and admitted, "It certainly made a deep impression on me." It was ironic that a Hollywood production served to introduce these senators to the harshest realities of rural poverty.[40]

The American Farm Bureau Federation (AFBF) and other representatives of large agricultural interests tolerated the FSA as a temporary relief measure during the late 1930s, though they were critical of FSA programs. However, personnel changes, along with wartime mobilization, converged to transform tolerance into a frontal attack on the agency and on what it had come to represent. In 1940 Henry Wallace left the Agriculture Department to serve as vice-president, and that same year Beanie Baldwin succeeded Will Alexander as director of the FSA, making the FSA a more inviting target. The AFBF considered Baldwin to be a militant, much like his former boss "Rex the Red" Tugwell, and it was outraged by his promotion to the directorship. The shifting balance of political power brought by the war increased the agency's vulnerability. The ensuing, prolonged struggle between conservatives and weakened supporters of the FSA contested the intent and consequences of New Deal reform for the South and its citizens.[41]

Malcolm C. Tarver, Democrat from Georgia, opened the campaign to dismantle the FSA in the spring of 1940 when he introduced several budget amendments that would restrict FSA operations and eliminate certain programs. Tarver was a veteran of seven terms in Congress and a longtime member of the Agricultural Subcommittee of the Appropriations Committee. He had been ambivalent about many of the rural rehabilitation projects of the FSA and charged that the cooperative farming associations were "very suspiciously related" to "sovietism." Tarver saw the migratory farm labor program as part of a plot to steal southern labor for large-scale farm operations in the West. The political bond that seemed to be growing between the FSA and labor and liberal groups in the North also made the agency suspect. In 1940 Tarver proposed an amendment to restrict the tenant purchase program; the amendment passed. Moreover, he provided a platform in Congress for the powerful AFBF, which had launched a full-scale investigation of the FSA in the hope of proving that the agency's programs were wasteful and unnecessary and politically subversive.[42]

As chairman of the Joint Committee for the Reduction of Non-Essential Federal Expenditures, Senator Harry Byrd was positioned to vent his longtime hostility to the New Deal. The committee presided over the dismantling of the Civilian Conservation Corps (CCC), the NYA, the WPA, the National Resource Planning Board, and the FSA. During the two-year legislative battle surrounding the FSA, regional organizations of large agricultural interests joined the AFBF in challenging the FSA's enforcement of wage, housing, and work standards for farm labor. Oscar Johnston, the Mississippi planter who had directed the Cotton Section of the Agricultural Adjustment Administration (AAA), testified for the National Cotton Council. He charged, "[The FSA] threatens the foundations of American agriculture and, through their contention for a minimum wage per hour for cotton picking, threatens to disrupt a fair and satisfactory system that has successfully operated in the Cotton Belt for over one hundred years."[43]

The debate over voting rights and privileges punctuated the hearings when Edward O'Neal, president of the AFBF, testified that the FSA was paying poll taxes for its clients in the southern states. Baldwin explained that his agency was not paying poll taxes directly but rather would allocate funds for the payment of poll taxes, if so requested, as a part of the overall loan to rehabilitate distressed farm families. Baldwin believed this was justified and contributed to the overall goal of the rehabilitation program. "We took the position that a person couldn't be a good citizen without being a voter and we couldn't do anything about the poll tax, so I told our people in the South to include the money in their loans, if these poor people could be registered so they could register and vote." Carter Glass, senator from Virginia, challenged Baldwin, saying that he doubted the right to vote had anything to do with rehabilitation. "I hope you bring before us all your rehabilitated Negroes from Alabama so I can have a look at them." The *New Republic* sarcastically reported, "The Byrd committee's all star cast of Senators from poll tax states were horrified by such a brazen belief in Constitutional guarantees." President Roosevelt publicly defended the FSA policy of including funds for the payment of poll taxes in household budgets and used the occasion to reiterate his strong opposition to the poll tax.[44]

During the hearings, it became clear that Baldwin himself was under attack. Baldwin recalled, "I had become a storm center of my own." At the start of a full Senate debate over appropriations for the FSA, Senator Kenneth D. McKellar, Democrat from Tennessee, questioned Baldwin's loyalty. McKellar said that he thought Baldwin was a Communist and was "not really in favor of our American institutions." He charged, "The teaching of Mr. Baldwin in regard to it being the duty of the Government to give away its money to people who will not work for it is fallacious and indefensible." Furthermore, he contended, Baldwin was a thoroughly incompetent administrator and probably the most extravagant one in government.[45]

Several southern senators challenged such blanket charges. In an eloquent defense of Baldwin, Senator John Bankhead of Alabama stated, "I have at all times found him to be a gentleman, a Virginia gentleman, and if any criticism could be made of him it is because of his generosity, possibly his tender heart toward relieving the sufferings of the poor farmers." Senator Richard Russell of Georgia noted that he and Baldwin had had some violent differences over the administration of the FSA, yet the charge that Baldwin was a Communist was ridiculous. Russell praised Baldwin as "an honest, sincere and patriotic American" whose "sole aim" was "to administer the program in the interest of the most underprivileged people on earth." Lister Hill, senator from Alabama, lauded Baldwin's efforts, saying: "If he has erred, his errors have been due, in my opinion, more to his zeal, and to his devotion to human welfare, human rights and human progress, than to any other things. . . . Mr. Baldwin has vision. He has the ability to project his mind and look down the corridors of time. If there is any one thing that America needs and has needed it is men of vision as her leaders in . . . Government. Mr. Baldwin is this type of public servant."[46]

Despite this personal vote of confidence from key southern legislators, Baldwin and the FSA continued to lose ground. Will Alexander recalled: "Senator Byrd and a lot of the meanest people in the place just had him [Baldwin] hand and foot. He couldn't move and the President knew it. So he let the axe fall." In the summer of 1942, Congress passed a compromise bill that reduced the budget for the FSA 43 percent below the president's request. The following spring a bill passed that transferred most of the FSA's responsibilities to the Extension Service, an arm of the AFBF, and virtually crippled the agency. Eleanor Roosevelt telegrammed her husband, urging him not to sign the bill. The president, however, followed through on his promise to congressional leaders to sign the conference report bill. Baldwin would have remained with the remnants of the FSA in the hopes of salvaging it, but the administration requested his resignation and offered him a position with the State Department, directing rural rehabilitation in postwar Italy. Instead Baldwin joined Sidney Hillman's newly established CIO Political Action Committee (CIO-PAC) as executive administrator.[47]

In December 1943 Palmer Weber resigned as staff director of Claude Pepper's Senate Subcommittee on Health and Education and followed Baldwin to the CIO-PAC. Weber had worked closely with Beanie Baldwin and the FSA on the issue of migrant labor and had organized hearings around the country in support of FSA programs during Baldwin's two-year struggle with the Byrd Committee. When the FSA was dismantled and a second soldiers vote bill was defeated late in 1943, Weber realized that the New Deal had come to a complete halt on Capitol Hill, largely due to southern obstructionists. The CIO-PAC shifted the focus of the battle for the New Deal to electoral politics, and Weber signed up, "determined to beat every Senator" he could "possibly beat who was reactionary."[48]

For Weber the defeat of a second soldiers vote bill was the last straw. During 1943, federal regulation of voting procedures for the armed forces supplanted the Geyer-Pepper anti-poll-tax bill as the primary battleground in the Senate during this session of Congress. The Green-Lucas bill, which Weber had helped to draft, aimed to further streamline voting procedures so that the eleven million members of the armed forces could effectively participate in the 1944 presidential election. The bill sponsors contended that since the federal government took men and women from their usual place of residence for war service, it was the federal government's responsibility to ensure that they should not lose their vote. The administration of forty-eight different types of ballots had obstructed the good intentions of the Soldiers Vote Act of 1942; a bare twenty-eight thousand had cast a vote in the 1942 elections. Under Green-Lucas, a bipartisan Federal War Ballots Commission would distribute federal ballots for use by members in the armed services; the ballots would be returned to the commission and forwarded to appropriate state election officials. Voter qualifications would be the same as those established by the respective voting districts, with one exception. Poll-tax payment would not be required for voting in federal elections.[49]

Southern senators met the Green-Lucas bill with a solid front of opposition, with the sole exception of Claude Pepper. Senator James Eastland, newly elected from Mississippi, along with Kenneth McKellar of Tennessee and John McClellan of Arkansas, offered a substitute bill recommending that the states pass legislation to facilitate the participation of members of the armed services in the 1944 elections. This token gesture would, at best, compound the problems of the 1942 Soldiers Vote Act. The debate that ensued was the most acrimonious to date. Senator Eastland spoke for the southern opponents when he accused Green-Lucas supporters of seeking a license to repeat the machinations of Reconstruction. The issue was not soldiers voting, he warned, but whether Congress should "turn the election machinery of the country over to an aggregation of power-crazed bureaucrats in Washington." The Eastland bill won the support of Republicans, who understood that a large soldiers' vote could easily provide Roosevelt a margin of victory in 1944. The passage of the Eastland bill by a vote of 42 to 37 ensured that Green-Lucas would not come to a vote.[50]

The passage of the Eastland bill fueled sectional rancor. CIO-PAC Chairman Sidney Hillman called it "brutal and cynical" and vowed that labor would make it an issue in the 1944 campaign. Roosevelt continued to support passage of the Green-Lucas bill, insisting that federal machinery was essential to ensure access to the ballot for members of the armed services. Senator Joseph Guffey of Pennsylvania, chairman of the Senate Democratic Campaign Committee, was more direct. In a statement to the press, he charged that northern Republicans and southern Democrats, under Harry Byrd's leadership, had conspired to deprive men and women in the armed forces of their vote. He called the maneuver the "most unpatriotic and unholy alliance" that had occurred in the U.S. Senate "since the League of Nations for peace in the world was defeated in 1919." Josiah Bailey of North Carolina responded to Guffey's accusation with an impassioned statement of southern solidarity and a stern rebuke of Guffey's scornful attack. "There can be an end of insults, . . . of toleration, . . . of patience," Bailey warned from the floor of the Senate. "We can form a southern Democratic party and vote as we please in the electoral college, and we will hold the balance of power in this country."[51]

Eastland greeted the passage of his bill as ending any chance for the enactment of anti-poll-tax legislation; southern Democrats had enough votes to defeat cloture. Palmer Weber agreed. Southern Democrats had demonstrated their ability to kill any program and defeat any bill that remotely challenged the political status quo in the South. The anti–New Deal coalition of Republicans and southern Democrats was locked in place. "It made me hellishly mad," Weber recalled. "At that very moment the CIO-PAC was getting under way. So I wrote a letter for Senator Pepper which he signed saying Mr. Weber will carry your bags for you anywhere, do anything, anytime, day or night. Give him a job." Weber moved to New York in December 1943 and joined the staff of the CIO-PAC as chief researcher and strategist on the South.[52]

The CIO-PAC, the brainchild of Sidney Hillman, aimed to turn back the tide of conservative reaction that threatened to sweep away what was left of the New Deal and defuse the hard-won gains of labor groups. A spate of antilabor legislation, culminating with the Smith-Connally Act of 1943, exposed the political weakness of the labor movement and the tentative nature of its achievements. The sharp increase in Republican victories at the polls in 1940 and 1942 challenged the viability and strength of the New Deal coalition and of its core element, the labor movement. At the same time, CIO membership had grown in quantum leaps during the war. The challenge, as Hillman viewed it, was to expand the terrain of traditional trade union political activity. The CIO-PAC sought to build party realignment from the ground up by organizing labor and the diverse constituency of New Deal liberalism into an articulate political movement capable of countering the powerful bipartisan coalition in Congress at the ballot box.

During the latter years of the war, the CIO-PAC reinforced efforts to democratize southern politics. Organizers navigated the fragile terrain of biracial politics and tapped into vibrant networks of labor and civil rights activists at a time when their ranks were rapidly growing. Union membership in the South multiplied during the war, NAACP branches proliferated throughout the region, and the struggle for voting rights heightened. Racial tensions and violence, however, accelerated in tandem and stoked the reactionary politics of racial and sectional chauvinism.

The war sharpened the process of political realignment initiated by Roosevelt and the New Deal. Supplementing steady Republican gains in 1938, 1940, and 1942, southern Democrats secured the balance of power in Congress and used their position to reassert the ideology of states rights' and white supremacy. At the same time, the "Four Freedoms" rhetoric of World War II not only heightened democratic aspirations and movements that had been manifested around the South during the 1930s but also drew national attention to the segregation system and its consequences. With the organization of the CIO-PAC, labor and New Deal activists sought to establish a political movement that could halt the conservative resurgence in national politics. Its success would depend on what happened in the South. And what happened in the South would depend, to a large extent, on how effective the national leadership and constituencies of the New Deal were in supporting the expansion of political participation in the southern states.

During this year we are going to concentrate much of our effort on securing the right to vote in primaries as well as the general elections throughout the South . . . a tremendous task which will not be completed but must be tackled.

THURGOOD MARSHALL to Arthur Shores, 15 March 1940

The work [of the Southern Conference for Human Welfare] is really as important as the war . . . because making the South a real part of the United States, and progressive in its racial and labor attitudes, is the finest work any one could do at the present time.

ELEANOR ROOSEVELT to James Dombrowski, 29 April 1942

5

War, Race, and Democracy

THE SOUTH IN TRANSITION

World War II hastened the integration of the South into the nation's economic and political life. Southern governors and development agencies lobbied hard for their share of federal dollars for defense-related activities, dollars that primed the pump of southern industrial development. The explosion of job opportunities in defense-related industries, North and South, and inductions into the armed services absorbed the surplus labor bottled up in southern agriculture. Wartime labor mobility advanced the nationalization of the southern labor market and drove the mechanization of southern agriculture.[1]

The demographic, economic, and political contingencies of the war made race and civil rights issues of national consequence. The war advanced the transformation of black culture and consciousness generated by the northward migration of the previous two decades. As Henry Louis Gates Jr. has written, World War II "did more to recement black American culture, which migration had fragmented, than did any single event or experience." For the nearly one million African Americans serving in the armed forces, the army became "a great cauldron, mixing the New Negro culture, which had developed since the great migration of the twenties and thirties, and the Old Negro culture, the remnants of traditional rural black culture in the South." At the same time, the massive movement of black southerners to centers of defense production in the North during the 1940s marked the largest internal migration in American history.[2]

The wartime emergence of civil rights as a national issue reinforced the development of a loosely organized effort among black southerners to challenge the racial barriers to citizenship. While the poll-tax bill stalled on Capitol Hill and southern senators gutted the Soldiers Vote Bill, the NAACP scored steady gains in the courts. The successful culmination of the two-decade legal challenge to the all-white primary in 1944 marked the first major victory in the effort to expand voting rights in the South. During the war years, the ranks of NAACP membership in the South swelled and supported a growing movement to expand political participation throughout the region. As anti-poll-tax activist Virginia Durr remarked, blacks had become the primary force in the New Deal–inspired movement to democratize southern politics.

As organized voter-registration efforts among blacks grew, arenas of interracial contact multiplied, from army barracks and centers of defense production to the ballot box. The full democracy promoted by the Southern Conference for Human Welfare (SCHW), the Southern Negro Youth Congress (SNYC), and by unions of the Congress of Industrial Organizations (CIO) competed with growing racial tensions and widespread appeals to white racial fears. Predictably, southern conservatives stirred the potent brew of racial pride and regional defensiveness never far from the surface of southern politics. More notable was the response of a large segment of white southern moderates and old-line interracialists; they met the heightened black consciousness and racial polarization of the war years by defending southern autonomy and the segregation system.

World War II magnified the nation's continuing accommodation of racial discrimination. "The Army," civil rights attorney and activist Charles

Houston observed, "insists on fastening the pattern of Mississippi and South Carolina on the entire country." Blacks were segregated in the army, restricted to servile posts in the navy, and barred from the marines. A group of black World War I veterans established the Committee on the Participation of Negroes in National Defense Programs in 1939 and lobbied for the desegregation of the armed forces. During hearings on a military appropriations bill, Houston recounted his bitter experiences during World War I and warned that black people would no longer tolerate the menial and degrading role to which they had historically been consigned. He advised the senators, "The morale of Negro citizens regarding national defense is probably at the lowest ebb in the history of the country." Houston reminded them that the problem was not merely one of wartime emergency. The government could no longer "expect Negroes to be valiant defenders in time of war when it ignore[d] them and insult[ed] them in time of peace."[3]

The infusion of new jobs and training to support the defense buildup exposed racial occupational patterns that resulted in wasted manpower, production delays, and millions of dollars in unnecessary expense. Robert Weaver, who worked in the Labor Division of the National Defense Advisory Commission, reported case after case of industries that recruited white workers from hundreds of miles away rather than employ black workers from the local population, aggravating problems of housing shortages and overcrowding. During the late 1930s white unemployment figures plummeted and black unemployment increased. As Weaver's classic study, *Negro Labor: A National Problem*, demonstrated, job discrimination knew no regional boundary. But it was most rampant in the segregated South. Weaver reported that Tennessee had collected $230,000 from the U.S. Office of Education to train workers for defense-related jobs through the spring of 1941; of this, $2,000 was used in defense courses for black workers. John Beecher, a government investigator, reported in March 1942 that among the thousands of workers who participated in federally funded training classes to prepare for defense-related jobs in Alabama, a mere 205 were black.[4]

By intensifying the flagrant disparities between the promise and the practice of democracy, the war fueled a national movement for civil rights. The black press, the NAACP, and A. Philip Randolph, president of the Brotherhood of Sleeping Car Porters, responded to growing mass discontent by pressuring the Roosevelt administration for full and equal inclusion of black Americans in the war effort. The *Pittsburgh Courier*'s "Double V" campaign announced that black Americans would wage a two-front battle in the coming conflict. When Roosevelt failed to meet demands that he enact an affirmative policy barring racial discrimination in defense industries and desegregating the armed forces, Randolph promised that ten thousand black Americans would march on the White House on 1 July 1941 and "demand the right to work and fight for our country." At the eleventh hour Roosevelt, Randolph, and NAACP Secretary Walter White arrived at a compromise. On 19 June Roosevelt issued Executive Order 8802, which prohibited discrimination in defense industries and in federal agencies and created the President's Fair Employment Practices Committee (FEPC) to implement the order.[5]

The creation of the FEPC was a major victory for Randolph's "March on Washington" movement. No-discrimination policies had been adopted by major New Deal agencies, including the Public Works Administration (PWA) and the Works Progress Administration (WPA). But now, for the first time, the federal government was officially and publicly addressing the issue of racial discrimination in employment. And, for the first time since Reconstruction, a federal agency was devoted exclusively to race-related problems. The lack of adequate enforcement powers, along with strong opposition in Congress and among local officials, greatly inhibited the effective working of the FEPC in the South. In the face of growing racial tensions and conservative ascendancy in Washington, however, the creation of such an agency served as a testimony to the effectiveness of black protest and supported the concept of national citizenship rights. Mary McLeod Bethune spoke for many when she wrote President Roosevelt that his order was "a refreshing shower in a thirsty land."[6]

The experience of black soldiers fueled the "Double V" campaign. More than 920,000 black men and women served in the segregated armed forces during World War II; 80 percent of the black troops were trained in the South. They were segregated into the least desirable sections of the camps, areas that were congested and lacking in adequate recreational facilities. During the war, the black press and the NAACP's *Crisis* magazine were filled with reports of the violence and insult endured by black American soldiers at the hands of local citizens, law enforcement authorities, and the U.S. military. In March 1941, the body of Private Felix Hall, from Montgomery, Alabama, was found hanging from a tree in a wooded section of Fort Benning, Georgia. Hall was in his uniform. The War Department would not rule out suicide even though Hall's hands and feet were bound. The murder was never solved. During 1942 there were numerous incidents of black soldiers being shot by military police; an armed bus driver murdered a black soldier in Mobile, Alabama; black soldiers were killed by local police in Columbia, South Carolina, Little Rock, Arkansas, and Alexandria, Louisiana. Early in 1942, racial tensions erupted into a race riot involving more than five hundred black soldiers in Alexandria, Louisiana; the number of racially charged outbreaks on southern military bases increased dramatically during the spring and summer of 1943.[7]

Responding to what was recognized as an explosive situation, the War Department initiated an investigation of policy toward black soldiers and conducted a public relations campaign highlighting the contributions of black soldiers to the war effort. NAACP counsel Thurgood Marshall advised that the War Department's reluctance to prosecute cases involving the murder of black servicemen in the South, as well as its overall failure to protect their civil rights, was destroying the morale of soldiers and civilians. Writer James Baldwin described the feeling of "helplessness and gnawing uneasiness" that plagued northern families who sent a son off to war. "Perhaps the best way to sum all this up is to say that the people I knew felt, mainly, a peculiar kind of relief when they knew their boys were being shipped out of the South to do battle overseas. It was, perhaps, like feeling that the most dangerous part of the journey had been passed and that now, even if death should come, it would come with honor and without the complicity of their countrymen. Such a death would be, in short, a fact with which one could hope to live."[8]

Southern whites had opened a second front against black people, the *Pittsburgh Courier* editorialized, and soldiers were often its victims. But racial violence and repression during the early 1940s was directed primarily against southern black civilians and the deeper changes that were struggling to take root in the region. There were thirteen reported lynchings during 1940–41; the victims included two fourteen-year-old boys, Charles Lang and Ernest Green, who were hung from a bridge in Shubuta, Mississippi, for allegedly frightening a young white girl. During the war there were reports of violent encounters on buses and streetcars as black people challenged segregation practices and abusive drivers. In Titusville, Alabama, a bus driver shot and critically wounded a black man for questioning his authority.[9]

Racial repression began to take on an overtly political cast. Shortly after Elbert Williams, a founder of the NAACP in Brownsville, Tennessee, launched a voter-registration campaign in 1940, he was lynched. That same year the Mississippi legislature enacted a law requiring that textbooks used in black schools exclude all references to voting, elections, civic responsibility, and democracy. In a bold stroke, Rev. James Arthur Parsons, pastor of four black churches in Tupelo, Mississippi, declared his candidacy, with the support of the National Negro Congress (NNC), for John Rankin's seat in Congress in 1942. Parsons abandoned the race when whites in Tupelo demonstrated "forcibly" that they did not approve "of the idea of a Negro running for Congress."[10]

Above, left to right. C. B. "Beanie" Baldwin, CIO-PAC Chairman Sidney Hillman, and Clark Foreman. In 1944 the CIO-PAC launched a nationwide campaign of voter education and registration aimed at countering the conservative gains in national politics. Baldwin and Foreman helped to link the CIO-PAC's program with similar efforts in the South. (Photograph courtesy of Mairi Fraser Foreman)

Facing page, top. Louis Burnham, executive secretary of the SNYC, addresses a wartime labor rally in New Orleans's Shakespeare Park, ca. 1943. Burnham emphasized the linkages between the extension of democracy at home, facilitating the maximum use of African American labor, and the struggle against fascist aggression abroad. Ernest Wright, Louisiana organizer for the SNYC, is partially visible at far right. (Photograph courtesy of Esther and James Jackson)

Facing page, bottom. Ella Baker (*second from right*), at a meeting in the NAACP's national office in New York, ca. 1942. Baker traveled throughout the South during the war years as assistant field secretary and director of branches for the NAACP. She played a critical role in expanding the association's membership base in the region while striving to make the national office more responsive to local issues and concerns. (Photograph by M. Smith; courtesy of the Library of Congress)

Top. Vice-president Henry Wallace walked the streets of Harlem with Adam Clayton Powell Jr. during the closing week of Powell's 1944 congressional campaign. Powell became the first black person elected to Congress from the state of New York. (Photograph courtesy of Marge Frantz)

Bottom. Attorney A. T. Walden (*center*), president of the Atlanta division of the NAACP, at an Atlanta polling place, listening to O. L. Walker explain that he cannot vote in Georgia's Democratic primary. When black people tried to vote, they were told their names could not be found on the registration lists. (Photograph from AP/Wide World Photos, 4 July 1944)

By most measures, the war exacerbated racial discrimination and repression in the South and underscored federal complicity with southern racial mores. But southern black political activists looked to the broad changes under way and to the opportunities inherent in them. South Carolina NAACP organizer Osceola McKaine observed in the spring of 1941: "We are living in the midst of perhaps the greatest revolution within human experience. Nothing, no nation, will be as it was before when the peace comes. . . . There is no such thing as the status quo." Organizers like McKaine encouraged black southerners to act on America's war aims; now was the time, as the country emerged on the international scene as a self-proclaimed bulwark of democracy, to lay claim to the guarantees of citizenship. This sentiment was widely shared throughout the region. NAACP field secretary Madison Jones reported from the South that the war had "caused the Negro to change almost instantly from a fundamentally defensive attitude to one of offense. If America meant her war aims, . . . if full democracy was to be brought to all peoples, then surely America in good conscience was compelled to begin at home with her thirteen million underprivileged black citizens."[11]

Developments during the 1930s had provided a foundation for the expansion of black political activism during the war years. Many of the organizers had come to political maturity in the 1930s, honing their skills and establishing networks through the student movement, CIO organizing drives, and New Deal programs like the Farm Security Administration (FSA) and the WPA. Black identification with the party of Roosevelt and the revival of the NAACP were primary mediating forces in the emerging civil rights movement. The NAACP provided the essential vehicle for meeting the escalation of black expectations and militancy that accompanied the war. NAACP membership in the South by the late 1930s was slightly more than 18,000. By the end of the war it approached 156,000.[12]

The NAACP created an infrastructure of support for black protest and politics. Local branches were linked by statewide Conferences of Branches and were further strengthened by their connections to a prominent national organization. After his appointment as NAACP special counsel in 1934, Charles Houston revived a deeply factionalized and demoralized organization in Texas, one worn down by a ten-year legal fight against the all-white primary. The Texas State Conference of Branches, established in 1936, spearheaded a final and ultimately successful assault on the white primary. Dr. Ralph Mark Gilbert, pastor of Savannah's First African Church, convened the first statewide meeting of the four existing NAACP branches in the late 1930s to establish a state conference. Gilbert traveled the state like a circuit rider, reviving old branches and helping to establish new ones, until there were more than fifty NAACP branches statewide. Levi Byrd, a plumber from Cheraw, South Carolina, led in establishing a South Carolina State Conference of Branches in 1939 to unite the eight existing branches in his state and their nearly 800 members. By 1945 there were forty branches and 10,639 NAACP members in South Carolina.[13]

The growth of the NAACP in the South during the late 1930s and early 1940s realized Houston's ambitions for the organization. Houston and Thurgood Marshall, who succeeded Houston as special counsel in 1938, cultivated a growing network of lawyers and community leaders throughout the South as they orchestrated the legal campaign against racial discrimination in public schools. The legal campaign was improvisational and exploratory as NAACP lawyers and local citizens mounted challenges to the facade of separate but equal. Following its victory in the 1938 *Gaines* case, the NAACP won a ruling, in the U.S. Court of Appeals in 1940, that overturned teacher salary differentials based on race in Norfolk, Virginia. Cases seeking access to graduate and professional schools and teacher salary equalization continued "bubbling up throughout the South" during the war years. But the slow, piecemeal nature of the legal campaign, along with the seemingly limitless capacity of the local officials to evade rulings and harass plaintiffs in NAACP cases, was a continuing source of frustration and disillusionment. As Houston, Marshall, and others had demonstrated, an active program of fieldwork and support was essential to sustaining local efforts.[14]

Ella Baker, southern field secretary for the NAACP during the war years, expanded on Houston's initiatives. Baker had deep roots in the rural South. She grew up in the small farming community of Littleton, North Carolina, and graduated from Shaw University in Raleigh in 1927. The "New Negro" movement drew her to Harlem just as the excitement and confidence of the twenties was cresting. But Baker thrived on the vibrant debates and organizing efforts that percolated throughout New York during the depression years. The depression had exposed the helplessness of the individual in the face of broad social and economic forces and drew Baker to collective action as a critical dimension of the democratic process. She participated in a wide range of community activities including the Young Negro Cooperative League and the Workers Education Project of the WPA, an experience that she easily transferred to her work in the South.[15]

Like Houston, Baker maintained that for the goals of the national NAACP to be achieved, an active and informed constituency at the local level was essential. Her work in the South challenged the elitist bias of the national NAACP leadership, which viewed the development of local chapters primarily as a source of increasing revenue. As field secretary, she spent six months of each year in the South, taking the NAACP to churches, schools, barbershops, bars, and pool halls; she helped to build chapters around the needs and concerns of individual communities and encouraged cooperation with labor unions and other progressive organizations. Baker reported that the expansion of NAACP membership during the war years brought "a new surge of identity" throughout the black community, including "some of the people who were not [working] class people."[16]

The NAACP, as Baker viewed it, was primarily a means for supporting the participation of people in what had to be their own fight. In describing her role, Baker explained that part of her job was to help people understand the violence they lived with "and how in an organized fashion they could help to stem it." People could act effectively in their own behalf "if they understood what was happening and how group action could counter violence even when it was perpetuated by the police . . . or the state." In the end, that was "the only protection" they had "against violence or injustice." Through the deliberate efforts of organizers like Baker, Houston, and Marshall, the NAACP provided a foundation for the growth of the southern movement during the war years.[17]

Whereas incidents of police brutality and the teachers' salary equalization effort encouraged participation in the NAACP, voting was the major impetus for the expansion of civil rights activities during the late 1930s and early 1940s. Before the New Deal, southern blacks were suspended between the lily-whitism of the Republican Party, which functioned primarily as a conduit for federal patronage in the South, and the outright exclusionary policy of most state Democratic organizations. The New Deal encouraged the expansion of black political participation, and in 1936 the national Democratic Party publicly invited blacks to identify with the party of Roosevelt. In the North, allegiance to the party of Roosevelt was measured in tens of thousands of black votes in the 1936 presidential election. In the South it was evidenced in a growing effort among blacks to surmount barriers to voting, particularly through the NAACP-sponsored campaign against the all-white Democratic primary, which effectively locked blacks out of the electoral process in eight southern states.

South Carolina offers a notable example of how a new generation of community leaders responded to the New Deal and World War II and built a statewide NAACP presence by the early 1940s. After the white primary fell in Texas in 1944, South Carolina became the primary battleground over the enforcement of that decision. By the mid-1940s black Carolinians were in the vanguard of the movement for voting rights and for full participation in the Democratic Party.

Longtime civil rights activist Mojeska Simkins recalled that when Roosevelt became president, "he took the jug by the handle. He tried to give the people who were down and had nothing something. . . . It was a shot in the arm for Negroes." Blacks responded by going to the polls. On 23 August 1936, a *New York Times* article announced: "Negro Vote Jumps in South Carolina." Based on heavy turnout in Richland County, some predicted that close to two thousand blacks would register to vote in the November election, far exceeding the seventy-five to one hundred that normally registered in that county. A member of the Richland County Board of Registrars attempted to explain the phenomenon by noting: "Every Negro I have registered so far has said he would vote for President Roosevelt. They say that Roosevelt saved them from starvation, gave them aid when they were in distress, and now they are going to vote for him." Similar trends in other industrialized areas around the state made it likely that more blacks would vote in the 1936 election than at any time in the previous forty years. This "wholesale registering of Negroes," the story noted, contained an element of danger according to some local observers. After Mississippi, South Carolina had the highest proportion of black citizens, composing 43 percent of the state's population. In nearly half of the state's forty-six counties, voting-age blacks outnumbered whites.[18]

During the 1930s, localized efforts among black South Carolinians to participate in the political process were of little consequence, since blacks were barred from voting in the Democratic primary, "the only real election." But fear of an aroused black electorate was never far from the surface, as was demonstrated in the textile town of Greenville, South Carolina. In the fall of 1938, only thirty-five blacks were on the voting rolls. During the following spring and early summer, a coalition of organizations, including the local NAACP, the Youth Council of the NAACP, the black division of the Greenville County Council, and the WPA's Workers Alliance joined to promote a voter-registration drive. There were several mass meetings in May and June. Arthur Raper, a founding member of the SCHW, addressed the local Interracial Council, emphasizing the essential importance of outlawing the poll tax and the white primary in order to redress economic and racial injustices; Mary McLeod Bethune urged that a mass meeting at Textile Hall "get representation"; and the NAACP Youth Council held two forums on democracy. The black clergy exhorted their congregations to register and vote. Simultaneously, the city turned down $800,000 in federal funds for public housing after black citizens had gained more than six hundred signatures in support of the grant. All of these factors contributed to a rapid escalation of black political interest. Black voter registration reached 324 by the end of June.

Hysteria gripped the white community when press reports claimed that as many as nine hundred blacks had registered. The police and the Ku Klux Klan terrorized black activists and supportive whites. William Anderson and J. C. Williams, high school students and leaders of the NAACP Youth Council, were arrested on trumped-up charges, and the white president of the Workers Alliance was arrested three times before election day. The Klan obtained a list of the registered black voters and published warnings in the local press, urging whites to stop black voter registration. Klan members ransacked the homes of eight black families in search of James Briar, head of the local NAACP and primary leader of the voter-registration campaign. Briar, an elderly public school principal, armed himself at the urging of a concerned friend. Police arrested him in October for carrying a concealed weapon, and the school board fired him. Walter White and civil rights attorney William Hastie appealed to the U.S. attorney general, warning that in the face of unbridled Klan activity, blacks in Greenville felt totally unprotected by state or federal authority and were arming themselves in desperation. In November only fifty-four black voters cast a ballot, whereas a record number of whites turned out. A total of 551 votes were cast in the municipal election.[19]

As an isolated, spontaneous movement, the voter-registration drive was easily squashed by the combined efforts of the local police, the white press, and the Ku Klux Klan. Yet the ill-fated effort heightened the sense of purpose and urgency that attended the founding meeting of the NAACP South Carolina State Conference of Branches in Columbia on 10 November 1939. James Briar recounted the "terrible happenings" in Greenville and won promises of support from the other participating NAACP branches. The newly elected president of the statewide group, A. W. Wright, reported to the national NAACP office that the Greenville branch needed help immediately, and he inquired about how the branch might obtain assistance from other branches around the country. "We are in great need of your presence," Wright added. He urged the national office to send a representative to meet with the newly established state conference.[20]

During the next two years local NAACP groups and newspaper publisher John McCray and his *Columbia Lighthouse and Informer* spearheaded a statewide movement to open the electoral process in South Carolina. The movement had its base in Columbia, where, as of 1941, Rev. James Hinton served as director of the NAACP State Conference of Branches and Mojeska Simkins served as secretary. Simkins's mother had helped to establish the first NAACP branch in Columbia in 1917, which Hinton was responsible for reviving in the mid-1930s.

The statewide contacts enjoyed by Hinton and Simkins were crucial to the vitality of the state conference. Hinton, a respected Baptist minister and a dynamic orator, also worked as district manager for the Pilgrim Life Insurance Company, a black-owned business headquartered in Augusta, Georgia. His responsibilities included establishing and overseeing branch offices throughout South Carolina. Simkins, a graduate of Benedict College in Columbia, worked as a state representative for the South Carolina Tuberculosis Association during the 1930s. Simkins and Hinton's efforts and networks were reinforced by newspaper publisher John McCray and his associate, Osceola McKaine, who revived the NAACP branch in Sumter and organized a statewide campaign to equalize teacher salaries.

Organized groups of black citizens had been attempting to vote in the Democratic Party primary since 1934. Each time the board of elections purged their names from the registration rolls, holding to a state Democratic Party rule that only those blacks who had continuously voted the Democratic Party ticket since 1876 were permitted to vote in the primary elections. In 1942 several hundred black citizens enrolled once again. This time they were invited to appear before the city board of elections and report on their eligibility to vote in the primaries.

Blacks, along with a few white supporters, filled the county courthouse to overflowing. Dr. Robert Mance, who had led the effort since 1934, offered what he called the "common sense view": that equal access to the ballot was essential to the freedom of whites as well as blacks. Mance was preparing to volunteer in the medical services of the army and was willing to shed his blood, but he resented coming home to a community where the whites could deny him his right to vote. R. Beverly Hubert, one of several white attorneys supporting an open primary, argued that barring blacks from the primary elections was, in effect, denying them suffrage and was therefore unconstitutional. He added that, if for no other reason, blacks should be allowed to vote in the primary because of the national emergency. Hubert's address elicited an outburst of applause from the blacks and astonished most of the whites at the hearing.

The election commissioners expressed sympathy with the group's request and agreed to place it before the State Democratic Committee. In the interim, however, they were obliged to implement current state policy; they purged the voting roll of all black enrollees. Regardless of the impending action of the state committee, the petitioners remained undeterred. "We have been fighting long and hard," Mojeska Simkins wrote the national NAACP office. "We mean to get on this matter now and go through to the end. This is our very best chance ever."[21]

R. Beverly Hubert was among five whites who submitted a resolution to the state Democratic convention on 3 May to repeal the rule barring blacks from participating in the Democratic primary. D. W. Robinson, an attorney, declared that a more serious question had never been placed before the state Democratic Party. Dr. J. Heywood Gibbes, spokesman for the group, said he had a feeling of genuine humility when drafting the resolution. He was convinced, he said, that a large element of the Negro citizenry was "now qualified in mind and character to take part in our form of government." Gibbes urged the convention not to "turn this thing down without prayerful consideration." He advised, "It's coming in one form or another." South Carolina had an opportunity "to light a spark that might find world-wide good in it." The convention voted the proposal down. Commenting on the proceedings, William Watts Ball, editor of the *Charleston News and Courier*, advised blacks to form their own party, hold their own primaries, and select their own representatives. Other white southerners had advocated allowing blacks to elect their own representatives, who would serve as advisory, non-voting delegates in the state legislatures.[22]

James Hinton responded immediately. Supplementing the NAACP branch network with subscriber lists to the *Columbia Lighthouse and Informer*, Hinton sent out a call to a statewide meeting "to do something constructive about the ballot." More than two hundred black men and women, representing twenty-one of the state's forty-six counties, met in Columbia on 19 May and established the South Carolina Negro Citizen's Committee (SCNCC). They agreed to promote voter registration and raise funds to support a legal fight for full voting rights. Within two months the committee had raised more than three thousand dollars. Hinton wrote Thurgood Marshall, "South Carolina is aroused as never before and we expect great things from this awakening." Marshall, who was preparing an appeal of the Texas primary case, traveled to Columbia in June 1942 to confer with Hinton and the local leadership. He instructed Hinton to have as many individuals as possible apply to vote in the primary elections and to complete affidavits when they were denied, being sure to indicate those serving in the armed forces. Marshall would then submit the affidavits to the Justice Department. In addressing a mass meeting sponsored by the state conference, Marshall praised their efforts and promised, "Nothing will stir us away from this action." By September the SCNCC had raised close to six thousand dollars, but the organization awaited the impending outcome of the Texas primary case before bringing suit.[23]

In April 1944 the U.S. Supreme Court dealt what would ultimately be the final blow to the all-white Democratic primary. *Smith v. Allwright* culminated a twenty-year legal campaign that revealed the changing contours of southern black activism and national developments and the seemingly inexhaustible capacity of southern lawmakers to maneuver around court rulings. Until the mid-1930s, the legal fight against the white primary was conducted by a handful of black lawyers and activists; most southern blacks viewed efforts to gain admission to the Democratic primary as an empty legal exercise, since few could imagine participating in a party committed to white supremacy. Just at the time that Roosevelt and the New Deal were causing black southerners to reassess the Democratic Party, a unanimous Supreme Court upheld the Texas white primary in the 1935 *Grovey v. Townsend* ruling, wiping out the slow but steady legal victories of the previous decade and leaving black veterans of that fight dispirited and disillusioned. The remarkable turnaround during the next nine years was a function of many factors. Charles Houston breathed new life into the white primary fight in Texas, which unfolded against the backdrop of a rejuvenated NAACP, a deepening identification of southern blacks with the national Democratic Party, and the transformation of the Supreme Court. The eight justices who voted to outlaw the white primary in 1944 were all Roosevelt appointees.[24]

Smith v. Allwright was the fourth time since 1927 that the Supreme Court had ruled on the exclusion of blacks from the Democratic primary in Texas. Twice before the *Grovey* decision of 1935, the Court had held that the primary, as regulated by state stature, violated the equal protection clause of the Fourteenth Amendment by excluding black voters. It never addressed the status of the primary as part of the electoral process. Texas lawmakers and the state Democratic Party proceeded to establish the Democratic Party as a private voluntary organization, separate from any state regulation and possessing the right to limit its membership. The *Grovey* decision sanctioned this arrangement. In an unrelated case involving fraud in primary elections in Louisiana, *U.S. v. Classic* (1941), the court fused the primary and the general election into a single process, opening the way for a challenge to racially exclusive primaries as a violation of the Fifteenth Amendment. In *Smith v. Allwright* the Court ruled that the relationship between state stature and the Democratic primary was such that the primary served as a quasi-governmental function and that, therefore, exclusion of voters based on race was a violation of the Fifteenth Amendment. Marshall acknowledged that the ambiguity of the Court's language "concerning the statutory scheme in Texas" might open the door "for the invention of new contrivances to bar Negroes from voting in primary elections." He advised the NAACP branches in all states affected by the Texas primary decision to turn out voters in the coming primaries and to prepare to challenge probable obstruction.[25]

"The Texas primary case was the beginning of a complete revolution in our thinking on the right of suffrage," said Luther Porter Jackson, founder of the Virginia Voters League. Palmer Weber later compared its significance to the 1954 *Brown v. Board of Education*. "Once the Supreme Court had opened the door in 1944," Weber recalled, "the NAACP charged into the whole registration and voting area very hard." Two weeks after the white primary ruling, thirty-six black delegates representing every southern state convened in Hot Springs, Arkansas, at the invitation of the Reverend Maynard Jackson Sr. and established the National Progressive Voters League. Participants included John Wesley Dobbs, founder of the Atlanta Civic and Political League, James Hinton of South Carolina, Roscoe Dunjee, editor of the *Black Dispatch* in Oklahoma City, national NAACP board member W. H. Hollins of Birmingham, and Dr. J. M. Robinson of Little Rock. The organization aimed to provide "guidance and orientation" in the use of the ballot for the "millions of newly enfranchised voters." Toward this end, it proposed to coordinate efforts among black voters throughout the United States and to integrate southern black voters into a broad liberal-labor coalition of voters. The league offered membership "to citizens of all shades of political thought in the hope that paths [could] be fashioned for the Negro voter to take his rightful place by the side of liberal political groups irrespective of race or class."[26]

Many black voting-rights activists and NAACP organizers saw their struggle as part of a larger movement uniting groups and organizations with shared economic and political interests. Several regional organizations supported the creation and expansion of such coalitions. Prominent among them were the SCHW, the SNYC, and Highlander Folk School. These organizations were guided by the assumption that an enfranchised, informed, and active electorate was essential to addressing the economic problems and injustices that plagued the South. They also believed that the segregation system stood as the greatest obstacle to establishing political and economic democracy in the region.

Few of these reformers underestimated the power of racial ideology reinforced by state law. But none doubted that it had to be met and steadily overcome, a challenge that required an exploratory and inventive approach. The CIO's commitment to racial equality provided a major source of support for the efforts of the SCHW, the SNYC, and Highlander. The organizations experimented with different tactics and strategies as they navigated the

South's racialized terrain, guided by the composition of their immediate constituency.

Former student activists, some of whom were affiliated with the Communist Party, organized the SNYC in 1937 as the counterpart to the National Negro Congress (NNC). While the NNC concentrated on organizing northern black industrial workers into the CIO unions, the youth-oriented SNYC sought to build a movement around challenges and opportunities peculiar to southern black youth and workers. Like the NNC, the SNYC cooperated with the CIO in appealing to the interests and concerns of black workers and strengthening their participation in the labor movement. SNYC organizers promoted workers' education and organization in urban and rural areas throughout the South. As noted earlier, in the aftermath of the SNYC founding meeting, SNYC members organized more than five thousand tobacco workers in Richmond for the CIO. During the war years the SNYC sponsored labor schools in New Orleans, Birmingham, and Richmond and at Hampton Institute and aided black workers in protesting discriminatory hiring practices and presenting grievances to the FEPC.[27]

The disfranchisement of southern workers, black and white, was a primary factor that distinguished the southern labor movement. Voting, SNYC organizers frequently explained, was essential to countering the antiunion, antiblack elected officials who dominated southern politics and exercised inordinate power in Washington. The SNYC's campaign for voting rights was creative and wide-ranging, combining education, organizing, "Right to Vote" rallies, publicity, appeals to the U.S. Justice Department, and lobbying efforts at the national conventions of the American Federation of Labor (AFL) and the CIO. The SNYC sponsored citizenship schools in Birmingham and New Orleans and worked with other organizations to help train "citizenship instructors" by sponsoring a compilation of voting requirements for each state and promoting the study of each state's constitution and laws. The SNYC and the SCHW cosponsored a National Anti–Poll Tax Week in the spring of 1941. It was widely publicized by the black press and succeeded in raising funds to support citizenship clinics and public forums. The SNYC's Caravan Puppeteers traveled around rural areas during the summer of 1942 using puppet shows to inform people about the anti-poll-tax campaign, voter registration, and the role of labor unions. In 1944, SNYC organizers, working with E. D. Nixon, chairman of the Alabama Voters League, launched a campaign to register ten thousand voters in Montgomery by July in order to make a better world for returning veterans.[28]

Highlander Folk School was established in 1932 to serve white industrial and rural workers in southern Appalachia. It became affiliated with the CIO in 1937 and quickly developed into a regional center for workers' education through a program of residential workshops and extension programs. Co-founder Myles Horton described Highlander as a place where people could "share their experiences and learn from each other and learn to trust their own judgement." Workers' education aimed to enable workers and union leaders to understand the world in which they lived while envisioning their roles in changing it. Programs included workshops on labor history, union problems, labor legislation, public speaking, economics, and labor journalism. Union officials, New Deal administrators, and representatives of the SCHW, as well as Highlander staffers, led these sessions, and union leaders from every state in the South attended. In response to the rapid rise in union membership during the war years, Highlander conducted extension programs for CIO unions in virtually every southern state; Highlander alumni were among the leadership of national, regional, and local unions.[29]

Organizers of Highlander agreed that cooperation between black and white workers was essential to the success of the labor movement in the South. The task facing Highlander, then, was to enable rural white workers to look beyond deeply ingrained racial attitudes and toward the broader interests of a biracial union movement. Staff members used a variety of approaches. Classes explored the connections between race relations and labor organizing, sociologist Arthur Raper assisted with workshops to break down racial prejudice, and black labor organizers visited Highlander as guest speakers. Organizers working through Highlander's extension program led in bridging racial barriers between white and black workers. Its residency program, however, remained limited to white workers until 1944, largely due to the reluctance of CIO unions to sponsor interracial sessions. Union leaders feared that to do so would undermine efforts to organize southern white workers.[30]

By 1940, Highlander cofounder James Dombrowski questioned the wisdom of maintaining a policy that accommodated the racial prejudices of white workers, even as a short-term strategy. Such a policy, he maintained, alienated black workers and only reinforced the race-baiting tactics of anti-union forces. He wanted Highlander to reconsider its position, as well as its relationship with the unions. But Dombrowski's concerns were never fully addressed, further exacerbating tensions between him and Myles Horton. At the end of 1941 Dombrowski resigned as chairman of Highlander's staff and assumed the position of executive secretary of the SCHW.[31]

The SCHW gained a talented administrator and publicist whose experiences complemented the Washington orientation of SCHW activists like Virginia Durr and Clark Foreman. Dombrowski was largely responsible for the successful establishment of Highlander. In the words of Myles Horton, "he did the solid work of coalescing the whole thing" and set Highlander on a sound administrative and financial basis. As a publicist, he focused national attention on the desperate condition of southern workers and on Highlander's effort to ameliorate them through unionization. Dombrowski engineered the production of Elia Kazan's *The People of the Cumberland*, a film about coal miners fighting for unions. The film premiered at the New School for Social Research in New York in 1938, and Eleanor Roosevelt hosted a private showing at the White House. Largely through Dombrowski's efforts, Highlander developed a network of supporters within the Roosevelt administration and among northern philanthropists.[32]

Dombrowski's social and political sensibilities were formed during the early years of the depression under the tutelage of Harry F. Ward at Union Theological Seminary. The son of a Tampa jeweler, Dombrowski went to Union after graduating from Emory University. Acting on Ward's advocacy that students immerse themselves in the struggles of their time, Dombrowski hitchhiked to the North Carolina Piedmont at the peak of the 1929 textile strikes. His experience there was formative and convinced him of the critical role of unions in countering the abject powerlessness bred into the lives of mill workers. Race was not a central issue among the nearly all-white textile workers, but it informed Dombrowski's studies at Union. He investigated how the Anglican Church in Virginia justified slavery with ethical canons, and he explored examples of interracial harmony in the late-nineteenth-century South for his Ph.D. dissertation on "The Early Days of Christian Socialism in America." He had concluded early on that racial discrimination was morally wrong and also subverted the possibility of advancing social and economic justice.[33]

Dombrowski joined the SCHW at a promising time. "The opportunity for progress on the race issue at the moment is enormous," Dombrowski observed early in 1942. As the one organization that enabled "whites and Negroes to get together in the South on a progressive program," the SCHW ensured that Dombrowski could act on his desire to advance full interracial cooperation. Dombrowski in turn played an essential role in revitalizing the SCHW. Scarcity of funds, the eclipse of New Deal reformism by the war effort, and administrative weakness had hindered its effort to gain a secure organizational base in the South. Shortly after Dombrowski joined the SCHW staff, Clark Foreman assumed the chairmanship. At that time the twenty-eight-member executive board included representatives from organized labor, the Young Women's Christian Association (YWCA), local and state chapters of the NAACP, the SNYC, the NNC, the National Anti-Poll-Tax

Committee, and black and white colleges. Under Foreman and Dombrowski's leadership, the organization embarked on a more deliberate course at the forefront of racial and political reform in the South.[34]

The SCHW's third regional conference, held in Nashville in April 1942, previewed the organization's postwar agenda. Dombrowski organized the program with the assistance of Frank Graham, Virginia Durr, Clark Foreman, John P. Davis, and William Mitch. Five hundred delegates attended. One-third of the delegates were black, and the majority of participants were affiliated with organized labor. Although wartime travel restrictions limited attendance, the Nashville conference hosted celebrated New Deal and civil rights figures, including Eleanor Roosevelt, who presented the Thomas Jefferson Award to Mary McLeod Bethune and Frank Graham. The Nashville meeting was the scene of Paul Robeson's first concert in the South.[35]

The role of the South in the national defense was the conference theme and provided an opportunity to expand on the "Double V" campaign. The way in which race impinged on the expansion of democracy at home was at the center of the conference deliberations. Robert Weaver, then serving on the War Labor Board, and Ira DeA. Reid, who was working as an investigator for the FEPC, reported on the persistence of racial discrimination in defense-related industries and its effect on the mobilization of southern resources for the war effort. The exigencies of war created a strong and vocal consensus within the SCHW against employment discrimination and for action to give concrete meaning to democratic rhetoric. "The old victories of human liberty can be preserved only in the revised versions of the new struggles for democracy," Frank Graham told the gathering. In his message to the conference, Franklin Roosevelt proclaimed that victory meant democracy would be "maintained as a vital strengthening force."[36]

The unity and the confident spirit that dominated the Nashville gathering were challenged internally when board member Frank McAllister revived his campaign for a resolution barring Communists from the SCHW. His action was triggered by an appeal made by Paul Robeson for Earl Browder's release from the federal penitentiary in Atlanta, where he was serving time for a passport violation. McAllister charged that the SCHW harbored "two or three" Communist Party partisans. He named one—SCHW board member John P. Davis, then director of the NNC. McAllister, who was a member of the Socialist Worker's Party and a southern representative of the American Civil Liberties Union (ACLU), proposed a resolution similar to one adopted by the ACLU in 1940. The ACLU resolution barred from its governing committees and staff any person who belonged to any political organization that supported totalitarian dictatorships or "who by his public declarations indicates his support of such a principle." It resulted in the "trial" of Elizabeth Gurley Flynn and her expulsion from the ACLU board. Executive secretary Roger Baldwin endorsed McAllister's proposal. As a trustee of the Marshall Fund, which had awarded the SCHW a one-thousand-dollar grant, Baldwin charged that the conference was in violation of the terms of the grant, which required, Baldwin said, "that no political influences . . . be allowed to color the conference organization."[37]

The SCHW had attempted to defuse the Communist issue during the "little red scare" of 1939–41 by adopting a resolution barring those who advocated the violent overthrow of the government or who belonged to organizations that did. But Foreman and Dombrowski refused to preside over a purge of the organization. They consulted with Virginia Durr, Frank Graham, and Lucy Randolph Mason in crafting their response, which articulated an action-oriented liberalism that would guide the SCHW through the postwar and early cold war period.

As part of their response, Foreman and Dombrowski challenged the substance of the charges as well as the implications of the policy that McAllister and Baldwin advocated. Though one might question the propriety of Robeson's using the Nashville meeting to issue a plea for Browder's release, Dombrowski asked Baldwin whether he would question Robeson's right to express his personal opinion on the subject or whether Baldwin would suggest that the committee in charge seek "to edit or censor in advance what platform participants said or sang." Reckless charges about subversive influences within the SCHW were an affront to the board's integrity, Dombrowski argued, and compromised the principles for which the ACLU had long stood. "As I understand the fight for civil liberties, the right to hold a conviction different from the norm is one of the basic rights for which the fight is conducted."[38]

Foreman drew attention to the paradox that a proponent of civil liberties would attempt "to force a democratic organization to exclude 'political intruders.' " The conference always had been and would continue to be open to all who were committed to advancing economic and political democracy in the South and were willing to meet on the basis of equality to discuss "our common problems." To adopt "a red-baiting, negative, undemocratic policy," Foreman countered, would put the conference at a much greater risk than a policy that allowed so-called fellow travelers to participate. He admitted to Baldwin that the conference would, therefore, be controversial and that there would be individuals and ideas with which neither he nor Baldwin agreed. But he added, "If there is merit in the democratic dogma, we should be delighted to have the opportunity to fight for our convictions on a fair battleground." He noted that there was no evidence that the battleground was not fair.[39]

Foreman questioned the factual basis of McAllister's charges and the nature of his concern for the SCHW. Since it was becoming increasingly common for individuals to take advantage of anti-Communist sentiment for personal gain, "it was all too easy to smear" an organization or an individual by alleging or implying improper motives. In implicating John P. Davis, McAllister did not charge that he was a member of the Communist Party but cited A. Philip Randolph's statement, made when Randolph resigned from the NNC, that suggested the organization was a Communist front. Foreman, who had known Davis since the early days of the New Deal, said he had no way of knowing Davis's political affiliations. Foreman observed that Davis, as an SCHW board member, had "been singularly free of the pettiness and formulistic activity" that Foreman associated with "the party-minded, whether Socialist or Communist." Foreman's long personal association with Davis suggested a man "sincerely working for the best interests of his people." Davis understood "better than many of his critics" that if the economic conditions of the South were to be improved, black and white people would have to put aside their differences and work together "toward the common end."[40]

For many southern activists and observers, the quest for ideological conformity seemed a senseless diversion as a wave of reaction and racist sentiment crested during the war years. Early in 1943 Thomas Sancton exclaimed, "The South is in a fevered state of mind." A two-month journey through Louisiana and Mississippi was a revelation for the Louisiana-born journalist. "I [finally] began to understand . . . the fatalism, the fear, the confusion, the spiritual suffering which made the Civil War possible."[41]

Far-reaching demographic changes stretched racial boundaries and stoked a siege mentality among white southerners. The sudden surge in population growth that accompanied industrial expansion in towns and cities throughout the South taxed housing, recreational, and transportation facilities, multiplying incidents of racial confrontations. Although blacks continued to endure widespread job discrimination and underemployment, the federal government's stated commitment to fair employment, along with evidence of expanding opportunities for black workers in defense industries, threatened to undermine the South's caste system. Widely reported incidents of racially motivated violence and rebellious outbreaks involving black soldiers fed racial fears and rumors. The revitalized ideology of democracy and freedom accompanying the war magnified scattered efforts by black southerners to secure voting rights. Defenders of the segregation system warned of a full-scale assault on states' rights and white supremacy.

Escalating racial tensions during the war years shook white southerners from the "racial dream world" that had pervaded their society and culture during the 1920s and 1930s. Historian Joel Williamson described this world as one in which the institutionalization of physical and social separation was accompanied by the total "escape of black people from the white mind." White southerners reconstructed and celebrated a mythical past. Black people were not to be found in school textbooks and had "very nearly evaporated from politics," except in the rhetorical flourishes of demagogues. The etiquette of paternalism nurtured a complacent faith in racial harmony, which was reinforced by "the sheer power of whites . . . to hold blacks in place and to enforce upon them prescribed behavior in the presence of white people." In the process, southern whites "lost all understanding of race as a primary determinant in southern culture." They "slipped further from an understanding of black life, and found themselves as a people separated from the nation."[42]

Race and "the Negro issue" dominated statewide primary races in South Carolina, Arkansas, Louisiana, and Georgia in 1942 in ways reminiscent of the campaigns that had accompanied the wave of disfranchisement and segregation laws at the turn of the century. In South Carolina and Louisiana, where blacks composed 36 percent of the states' populations, candidates and press editorials warned that if blacks obtained the right to vote, they would hold the balance of power. At several polling places in Louisiana, police removed blacks lined up to vote, charging them with disturbing the peace. In an unsuccessful challenge to Senator Allen Ellender in Louisiana, E. A. Stephens ran exclusively on the race issue and warned, "Colored organizations are sitting around midnight candles, and I only wish I could tell you what was taking place."[43]

Eugene Talmadge's racially charged gubernatorial campaign in Georgia was accompanied by a campaign of racial terror. The Georgia Home Guard issued a riot alert and advised that it was not safe for white women to go out alone. A district commander of the Georgia highway patrol testified that the commissioner of the state highway patrol had ordered highway police "to stop and search all colored persons found on the road after 9 P.M." The commissioner had stated, "Use your black jack on them whenever you can." Governor Talmadge mixed his virulent racism with a purge of the state university system, causing the system to lose its accreditation and helping Ellis Arnall to defeat the incumbent governor. Talmadge's defeat and the unsuccessful challenges by Stephens in Louisiana and Cole Blease in South Carolina suggested the limits of racial extremism but did not temper the increasing potency of the race issue. Though protesting Talmadge's pernicious race-baiting, Arnall had reassured Georgia voters, "If a nigger ever tried to get into a white school in my part of the state the sun would never set on his head, and we wouldn't be running to the Governor or the State Guard to get things done either."[44]

The FEPC's investigation of discriminatory practices in southern-based defense industries and training in June 1942 further fused racial and sectional loyalties into an aggressive defense of "the southern way of life." In preparation for the Birmingham hearings, FEPC Chairman Mark Ethridge tried to persuade black FEPC member Earl Dickerson to stay away from Birmingham on the grounds that he feared for Dickerson's safety. The Mississippi-born Dickerson responded, "If honestly trying to get some benefits from this area for the 9,000,000 Negroes who live in the South is going to jeopardize my life, I am willing to do it." Dickerson condemned the committee's gingerly approach to the Birmingham hearings for encouraging white southern recalcitrance. Nevertheless, Ethridge attempted to reassure the white South by opening the hearings with a statement that attacked black leaders who had "adopted an all or nothing attitude." He promised, "No power in the world—not even . . . Allied and Axis [armies together] . . . could now force the Southern white people to the abandonment of the principle of social segregation." Ethridge's indulgence of white southern sentiment dismayed and angered black leaders and failed to contain the furor sparked by the hearings.[45]

The FEPC field investigations and hearings documented racial discrimination in defense training programs in every southern state. Widespread racial discrimination in defense-related industries was supported by restrictive union policies and management hiring practices. Ira DeA. Reid found that blacks were not being denied defense work; rather, they were restricted to unskilled jobs. Southern-based industries imported thousands of white workers, and tolerated labor shortages, while black workers remained underemployed or unemployed. Field investigator John Beecher reported that a Mobile shipyard refused to upgrade black workers, dismissing the idea as "impractical and utopian"; at another shipyard, the AFL's Mobile Metal Trades Council eliminated all skilled blacks from its rolls.[46]

Public exposure of employment discrimination was the FEPC's primary means of nudging the offending employers to abandon such practices, a tactic that met with uneven success outside of the South. In the South, FEPC investigations had minimal impact on the workplace but far-reaching social and political implications. The Birmingham hearings showcased the contending forces of racial equality and white southern tradition. Black FEPC committee members Earl Dickerson and Milton Webster occupied positions of authority and questioned white witnesses, challenging them in a way that breached southern racial practice. Black professionals testified as experts, and black workers accused unions and employers of discrimination. Birmingham had not witnessed such an affront to racial mores since the founding meeting of the SCHW in that city four years earlier.

The hearings offered an inviting platform for defenders of white supremacy and for longtime opponents of New Deal reformism and the CIO unions. Alabama Governor Frank Dixon, the nephew of Thomas Dixon, author of *The Clansman* and other white supremacist novels, accused the FEPC of "operating a kangaroo court obviously dedicated to the abolition of segregation in the South." Dixon's charge that the Roosevelt administration was using the war emergency to end the color line joined a chorus of southern politicians from Washington to the Deep South. The FEPC hearings became a lightning rod for southern defiance of federal policy and a closing of the ranks against outside intervention. To much fanfare, the Alabama governor refused to sign a contract with the Defense Supplies Corporation for cloth made in prisons because he charged that its required nondiscrimination clause violated Alabama law. South Carolina Governor Olin Johnston reassured a reporter at a meeting of southern governors: "South Carolina is fully able to take care of the race question without outside interference.... The white people of this state have successfully run this government for generations and ... we intend to run it as we have in the past." In a speech to South Carolina's Defense Force (the state guard), Johnston stated, "If any outsiders come into our state and agitate social equality among the races, I shall deem it my duty to call upon you men to help expel them."[47]

By 1943, sociologist Howard Odum observed, the region had slipped into "a new pro-South tempo . . . highly motivated for self defense," ready to guard against and root out those subversive elements eating at the foundations of "southern" racial harmony. The possibility of indigenous efforts growing out of black communities was hardly entertained. Most whites, rationalizing that southern blacks were content, dismissed the idea that blacks would or could act independently. New Deal reformers, Communist Party organizers, and the CIO earned distinction as the new abolitionists, but Eleanor Roosevelt was the most notorious of all. Following a seventy-thousand-mile bus trip around the United States, a South African journalist marveled at the bitter opposition to the First Lady, particularly among white southern men. Journalist Thomas Sancton wrote in 1943, "Mrs. Roosevelt is the most hated symbol of the white middle class since Harriet Beecher Stowe."[48]

Eleanor Roosevelt's unique relationship to the South was shaped by her participation in the New Deal. Before going to Washington, she had had little contact with the region. She rarely accompanied her husband to their cottage in Warm Springs, Georgia, because, her biographer explains, "the atmosphere of the rural South with its poverty and degradation of the Negro depressed her." But her concerns about social and economic injustice and the role of the government in meeting these problems drew her attention to the South. She was at the center of the network of southerners who administered the most progressive programs of the New Deal, people such as Aubrey Williams, Will Alexander, and Clark Foreman. She served as an advocate for the Southern Tenant Farmers Union (STFU) and learned about the challenges facing organized labor in the South from Lucy Randolph Mason and Highlander Folk School. Her close association with Mary McLeod Bethune and the NAACP's Walter White informed her understanding of the realities of black life in the South and of how racial discrimination thwarted efforts to advance social and economic justice. The SCHW, which she helped to found, and the anti-poll-tax campaign maintained her active and enthusiastic support.[49]

Eleanor Roosevelt's public association with black people and her frequent endorsement of the ideal of human equality and equal opportunity attracted ridicule during the 1930s. The *Rosslyn (Virginia) Chronicle* reported that in a speech Mrs. Roosevelt delivered to a black gathering in 1936, she used the word "equality" twelve times and "equal" six times. The paper referred to a photograph of the First Lady sitting beside a black woman at a welfare gathering—"so close their bodies touched." That same year an issue of the *Georgia Women's World*, a publication of the Atlanta-based National Women's Association for the Preservation of the White Race, had a cover photograph of Eleanor Roosevelt being escorted by a black professor at Howard University. An article attacking Mrs. Roosevelt charged: "Surely no other roamed the country at will as she does . . . surely the white women of the nation, at least those of the South, have not shared the cordial comradeship which is so freely bestowed to and among the Negroes of the nation. Walter White and the other Negro boys who ran the streets of Atlanta a quarter of a century ago seem to find special favor in the eyes of Madam Roosevelt." Eugene Talmadge, governor of Georgia and a bitter foe of Franklin Roosevelt's, distributed three thousand copies of this publication at the "grass roots" convention he convened in Macon, Georgia, in 1936 in a futile attempt to challenge the president. Such attacks had a limited audience beyond extremist groups in the 1930s.[50]

By the war years, however, few southerners were neutral about Eleanor Roosevelt. Her pronouncements during the war were consistent with earlier ones, but they resonated throughout the South. "There must be equality before the law, equality of education, equal opportunity to obtain a job according to one's ability and training and equality of participation in self government," she wrote in the *Ladies' Home Journal* in the fall of 1941. She challenged those who argued that recognition of inequities at home was a deterrent to the war effort. Echoing black demands she said, "I do not see how we can fight this war and deny . . . rights to any citizen in our own land." Although she often urged patience on the part of black citizens, she was sensitive to the pain of endurance. "How many nights! he has waited for justice." And patience did not mean idleness. "We must keep moving steadily forward," she wrote in 1942.[51]

Rumors, letters of protest to the White House, and press reports and commentary held Eleanor Roosevelt responsible for a new spirit of "rebelliousness" evident among southern blacks. A Texan who described himself as a supporter of the president's struck a common theme when he wrote FDR: "The national publicity and attention that is being given the Negro is fast ruining the southern Negro. . . . The efforts of Mrs. Roosevelt to help them are being greatly misrepresented by the Negroes and is [sic] causing them to become belligerent and extremely bad-mannered." The most fantastic expression of this charge was the "Eleanor Clubs," allegedly organized by black domestics at the behest of the First Lady for more pay, more privileges, less hours, and less work. Rumors about the Eleanor Clubs flooded the South during 1942 and 1943 in many imaginative variations. A common motto attributed to the clubs stated, "A white woman in every kitchen by Christmas." Several investigations, including one by the Federal Bureau of Investigation (FBI), found no evidence that any such clubs existed. The rumors were fed by a shortage of domestic help due to better-paying opportunities in defense industries and to the organization of black women into clubs and branches of organized labor.[52]

Eleanor Roosevelt's presence at a dance for servicemen in Washington, D.C., struck at the heart of the southern caste system and drew a storm of protest. The CIO sponsored the dance at a nonsegregated canteen, and black and white women attended as hostesses. Representative Charles McKenzie of Louisiana led the attack on the First Lady from the floor of the U.S. Congress. "How can anyone be party to encouraging white girls into the arms of Negro soldiers at a canteen dance while singing 'Let Me Call You Sweetheart'? . . . Do these people have no regard for the traditions of the South and the culture of the white race?" A flurry of letters to the White House followed, defending racial purity and chastising Mrs. Roosevelt for lending "her presence and dignity to such a humiliating affair." A group of women from Lynchburg, Virginia, wrote President Roosevelt that though they would not deny the Negro "his legitimate rights," they did not approve "sacrificing upon the alter of so-called patriotism the white womanhood of this country to boost the morale of the Negro soldier in this war." The mayor of Uniontown, Alabama, protested the First Lady's behavior to FDR: "[It is] a DIRECT slap in the face of your supporters in the South. . . . We will never stand for SOCIAL EQUALITY." A Mississippian warned Mrs. Roosevelt that her behavior would ultimately lead to a race war: "Minorities will all be killed and crusaders [put] out of work. . . . We in Mississippi know how to deal with this or any other problem that threatens 'our way of life.' "[53]

Early in 1944, a disgruntled Tennessean charged that Eleanor Roosevelt was indirectly responsible for a shoot-out between black soldiers and two white law enforcement officers in Ripley, Tennessee, in which one soldier was killed and an officer wounded. W. T. Straub of Memphis sent news clippings of the incident to Mrs. Roosevelt and said that her campaign for social equality precipitated such incidents of interracial violence. The First Lady sent a brief reply: "These articles are sad reading for you—not me." "Flabbergasted" by this "cryptic" response, Straub and the *Memphis Commercial Appeal* insisted on an explanation. The paper excerpted a response sent by a secretary to Roosevelt: "Mrs. Roosevelt meant that not she, but the South is responsible for things like that because of the condition there caused by discrimination against the Negro. Certainly she was not responsible for them. If she'd died in her cradle, conditions there would still be the same as they are."[54]

The *Commercial Appeal* was outraged. In a widely distributed editorial, the paper denounced this "second hand evasion." It added: "Mrs. Roosevelt denies the patient, sympathetic efforts of the real leaders of both races in the South. It shows that she blames southern whites exclusively for any trouble and disregards her own either ignorant or intentional role as meddler and agitator. . . . She has been disrupting the natural processes through which the people of the South, white and colored, have been working through the years to ever more satisfactory relations. If Mrs. Roosevelt is neither able nor willing to be intelligent, kindly, impartial, understanding and sympathetic in this matter, let her keep her nose out of it."[55]

That the South was at a critical juncture in its racial and social development was indisputable. Black protest of racial discrimination in the war effort, along with the steady escalation of racial tensions and violence in the South and in the North, peaked in a crescendo of interracial violence and rioting during the spring and summer of 1943. Hundreds of black soldiers rebelled at Camp Stewart in Georgia and Camp McCain and Camp Van Dorn in Mississippi; there were numerous racially charged outbreaks at other military installations. In Mobile, white workers rioted for two days when the Alabama Dry Dock and Shipbuilding Company attempted to implement an FEPC order to upgrade black workers. During a seven-week period that summer, racial tensions erupted into full-scale rioting in cities from Harlem to Los Angeles, with Detroit surpassing all other cities in deaths and destruction. The Social Science Institute at Fisk University estimated that there were 242 incidents of interracial violence and rioting during 1943.[56]

Warnings abounded that the country was fast approaching a surge of violence that would surpass the post–World War I "Red summer" of lynchings and race riots. Yet there had been far-reaching changes since 1919, changes that had fundamentally altered the nature of race relations in the South and provided the legal and political underpinnings for a continuing attack on the segregation system. These changes, however, were not widely appreciated or acknowledged among white liberals nationally or in the South. Indeed, the racial crisis of the war years revealed critical interpretive differences among liberals about the New Deal, the political developments of the 1930s, and the significance of race as a national issue, differences that had important consequences for liberal Democrats in the postwar period and for the emerging civil rights movement. The perspectives and politics of traditional southern liberals, known also as moderates, and of the New Deal activists of the SCHW illustrate this division.

Jonathan Daniels, a North Carolinian who served as race relations adviser to FDR during the war years, typified the views of white southern moderates who contended that the racial crisis of the war years was primarily a problem of black protest. "We thought we had to get a little justice to keep them [black Americans] in line," Daniels recalled. "Throw a little meat to the lions." In seeking the source of protest, southern moderates identified the black press, militant northern black leaders, and outside agitators like Eleanor Roosevelt. Daniels referred disparagingly to Mrs. Roosevelt as positioned "to the extreme left on the racial thing." Southern moderates dismissed efforts to support or legitimize the wartime movement for democracy at home as dangerous, irresponsible, and potentially disloyal, a view that had currency within the Roosevelt administration. During the war, the

Justice Department and the U.S. Post Office maintained widespread surveillance of the black press.[57]

The racial and political attitudes of white southern moderates like Daniels reflected the interracial movement that grew up around the Commission on Interracial Cooperation (CIC) and remained largely unchanged by the forces that gave rise to the New Deal–inspired SCHW. Traditional southern liberalism was guided by the assumption that the "better class" of white southerners would and should control the direction and pace of change in race relations in the South. That was the abiding lesson of the Reconstruction era and the Populist movement. Moderates maintained that Reconstruction was a fatally flawed experiment that had invited thievery and chaos, exposed the political ineptitude of the freedmen, and brought about the dismal state of southern politics. The necessary battle waged to "redeem" the South from Radical Republicans resulted in the one-party state, and its attending limitations, feeding the insurgency of the 1890s. Whereas southern New Dealers held that C. Vann Woodward's study of Populist leader Tom Watson suggested the potential of class-based political alliances for economic reform, moderates argued that it demonstrated the enduring hold of racial and regional folkways and exposed the demagoguery inherent in popular democratic movements. To such a mentality, the CIO's organizing drives, Roosevelt's intervention in the 1938 primary elections, and growing black demands for full citizenship rights were harbingers of chaos and reaction.[58]

Seasoned by the popular democratic impulses of the New Deal and the labor movement, the founding of the SCHW in 1938 marked a significant departure from the interracial movement born in the aftermath of World War I. Several former and longtime participants in the CIC, like Arthur Raper, Clark Foreman, and even CIC founder Will Alexander, embraced the SCHW as a natural extension and continuation of the work begun by the CIC. But for others, the SCHW's close ties to the Roosevelt administration, its efforts to build a political program with mass appeal, and its resolution not to hold segregated meetings ran against the grain of southern liberalism and the interracial movement. During the SCHW founding meeting, Mark Ethridge, editor of the *Louisville Courier-Journal*, convened a small group to consider Howard Odum's plan for a new regional organization. A follow-up meeting, consisting mostly of journalists and academics, met in Atlanta, with Charles S. Johnson present as the sole black participant. Countering the perceived militancy of the SCHW, the group reaffirmed its commitment to slow, carefully moderated change and declared, "Since our conditions are products of a long existent economy, remedial action will require a relatively long period of time."[59]

The growth of black political activism during the war, along with heightening racial tensions, compelled white southern liberals to clarify their position on segregation. Mark Ethridge's famous declaration at the FEPC hearings in Birmingham was reinforced in widely publicized articles and statements by southern journalists such as Virginius Dabney, Ralph McGill, and John Templeton Graves. Graves declared: "Segregation in the South is not going to be eliminated. This is a fact to be faced, but it does not preclude a constant improvement in the Negro side of jim crow." In 1942, McGill began qualifying his discussion of race relations in the South by asserting, "Anyone with an ounce of common sense must see . . . that separation of the two races must be maintained in the South." Southern liberals became part of what Odum described as the "new pro-South tempo," defenders of southern folkways and the "southern way of life," the white racial dreamworld in which the status of blacks was forever separate and inferior.[60]

Where one stood on the segregation issue became a test for legitimacy in what some regarded as the jealously guarded field of race relations in the South. Neither the NAACP nor the SCHW advocated or agitated for the immediate dismantling of the segregation system. Indeed, the NAACP's legal campaign to equalize teachers' salaries and provide equal access to publicly funded graduate and professional schools complemented southern liberals' pronounced commitment to ensure the equality promised under "separate but equal." And southern liberals supported the abolition of the poll tax, the central focus of the SCHW's lobbying activity. But both the SCHW and the NAACP were labeled as extremist by southern moderates because they failed to endorse the maintenance of segregation.

The SCHW, the NAACP, and Highlander Folk School were steadily redefining the debate. Although most white and black activists acknowledged that the end of segregation as a short-term goal would be self-defeating, they acted on the assumption that a racial caste system and a democratic society were "not only incompatible but impossible." SCHW and Highlander activists trusted that in the process of addressing common social and economic problems in the South through political education and interracial action, increasing numbers of whites would surmount their racial prejudices; the efforts of these activists slowly bore this out. To insist on an immediate end to segregation might have been unwise and unachievable. But to be apologists for the segregation system, even as a temporary political strategy to reassure whites, would have denied the fundamental purpose of their efforts.[61]

The ways in which the liberal obsession with segregation stiffened the contours of the old interracial movement were evident in the process that preceded the founding of the Southern Regional Council in 1944. In response to the worsening racial situation during the war years, Gordon Hancock, a black professor at Virginia Union University, and Jesse Daniel Ames, head of the Association of Southern Women for the Prevention of Lynching, initiated a series of meetings that aimed to broaden the dialogue among the CIC's constituency, the "better class" of both races. Three meetings were held in all, starting with an all-black meeting in Durham in October 1942, followed by an all-white meeting in Atlanta, and then a meeting of representatives from both groups in Richmond. The parties agreed, largely at Ames's insistence, that federal employees and northern blacks be excluded from the gatherings. Will Alexander argued, to no avail, that such a policy wrongly suggested that southern racial concerns could be examined apart from a national context. As an employee of the Roosevelt administration, Alexander was barred from the discussions.[62]

Black delegates did not follow Ames's recommendation that they avoid the segregation issue. They began the "Durham Manifesto" by stating, forthrightly, their opposition to the principle and practice of compulsory segregation. But they did not argue for its immediate dismantling, focusing instead on specific economic, social, and political reforms for immediate attention and action. Meeting in Atlanta, their white counterparts worried lest they be labeled a racial equality organization. At Ralph McGill's request, a stenographer recorded the meeting to ensure that no one's position was misrepresented. The Atlanta group emphasized the importance of accommodating a broad consensus of white opinion. They resolved that the South had a responsibility to administer segregation laws equitably and advised that this could be done by appealing to white goodwill and self-interest. Commenting on the Atlanta gathering, the *Crisis* magazine said the discussion was helpful but was limited by an outdated mindset. "Guardianship," the *Crisis* advised, "is no substitute for citizenship."[63]

When the delegates from Durham and Atlanta met in Richmond, blacks and whites voluntarily segregated themselves by race, suggesting deeper divisions. In a letter written to Virginius Dabney before the Richmond meeting, the patient, accommodating Gordon Hancock expressed his dismay at the failure of the Atlanta group to even consider the end of racial segregation as an ultimate goal. Dabney interpreted such a suggestion as an "all-or-nothing" attitude and emphasized the need to reassure whites who feared that the aim of such discussions was the end of segregation. Dabney failed to acknowledge his own expectations. After news of the Hancock-Dabney exchange circulated, McGill and several other white participants decided to avoid the Richmond meeting. Black frustration spilled over into the discussion at Richmond. Hancock warned the whites present that if the pace of change did not quicken, they would be forced to deal with northern black militants. Ashby Jones, a CIC founder, countered that Hancock's belligerent attitude risked alienating white allies. Howard Odum urged a more conciliatory approach on the part of the white participants. Even if they were "not sincere," he advised, white participants needed to say that they understood and appreciated working with "Negro leadership of the best type." Reporting on the subsequent establishment of Odum's long-awaited Southern Regional Council, J. Saunders Redding observed that the council was still "pretty effectively enslaved by the segregation issue." Its leaders were "worn gears" in what was, at best, "a reconditioned machine."[64]

Confined by racial and sectional identity, traditional white southern liberals had become apologists for the segregation system. In a 1943 essay, Thomas Sancton compared two strains of southern liberalism that had emerged during the war years. Sancton acknowledged that people like Virginius Dabney, Mark Ethridge, and John Templeton Graves had, in the past, contributed to a liberal spirit in the South. But he found it hardly comprehensible that these men could "in the midst of this Four Freedom War . . . state baldly that the Negro must always expect to be jim crowed in the South." Still in their fathers' shadow, he explained, they had retreated to the "liberalism of yielding, yielding on points of justice rather than an active . . . effort to create justice and extend it through the whole broad field of race relations." He did not question the sincerity of their stated concern that black people would suffer most if the racial situation continued to worsen. But Sancton suggested that their words and actions betrayed another motivation. "Deep down in his white soul," he had a less selfless fear of a time when "the race of serfs which he hoped to lead gradually to a higher plane of freedom and welfare" would suddenly slap "his friendly hands away and say 'the hell with you; I want democracy and I want it now.'"[65]

The emergence of a black-led movement for "full and unconditional equality of citizenship" created possibilities for a new liberalism capable of bringing "some order to the economic and racial chaos" created by "traditional politicians" of the South, Sancton wrote. The success of the movement would depend on the capacity of white southerners to move beyond racial prejudice and ideology and join with black southerners as allies in advancing the economic and political liberalization of the region. As black journalist Louis Martin explained in a 1942 article "To Be or Not to Be a Liberal," the true liberal was neither a friend nor a foe of black people but was one who believed and acted on the principles of democracy that were "everywhere professed." For the white southern liberal this was, he added, a heroic and revolutionary role.[66]

The new southern liberalism abandoned the notion of "self-reconstruc-tion"—a defining principle of traditional liberals—as legally, politically, and tactically flawed. A southern liberalism operating exclusively within the parameters of a caste system was mired in fatalism and doomed to power-lessness. The movements for change that had emerged during the New Deal era in conjunction with organizations such as the NAACP, the SCHW, the SNYC, and Highlander were reinforced by their interactions with the Roose-velt administration and liberal and labor groups outside of the South. Local organizing efforts were joined by lobbying on Capitol Hill for anti-poll-tax legislation and a permanent FEPC. As a result of the NAACP's legal campaign in the South, the Supreme Court had begun to enforce compliance with the intent of the Fourteenth and Fifteenth Amendments. More aggressive fed-eral action and support, Sancton wrote, was essential to securing the trans-formation of southern race relations and politics. "States Rights! Unless some administration in Washington gets the political and moral guts to make the race problem . . . the concern of the nation, the Negro faces hopeless odds." The South would remain "chained to the deadly ideology of another century."[67]

Gunnar Myrdal's *An American Dilemma: The Negro Problem and Ameri-can Democracy*, published in January 1944, gave resonance to the voices for change in the South. Researched and written during the war years, it docu-mented the pervasive, institutionalized nature of racial oppression in all facets of American life while capturing the dynamic and rapidly changing terrain of black protest and race relations. Myrdal's study established what an increasing number of Americans already acknowledged—that the denial of elemental civil and political rights to black Americans under the guise of "states' rights" betrayed and compromised the fundamental premise of a democratic society and was a problem of national and international conse-quence. The convergence of an aggressive black movement for full citizen-ship with the democratic rhetoric and aspirations of the war effort, Myrdal predicted, would make racial equity and justice the central challenge in defining the nature of America's postwar society. Myrdal was cautiously optimistic, anticipating that the revival and expansion of the progressive trends of the New Deal would reinforce and nationalize wartime civil rights efforts.[68]

As the end of the war approached, Franklin Roosevelt proclaimed a "sec-ond Bill of Rights," which promised to revive the New Deal and energize postwar liberalism. "True individual freedom," the president asserted in his 1944 State of the Union message "cannot exist without economic security and independence." The rights to a job, to decent housing, to adequate medi-

The future belongs to those who go down the line unswervingly for the liberal principles of both political democracy and economic democracy regardless of race, color or religion.

HENRY WALLACE, 1944 Democratic Convention

Thank God South Carolina is still part of the United States. Unless and until she once again secedes from the Union, she shall be compelled to obey the courts.

OSCEOLA McKAINE, May 1944

6

Democrats at the Crossroads, 1944

In April 1944, black newspaper publisher John McCray and his colleague George Elmore sat alone in the gallery of the South Carolina statehouse observing an emergency session of the state legislature. Governor Olin Johnston had convened the legislators immediately following the Supreme Court's *Smith v. Allwright* decision overturning the white primary. In South Carolina, where voting-age blacks were in the majority in nearly half of the state's forty-six counties, the governor pledged that he and the legislature would do whatever was necessary "to maintain white supremacy." The special session provided a forum for denouncing President Franklin Roosevelt, the New Deal, and "the dictatorship of the North." As McCray and Elmore looked on, the legislators affirmed that the Democratic

Party of South Carolina would remain a white man's party, and they proceeded to repeal all remaining laws referring to the Democratic Party and
primary elections so that the elections would remain completely separate
from state regulation.[1]

South Carolina, bastion of nullification and secession, led white southern
resistance to the Court's ruling on the white primary. The state's defiance
invigorated the movement among black Carolinians to obtain unrestricted
political rights. Starting with "fourth term for Roosevelt" clubs, John Mc-
Cray and Osceola McKaine organized the South Carolina Progressive Democratic Party (PDP) in the spring of 1944 to ensure that blacks could participate in all phases of the election that year. The PDP had the support of the
state leadership of the National Association for the Advancement of Colored
People (NAACP) and became, in effect, the "voters league" arm of that organization. In a hastily organized convention following the legislature's special
session, the PDP elected its own slate of delegates to represent South Carolina at the 1944 Democratic national convention. By the end of July, the
PDP claimed 45,000 members.[2]

Two delegations from South Carolina vying for recognition at the national convention threatened to explode the uneasy accommodation that the
national Democratic Party had maintained between its northern black constituency and its white supremacist southern wing. The PDP challenge, Mc-
Cray explained, was aimed at the national level: "[The] national [Demo-
cratic] Party is as responsible as the state party for the denial of membership
to Negroes in that it tolerates discrimination in the South." McCray warned
that if the PDP delegates were not seated, the Democrats would risk losing
black voters in key northern states. Senator Burnett Maybank, a leading
member of South Carolina's regular delegation, was equally blunt about the
implications of the PDP challenge. "As a Southern Democrat," Maybank
proclaimed, "I do not propose to be run out of my Party by either the
Negroes, the Communists or Northern agitators . . . it will be my purpose to
see that our Party stands where it always has—[for] states rights and white
supremacy."[3]

The Democratic National Committee (DNC) brought representatives of
the PDP to Washington one week before the convention in a futile effort
to discourage the challenge. Democratic National Committeeman Robert
Hannegan, vice-chairman Oscar Ewing, and black freshman Congressman
William Dawson met with three PDP members led by John McCray. Appealing to the PDP's allegiance to Franklin Roosevelt, they argued that a challenge to the regular delegation might rupture the party and cost the president the election. McCray recalled his response: "Gentlemen, we are going

to Chicago. Now if you care to, you can start talking from that point." The discussion continued. Ewing assured the PDP group that the Roosevelt administration would continue to work through the federal courts to secure full voting rights for blacks. The PDP, in turn, would make its challenge in Chicago but pledged to support Roosevelt's reelection regardless of the outcome. McCray reported that both sides had agreed to a course of action "of mutual benefit to the national Democratic Party and the PDP."[4]

On the Monday of convention week, the PDP delegation and several of the regular South Carolina delegates, led by Senator Maybank, arrived in Chicago for a conference with DNC leaders. After hearing both sides, a closed meeting chaired by Oscar Ewing unanimously favored seating Senator Maybank's delegation. The PDP was disqualified because it had neglected to follow party rules that required precinct and county meetings as preliminary to the establishment of a party and the selection of delegates. The PDP abided by the DNC's decision and did not take its fight to the credentials committee. However, it did try to find a black delegate or a delegate representing organized labor to present its case on the floor of the convention. McCray recalled that the handful of black delegates had no power and that the labor people were caught up in the struggle to renominate Vice-President Henry Wallace. "Plus," he continued, "South Carolina was one of those states. Anyone who had any sense steered around us. Like Mississippi."[5]

Although they failed to dislodge the regular delegation, PDP organizers took satisfaction in having carried their challenge to Chicago. Their effort to organize South Carolina's black voters into an alternative statewide Democratic Party continued. For southern conservatives, the defeat of the PDP challenge was but a footnote to the broader struggle over the future of the Democratic Party and their place in it, particularly in the wake of the *Smith v. Allwright* decision and the emergence of the Congress of Industrial Organizations Political Action Committee (CIO-PAC) as a force in national politics. Vice-President Henry Wallace, however, loomed as the primary target of southern Democrats determined to hold their ground.

In accounts of the 1944 Democratic convention, the unprecedented challenge by an all-black delegation has been overshadowed by the contest over the vice-presidential nomination and the emergence of Harry Truman as Roosevelt's heir apparent. But these developments were interrelated in important ways. The politics surrounding Truman's victory and the defeat of Wallace reflected the growing polarization within the national Democratic Party between the constituencies mobilized by the New Deal. By 1944, Wallace personified the New Deal and the coalition of black, labor, and urban voters that challenged the dominance of conservative southerners. Despite its ultimate defeat, the movement to renominate Wallace, a movement orchestrated largely by the newly established CIO-PAC, created a momentum that carried the battle for a liberal, racially progressive Democratic Party beyond the Chicago convention.

Founded in the summer of 1943, the CIO-PAC rocked the political establishment and revived the sagging ranks of the New Deal coalition. "Everyone was gloomy when we started," CIO leader Sidney Hillman recalled. "Then liberals seemed to spring up from the ground everywhere." Hillman and his associates were engaged in building a political machine rooted in the national network of local CIO unions and city and state industrial councils and embracing liberals, progressives, and civil rights activists. The CIO-PAC divided the nation into fourteen regional centers and organized downward into states, cities, wards, and precincts. It created special divisions to concentrate on issues concerning blacks, women, and youth. In a brilliant stroke, Hillman established the National Citizens Political Action Committee (NCPAC) as the nonlabor affiliate of the CIO-PAC. NCPAC became an influence network, institutionalizing "the CIO's relationship to prominent opinion-making, policy-shaping, and power-dispensing circles in Washington and New York." *Time* magazine said that the CIO-PAC was "everything which all of labor's political movements in the past were not," that is, "sophisticated, thoroughly professional," and "backed with money, brains and an army of willing workers."[6]

"The People's Program of 1944," the CIO-PAC's platform, anticipated the challenges of postwar reconstruction, proposing an agenda that expanded on the program of economic and social security initiated by the New Deal. It was broad and derivative, projecting a vision of postwar America that had been popularized by the "Four Freedoms," by Henry Wallace's widely acclaimed 1942 speech "The Price of Free World Victory" (better known as "The Century of the Common Man"), and by Roosevelt's appeal for an "Economic Bill of Rights." Such aspirations were but the opening salvo in what promised to be a fierce political battle.

Organized, informed, and active voters, Hillman believed, were essential to meeting the entrenched power of southern conservatives and corporate lobbyists who dominated wartime Washington and the inner councils of the Democratic Party. Voter education, registration, and organization were at the core of CIO-PAC efforts. The CIO-PAC's Research Division pioneered new techniques of voter education and electioneering, paying "close attention to the ethnic complexities of American politics." It monitored national election trends to target how the CIO-PAC should allocate its resources; compiled and disseminated the voting records of members of Congress on key issues, such as the Soldiers Vote Bill; and devised special tactical approaches to reach women, black voters, and nationality groups. During 1944 the Research Division blanketed the nation with eighty-five million flyers and pamphlets. It was a political-information campaign of unmatched "cleverness, effectiveness and volume," wrote the *New York Times.*[7]

The CIO-PAC orchestrated an aggressive voter-registration effort. Union membership lists were broken down by ward and precinct to aid organizers in local get-out-the-vote campaigns. In many places the CIO-PAC moved voter-registration booths into the factories. The need for a concentrated voter-registration effort was most pressing in the South, where, as of March 1944, a mere 10 percent of the CIO's membership were registered voters. In localities throughout the region, the CIO-PAC aided union members in paying their poll tax and sponsored black and white fieldworkers to get out the vote.

One of the CIO-PAC's unique features, reported the *Chicago Defender*, was "its integration of Negroes" into its organization. Another unusual feature of this national liberal-labor organization was its inclusion of the so-called Solid South. Southern New Dealers affiliated with the National Committee to Abolish the Poll Tax (NCAPT), the Southern Conference for Human Welfare (SCHW), the NAACP, southern CIO unions, and other regional organizations staffed strategic CIO-PAC positions. Beanie Baldwin served as assistant chairman of the CIO-PAC; Palmer Weber was head of its Research Division; and Clark Foreman joined the CIO-PAC in the spring of 1944 as executive secretary of NCPAC. George Mitchell, who had worked with Baldwin in the Farm Security Administration (FSA), was director of the southern region. The CIO-PAC's southern program was suited to the peculiarities of the region. The effort to get out the vote implicitly challenged voting restrictions based on the poll tax and on race. In addition to paying poll taxes, the CIO-PAC made a deliberate effort to register black voters by working through the unions and by employing black field organizers. Henry Lee Moon worked in the national CIO-PAC office but spent much of 1944 in the South organizing black voters around key campaigns.[8]

The CIO-PAC scored several notable victories in the spring primary elections, during which it campaigned against three members of the House Un-American Activities Committee (HUAC). HUAC Chairman Martin Dies, who had charged Hillman with aspiring to be the next "Red Chief of America," withdrew from the primaries when it became clear that the CIO-PAC had organized strong opposition among the oil and ship workers in Dies's district. Dies's withdrawal came on the heels of the defeats of two other HUAC members, Joe Starnes of Alabama and Frank Costello of California. According to George Mitchell, the work of the CIO was key in swinging the vote to Albert Raines, Starnes's challenger. The CIO-PAC's strength and the viability of New Deal liberalism were also felt in other primary elections, most notably in senatorial primaries in Florida and Alabama, where the CIO-PAC concentrated resources and organizers. In both campaigns, challengers to Claude Pepper and Lister Hill linked the incumbents' strong New Deal records to the erosion of white supremacy. The resounding victories of Pepper and Hill were greeted as a measure of Roosevelt's enduring support in the South even as nascent "Dixiecrats" flirted with open revolt.[9]

Southerners waged their counterattack from Capitol Hill, spotlighting the CIO-PAC's "Russian-born" leader, floating charges of political subversion, and exposing the CIO-PAC's close connections with the Roosevelt administration through people such as former FSA administrator Beanie Baldwin. During the months leading up to the convention, the CIO-PAC took a relentless drumming from Rules Committee Chairman Howard W. Smith of Virginia, who accused the CIO-PAC of violating laws regulating campaign procedures and financing. An investigation by the Federal Bureau of Investigation (FBI) cleared the CIO-PAC of any wrongdoing, and Hillman convincingly answered CIO-PAC critics during his testimony before the Senate Committee on Privileges and Elections. By the time the Democratic convention convened in July, the CIO-PAC had invigorated the New Deal coalition, and Hillman had secured his place as one of the most powerful men in the Democratic Party.[10]

Rumblings among the southern delegations added to the suspense of what promised to be no ordinary Democratic convention. The dual-delegate challenge from South Carolina was matched by competing delegates from Texas, where an anti–New Deal faction won control of the state party machinery. Pro-Roosevelt delegates bolted and elected their own slate of delegates; the convention split the seats between the two groups. Mississippi, Louisiana, and Virginia pledged their delegates to Senator Harry Byrd of Virginia, the uncrowned leader of conservative southerners; Byrd delegates were also represented in four other state delegations. The Georgia delegation, led by liberal Governor Ellis Arnall, was the exception. It brought a full slate for Roosevelt and Vice-President Henry Wallace.[11]

With Roosevelt's nomination assured, the contest between the Democratic Party's competing constituencies focused on the vice-presidential nomination. Roosevelt's failing health and the speculation that he would not live to complete a fourth term heightened the stakes. Southern conservatives formed a solid block of opposition to the renomination of Wallace; they warned that his removal would be the minimal price for maintaining party unity. The CIO-PAC and black leaders were equally adamant in their support for Wallace. "Colored delegates have no second choice," said Congressman William Dawson. NAACP Secretary Walter White warned, "Any substitute for Wallace will be construed as further surrender to the reactionary Southerners by the Administration." That Wallace's bid for renomination was doomed by party insiders before the Democrats convened heightens the significance of what happened in Chicago and its consequences.[12]

Henry Agard Wallace was, by all accounts, a rare breed of politician. His rise to national prominence was one of the accidents of the New Deal. "Minds of his breadth of interest and learning have appeared in American public life rarely, if at all, since the days of Thomas Jefferson and the Adames," reported *Fortune* magazine in 1942. Wallace was one of the primary architects of the New Deal and its foremost propagandist. He believed that the ultimate success of the New Deal depended on a revolution in public attitudes toward government and politics. Roosevelt's reforms had initiated such a transformation by creating a powerful coalition of voters in support of an activist, socially responsive federal government. Wallace led the fight for the complete liberalization of the Democratic Party so that it might become an effective vehicle for advancing economic and political democracy and might offer a clear alternative to the conservatism of the Republican Party.[13]

Wallace was the third in a line of preeminent agrarian intellectuals and reformers. The Wallaces were progressive Republicans with roots stretching back to the abolitionist movement. Wallace's grandfather Henry Wallace and Wallace's father, Henry C. Wallace, led their Iowa communities in meeting the technological and nationalizing trends of the post–Civil War era. Their lives and politics were shaped by a sustained effort to modernize agricultural education and to organize farmers into an informed and effective political force. Through the Iowa Agricultural College, farmers associations, and the pages of *Wallace's Farmer*, they worked to promote scientific agriculture and its application. The Wallaces studied and explained those economic developments and structural changes that affected the livelihood of farmers but were beyond their immediate control. Positive intervention by the federal government, according to the Wallaces, was essential to countering the waste and inequity that accompanied rapid industrial growth, often at the expense of farmers. The eldest Wallace was a leader in the agrarian reform movement that swept the South and the Midwest in the late nineteenth century, but his support for Populism wavered as that movement was eclipsed by what he perceived as evangelical zeal and nostalgia. Though nominally Republicans, the Wallaces maintained a pragmatic political approach, informed by the tenets of the Social Gospel and a belief in popular democracy.

From his earliest days, Henry A. Wallace imbibed the agrarian culture and intellectual vitality that dominated the Wallace household. The expansive reach of Wallace's mind and an indomitable curiosity became defining characteristics. He was born in 1888 and was, as one biographer notes, to a large extent "a self-made technician and educated man." By the age of sixteen, Wallace was already a pioneer in the development of hybrid corn. He took his college degree at Iowa State, where he majored in agriculture and genetics but also pursued history, economics, mathematics, and religion, seeking a deeper understanding of subjects that interested him. He created his own field of specialization in early American civilizations and traced the adaptation of corn to changing climates and soils in the Americas. He hired a Drake University professor of mathematics to explain how calculus could be applied to determine the precise influence of rainfall on corn yield, and he became an expert in biometrics. During the summer of his twenty-first year, Wallace followed the migration of Midlanders west to California and reported on his three-month trip in a series of articles titled "On the Trail of the Corn Belt Farmer."[14]

Like his father and grandfather, Wallace could not avoid politics and public affairs, despite his natural inclination to the more contemplative and solitary pursuits of science, mathematics, and farming. As assistant editor and then editor of *Wallace's Farmer*, he continued to provide its readership with practical advice along with economic and political commentary and analysis. His father's appointment as secretary of agriculture in 1921 enabled the Wallaces to apply ideas that had long been percolating in the Iowa cornfields to problems that were national in scope. Henry C. Wallace modernized the Department of Agriculture and paved the way for federal assistance to agriculture. He enlisted the talents of leading economists and statisticians to chart a way out of the defeating cycle of price-production fluctuations that plagued agriculture, and he institutionalized the arrangement in the Bureau of Agricultural Economics. During his father's tenure as secretary, Henry A. became a leading participant in the emerging network of economists, agricultural leaders, and members of Congress who framed a national farm program.[15]

Wallace continued to spend stretches of time in Washington after his father's death in 1924, organizing support for the McNary-Haugen farm relief bill and for a series of bills to regulate farm output. As he lobbied southern and western agrarian representatives, he displayed what one contemporary called "a real nose for politics" and demonstrated great acumen and skill in building a coalition around a new approach to farm problems. Wallace found this aspect of politics challenging and worthwhile. But he lacked a strong party affiliation. The narrowly partisan focus of both parties inhibited the development of the kind of national leadership that Wallace believed was essential to meeting the challenges of a modern industrial society. The Republican Party's unswerving devotion to the laissez-faire business creed caused Wallace to end his tentative Republican affiliation. Wallace supported Robert M. La Follette's third-party candidacy in 1924 and supported Democratic candidate Al Smith in 1928, but only after Wallace failed to persuade Governor Frank Lowden of Illinois to run on a third-party ticket. Wallace, however, campaigned enthusiastically for Franklin Roosevelt in 1932. Roosevelt endorsed the basic farm program that had evolved since the 1920s. Moreover, Wallace believed that in meeting the economic emergency, Roosevelt was uniquely suited to orchestrate a long-overdue reordering of the country's political and economic system.[16]

Appointed secretary of agriculture in 1933, Wallace presided over what was arguably the most ambitious, innovative, and successful New Deal program. It drew on a wide and eclectic range of talents and interests, which included its traditional agribusiness constituency, the network of agrarian economists and service intellectuals that had grown up during the previous decade, and the new generation of urban intellectuals who provided the yeast of New Deal reformism. Under the Agricultural Adjustment Administration (AAA), the centerpiece of the farm program, farm prices rose steadily until the recession of 1938. The AAA involved hundreds of thousands of farmers in the planning and implementation of acreage reduction and in the setting of marketing quotas through county committees and farm clubs. Although the inherent localism and volunteerism of the program unavoidably bolstered the power of conservative rural pressure groups, the program also expanded economic democracy in consequential if often contradictory ways. The market-quota referendum of the late 1930s, which included all farmers on a one-man, one-vote basis, was an important departure for black and white sharecroppers in the South; political scientist Ralph Bunche saw it as a first step in the reenfranchisement of southern blacks.

Wallace and his advisers combined tough-minded realism with political agility and a questioning and pragmatic approach to the complex range of problems they confronted. Unlike the National Recovery Administration (NRA), which was dealt a fatal blow by the Supreme Court, the AAA quickly bounced back after the Court ended its first program. The AAA was revised, incorporating new programs and revising old ones as it went. Under Wallace's leadership, the Department of Agriculture managed to balance the need to maintain southern conservative support for the AAA, support critical to its success, with internal and external pressures to address the problems of tenant farmers and sharecroppers, often victims of AAA policies. The Resettlement Administration (later the FSA) consolidated and broadened the New Deal attack on rural poverty. In the process of expanding the reach of the farm program, Wallace exposed himself to southern rural poverty by taking a two-thousand-mile automobile trip along the back roads of the Mississippi Delta. It was a sobering experience, one with important consequences for his political development.[17]

Through speeches, pamphlets, and books, Wallace helped shape and define the meaning of the New Deal. He referred to it as the process of economic democracy, essential to redressing the "trail of economic insecurity and waste of human and natural resources" left in the wake of unbridled technological and industrial development. Wallace explained that in striking down the early New Deal program, the Supreme Court exemplified the obstacles that had persistently thwarted the development of a modern political economy. "Unity in the name of the general welfare has too long been delayed by those who have made the theory of [individual and] States Rights a refuge for anti-social activity," he wrote in *Whose Constitution*. The effective organization of agrarian interests and the growing strength of labor were important developments, but not sufficient. Politics and government, Wallace urged, must provide an arena, a mechanism for directing economic planning in behalf of the general welfare. The fundamental question before the American people, Wallace wrote in 1936, was whether the nation could preserve "the ability of our government to meet nationally the problems" that had become "national in scope."[18]

By 1940, Wallace represented the progressive, activist wing of an increasingly divided Democratic Party. Conservatives and party stalwarts like DNC member James Farley firmly opposed Wallace's candidacy for vice-president. New Deal administrator Harry Hopkins and cabinet secretary Harold Ickes tried to persuade the president to select someone else. But Roosevelt insisted on Wallace as his running mate and made his own acceptance of the presidential nomination conditional on his selection. Roosevelt told Labor Secretary Frances Perkins that he wanted Wallace as vice-president not only because Wallace had a strong following among liberals and labor but also because Wallace would help the "people with their political thinking." Eleanor Roosevelt, as her husband's emissary to the Democratic convention in Chicago, explained that if the strain of a third term proved to be too much, the president felt that Wallace was "the man who could carry on best" in times such as the present. The convention teetered on the verge of schism but finally endorsed the president's choice.[19]

Wallace transformed the office of the vice-president. *New York Times* reporter James Reston marveled that he had become "the administration's chief man on Capitol Hill, its defense chief, economic boss and no. 1 postwar planner." Reston noted, "He is not only Vice President, but 'Assistant President.'" Wartime mobilization expanded the challenges and possibilities facing the government; in his effort to reconcile both, Wallace went head to head with resurgent business interests and their conservative supporters in Congress. The contest was played out between the Bureau of Economic Warfare (BEW), which Wallace chaired, and the Commerce Department, headed by Texas oilman Jesse Jones. Impatient with Jones's "banker mentality," which frustrated loan applications and slowed procurement procedures, Wallace pushed to expand the scope of the BEW's authority and hasten the process. Jones and his constituency charged that Wallace was angling to internationalize the New Deal. Of particular concern was the modest labor-standard clause that the BEW included in procurement contracts with private companies in Latin America, providing for a minimum wage and health standards. Wallace held that such a provision was in accordance with the Atlantic Charter. The ongoing contest between Wallace and Jones, as many commentators noted, was one of the defining contests in wartime Washington. When it reached a critical impasse in the summer of 1943, Roosevelt bowed to conservative pressure and abolished the BEW.[20]

While Roosevelt substituted "Dr. Win the War" for "Dr. New Deal," Wallace tied the "Four Freedoms" aspirations of the war to a continuation and expansion of the New Deal in the postwar era. His May 1942 address "The Price of Free World Victory" was his manifesto. Using the metaphor of a continuing people's revolution, Wallace internationalized the vision and values that shaped his New Deal philosophy. The march toward freedom appealed to individual dignity and social justice, emphasized human rights over property rights, and strove toward cooperation over competition. Expanding on Roosevelt's "Four Freedoms," Wallace said that freedom from want was necessary to the realization of democratic freedom worldwide. It was technologically possible to ensure that all people had enough to eat. What was necessary was the political will to move beyond the selfish economic interests that drove the military and economic imperialism of the nineteenth century, leading the world to economic chaos and war. A secure peace would be one that sought to advance the general welfare worldwide. In a veiled reference to *Time* magazine publisher Henry Luce's proclamation of "the American century," Wallace countered that the postwar era must inaugurate the century of the common man. "There can be no privileged peoples," he warned. "We in the United States are no more a master race than the Nazis. And we cannot perpetuate economic warfare without planting the seeds of military warfare."[21]

By virtue of this speech, *Fortune* magazine declared that Wallace had emerged as "one of the major prophets of the postwar world." The speech was translated into twenty languages; federal agencies responded to requests for hundreds of thousands of copies. Supporters compared it to Lincoln's Gettysburg Address; Clare Booth Luce called it "globaloney." Assistant Secretary of State Adolph Berle chided Wallace for his "talk about revolutions." Commenting on the strong opposition the speech aroused, Wallace admitted that it "was a little like letting the genie out of the bottle" so far as the State Department and conservatives generally were concerned. At the same time, the speech enjoyed wide popular support and interest and was hailed by Eleanor Roosevelt and other leading liberals. Wallace continued to promote its themes and ideas, pressing for the Democratic Party to embrace its basic principles.[22]

Wallace's hopes for the postwar era anticipated that the Democratic Party could facilitate the political mobilization necessary to carry forward the progressive agenda of the New Deal. By the late 1930s he had also concluded that the future of liberalism and progressive reform would be doomed by continuing compromise with the anti–New Deal southern bloc. Relying on the ideology of states' rights, southern conservatives thwarted the democratic process down to its most basic element, the right to vote. So long as the power of conservative southerners remained unchecked, the region would remain an economic and political backwater, and the liberal coalition of the Democratic Party would be neutralized. Like Roosevelt, Wallace welcomed the rising tide of liberalism in the South and counted its political representatives, such as Claude Pepper, among his closest allies. But Wallace took the fight for a liberal South further than Roosevelt when he attacked racial discrimination as a central challenge to the effective workings of democracy in the South and in the nation.

Wallace's growing responsiveness to black concerns and racial issues was evident after the 1936 election. It was probably motivated by a combination of factors, including his trip through the rural South, the decision to pursue a more reformist course in the Department of Agriculture, and the dramatic crossover of black voters into the Democratic Party. But his credibility as a sincere spokesman for racial justice was earned by his response to the rise of fascism in Europe. On Lincoln's birthday in 1939 Wallace delivered a major address in New York. "The Genetic Basis of Democracy" attacked ideas of racial superiority as unscientific and explored the political and economic motivations for racial prejudice. Germany provided a horrific example of a society consciously and systematically promoting the idea of racial supremacy. Wallace debunked the basis of such a theory, observing that no nationality in Europe was a greater "mixture of tribes and breeds" than the Germans. He asked his audience to consider the roots of fascism and confront those conditions that threatened the survival of democracy in America. Reflecting on his tour through the South, Wallace observed that ignorance and economic distress were the breeding grounds for demagogues. He dismissed the idea that poor whites were genetically inferior. They were the products of bad diets and poor education, living in "tumble down cabins" and enduring a monotonous daily routine that easily led to hatred and violence. Racial and economic prejudice represented a failure of America's political and economic system. Wallace expanded on the themes of this speech when he went to Tuskegee later in the year to visit agriculturalist George Washington Carver, whom he had known since childhood. He told a mostly black audience of farmers and educators that one of the most effective ways of strengthening democracy was to end prejudice, whether racial, religious, or economic.[23]

By 1940 Wallace had articulated strong racial concerns and integrated them into his vision for democratic reform in a way that was unprecedented for a national political figure in the twentieth century. He was an active supporter of black America's wartime "Double V" campaign. Addressing the all-black Capitol Press Club, the vice-president insisted that winning the war abroad must also mean winning the war at home against bigotry, prejudice, and lack of opportunity. He talked about the discrimination and brutalities heaped on black soldiers and observed that the necessity of such a discussion, "in the midst of a war to preserve and extend democracy," was "a particularly unhappy commentary upon the practice of democracy in our own country." He continued, "It seems incredulous that we should have to say over and over . . . the simple truths that Negroes in America . . . are among the members of our oldest families, that they have made vast contributions in labor and loyalty to America and that they are entitled to the rights and privileges of Americans . . . but say it we must."[24]

Wartime racial violence peaked in Detroit in July 1943 with a riot that claimed the lives of twenty-five blacks and nine whites. Wallace visited the city several days after the riot and addressed a crowd of twenty thousand people. His speech placed the issue of racial justice and tolerance at the center of the challenges facing America in the postwar world. "Education for tolerance will be just as important as the production of television," Wallace predicted. The choice was between extending democracy, social safeguards, and educational and economic opportunity for all or returning to abundance for the few. America's ability to practice democracy at home would determine the nature of its leadership in securing the peace abroad. "We cannot plead for equality of opportunity for people everywhere and overlook the denial of the right to vote for millions of our own people," Wallace explained. He praised the efforts of organized labor to enlighten public opinion and warned that racial and antilabor violence were the tools of powerful groups hoping to use the war emergency to roll back the social gains of the previous decade. Wallace appealed to the schools, the churches, and the press to join in educating the American people about "the fundamental decencies and understandings" that were essential if U.S. power was "to be a blessing to the world and not a curse."[25]

Wallace's Detroit speech drew a decidedly mixed response. It articulated the hopes and aspirations that the CIO and progressive New Dealers harbored for the postwar period, and it won their broad support. The *Birmingham World* echoed a common response among African Americans when it praised Wallace's message as one of "vision and courage." The *New York Times*, by contrast, called parts of the speech "reckless" and warned that Wallace's appeal to the "ultra-liberals" would jeopardize his prospects for renomination in 1944. Others joined the chorus, calling Wallace "an extreme liberal," "an impractical idealist," "the creature of radical New Dealers and the CIO." For his part, Roosevelt said the speech was "splendid" and commented on its favorable reception in most quarters, adding, "You drew blood from the Cave Dwellers!"[26]

By the time the Democratic convention met in Chicago the following summer, Henry Wallace's candidacy, more than any other issue, defined the divisions within the Democratic Party. A Gallup poll on the eve of the convention reported that Wallace was the three-to-one favorite among Democratic voters nationally and that he commanded a substantial degree of southern support, 43 percent according to a 6 June Gallup poll. Significantly, his strongest support had shifted from rural America to urban-industrial areas. Among the rank and file of the Democratic Party, support for Wallace was much broader in 1944 than it had been in 1940. But in terms of Democratic Party officials, opposition to Wallace's candidacy for another term as vice-president was stronger and more determined than it had been in 1940. And, unlike in 1940, Roosevelt declined to resist the tide running against Wallace among the Democratic Party leadership. When the convention opened in mid-July, the party machinery was in gear to defeat Wallace's renomination and offer Harry Truman in his stead, though Roosevelt remained noncommittal publicly.

The outcome of the convention seemed anything but inevitable when the delegates arrived in Chicago. Energy, expectations, and ambitions ran high. The drama that unfolded threatened to reel beyond the control of DNC chairman Robert Hannegan and his collaborators. Just as Hannegan was completing the carefully scripted plan for Truman's nomination, Wallace arrived in Chicago prepared to lead his own fight. He told a jammed press conference that he was in it "to the finish." When asked about the president's feeble endorsement, Wallace replied that Roosevelt had done all he expected the president to do; he agreed with the president that "there should be nothing in the nature of dictation." Reporters speculated that the majority of delegates were for Wallace. The CIO-PAC was prepared to provide the pro-Wallace forces with organizational support. CIO-PAC members numbered nearly one hundred delegates or alternates, and the CIO was represented on each of the major convention committees. Indeed, the CIO-PAC was the "wild card" in a political ritual long dominated by back-room deals and party bosses.[27]

Wallace took the offensive on the opening day of the convention. In a ringing speech seconding the nomination of Franklin D. Roosevelt, he told the delegates that the Democratic Party must be a liberal party; its future depended on it. Republicans had the best conservative brains and the wealthiest corporate supporters. Liberalism, Wallace explained, was an affirmative philosophy based on "both political democracy and economic democracy regardless of race, color or religion." Southerners, one newsman reported, "got a heaping dose of brine in their open wounds as Henry Wallace, no longer ill at ease, rubbed the word 'liberal' eleven times in his brief platform appearance." Wallace proclaimed: "In a political, educational and economic sense, there must be no inferior races. The poll tax must go. Equal educational opportunities must come. The future must bring equal wages for equal work regardless of sex or race." Several southern delegates walked out of the convention hall. An English editor described Wallace's speech as more than an endorsement of the social program of the New Deal; it was "a startling act of courage," for Wallace defied the South. In his vision for the future of the Democratic Party, Wallace made it clear that the party could no longer accommodate the conservative and racially discriminatory practices of southern Democrats.[28]

Wallace's speech "got the most honest ovation of the convention, three minutes of real cheering," reported *Time* magazine. Robert Hannegan quickly called a press conference and endorsed Harry Truman. Meanwhile

CIO-PAC delegates, under the direction of Beanie Baldwin, were working to mobilize delegate support for Wallace. Finding no organizational support behind Wallace, Baldwin hastily convened a meeting of CIO-PAC regional directors that evening to plan a strategy and recruited Claude Pepper, Pennsylvania Senator Joseph Guffey, Georgia Governor Ellis Arnall, and Oscar Chapman, assistant secretary of the Department of the Interior, to manage the campaign for Wallace on the floor of the convention. They were joined by Harold Ickes who, having realized that the anti-Wallace campaign had the active support of the urban bosses, led a revolt of the Illinois delegation into the Wallace camp.[29]

On Thursday evening Roosevelt's acceptance speech was broadcast into the convention hall from the West Coast, where the president was inspecting defense installations. After his speech, CIO-PAC delegates from every corner of the stadium began parading and chanting, "We want Wallace." The action quickly grew into an enormous floor demonstration. Mayor Ed Kelley had packed the galleries with some five thousand "loyal Democrats" from Chicago, only to have them join in the demonstration for Wallace. Osgood Williams, of the Georgia delegation, recalled: "The convention floor was packed to the danger point. Those delegates really wanted Wallace. They really wanted him. . . . there was total dedication and commitment. . . . It was perfectly apparent that if a vote was taken, Wallace would have gotten the nomination in spite of Roosevelt."[30]

As the demonstration gained in volume and enthusiasm, Claude Pepper also concluded that if Wallace's name was put into nomination that night, he could carry the convention. Pepper moved to get recognition from the convention chairman, Senator Sam Jackson. Jackson ignored Pepper and would not turn on his microphone. Pepper recalled, "I jumped up, waved my banner and everything, and he wouldn't pay me any attention; he knew what I was after." So Pepper pushed through the crowd and made his way to the platform. Meanwhile, Hannegan and Mayor Kelly told Jackson to adjourn the convention. When Jackson protested that "the crowd was too hot," Hannegan insisted. Just as Pepper reached the top step of the platform, the chair motioned that the convention be adjourned. The stadium "rocked with a chorus of no." Jackson announced, "The ayes have it."[31]

Hannegan and his legions worked through the night whipping delegations into line, reportedly backed up by direct calls from the president. J. P. Mooney, CIO-PAC member and Alabama delegate, recalled that he and future governor and Alabama delegate-at-large James Folsom were summoned to Sidney Hillman's suite shortly before dawn. Hillman, choosing to be on the inside of the party leadership's consensus, had agreed to support Truman before the convention but had not interfered with the CIO-PAC's efforts in behalf of Wallace. However, he advised the Alabama delegates and all other CIO affiliates that if Wallace did not make it on the first ballot, they should vote for Truman.[32]

When the convention opened on Friday, Harry Truman joined Hannegan under the speakers' stand and greeted a parade of delegates for three hours. The vice-presidential nominating process began later that afternoon. In an effort to avoid a repeat of Thursday evening's demonstration, Mayor Kelly tightened restrictions on entry to the hall, and convention managers put a clamp on the organ. But even in a half-filled stadium, demonstrations erupted every time Wallace's name was mentioned, and a fifteen-minute demonstration greeted his nomination. Governor Arnall of Georgia and Senator Pepper of Florida seconded Wallace's nomination. Pepper challenged the delegates, "Let us not tell the democratic people of the world that Henry Wallace is too democratic for a Democratic national convention." Wallace led the balloting with 439 votes, Truman took 319, and favorite sons held the balance with 393. There was no recess. The second ballot followed immediately, excluding ticket holders for the evening session. Wallace's lieutenants, most of whom were on the convention floor for the first time, were no match for the seasoned professionals. With the galleries practically empty, Truman swept the convention with 1,031 votes; Wallace trailed with 105.[33]

Wallace's supporters felt cheated by the way victory was snatched from their candidate and were dismayed by the president's acquiescence if not active collaboration in the deed. Mark Ethridge, editor of the *Louisville Courier-Journal* and former member of the Fair Employment Practices Committee (FEPC), told Roosevelt that the president had made "the biggest moral and political mistake of [his] career." Speaking as a native Mississippian, Ethridge explained, "The Southern revolt . . . was the revolt of the Ku Klux minded and the tight-minded Bourbons against a New Deal they never liked and were determined to knife whenever they got the chance." He endorsed Pepper's claim that Wallace "bore the scars of many a dagger" aimed at the president. Roosevelt's role in the Chicago maneuverings left Ethridge "sick and bewildered." How could the Democratic Party "have any moral force or expect to appeal to people who value moral force" when it played "the shell game"? Whatever Roosevelt had gained by "giving into the revolters and the bosses" had been lost in the "heart" that Roosevelt had taken out of the people. They were "disillusioned . . . and angry that the combination of southern white supremacy and northern political cynicism was appeased."[34]

For black Americans, the Chicago convention prompted a searching examination of their uneasy alliance with the Democratic Party. The memory of New Deal gains and hopes that had drawn blacks to the party of Roosevelt was receding in the wake of current realities: discrimination in the armed forces; the failure of the Roosevelt administration to aggressively enforce the Fair Employment Practices Act; the president's silence in the face of wartime race riots. As the *Pittsburgh Courier* headline announced "Democrats Sell Race, Wallace to Buy South," many speculated how black voters should and would respond, particularly in large northern states where the black vote was often pivotal.[35]

Black Americans had looked to the Democratic convention to adopt a strong racial plank and to renominate Wallace. The *Chicago Defender* called the convention's watered-down racial plank "a masterpiece of evasion"; Walter White called it a splinter. But it was Wallace's defeat that was most disturbing. "It was Wallace," said the *Defender*, "who represented more than any platform exactly what the Negro wanted from the Democratic Party. . . . Wallace was the platform." Charles Houston protested "the way the Democrats ditched Wallace." Houston added, "He represents the progressive position colored people must support." Historian Rayford Logan called Wallace's defeat a "tragic blow to the cause of liberalism and democracy" and doubted whether either party contained "sufficiently strong elements to implement the Declaration of Independence [or] the fourteenth and fifteenth amendments." Logan speculated on the need for a third party combining liberal elements from both major parties, from the Socialist Party, and from other "lovers of true democracy," but he added that organizing such a party would be "almost impossible." Walter White wondered if "the debacle at Chicago" would "be enough to stir up decent people to a realization of their peril."[36]

Although many Democrats felt betrayed, Wallace's strong showing at the convention provided liberals with renewed hope and direction. Senator George Norris said that Wallace was riding a progressive wave that might "well have carried him over the political reefs" if it had not been "for the determined opposition of the Party leaders." Never before in American history, reported the *New Republic*, had someone "so far to the progressive left so sweepingly received the approval of the large mass of people . . . nor even come close to breaking the hold of the professional politicians." Claiming that Wallace had surpassed Roosevelt in stature, the NAACP's Walter White predicted that Wallace's courage and integrity would help keep faith in the democratic process alive. With his convention speech, wrote the *Chicago Defender*, Wallace had provided progressive Democrats with a "sterling platform" to guide them in the battles to come. Political commentator Bruce Bliven expressed a widely held sentiment when, in the aftermath of Chicago, he concluded that liberals were in a stronger position politically than they had ever been.[37]

The CIO-PAC and NCPAC provided the primary institutional structure for organizing the liberal and progressive elements of the Democratic Party into an integrated political movement. Throughout the fall campaign season, the CIO-PAC continued to distinguish itself as a major political force. "Hillman's committee," as its opponents disparagingly called it, was noted for being more viligant and successful than traditional Democratic organizations and a formidable rival to old-line political machines in getting out the vote. Analysts credited the CIO-PAC's registration drive with causing a much larger voter turnout than expected, which was in Roosevelt's favor. Roosevelt received 53 percent of the vote, his smallest majority in four elections. The CIO-PAC's effort may well have provided the margin between victory and defeat. By the end of 1944, supporters and critics agreed that, for the moment at least, the CIO-PAC occupied a position of tremendous strategic importance in American politics. One analyst speculated, "The PAC twins . . . may well be riding a tidal wave which will sweep away traditional alignments and profoundly change existing political patterns."[38]

Could the CIO-PAC sustain the momentum generated by the 1944 campaign and build a political movement capable of countering the conservative ascendancy in the Democratic Party? What happened in the South would be a determining factor. Following a tour of the region before the fall election, Henry Wallace observed, "A spirit of liberalism is abroad in the South." And he added, "If we are to have a great liberal party in this country the South must participate." Within a week after the election, Clark Foreman and SCHW Executive Secretary James Dombrowski, who had taken leave from the SCHW to work in NCPAC's national office during the campaign, submitted a proposal to the board of the CIO-PAC analyzing the political situation in the South and outlining a strategy for realizing the CIO-PAC's objectives in the region. The proposal emphasized that close attention to the southern situation was essential to advancing the CIO-PAC's program nationally.[39]

Southern obstructionism, Foreman and Dombrowski explained, could easily be the undoing of the revival of progressive forces evident in the 1944 campaign. The power of southern conservative Democrats in Congress remained largely unchecked and unchallenged. There, acting in concert with Republicans, they led in rolling back the gains of labor, in thwarting the extension of social welfare legislation, and in sponsoring laws that would constrict the sphere of legitimate political activity. These efforts were matched on the state level. Southern state legislatures were hotbeds of antilabor legislation, threatening to neutralize the dramatic gains scored by organized labor during the war. As the result of an intensive lobbying campaign by a fundamentalist, right-wing organization called "Christian America," voters in Florida and Arkansas had already adopted "Right to Work" constitutional amendments. Similar legislation was pending in Texas, Louisiana, Tennessee, Mississippi, and Alabama.

The South of political reaction, the South of Theodore Bilbo, Martin Dies, and Harry Byrd, was a potent brew of racism and antilabor appeals. It "spoke the loudest," had "the heaviest financial backing," and with "the advantage of a Congressional forum," got the most publicity. But in actuality it represented a minority of southerners, the scant 20 percent who went to the polls. What of the other South, the "silent South," the great majority of southerners who remained disfranchised by the poll tax, the white primary (in spite of the Supreme Court ruling), and a host of other legal and extralegal restrictions, as well as the consequences of decades of political exclusion? Here lay the seedbed for a genuinely liberal and progressive movement. Moreover, in the aftermath of the changes released by the New Deal and World War II, the potential was ripe for realization.[40]

The report explored the combination of developments that had created a window of opportunity in the South, an opening toward liberalism and political democratization. The nationalizing trends of the previous decade and "the logic of the South's economic development" drove it in a liberal direction. No other region had benefited more from the New Deal or from the infusion of federal dollars during the war. Industrial growth and federal activism supported the rapid growth of the labor movement, creating possibilities for new political alliances and constituencies. By 1944, union membership in the South reached 400,000 for the CIO and 1.8 million for the American Federation of Labor (AFL). Beyond expanding the ranks of industrial unionism, the national CIO's firm stand against racial discrimination had created an arena for interracial action and had won the respect and support of black southerners, who composed one-third of the South's population. The efforts of organized labor and the progressivism of the New Deal also reinforced and complemented the growth of southern liberalism. By 1944 indigenous groups of progressive ministers, editors, educators, and writers were evident in communities throughout the region.[41]

Yet these developments did not make the liberalization of the region's political structure inevitable. As evident in the early success of the right-to-work movement and in state defiance of the *Smith v. Allwright* ruling, the forces of economic and political reaction remained entrenched and beyond serious electoral challenge. An organized campaign to enfranchise the disfranchised was essential to reaping the changes of the previous decade and resisting the conservative reaction that had already begun. To be effective, it would have to be waged on two fronts. The report of Foreman and Dombrowski endorsed the continuation and expansion of legal efforts to enforce the white primary decision and of lobbying campaigns in Congress and the state legislatures to repeal the poll tax. A simultaneous effort to expand voter registration and participation was equally important and, in the short term, vital to sustaining a progressive movement and building support for the removal of voter restrictions. The report outlined the key Senate and statewide races coming up in 1946, stressing the urgent need for quick and decisive action on voter registration.

Foreman and Dombrowski concluded by proposing a plan for mobilizing the liberal South for political action through the SCHW. The plan combined a public relations drive to present the essential facts about the South in the areas of politics, economics, and race relations with an organized campaign to eliminate franchise restrictions and get voters to the polls. In essence, the techniques pioneered so successfully by the CIO-PAC were to be "adapted to the South by Southerners." As a preliminary step, the SCHW proposed to organize statewide committees of liberals to cooperate with labor in lobbying state legislatures and in organizing voter-education and voter-registration drives. The memo concluded by requesting that the CIO help fund the expansion of the SCHW program in what would effectively be an extension of the CIO-PAC's southern operation.[42]

Palmer Weber, Beanie Baldwin, and Lucy Randolph Mason lobbied in behalf of the Foreman-Dombrowski proposal, which had the support of Eleanor Roosevelt and CIO President Philip Murray. Late in November the executive board of the CIO unanimously endorsed the SCHW as "the natural and appropriate spearhead of liberal forces in the South" and recommended that the CIO support the SCHW in its efforts to end discrimination, maximize the region's voting population, and "express the true liberalism of our great southern states." By the end of the year, CIO unions had pledged thirty-five thousand dollars to the SCHW for 1945, helping to launch the SCHW on its most ambitious period.[43]

Following the Chicago convention, the PDP held its own convention and nominated Osceola McKaine for the U.S. Senate. McKaine's candidacy was a part of the PDP's evolving program of black voter registration and its effort to build a new Democratic Party in South Carolina. The PDP embarked on a statewide campaign, organizing from the precinct level up, sponsoring county conventions and establishing PDP clubs. It solicited funds from black veterans and native South Carolinians living in other states to support what it claimed was the opening wedge in the movement to restore full political rights to black southerners. The PDP also sought to educate white South Carolinians and "show them the Negro that Mr. Smith ["Cotton" Ed Smith] and Mr. Johnston [senatorial nominee-elect Olin D. Johnston]" did not know. The PDP welcomed white support and expressions of interest. But as John McCray emphasized, "Our [main] purpose in South Carolina is to vote."[44]

Osceola McKaine was the first black man to run for statewide office in South Carolina since Reconstruction. His candidacy challenged Governor Olin Johnston, the Democratic Party's candidate for the Senate seat of "Cotton" Ed Smith. From late summer through the fall, McKaine campaigned in nearly every county. He reminded his listeners of the critical importance of black political participation to democratic movements present and past. The proud history of black Carolinians during Reconstruction was woven through his speeches as McKaine recited the "awakening of progressive forces" stirred by Roosevelt and the New Deal. Those forces, he explained, had been heightened during the "Four Freedoms War" and given eloquent voice by Henry Wallace, who had supported the struggle of black people "even when he knew that perhaps his advocacy of equal opportunity for Negroes in all fields would cost him the nomination for vice-president of the United States." The nationalizing influence of the New Deal and the war had penetrated the South, changing many white southerners and emboldening others to express their democratic convictions openly, providing crucial allies in the movement for full citizenship. McKaine was careful not to paint an overly optimistic picture. The struggle to vote would be "painful, bitter, without glamour . . . a continuing struggle." But if black men and women rejected the idea of being a "ruled" group, they "must be willing to make every sacrifice necessary to obtain the right to vote."[45]

The PDP's ambitious fall campaign was met by a variety of devices to deter black voter registration and by widespread fraud and intimidation on election day. McKaine's supporters reported that the ballots the PDP had printed and distributed to polling places throughout the state were not available in many voting stations. In the only state that did not have a secret ballot, many first-time voters were simply handed the lily-white ticket or were not given any ballot at all. In Richland County, prospective voters had to beg for the PDP ticket. Others reported that the police who were assigned to precincts attempted to influence blacks to vote certain tickets or mark the PDP ballot in such a way as to invalidate it. In Greenville County, most of the PDP ballots were not counted. The actual votes McKaine might have received, or actually received, cannot be known; according to the state's tally, McKaine scored 3,214 votes.

Reporting on the election to NAACP Legal Counsel Thurgood Marshall, John McCray wrote: "We have had a hell of a job beating down the fear in these people, in getting their trust and hopes and don't intend to see them come down with their ballot . . . to be robbed, intimidated and frustrated." The PDP and the state NAACP organized the collection of affidavits documenting irregularities and illegal practices during the registration period and the general election. Marshall submitted the affidavits to the Justice Department, along with a brief requesting that criminal action be taken against state election officials in South Carolina. Meanwhile, McKaine and the PDP contested the seating of Olin Johnston in the U.S. Senate, charging unfair election practices. The Senate failed to investigate the complaints, and the Justice Department did not bring any charges against South Carolina's elected officials.[46]

The PDP remained undefeated. Like the efforts of Wallace's supporters in 1944, the efforts of the PDP were not confined by conventional measures of political success. Both groups engaged the changes and possibilities created by the New Deal and the war as they sought to complete the liberal-labor realignment initiated by the New Deal. If the Democratic Party was to provide the national vehicle for framing these efforts, the South stood as the primary battleground for carrying them forward. During 1945 and 1946, the CIO-PAC, the SCHW, the PDP, the NAACP, and a host of other organizations coalesced in a regionwide movement to democratize southern politics. Early in 1945 at a voting rally in Birmingham, Alabama, McKaine remembered those "first bright days of Reconstruction [when] the legislatures controlled by the newly freed slaves and the emancipated poor whites gave to our region its first democratic governments." It was time, he said, for "history to repeat itself."[47]

For the Negro the summer and fall elections of 1946 offer the best opportunity to advance which he has had in a generation. In most southern states the ballot box is open to him, and in every southern state the liberal organizations, representing the divided [white] South, are depending upon him.

LUTHER P. JACKSON, 11 May 1946

I keep remembering that every day, every conversation in the field is a necessary investment, something no one ever tried before, at least not in the South. Whether we break through this time or not, we are going to break through sometime.

PALMER WEBER, August 1946

7

Organizing the Southern Movement

VOTER REGISTRATION AND POLITICAL ACTION, 1945–1946

Max Lerner voiced an opinion common among political commentators when he noted early in 1946 that the South would be pivotal in determining whether Congress was "really Democratic or Republocratic." Those Democrats who had joined with Republicans to roll back the New Deal—Democrats such as Senator Theodore Bilbo of Mississippi, Senator Harry Byrd of Virginia, and Senator Kenneth McKellar of Tennessee— still dominated the Washington scene. But the region's political direction in the aftermath of the war was less than certain. It was the region, Lerner wrote, that was "still most fluid politically," that still had "to come to political consciousness." It could "move in almost any political direction." Union membership had more than doubled during the previous five years, and the Congress of Industrial Organizations (CIO) and the American Federation of Labor (AFL) each launched major organizing drives during 1946. In many states, blacks voted in the Democratic primary for the first time in 1946. Returning veterans also added a new dimension to the region's political landscape.[1]

Labor and civil rights activists were cautiously optimistic. During the preceding decade a combination of forces had created an opening for racial tolerance and political democracy in a society steeped in segregation and white supremacy. New Deal programs, CIO organizers, lawyers for the National Association for the Advancement of Colored People (NAACP), liberal newspapermen, and Socialists and Communists had, in the words of social scientist St. Clair Drake, "softened up the South." The war accelerated the pace of change in all areas of southern life, creating new expectations and broadening the possibilities for change. Paralleling the growth of organized labor during the war, the southern civil rights movement scored impressive gains in the courts and in the field. In June 1946, the Supreme Court ruled in favor of NAACP plaintiff Irene Morgan and barred racial segregation in interstate travel. Moreover, the Justice Department's recently established Civil Rights Division suggested that the federal government was prepared to assist in enforcing court rulings. Citing a ruling by the Fifth Circuit Court of Appeals, the solicitor general of the Justice Department announced in the spring of 1946 that any state or party official who attempted to prevent a person from voting due to race would be prosecuted by the Justice Department under the criminal code.[2]

During 1945 and 1946, the NAACP, the CIO Political Action Committee (CIO-PAC), the Southern Negro Youth Congress (SNYC), and the newly established state committees of the Southern Conference for Human Welfare (SCHW) created a loose regional coalition to promote the democratization of southern politics. This effort complemented the CIO's ambitious postwar organizing drive. But it was a separate endeavor, committed primarily to organizing a biracial political movement capable of challenging the conservative control of state Democratic parties. Fieldworkers for the sponsoring organizations supported voter-education and voter-registration efforts, linked individuals and communities throughout the South, and played a critical role in gathering information on local political developments and the status of race relations. Such efforts helped to focus national attention on liberal political movements in the South as segregationists fought to hold their ground.

Though motivated by the vision of a biracial democracy, organizers had to work within the constraints of a segregated society. Race, as a social, legal, and cultural reality, had shaped the political consciousness of white and black southerners for generations. For white southerners, politics had long been the vehicle for maintaining white privilege and states' rights. The political sensibility of black southerners was informed by a belief in racial equality and federally protected citizenship rights; it sustained the undercurrent of resistance to the segregation system. Thus, in the movement of the mid-1940s, black and white southerners offered different kinds of opportunities and challenges to those who worked to move the South beyond the politics of racial difference.

Blacks were "the generating force" of the southern movement, voting-rights activist Virginia Durr explained. The NAACP's legal successes, along with the growth of NAACP branches, black civic organizations, and biracial unions, broadened the parameters for black activism. Henry Lee Moon, who went south as a field organizer for the CIO-PAC during 1944–46, marveled at the changes that had taken place since he had last been in Alabama in the late twenties. At that time Moon had been a young administrator at Tuskegee Institute. His determination to resist Alabama's system of disfranchisement had been discouraged by colleagues who warned that his lonely protest could only bring dire consequences. "My thoughts," he recalled, "were beyond my real capacity to act." Some fifteen years later, the changes were astounding. Everywhere he went, Moon found "a politically inspired people . . . who were registered and making the fight to get more registered." He reported, "Negro groups, sometimes in collaboration with labor and progressive groups, sometimes alone, were setting up schools to instruct new voters in the intricacies of registration, marking the ballot, and manipulating the voting machine."[3]

Ella Baker expanded on her work as director of branches for the NAACP. During 1945 and 1946 she convened a series of regional leadership-training conferences for NAACP branch leaders, whose ranks had multiplied during the war years. Montgomery NAACP officials E. D. Nixon and Rosa Parks were among the participants in the 1946 meeting in Jacksonville, Florida. Baker emphasized the importance of backing up the legal victories that had been "won against the white primaries with vigorous voter registration and education campaigns." She urged cooperation with the CIO-PAC and other progressive organizations, particularly the SCHW and its newly hired field secretary, Osceola McKaine.[4]

Osceola McKaine was, according to Henry Lee Moon, "easily the most outstanding and effective mentor in the southwide drive." Palmer Weber had vivid memories of McKaine as a brilliant organizer and as a tall, physically imposing man, "so black he was blue." McKaine's personal experience embodied the determination and hopes of several generations. At fifty-two years of age, he had spent most of his life seeking the freedom and opportunity denied African Americans. McKaine left his native Sumter, South Carolina, in his early teens to obtain an education in the North. He served in France during World War I and won a commission as a first lieutenant, one of the first of his race to be so designated. It was a distinction he held proudly; associates called him "lieutenant" for many years thereafter.[5]

Like many of his contemporaries, McKaine experienced a heightening of his racial consciousness during his service in France, where black soldiers were the target of racist propaganda and assault leveled by their white comrades-in-arms. McKaine and several fellow officers founded the "League for Democracy" in Le Mans, France, for their "mutual protection and advancement." After the war, the New York–based league sought to build "a thoroughly coordinated, organized effort" to keep the militant spirit of the race alive and make "democracy safe for the Negro." The league held mass meetings, established chapters, lobbied for an end to all forms of discrimination in the military, and supported demands for full voting rights, equal economic opportunity, antilynching legislation, and an end to Jim Crow. McKaine served as the national field secretary and was among the organization's most popular speakers. He won the attention of U.S. military intelligence as "an energetic young man of excellent education and ability" and was singled out for advocating that blacks meet violence with violence.[6]

The anti-black violence and racial repression that swept the nation in 1919 became intolerable for McKaine. "He was very angry . . . militant," his brother recalled. "He had no stomach for what was going on."[7] He finally left New York and returned to Europe, settling in Ghent, Belgium, where he opened a supper club. It won wide acclaim for its "exclusive clientele and floor shows of high quality." McKaine became fluent in four languages and traveled widely in Europe, enjoying a freedom that would have been impossible in America. His twenty-year sojourn in Europe, however, came to an abrupt end when Hitler invaded Belgium. After nearly a thirty-year absence, McKaine returned to his hometown of Sumter.[8]

The racial atmosphere in Sumter in 1939 was better than McKaine had anticipated, but the level of political activity in the black community was minimal. He led the revitalization of the Sumter branch of the NAACP and served as its executive secretary. Responding to the national NAACP campaign to equalize teachers' salaries, McKaine raised money—from ten prominent black businessmen in Sumter—to travel the state and organize

South Carolina's teachers and their communities behind a legal challenge. McKaine became acquainted with publisher John McCray and joined his *Columbia Lighthouse and Informer* as associate editor, beginning a partnership that energized black activism throughout the state, particularly through the organization of the Progressive Democratic Party (PDP).

McKaine joined the SCHW as a field organizer early in 1946. Clark Foreman and Jim Dombrowski had discussed the position with McKaine and with John McCray in light of the great success of the PDP in organizing black voters in South Carolina. They also consulted with Luther Jackson, head of the Virginia Voters League. Jackson's teaching schedule at Virginia State University and McCray's responsibilities as publisher of the *Lighthouse and Informer* limited their ability to travel through the South for extended periods. Moreover, of the three, McKaine was the most experienced organizer. McKaine welcomed the opportunity to extend his efforts beyond South Carolina and appeal to the expectations of a new postwar generation.[9]

McKaine's first tour as SCHW field secretary in January 1946 began in Birmingham, Alabama, where he participated in what was probably the first organized march for voting rights in the city. In a striking public display, one hundred black World War II veterans, dressed in their uniforms and carrying their discharge papers, marched through the main streets of Birmingham to the courthouse, where they planned to register to vote. "Lieutenant" McKaine accompanied them, as did Louis Burnham of the SNYC. When the board of registrars requested that the veterans interpret parts of the constitution, they refused; Alabama merely required the ability to read as a condition of registration. Nevertheless, the board rejected the majority of the veterans. Burnham appealed to white veterans, who had fought fascism, to support the fight for democracy on the home front. The black veterans who had been turned away filed an appeal in the circuit court.[10]

Travels throughout the South during 1946 offered McKaine a window on the growth of black political activity and the fluidity of race relations. He was, noted Jim Dombrowski, a very practical operator. He organized his schedule around local voter-registration periods and primary elections. Before his arrival, he sent instructions to the secretaries of each state SCHW committee, advising them what needed to be done before his visit in order to facilitate his work. This included the preparation of a list of the names and addresses of the following: "the heads of all ministerial alliances or associations (and the days, places and hour of their assemblage); the heads of city and county teachers associations, college fraternities, sororities, Elks, Masons, medical educational associations, labor unions, civic groups, educational institutions, PTAs, important political and social clubs, beauticians,

Above. Osceola McKaine (*third from left*) with the staff of the supper club he owned and managed in Ghent, Belgium, during the interwar years. After Hitler invaded Belgium in 1939, McKaine returned to Sumter, South Carolina, and became a leading organizer of the movement to expand black participation in the electoral process. (Photograph courtesy of the South Caroliniana Library, University of South Carolina)

Facing page. John McCray, publisher of the *Columbia Lighthouse and Informer* and chairman of the South Carolina Progressive Democratic Party, addressing the SNYC-sponsored Youth Legislature, held in Columbia, South Carolina, in October 1946. Clark Foreman, president of the Southern Conference for Human Welfare, and Rose Mae Withers, chair of the Southern Negro Youth Congress, are seated to the left. (Photograph courtesy of the South Caroliniana Library, University of South Carolina)

Top. "Lend a hand to Dixieland." The New York Committee of the Southern Conference for Human Welfare was organized in 1945 to focus national attention on the struggle in the South and to raise money for the Southern Conference's efforts. Branson Price (*third from left*) was the executive secretary of the New York office. (Photograph courtesy of Branson Price)

Bottom. North Carolina students formed a Wallace for President Committee in August 1947, following Wallace's visit to Chapel Hill. Marge Frantz (*seated near center with her back to the camera*) was a primary organizer of students for Wallace. (Photograph courtesy of Marge Frantz)

YMCAS, YWCAS, USOs and businessmen's organizations. Also printers prepared to do rush work." McKaine requested the names of people willing to permit the use of their automobiles free of charge or at a minimum price "to help a good cause." Temporary office space was also needed, with access to a telephone, possibly in the office of a doctor, newspaper, or labor union. For housing he preferred "a modest home with bath and telephone." He explained: "In the finer homes there is likely to be too much entertaining and long drawn-out conversations, with libations late into the night. . . . As a rule, Negro hotels are noisy, very expensive and with few facilities." McKaine emphasized the need for quiet, uninterrupted rest after "14 or 15 hours of hard work."[11]

McKaine reported from Norfolk, Virginia, "The Negro and labor groups . . . are very active politically and are fervidly seeking political direction." There was great interest in the SCHW, and McKaine attended many "bull sessions" to discuss its program and philosophy. He noted that Jerry O. Gilliam, "Negro head of the Eureka Lodge with 1700 members," gave McKaine five dollars and "promised to involve his organization to the fullest extent." The Eureka Lodge had donated five hundred dollars to support legislation for a permanent Fair Employment Practices Committee (FEPC) and two hundred dollars to the anti-poll-tax campaign.

Following McKaine's visit, S. H. Bell, district manager of the Southern Aid Society of Virginia, an insurance company, wrote Dombrowski that McKaine had provided several organizations with "wonderful assistance in putting over certain community projects." He reported that several blacks in Norfolk had decided to run a black candidate in the city council election in June and requested that McKaine return to help. "We feel certain that he can be of great assistance in formulating the strategy and charting the blue print for us to follow." Dombrowski responded that McKaine was already scheduled in Tennessee in mid-April and in North Carolina until 12 May but could visit Norfolk after then. In June, Victor J. Ashe, a black candidate for the Norfolk City Council, placed seventh in a field of nine. He polled 2,967 votes, which included nearly all of the black vote and roughly 500 votes from whites.[12]

McKaine visited every southern state. His field reports described a veritable sea change in the political aspirations of black southerners. During a short registration drive in Birmingham, the number of black voters more than doubled. The last voters McKaine helped to register in Birmingham were two black firemen employed by the L&N Railroad; they each had to pay thirty-six dollars in cumulative poll taxes in order to register. But they were willing to pay the fee because they believed that voting was essential to protecting their right to work and ultimately in removing the barriers that prevented them from becoming engineers. "Such actions and motives," McKaine reported, "can be multiplied by the hundreds." A seventeen-day registration drive in Savannah boosted the number of black voters from 8,000 to 20,000. The black vote grew from 1,200 to 4,900 in Augusta and aided in the defeat of the "Cracker" machine of Roy Harris, who had dominated county politics for fifteen years. In Durham, a twelve-day drive saw the number of black voters climb from "a doubtful 3,000" to "an effective 5,500." In each case, the gains took place in spite of delaying tactics on the part of registrars.[13]

This "third revolution," as McKaine called it, was fueled by a change at the most fundamental level. People had come to a new understanding: "The use and nonuse of the ballot can determine whether they have a job or become jobless; whether they shall have adequate schools and school bus transportation for their children or whether the present handicaps to their educational and personality development shall continue or become intensified." As growing numbers sought to secure the vote, black leaders acted with courage and boldness in advocating political action to improve the conditions of the group. The 1946 registration drives had demonstrated the effectiveness of organization: "An aggressive and energetic leadership can and will increase the number of Negro voters in an area or city despite all previous conditions or attitudes which have exerted influence to keep that vote limited." Furthermore, McKaine observed that the growth of black political strength enabled white southern liberals to be "more vocal, more consistent and more steadfast in their efforts to bring democracy to Dixie."[14]

V. O. Key described the SCHW as "one of the most conspicuous agencies in exciting the electorate" in the immediate postwar years. SCHW state committees provided a base for organizing black and white southerners around a program of political action. During 1945, the SCHW established state affiliates in Georgia, Virginia, Alabama, and North Carolina, state organizing committees in South Carolina, Louisiana, Texas, Arkansas, Tennessee, and Florida, and SCHW chapters in New Orleans, Memphis, Columbia, and other cities. The Southern Patriot, the SCHW's monthly newspaper, helped knit these groups together. It reported on political events and activities in southern states and in Washington, monitored state and federal legislation, and published in-depth reviews of the status of public health and public education in the southern states, underscoring the consequences of segregation for blacks and for the region at large. From 1943 to 1945, the Patriot's circulation tripled, to more than seventeen thousand.[15]

Endorsement of the SCHW southern organizing effort by the CIO was seconded by the NAACP's executive board late in 1944 and by attorney Thurgood Marshall. During 1946, local and state organizations gained over one thousand members a month. Though drawn mostly from the middle class, membership and leadership varied from state to state, reflecting the particular concerns and political configurations of each place. These groups, however, were distinguished by their biracial composition, the prominent role of women, a strong support for organized labor and fair employment, and an emphasis on political action at the local and state levels. It was, Jim Dombrowski recalled, a hopeful time, when "a great spirit of reciprocity and cooperation" united and inspired the Left.[16]

Georgia was one of the most promising arenas for liberal political action in the South. Ellis Arnall galvanized civic-minded groups in Georgia when he challenged Eugene Talmadge for the governorship in 1942 and won by a wide margin. Arnall was an active proponent of electoral reform. Early in his term, he lowered the voting age to eighteen; in February 1945 he persuaded overwhelming majorities in both houses to vote to abolish the poll tax. The *Atlanta Constitution* called the poll tax repeal "a symbol of an awakening in the South." Clark Foreman hailed Arnall's "bold progressivism" and predicted that the end of the poll tax in Georgia would boost voter participation among blacks and whites.[17]

Publicly, Arnall did not stray far from the racial prejudices of most white Georgians. He made his support of segregation clear during the 1942 campaign, and he called the Texas white primary decision a "blow to liberalism." But as Arnall's liberal support became more secure and his national stature grew, he responded positively to the reality of an expanding black electorate. When the U.S. Supreme Court declined to review *Chapman v. King*, a ruling that struck down efforts by the Democratic Committee in Macon to bar blacks from the primary elections, Arnall refused to call a special session of the legislature to repeal the state primary laws. He declared that he would not be party to any "subterfuge scheme" to prevent blacks from voting, thus ensuring that the 1946 primary elections would be open to blacks in Georgia. A. T. Walden, a leading black lawyer and founder of the Georgia Association of Democratic Clubs, said that black Georgians generally felt Arnall was "honest and sincere in his expressed liberal views and actions." Walden added, "They think he is as liberal as it is possible for a white man to be and hold public office in the South."[18]

The SCHW's Committee for Georgia worked to build a statewide political organization capable of sustaining and expanding Arnall's reform initiatives. Headquartered in Atlanta, it drew on traditions of civic activism in the black and white communities. Lucy Randolph Mason served as vice-chairman of the group, and Benjamin Mays, president of Morehouse College, was secretary-treasurer. Board members included Grace Hamilton, director of the Atlanta Urban League and a leading black voting-rights activist, Josephine Wilkins of the Georgia Fact-Finding Committee and the League for Women Voters, and CIO Director Charles Gilman.

Margaret Fisher, a native of Andrews, North Carolina, was the acting director of the Georgia committee. She had worked as the regional liaison officer between the War Manpower Commission and the FEPC during the war and then for the Southern Regional Council. Fisher left the council to go to work for the Georgia committee because it offered an opportunity to push beyond racial barriers and establish a political base of operation for young progressive southerners. Only in her mid-twenties, she was, by most accounts, a seasoned political operative who combined savvy with the finely honed skills of a stump speaker. She campaigned before civic, religious, and labor groups for "more and better schools, expanded public health services, increased employment opportunities, an unrestricted ballot . . . [and] more adequate housing . . . in order to have a healthy, prosperous and democratic state."[19]

Reporting on the possibilities created by the SCHW in Georgia, Lucy Randolph Mason exclaimed, "We are touching tap roots of democracy in this state and are going to release new forces for good and right." The Georgia committee orchestrated a public-information campaign through a variety of publications including a monthly newsletter, "Let the People Know," and a pamphlet, "Your Part in Georgia Politics," published in cooperation with the League of Women Voters. Through organized letter-writing campaigns and work in the Georgia statehouse, the Georgia committee lobbied representatives on a variety of issues, including opposition to right-to-work legislation and the Georgia white primary bill. Commenting on the work of the committee, CIO-PAC Regional Director Dan Powell proclaimed that the citizens of Georgia were "politicized as not since the days of Watson and the Populist movement."[20]

The "machine rule" of Senator Harry Byrd provided the rallying point for progressive Democrats in Virginia, where only 11 percent of eligible voters were registered. Virginia Durr and Luther Porter Jackson, leading strategists in the voting-rights movement, cochaired the SCHW's Committee for Virginia. Jackson, a professor of history at Virginia State University, was the founder and director of the Virginia Voters League, a statewide black voter-registration organization. The SCHW's national office allocated one thousand dollars to the Virginia committee specifically for black voter registration. Jackson divided the funds among black activists throughout the state.

The committee's executive board included black and white representatives from colleges, businesses, and labor. Black participants included P. B. Young, publisher of the *Norfolk Journal and Guide* and FEPC commissioner, Vivian Carter Mason, executive director of the National Council of Negro Women, and Jerry Gilliam, a Norfolk postman. Boyd Patton, the statewide director of the CIO, and Charles Webber, state director of the CIO-PAC, were among the labor representatives. Other board members included a veteran of the woman's suffrage movement, rector of the Episcopal Church in Hampton, a professor from William and Mary College, and the president of a paper company in Richmond. Moss Plunkett, the leading organizer of liberal Democrats in opposition to the Byrd machine and candidate for governor in 1945, worked closely with the committee's executive director, Virginia Beecher, the wife of poet John Beecher.[21]

Senator Harry Byrd had reigned as the political boss of Virginia for nearly two decades. He presided over a closely knit state Democratic organization of seventeen thousand officeholders and commanded their complete loyalty. In 1946, when a group of independent Democrats attempted to participate in a Norfolk meeting to elect delegates to a statewide Democratic Party convention, they were ignored and then finally evicted from the hall. When they convened outside the hall, party leaders ordered the streetlights turned off. The group met in the glow of cigarette lighters and flashlights.[22]

In 1946, the CIO-PAC and the Committee for Virginia supported Richmond attorney Martin A. Hutchinson to run against Byrd in the Democratic primary. It was the first time Byrd had had any opposition since he was elected to the U.S. Senate in 1933. Byrd, who bragged that his hand-picked governor, William M. Tuck, was the nation's number-one strike-breaker, led the coalition of antilabor Democrats and Republicans. Although few expected Hutchinson to break the grip of the Byrd machine, observers anticipated a strong showing on the part of Byrd's opponent, who was expected to draw support from labor, black voters, and veterans. One of the most promising developments during the primary season was the registration of forty thousand blacks despite the obstructive tactics of Virginia registrars.[23]

Based in Birmingham, the SCHW's Committee for Alabama continued much of the work initiated during the 1930s by the Communist Party and CIO activists around civil liberties and voter registration. Among the leading members of the committee were Louis Burnham of the SNYC, New Deal administrator Aubrey Williams, who returned to Alabama in 1945 as publisher of the *Southern Farmer*, and Pauline and Malcolm Dobbs, who served consecutively as the committee's executive director. The Alabama committee had additional chapters in Montgomery, Mobile, and the University of Alabama at Tuscaloosa.

The Alabama committee's emphasis on voter registration and education complemented the efforts of the NAACP and its Birmingham representative, attorney Arthur Shores, who had systematically challenged discriminatory registration practices since 1937. Shores's procedure served as a model for other NAACP branches in Alabama. The threat of successful litigation often resulted in the registration of the plaintiffs. Representatives of the Alabama committee monitored the registrar's office in an effort to pressure registrars to treat blacks fairly. Malcolm Dobbs accompanied the black veterans who marched to the courthouse in Birmingham to register to vote in January 1946, and he assisted with the legal challenge made by veterans whose applications were rejected.[24]

Palmer Weber and Clark Foreman recruited Mary Price to organize the SCHW state committee in North Carolina. Price, a native North Carolinian, had spent her teen years in Chapel Hill before moving to New York in the 1930s. She returned to Chapel Hill in 1945 and, with the support of University of North Carolina President Frank Graham, organized what was probably the largest and most active state committee. Rev. Lee Shepard, a Baptist minister at one of the largest churches in Durham, chaired the Committee for North Carolina. Lawrence Wallace, a businessman and state senator, served as vice-chair, along with Charlotte Hawkins Brown, founder and president of Palmer Memorial Institute. Other black board members included the newspaper publisher Louis Austin, Durham attorney and NAACP counsel Conrad Pearson, and G. W. Logan, a Durham businessman. The membership included seven college presidents, a handful of manufacturers, industrial workers, domestic workers, small business owners, and a large college student contingent, many of whom were veterans. A number of individuals supported the committee financially but declined to have their names publicly associated with the organization.

Like the other state committees, the North Carolina committee concentrated its resources on increasing voter education and registration and lobbying the state legislature. Mary Price spent half of her time in Raleigh as a registered lobbyist, campaigning for minimum-wage legislation for workers not covered by federal legislation, for appropriations to equalize educational expenditures for both races, and for opposition to right-to-work legislation. *Citizens in Action*, a monthly committee publication, examined public issues and informed readers of voter registration dates and procedures.

The North Carolina committee sponsored a statewide voter-education effort and monitored voter registration. When registrars in Surry County refused to register two black veterans, Price protested to the county board of elections. She reminded local officials of a recent case in Washington, North Carolina, in which a registrar was convicted by a grand jury for refusing to register a black man and was sentenced to a prison term. The veterans, who were students at A&T College, were finally registered, along with thirty other black people in the predominantly white rural county.[25]

John Hope Franklin, then a young professor at North Carolina College for Negroes, was on the North Carolina committee. One of his most vivid memories of that time points to another dimension of the role of the SCHW as an agent of change. Recounting a committee meeting at the Washington Duke Hotel in Durham, Franklin recalled that when lunchtime came, the hotel refused to serve the black members of the group in the dining room. In response, white members "went out to the white places and brought food in and we all ate together. For the 1940s this was real wild stuff . . . but they did it. That's the kind of thing Mary Price and them were doing."[26]

The SCHW's success in establishing a regional presence was dependent in large part on the financial support of the CIO. At the same time, the SCHW program of voter education and political organization was important to advancing the CIO's agenda. In 1944 CIO President Philip Murray announced that the drive to organize southern workers was "a civil rights program . . . which not only encompassed the organization of workers into unions . . . but the freedom of southern workers from economic and political bondage [and] . . . to exclude . . . from the South all types of racial and other forms of discrimination." The CIO had made significant breakthroughs in southern-based industries and recruited large numbers of black workers, especially in industries such as mining and metals, tobacco, and maritime. These unions produced a corps of politically progressive organizers, white and black, and they worked closely with the CIO-PAC and the SCHW.[27]

Whereas wartime industrial growth secured the CIO's presence in the South, it also deepened the racial discrimination and tensions that plagued the southern labor movement. Rural whites, with no union experience, swelled the ranks of organized labor during 1942 and 1943 and "transformed the political dynamic of the industrial union movement." Union education programs could not begin to meet the demand created by the war. Meanwhile, as black expectations rose, the color line hardened. Occupational segregation, unequal wage scales, and discriminatory job classifications characterized wartime industries, the FEPC notwithstanding. The AFL policy of racial exclusion ensured that blacks were frozen out of the expanded lines of skilled crafts generated by the war.[28]

Postwar adjustments aggravated racial hostilities. Competition for jobs increased as war industries disbanded and veterans returned home. Cutbacks in overtime hours and rising inflation squeezed wages. Starting late in 1945, worker anxiety and resentment exploded into a year-long wave of strikes across the nation. In the South, however, the internal contest over the racial terms of unionism threatened to immobilize the CIO as it prepared for its most ambitious organizing drive. Relatively few white unionists had embraced the CIO's vision of a racially egalitarian union movement. As blacks became more assertive in the workplace and the political arena, many whites retreated to the defense of racial privilege. The Ku Klux Klan resumed open activities early in 1946. Manufacturers, politicians, and the AFL stoked white fears in their effort to discredit the CIO as a subversive organization.

Racial polarization enhanced the position of conservative CIO leaders who were inclined to accommodate organized labor's largest constituency in the South, white workers. They could convincingly argue that any challenge to white racism was a futile and potentially fatal diversion from union building in the segregated South. Conservative unionists warned that the AFL stood ready to make even greater inroads in the South at the expense of the CIO's alleged racial liberalism, an important consideration as the CIO finalized plans for its southern organizing drive.

Launched in May 1946, "Operation Dixie" carried out this conservative approach. Van Bittner, director of the southern drive, presided over a tightly run operation. Staff members and fieldworkers were not permitted any formal affiliation with the CIO-PAC. Bittner excluded left-wing trade unionists and turned down the offer of Highlander Folk School to assist with training. There were more black organizers working for the AFL's southern organizing drive than for the CIO's. Operation Dixie concentrated its limited staff and resources on the textile industry as key to success in the South. Ironically, some of the CIO's most important gains were among black workers concentrated in other industries.[29]

As the CIO moved to the right, the CIO-PAC sought to expand black and white cooperation in the political arena. Palmer Weber was the primary strategist for the CIO-PAC's southern effort. Since his earliest days as a student radical, Weber had challenged the ideology of white supremacy and its institutional and social manifestations—as a labor organizer, a congressional staff member, a lobbyist for the National Committee to Abolish the Poll Tax, and research director for the CIO-PAC. In the process, he helped to weave a network of black and white activists for whom full racial justice and equality was fundamental to any program for economic and political reform. The NAACP acknowledged Weber's unique role in 1946 when it elected him to the national executive board; he was the first white southern man to serve on the national board.

The demise of the all-white primary created a critical opportunity to organize a coalition of black and white voters through the Democratic primary. The liberalization of southern politics, Weber had long argued, was dependent on the growing strength of the black vote and a fuller appreciation among liberal whites of its progressive potential. In 1946, the potential for a large black voter turnout was greater than at any other time since the turn of the century. Weber, who traveled extensively through the South during the first half of 1946, focused heavily on supporting black voter registration and participation. In January he accompanied Mary McLeod Bethune on a ten-day SCHW-sponsored tour of major southern cities, a trip that combined public rallies to get out the vote and private meetings with local black leaders. The CIO-PAC helped fund organizers to work with NAACP state conferences of branches on voter registration, and Weber prevailed on CIO-PAC Chairman Sidney Hillman to send Henry Lee Moon south as a full-time organizer for the CIO-PAC.

Working with a shoestring budget and a handful of field organizers, the CIO-PAC's effort among union members won wide support among black workers and tested the limits of racial tolerance among white southern workers. Sharing a platform with Osceola McKaine at a mass meeting in Columbia, South Carolina, Weber proclaimed that the CIO drive was "the best thing" that had "happened in the South since the Civil War." But he stressed the importance of a no-discrimination policy as a fundamental principle of the CIO and warned that the CIO was "doomed if the Negro and white workers fail[ed] to come to a sympathetic understanding." When Weber delivered a similar speech before a group of white steelworkers in Alabama, they threatened to kill him if he ever returned. In April 1946 Luther P. Jackson reported that the CIO-PAC was spreading in the South as fast as it could recruit members, black and white. Its visibility and its success sharpened the lines between CIO-PAC activists and the organizers of Operation Dixie.[30]

Shortly after Operation Dixie began, an exchange between McKaine and the CIO national office exposed the widening gulf between the CIO and its progressive affiliates. In a private letter to CIO Vice-President Allen S. Haywood, McKaine welcomed the start of the CIO's southern drive. However, he expressed concern that a number of white organizers in the South failed to act in accordance with the CIO's policy barring racial discrimination. "The attitudes of certain . . . white CIO organizers in this region . . . could readily be mistaken for AFL or Railway Brotherhood if one judged them by their racial attitudes and approaches." McKaine advised that they "be told that the CIO expects them . . . whenever and wherever . . . possible to practice what the CIO professes."[31]

McKaine's letter coincided with a Harlem rally to raise money for the CIO's southern organizing effort. In a public statement that aimed to disassociate Operation Dixie from the Harlem event, Bittner charged, "No crowd, whether Communist, Socialist or anyone else will be permitted to mix up in this campaign." In response to McKaine's letter, he added, "And that goes for the Southern Conference for Human Welfare or any other organization living off the CIO."[32]

Bittner's outburst signaled that the national CIO was reevaluating the political alliance it had forged with southern progressives and civil rights activists. In the short term, however, Bittner retreated and reassured SCHW officials of his desire to cooperate with the organization. A fragile truce prevailed during 1946 as the CIO-PAC, the SCHW, and the NAACP concentrated their energies and attention on southern primary races. Gubernatorial contests in Georgia, Alabama, and Texas provide a measure of these efforts and suggest emerging patterns of postwar southern politics.

Georgia's primary season was preceded by a special congressional election in Atlanta in February 1946 to fill a vacated seat. It was the first election since the abolition of the poll tax. Since the challenge to Georgia's white primary was still pending in the courts, the special election in Atlanta offered a unique opportunity for black voters to test their strength in the general election. The NAACP, the Atlanta Civic and Political League, the *Atlanta Daily World*, and other groups organized a voter-registration campaign that more than doubled the number of registered black voters in the city, from 3,000 to 6,876. Tom Camp, who had the support of Georgia Power and the Georgia Railroad Association, was the favored candidate, followed by Helen Mankin.[33]

Mankin was distinguished by her liberal record as a state legislator and as sponsor of Georgia's labor and child welfare legislation. She won the endorsement of the CIO-PAC and the SCHW's Georgia committee and actively courted the black vote. At their invitation, she met with black leaders at the Butler Street Young Men's Christian Association (YMCA), whereas Camp neglected to respond at all. The Camp campaign did not raise the race issue but did charge that Mankin was supported by a front for "New York East Side Communists," the CIO-PAC. Black leaders carefully navigated the racially charged politics of 1946 and waited until the eve of the election to recommend Mankin to the black electorate. After the polls closed on election day, Camp led by 156 votes with all but one precinct reporting. The final precinct was Ashby Street School, comprising a large black community adjacent to Atlanta University. When those votes were counted, Mankin had won by 800 votes.[34]

The race issue moved to the center of Georgia politics in April 1946 when the Supreme Court upheld a lower court decision that blacks were entitled to vote in Georgia's Democratic primary. The *Atlanta Constitution* reported that the Court's decision heightened prospects that Georgia would be the first Deep South state to witness the mass enfranchisement of blacks. Georgia House Speaker Roy Harris and former Governor Eugene Talmadge immediately began laying their individual plans to ride the issue of black voting to the governor's mansion. Harris, a twenty-four-year veteran of the legislature, was known as the smartest organizational man in Georgia politics. He had managed the successful gubernatorial campaigns of E. D. Rivers and Ellis Arnall, both considered to be "New Deal" governors, and Harris himself had a relatively liberal record. But in April 1946 he made the restoration of the white primary the central issue of his reelection campaign in Augusta and demonstrated his ability to "outholler Talmadge on the Negro issue."[35]

As mentioned earlier, Osceola McKaine aided in a voter-registration drive in Augusta that boosted the number of registered black voters to 4,700. Although Harris's opponent, newspaper publisher William Morris, defeated the incumbent by nearly 5,000 votes, the *Atlanta Constitution* estimated that only 2,000 of them came from black voters. In many wards, blacks were left standing in line at the polls all day, only to be turned away when the polls closed. But Harris blamed his loss on "5,000 Negroes who were instructed by an Atlanta Negro attorney just how to vote." He predicted that there would be 12,000 blacks registered to vote by 1 July and warned, "The things they advocate will wreck and destroy this state."[36]

After Harris failed to win reelection to the state legislature, he chose not to run for governor and joined former rival Eugene Talmadge's campaign. Talmadge revived his sagging political fortunes by running on a platform that promised the people of Georgia "a Democratic white primary, unfettered and unhampered by radical, communist and alien influences." Pointing to Harris's defeat, he cautioned what would happen if blacks continued to vote in the primary: "You will have to go to their homes . . . shake hands with all of them, and kiss their babies if you want to be elected. If you don't want to do this you will have to voluntarily retire from office and let the scalawags take charge." He foretold the result if white people failed to maintain control of Georgia: "Our jim crow laws are gone, and our pretty white children will be going to school with Negroes, sitting in the same desk."[37]

Black leaders throughout Georgia had been preparing for an open primary since the Supreme Court had ruled on *Smith v. Allwright* two years earlier. In June 1944, Atlanta attorney A. T. Walden led in establishing the Georgia Association of Democratic Clubs, which included fifty-five clubs statewide. These clubs provided the nucleus for local registration efforts, which accelerated in anticipation of the 17 July primary. Atlanta blacks established the All Citizens Registration Committee to coordinate the registration efforts of various community groups and organizations. The committee divided black neighborhoods into wards, precincts, and census tracts and blocks, assigning workers for each of the twelve hundred blocks where black families lived. Nearly nine hundred volunteers canvassed door to door, collecting the names of registered voters and urging the unregistered to register. This effort was reinforced by weekly pleas from the pulpit. When the books closed on 4 May the number of registered black voters in Atlanta's Fulton County had increased from slightly less than 7,000 to 24,137. Statewide, the number of registered black voters climbed from 20,000 to 135,000. This figure represented 20 percent of the state's black population, a percentage that far exceeded the proportion of registered black voters in any other southern state.[38]

Despite the vastly increased number of black voters on the rolls, none of the gubernatorial candidates addressed a black audience. Talmadge's opponents, James Carmichael and E. D. Rivers, avoided any hint of racial liberalism. Carmichael, who was supported by the liberal Arnall faction, declared in his opening campaign statement, "While I believe in helping the Negro . . . I will never . . . permit the mixing of the races in Georgia . . . in any manner . . . which violates southern traditions." Carmichael did pledge to obey the Court's decision on the white primary.[39]

The CIO was divided over which candidate to support and reluctantly endorsed Carmichael in spite of his poor labor record. Black organizations did not officially endorse any candidate, but most supported Carmichael. In this election, black leaders emphasized that the act of voting was of primary importance. Due to widespread purging of voting lists, slowdowns on election day, and outright intimidation, only 85,000 blacks voted. The great majority cast their ballot for Carmichael, who carried the popular vote by a margin of 15,000 votes. Talmadge, however, won the election handily, taking the county-unit vote by two to one. He dismissed Carmichael's lead in popular votes as due exclusively to the black vote and to the "Moscow-Harlem zoot suiters trying to take over Georgia." Henry Lee Moon observed that by making race the issue of his campaign, Talmadge created the bloc voting he decried. "The inescapable logic of the situation compelled colored voters to support the candidate who had the best chance of defeating an avowed enemy."[40]

Even with a county-unit system that favored the rural areas of the state, there is evidence that Talmadge would have lost if not for widespread fraud and purging of the voting rolls. Although there was a greater proportion of registered black voters in urban areas, there had been a notable increase in voter registration in rural areas, where the majority of black Georgians still resided. Talmadge's campaign strategists supplemented appeals to white supremacy by openly advocating that county officials should purge black registrants from the rolls as unqualified under Georgia code. Talmadge led the charge, demanding that three thousand black registrants on the Fulton County voting rolls be removed for alleged criminal records. In a number of counties, officials dispensed with procedural formalities and purged black voters en masse without any explanation regarding individual qualifications. Appeals by black voters resulted in the issuance of injunctions by federal judges in a few instances, but these were not enforced by court supervision of the registration-voting process. Through purges, slowdowns, and other electoral irregularities, the Talmadge campaign succeeded in decisively swinging fifty-six counties into Talmadge's column, providing the key to victory. Although the purges were reported in the press and investigated by the Federal Bureau of Investigation (FBI) on a large scale, the Justice Department decided not to attempt to indict Talmadge because the successful prosecution of such a case was highly unlikely.[41]

The intensive and well-publicized campaign against black voters in Georgia generated widespread racial violence and intimidation. Night riders warned that blacks who voted invited retribution. In Meriwether County, four hundred of the eight hundred black voters were purged, providing Talmadge with a margin of seventeen votes. In Greenville, the county seat, a cross was burned in the black section of town on the night before the primary. White people picketed the polls in the textile mill section of Manchester, warning blacks not to vote. In Grady County, the FBI investigated reports that white men firing guns drove through the black residential area. In Taylor County, Georgia, a sign posted on the local black church warned "The first Negro to vote will never vote again." Maceo Snipes, a World War II veteran, voted in Taylor County. That night four men dragged him from his home and shot him.[42]

In rural Walton County 60 blacks voted in the primary elections; 332 blacks in Monroe, the county seat, cast ballots. Walton County, which boasted the highest average yield of cotton per acre of all southern counties in 1945, was known for keeping black sharecroppers in virtual peonage.

Three days before the primary election, Roger Malcolm, a sharecropper, was arrested for stabbing his landlord. Two weeks later Loy Harrison, a prosperous farmer, posted the six-hundred-dollar bond for Malcolm. Malcolm's wife, Dorothy, her sister May Dorsey, and May's husband, George, who had just completed five years of service in the U.S. Army, accompanied Harrison to the jail. The Dorseys worked for Harrison. As Harrison drove the two couples home, twenty-five men ambushed his car. They took the Malcolms and the Dorseys to a nearby riverbank and murdered them, execution style.

By the time the FBI and the Georgia Bureau of Investigation (GBI) arrived on the scene, most of the physical evidence had been destroyed. Loy Harrison said he had not recognized any of the mob members. Investigators met a wall of "careful ignorance" when they interviewed townspeople about the murders. Some people were fearful. Others were complacent. One local explained: "This things got to be done to keep Mister Nigger in his place. Since the court said he could vote, there ain't been any holdin' him down." The funeral announcement for the four victims was posted above a placard assuring blacks of their right to vote in the recent primary elections. Bold letters said, "U.S. Ready for Prosecutions in Negro Balloting."[43]

A climate of terror and lawlessness hung over Walton County. But blacks in Monroe and many in surrounding rural areas demonstrated a "new consciousness," wrote an investigative reporter. They were beyond fear. "The night the murders occurred," he observed, "cops went through the Negro section of town and told everyone to go home. Many younger ones went home, got their guns, and came back downtown again." These men, many of them returned veterans, were not looking for trouble but planned to be ready when it came. "Although they know if they defend themselves against the white people they will be killed, they think it will be sufficient compensation if they can 'take two-three of them crackers along.'"[44]

Black voting-rights activists met the Talmadge-inspired campaign of terror by calling for expanded organizational work in the state's rural areas. A. T. Walden and Grace Hamilton proposed a statewide program of civic education to maintain the interest and momentum created during the spring voter-registration drives and to expand on preliminary contacts they had established with local leaders in 120 counties. A grant proposal requesting thirty-one thousand dollars to support such an effort explained that they aimed to overcome the apathy and ignorance resulting from fifty years of exclusion from Georgia politics and to counter the fear and intimidation that had met black efforts to vote. The program would provide training and support for local leaders, who in turn could prepare the local populace for "constructive social action." The proposal, however, was not funded. Looking back some forty years later, Grace Hamilton explained the situation in 1946: "We knew how to work with the resources in the community, but we didn't have the contacts with the foundations."[45]

In neighboring Alabama, the Folsom-Ellis contest sustained the belief that democratic change was possible in the postwar South. James E. Folsom, a thirty-seven-year-old insurance salesman and veteran of World War II, took the political pundits by surprise with his folksy campaign to scrub the capitol clean and let the "the cool green breeze of democracy" fill its halls. Folsom, who had been a delegate for Henry Wallace at the 1944 convention, was a political outsider, and he used his position to full advantage. He campaigned for a "People's Program" to reclaim the government from the "Big Mules" and Black Belt interests that had long dominated. He promised to restore democracy by abolishing the cumulative poll tax, reapportioning the state legislature, and revising the 1901 constitution so that it would provide for equal representation throughout the state: one man, one vote. Folsom opposed the Boswell amendment, Alabama's answer to *Smith v. Allwright*, which by virtue of an understanding clause would empower local registrars to decide who was fit to vote. He also pledged to improve public education, increase teachers' salaries, expand state aid to individuals not covered by social security, and provide farm-to-market roads. Countering the trend in other southern states, Folsom endorsed the right of workers to organize and bargain collectively, and he welcomed the endorsement of the CIO-PAC.

Folsom's opponent, Lieutenant Governor Handy Ellis, led the charge that Folsom's social programs would bankrupt the state, and he played up Folsom's connections with the CIO. The *Dothan Eagle* warned that the CIO-PAC was associated with the Communist fringe and was working with the NAACP to abolish segregation. The SCHW's Tex Dobbs marveled, "The race issue and CIO domination are thrown at Folsom in every part of the state, but he refuses to depart from his progressive program." The majority of voters failed to be distracted. On election day, Folsom defeated Ellis by the largest vote ever received by a candidate for governor in Alabama: 200,256 to 141,917.[46]

Folsom's landslide victory was not dependent on the support of the CIO-PAC, or of the SCHW, or of the black vote. His campaign, however, had provided a vehicle for strengthening a progressive biracial coalition. Dobbs reported that the union leadership in Alabama, particularly the AFL and the Railway Brotherhood, opposed Folsom. The CIO leaders got on board only after "rank and file sentiment forced them into line." They initially endorsed Ellis, on the assumption that he was favored to win. CIO-PAC organizers J. P. Mooney and Bill Aycock spearheaded the CIO's campaign for

Folsom. Palmer Weber, Dan Powell, and Al Reitman provided essential help in getting the labor vote out for Folsom and taught local organizers "a great deal about ward and precinct politics." In Jefferson County, the CIO-PAC provided cars to carry workers to the polls, an action that helped provide Folsom with the margin of victory in a county that had gone for Ellis in the first primary.[47]

Folsom won an estimated 90 percent of the approximately 6,000 black votes cast. Even though the number of black voters in 1946 represented a notable increase over the 2,000 registered in 1940, it was still a very small fraction of the black voting-age population. Dobbs reported to Clark Foreman that one of the greatest political challenges in Alabama was "forcing the board of registrars to register Negro voters." Dobbs advised Foreman that the SCHW should press Folsom on two major concerns: a liberal appointment to head the state Department of Labor; and the appointment of progressives to the county board of registrars. The governor was responsible for one appointment on the three-member county board of registrars. Dobbs predicted that if Folsom appointed registrars who did not discriminate against black applicants, this would pave the way for blacks to gain the right to become registered without the delays and runarounds that they currently experienced in every county. "By 1948 we should be able to increase Negro registration from its present low of 6,000 to 200,000 *if* decent registrars can be appointed."[48]

Folsom made an effort to expand voting rights through the appointment of registrars, but in many counties it was difficult to find a white individual willing to register blacks. In the few cases where he succeeded in appointing fair registrars, the results were dramatic. Herman Bentley, a Folsom appointee to the Macon County board of registrars, was responsible for more than quadrupling the number of registered black voters in that county during his two-year tenure. Bentley, a Notasulga farmer, saw no reason to deny blacks in Tuskegee the right to vote. When asked to explain his enlightened views, he responded: "Them folks out there got more sense than I got. How can I fail to register them?"[49]

The governor's race in Texas was among the more closely watched races nationally as a referendum on the New Deal and the state Democratic Party. Homer Rainey and Beuford Jester emerged as the two leading candidates following a bitterly contested twelve-man race, and they faced each other in a runoff. Labor and liberals rallied behind the candidacy of Rainey, the popular former president of the University of Texas who had been fired by the board of regents in 1944 after a dispute over academic freedom. Rainey held conventional New Deal views and ran on a platform of progressive taxation and increased state spending for public education and welfare programs. Jester was the candidate of the Texas Regulars, who had bolted the Democratic convention in 1944 in opposition to a fourth term for Roosevelt. He promoted limited government and no tax increases.

Palmer Weber spent the last week before the runoff election in Texas in a final effort to turn out the vote for Rainey. He wrote of "the painful, first hand experience of CIO weakness." Many potential supporters were "psychologically whipped." The CIO-PAC machinery was in the worst shape of all CIO-PAC organizations in the South with the exception of Birmingham. CIO officials, Weber noted, were "sitting around in twos and threes doing absolutely nothing." Weber's frustration with red-baiting labor organizers who shunned political activity exploded: "The scum the labor movement pays to conduct its business is incredible. They don't know what the word work means. Such poverty of mind and spirit. They are like hogs at a trough."[50]

Black voting activists offered a study in contrast to the ineffectual CIO-PAC. This was the first open primary since the *Smith v. Allwright* ruling. Weber had several sessions with local black leaders and with NAACP officials around the state. He met with Osceola McKaine, Henry Lee Moon, LeRoy Carter, and two local organizers to help map out the work for black voter turnout. McKaine covered northern Texas, Carter took the middle of the state, and Moon organized the Gulf coast. "All five showed tremendous espirit de corps and were obviously deep in work," Weber reported.[51]

The campaign to unite black voters behind Rainey, however, experienced a serious setback when Rainey issued a statement advocating separate polling places for blacks and whites. Coming less than a week before the election, the comment appeared to be a desperate attempt on the part of the candidate to project a more conservative image among white voters. Carter Wesley, owner of a chain of black newspapers, withdrew editorial support from Rainey and advised blacks to "go fishing" on election day. Weber and several black activists attempted to mollify Wesley, to no avail. "I think he is deeply hurt by Rainey's super stupid statement," Weber wrote, "but he also figures Rainey to lose."[52]

The red-baiting and personal smears that dominated the Rainey-Jester campaign foreshadowed the 1950 senatorial races in Florida and North Carolina. Jester engaged in a relentless campaign to portray Rainey as a pawn of radical left-wing groups and "a threat to all American virtues." Several days before the election, Weber was prepared to admit defeat. He concluded that the opposition had "so clouded Rainey with communism, atheism, homosexuality, etc. that these essentially simple people" were "completely confused." He added, "The organization doesn't exist to get them clear."

Another Rainey supporter observed that the candidate contributed to the confusion by taking a defensive posture and backsliding on labor and civil rights issues, weakening his support among both groups.[53]

As the governors' races in Alabama, Georgia, and Texas suggest, the 1946 primary elections upset longtime political patterns in some places while illustrating the enduring power of racist appeals, electoral fraud, and political demagoguery in others. Senator Theodore Bilbo and Congressman John Rankin of Mississippi, two of the most virulent racists in Congress, won reelection, Bilbo after embracing the Ku Klux Klan and publicly inviting whites to forcibly keep black voters from the polls. Senator Byrd of Virginia and Senator McKellar of Tennessee, both high on the CIO-PAC's list for defeat, easily won reelection.

But as the *Nation* editorialized, "There are some drops of southern comfort to be squeezed out of the past week's primaries." In addition to a strong showing in the Georgia governor's race, candidates supported by the CIO-PAC won three congressional seats in the state. In a major upset, textile workers in Dalton ousted Congressman Malcolm Tarver, who had been undefeated for forty years. In Alabama, John Sparkman, Democratic whip in Congress, won a sweeping victory in his bid for the Senate, with the support of the CIO-PAC. Florida elected Spessard Holland to the Senate over an opponent who made race the chief issue of his campaign. A young veteran, George Smathers, unseated a leading member of the southern bloc in Congress, Clarence Cannon of Miami. There were notable gains for more moderate congressional candidates in North Carolina and Virginia. In McMinn, Tennessee, a nonpartisan citizens committee, led by veterans, succeeded in challenging a fraudulent election and reversing the outcome.[54]

Even in Mississippi, Bilbo's brazen effort to keep blacks from the polls failed to dampen the "new consciousness" evident among black southerners in the Deep South. In the aftermath of the primary, fifty Mississippians filed a complaint with the U.S. Committee to Investigate Campaign Expenditures and called for an investigation of the Bilbo campaign. Nearly two hundred blacks from all parts of the state showed up for the committee hearing in Jackson; the majority were veterans. Sixty-eight black men and women testified, documenting the pervasive pattern of unlawful behavior and racial terrorism that had characterized the senatorial primary. The Democrats on the committee, all southern, voted to exonerate Bilbo; the Republican minority condemned him. Bilbo's failing health eventually kept the issue of his seating from coming to a vote in the Senate.[55]

The black vote was the big story of the 1946 primary elections in the South. An estimated 600,000 black southerners registered to vote in 1946, far exceeding the previously recorded estimate of 200,000 for 1940. This phenomenon suggested to some that the realignment of Democratic Party politics in the South was under way. University of Florida Professor William Carleton viewed the increase in black voting as "a boon to liberals in their fight within the [Democratic] Party to gain and keep party control." He confidently predicted, "The cry 'nigger' employed to divide the liberal forces is losing its old magic." Jack Kroll, Sidney Hillman's successor as national director of the CIO-PAC, claimed partial credit for his organization in the successful outcome of key primary races in the South. But he acknowledged that this incipient challenge to "the reactionaries . . . in their strongholds" was driven largely by the surge of black political participation and the legal victories of the NAACP. Reporting on the "aroused citizen's movement in Georgia," CIO-PAC organizer Dan Powell suggested the possibility of establishing an independent Democratic Party in that state, with black voters forming the core group. Powell estimated that such a party could draw 125,000 black votes, 30,000 CIO votes, and 50,000 AFL votes, along with liberal support.[56]

Whether or not growing black political participation previewed the liberalization of southern politics was less than certain. There were compelling signs that it was a singular development, bereft of the supporting components deemed essential to building a new democratic coalition in the South. Indeed, there was much evidence that gains in black voter registration, the growth of the NAACP, and other signs of a new militancy among black southerners were easily manipulated to heighten white fears and elevate race to a defining and divisive issue in the postwar South.

Reports of interracial violence abounded during 1946, starting with a February race riot in Columbia, Tennessee, which pitted black veterans and their community against the police and the national guard. It left four white policemen wounded, two black men dead, and more than one hundred blacks arrested. During the two months following the primary elections, there were nine lynchings in the South. In November Isaac Woodard, a twenty-seven-year-old black veteran, was blinded by the police chief of Aiken, South Carolina, after an altercation with a bus driver. A national campaign on Woodard's behalf succeeded in securing the indictment of Police Chief Lynwood Shull, who was tried in federal court in Columbia, South Carolina, in the first civil rights case ever heard in the state. The jury acquitted Shull. No one was ever arrested for the mass lynching in Walton County, Georgia. With the escalation of racial violence and the spread of the Ku Klux Klan, it appeared that the South might easily succumb to a wave of reaction reminiscent of the "Red summer" of 1919. Secretary Walter White of the NAACP declared that blacks might have to resort to armed resistance to defend their lives.[57]

The SCHW convened its fourth regional meeting in New Orleans at the end of November. Fifteen hundred southerners attended; more than half of the delegates were black. Palmer Weber, Osceola McKaine, Walter White, Ellis Arnall, Claude Pepper, Aubrey Williams, Clark Foreman, and Mary McLeod Bethune were among the speakers who reflected on the significance of the 1946 primary season in the South. They recounted how the effort to defeat the southern reactionary bloc, an effort initiated by Roosevelt in 1938, had scored significant breakthroughs in Georgia and Alabama and modest gains elsewhere. Even when the winning candidates did not differ fundamentally from the incumbents they replaced, Weber noted the importance of shaking "some of the old gang loose from important committee chairmanships." In a rousing speech emphasizing the importance of voting and political action, Mary McLeod Bethune urged sustained efforts to abolish the poll tax and mob violence and to end segregation and discrimination. "With the franchise we must get our justice. Let us give volume and vital significance to the philosophy [of the SCHW]."[58]

By the end of 1946, a political movement had emerged in the South, one that revived the democratic promise of Reconstruction and moved beyond the tentative interracialism of the Populist movement. It was rooted in the ethos of the New Deal, the Popular Front politics of the 1930s, and the democratic ideology of World War II and was a part of the national effort to secure the full liberal realignment of the Democratic Party. For this movement, as for Reconstruction, reenfranchised black voters formed the core of the liberal-labor coalition dedicated to establishing a democratic economic and political order in the South. The electoral fraud, mob violence, and racial intimidation that surrounded the voting-rights drives underscored the fact that such efforts were ultimately dependent on a national commitment to act decisively on a broad interpretation of constitutionally protected rights. That likelihood, however, became increasingly remote as the politics of the cold war eclipsed the confident liberalism of the New Deal.

We cry for action—and I think the time is very short.

Virginia Durr to Luther P. Jackson, June 1947

8

The Closing Circle of Democratic Party Politics

BREAKUP OF THE NEW DEAL COALITION

Commenting on Washington in the early days of Harry Truman's administration, journalist I. F. Stone lamented, "The fizz was out of the bottle." Whereas the social engineering of the New Deal had been interred during the war, Franklin Roosevelt's death gave it a grim finality. Truman replaced all but four of his predecessor's cabinet members. Conservative southerners, party regulars, political cronies, and businessmen staffed the new administration. The "human spark plugs . . . who had made the New Deal possible," Stone noted, were absent. Senator Claude Pepper confided in Commerce Secretary Henry Wallace that the White House appeared to be ushering in a new era of normalcy reminiscent of the post–World War I administration of Warren Harding.[1]

President Roosevelt's death on 12 April 1945, amplified the uncertainty surrounding the transition to peace. During his twelve-year tenure, Roosevelt had steered the nation through depression and war, vastly expanding the role of the federal government in American life and creating a veneer of continuity. But he left an ambiguous legacy, wrought with contradictions. By the time of his death, American political culture was deeply rooted in the war experience and in the assumptions and expectations it had created. Defense mobilization, built on the institutional legacy of the New Deal, redirected federal priorities toward national security concerns. Record-breaking amounts of federal dollars fueled the "arsenal of democracy," securing full employment and contributing to the most progressive redistribution of income in this century. The sharp-edged politics of the 1930s were subsumed by a national mood of solidarity and purpose, which fused ideals of democracy with the dogma of Americanism.[2]

Harry Truman inherited an economic and political order that had been shaped by the prerequisites of war. Industrial leaders and military officials, buttressed by the ascendancy of conservatives in Congress, dominated the war agencies that transformed Washington; New Dealers and labor leaders served in a subordinate capacity. Four months into Truman's term, the war ended with the dawn of the nuclear age and the emergence of the United States as the world's preeminent power. The parameters of presidential leadership and initiatives were determined largely by the institutional legacies of the war and the urgency attending reconversion.

The vitality of New Deal liberalism in the postwar era would be determined in large part by the ability of its core constituencies to define a postwar program and organize themselves into an effective political force. To a large extent, this would be a function of their evolving relationship with the new administration. During the first year, labor, liberals, and civil rights activists cohered in opposition to Truman's pronounced tendency to compromise the advances that had been secured during the previous decade. By early 1946, however, the incipient cold war began to eclipse domestic issues as the defining element of postwar politics. This development tested postwar liberalism in ways that ultimately divided the New

Deal coalition and led to the emergence of a third-party movement for Henry Wallace.

In September 1945, President Truman presented the outlines of his domestic program to Congress, briefly stirring the hopes of progressives. Its provisions included a full-employment bill, an increase in the federal minimum wage, a permanent Fair Employment Practices Committee (FEPC), unemployment compensation, and legislation for public housing. But the president's actions and pronouncements during the next year set a tone that emphasized the limits of his ability to press for a liberal agenda. Truman's deteriorating relations with labor, his retreat from support of the FEPC and a federal anti-poll-tax bill, and the widening rift between Truman and prominent New Dealers suggested that the president lacked any basic commitment to the social democratic thrust of New Deal reform.

Barely six months into Truman's presidency, labor protested the inequities of the reconversion process with the greatest strike wave in American history. Federal policy, established under Roosevelt, offered federal assistance and subsidies to ensure the quick and smooth transition of large defense contractors to a peacetime economy. It left workers to fend for themselves as layoffs mounted, wartime wages declined, and economic dislocation plagued large segments of the labor force. Facing an aggressive business community and a strong antilabor bloc in Congress, the Truman administration showed little inclination to moderate the process. Labor discontent boiled over from November 1945 until May 1946; strikes closed down nearly every major American industry.

The strikes polarized public opinion and turned Truman's seeming disinterest in the plight of labor into open contempt. He retreated from his support of the full-employment bill and proposed drastic antilabor legislation that included the drafting of striking railway workers. The extremism of the president's proposed legislation drew Republican leader Senator Robert Taft, normally not a labor ally, into the ranks of the opposition. Eleanor Roosevelt worried that Truman relied on his military advisers too heavily. Although the bill failed, the new president had demonstrated his intention to use the powers of government against striking workers.[3]

During his first year in office, President Truman's actions on racially significant policies, along with his appointment of southerners to key administration positions, favored the conservative wing of the Democratic Party. In the spring of 1946, in what appeared to be a major concession to southern conservatives, Truman stated that the poll tax "was a matter for the southern states to work out." SCHW President Clark Foreman responded that such a pronouncement indicated that Truman had given up the fight for New Deal legislation and "would not run for reelection." Several days later Truman issued a qualification and added his support for federal legislation as well.[4]

The president's public support for a permanent FEPC was seriously compromised when he blocked the FEPC's directive requiring the Capitol Transit Company to end racially discriminatory hiring and promotion practices. In December 1945 the president tabled an FEPC directive ordering an end to racially discriminatory hiring practices by the District of Columbia Transit Company, even though the transit company was temporarily under the jurisdiction of the federal government. In a similar case involving the Philadelphia Transit Company a year earlier, Roosevelt's action had resulted in the hiring of eight black motormen. The *Crisis* magazine of the National Association for the Advancement of Colored People (NAACP) said that Truman's action, and his refusal to even discuss the directive with the FEPC, "cut the authority—and life—from the FEPC."[5]

FEPC Commissioner Charles Houston resigned from the FEPC and publicly charged that the president's failure to implement the directive raised "fundamental questions of the basic government attitude towards minorities." In his letter of resignation, Houston continued, "Since the effect of your intervention in the Capitol Transit case is not to eliminate discrimination but to condone it you not only repudiate the committee, but more important you nullify Executive Orders themselves." He warned, "The failure of the Government to enforce democratic practices and to protect minorities in its own capital makes its expressed concern for national minorities abroad somewhat specious." Houston distributed copies of his letter widely, including to several foreign embassies.[6]

"The constant dropping of original New Dealers and Roosevelt followers," observed newspaper man Leon Washington, "is narrowing Truman's official family down to party hacks and lame duck southerners." Harold Ickes's departure from the cabinet in February 1946 punctuated a distressing trend. After unsuccessfully protesting the appointment of oilman and lobbyist Edwin Pauley as undersecretary of the navy, Ickes told a national radio audience that he could no longer retain his "self respect and stay in the Cabinet of President Truman." Robert Weaver quietly left the administration, noting that the possibilities for implementing racially enlightened policies had dried up.[7]

The year 1946 was a formative one for Democratic Party politics in the post-Roosevelt era. By the end of his first year in office, the goodwill and cautious optimism that had greeted Harry Truman was spent. The pattern of his domestic policies stood as a bold challenge to the vitality of liberals, labor, and civil rights proponents as a force within the Democratic Party. At the same time, the basis of the New Deal coalition was being challenged by a vocal segment of liberals and leading figures in the Congress of Industrial Organizations (CIO). Fought in the shadow of the emerging cold war, this internal struggle over the role of liberalism in postwar America was critical to the outcome of the 1946 midterm election and its consequences.

If Truman's domestic policies were divisive and often lacked a clear focus, the abrupt shift in the status of the Soviet Union from ally to adversary invited decisive presidential leadership. A postwar foreign policy premised on Soviet expansionism and subversion changed the context of domestic politics. The onset of the cold war reopened the debate within labor unions and among liberals, simmering since the days of the Nazi-Soviet Pact, on whether or not Communists should be barred from their organizations. During 1946, the Union for Democratic Action (UDA) elevated domestic communism as a more important issue than the performance of Congress and the Truman administration and as the major challenge confronting the liberal movement. In its aggressive challenge to the politics of the Popular Front, the UDA and its supporters helped to shape the new political ortho-doxy of the cold war. Southern progressives and civil rights activists, in league with the CIO and the National Citizens Political Action Committee (NCPAC), led the resistance to what they viewed as a potentially fatal blow to the political foundation of democratic reform.

Several developments during 1946 highlighted the deepening divisions within the ranks of the Democratic Party over the course of foreign policy and its relationship to domestic politics. Competing efforts to inform the public debate were made by former British Prime Minister Winston Chur-chill, in his infamous "Iron Curtain" speech, and Henry Wallace, in his first major public critique of American postwar foreign policy.

On 5 March 1946, with President Truman at his side, Churchill publicly heralded the onset of the cold war in a bold call for an Anglo-American military alliance against Soviet expansionism. He traced Soviet penetration of Eastern Europe and warned of the insidious work of Communist subver-sives and fifth-column activity in countries throughout the world. The Ca-nadian government's uncovering of a Soviet atomic spy ring just weeks before gave immediate credence to this dire warning. Political commentator Max Lerner wrote that Churchill had rolled up "into a single image all the fears" invoked by the Soviets "since the Russian Revolution almost thirty years ago." In the short run, strong press criticism of the harsh tone of

Churchill's speech caused Truman to disassociate himself from it. But Churchill's exaggerated appraisal of Soviet actions and intentions provided popular imagery for the Truman administration's evolving foreign policy.[8]

Secretary of Commerce Wallace, the last holdover from the Roosevelt administration, was the sole member of Truman's cabinet to voice opposition to the administration's get-tough policy with the Soviets. Wallace outlined his concerns in a long letter to the president in July, warning of an arms race with Russia. Frustrated by his inability to stimulate a reconsideration of American policy within the administration, Wallace went public in September at an NCPAC-sponsored rally in Madison Square Garden. After Wallace had cleared the text of his speech with the president, Truman publicly claimed that it was "exactly in line" with the State Department's policy toward the Russians. Palmer Weber, research director for the CIO-PAC, read the text while waiting with Wallace under the stage at Madison Square Garden; Weber advised Wallace that the speech would cost him his cabinet post.[9]

Wallace challenged the basis of the postwar policy that had been articulated by George Kennan earlier in the year and that was then being negotiated by Secretary of State James Byrnes. Kennan's containment strategy assumed that the Soviet Union, though weakened, was an expansive, totalitarian power, impervious to reason and responsive only to force. Accordingly the United States need not be concerned with the Soviets' legitimate interests; there were none. The containment of Soviet power should be America's singular goal. As historian Melvyn Leffler has explained, "Kennan's unambiguous appraisal of Soviet intentions and motives, his didactic tone, and his self-confident belief in the West's potential superiority and the Kremlin's inherent weakness" were greeted with enthusiasm throughout the upper ranks of the State Department and War Department and by a number of Truman advisers, including Clark Clifford.[10]

To assume that the Soviet Union was the enemy and to embark on an exclusively confrontational and militaristic approach, Wallace argued, would be gravely misguided and even reckless in the atomic age. Wallace urged a more reasoned approach to America's role in securing peace with the Soviet Union, a role that was not dictated by British balance-of-power concerns. He warned against a false sense of security based on America's temporary monopoly of the atom bomb; such an advantage made it imperative for America to lead in negotiating a postwar settlement that would permit both powers to coexist safely and peaceably. This required the recognition of the Soviet Union's legitimate spheres of influence in Eastern Europe, just as the United States claimed similar hegemony in Latin America and Western

Europe. Wallace emphasized that he was not advocating appeasement or underestimating the irreconcilable ideological differences that separated the two powers. But the United States must, at the very least, make an effort to establish a basis for cooperation with the Soviet Union. Toughness, Wallace predicted, would only beget toughness and would squander a critical opportunity.

Wallace considered the domestic implications of a policy that sought to demonize the Soviet Union by stirring mass prejudice, fear, and ignorance and compared it to the tactics long used by reactionary elements in the United States. The recent lynchings in Monroe, Georgia, Wallace explained, illustrated the ways in which blind hatred bred violence and lawlessness. And the persistence of state-sanctioned racial prejudice in the United States, Wallace added, seriously compromised America's ability to serve as a positive force for democratic values worldwide. "If we are to work for peace in the rest of the world," he advised, "we here in the United States must eliminate racism from our unions, our business organizations, our educational institutions and our employment practices."[11]

Senator Claude Pepper joined Wallace on the platform and delivered a more scathing indictment of the Truman administration's "blundering foreign policy." But it was Wallace's speech that drew the fire of the press and leading Democratic Party officials. They charged the secretary of commerce with undercutting Secretary of State Byrnes, who was then meeting with the Russians to negotiate Eastern European peace treaties. Truman vacillated and tried to back away from his earlier endorsement of the speech. Finally, under pressure from Byrnes, who impugned Wallace's loyalty, Truman wrote Wallace a brief, rude note firing him. Wallace suggested that the note be swapped for something more suitable for public consumption. That was done, and the original note was destroyed. In his diary entry for that day Truman referred to Wallace as "a pacifist 100 percent." He added, "The Reds, phonies and 'parlor pinks' seem to be banded together and are becoming a national danger."[12]

The limits of dissent on foreign policy had been tested. Liberals hailed Wallace for at last opening the State Department's policy to public scrutiny and debate and for creating the possibility for some reorientation. The black press reported favorably on Wallace and expressed the widespread cynicism within the black community over the administration's reliance on South Carolinian Byrnes as its international spokesman for democracy. But a national poll found that, overall, Americans favored Byrnes over Wallace by nearly 5 to 1. In the aftermath of the Madison Square Garden speech, the campaign speakers bureau of the Democratic National Committee (DNC) scratched Wallace and Pepper from the party's official list of campaign speakers. DNC Chairman Robert Hannegan modified the policy and agreed that local and state Democratic committees were free to sponsor Wallace and Pepper, the party's most popular speakers. The national party, however, would not sponsor Wallace. For his part, Wallace continued to campaign, at his own expense, for the election of liberal Democrats.[13]

Less than two weeks after Wallace's dismissal from the cabinet, liberals and laborites participated in a "Conference of Progressives" sponsored by the NCPAC, the CIO Political Action Committee (CIO-PAC), and the Independent Citizens Committee of the Arts, Sciences, and Professions (ICC-ASP). Clark Foreman, the NAACP's Walter White, James Patton of the National Farmers Union (NFU), and former Secretary of the Treasury Henry Morganthau Jr. were among those who signed the call to the conference. Three hundred delegates from thirty-five states attended the two-day meeting, which has been described as "one of the widest and most representative assemblies of liberals ever brought together." CIO President Philip Murray hailed the conference as "one of the most important of its kind ever held" and hoped it might finally realize the long-felt "need for a broad people's movement to lay the foundation for political democracy through political action." It served as a final pep rally to get out the vote in November and created a continuations committee to plan for the establishment of a consolidated organization after the election.[14]

The conference platform outlined major principles of foreign and domestic policy. Reiterating Wallace's critique, it advocated that the United States should lead in reviving the wartime spirit of Allied cooperation, proposed international control of atomic energy, and opposed American efforts to secure military bases around the world. The domestic platform called for the revitalization and expansion of New Deal reforms, emphasizing the federal government's essential role in ensuring a minimum of economic security, educational opportunity, and political rights for all citizens. The platform advocated passage of a federal civil rights bill "to put into law the protection guaranteed by the 14th and 15th amendments and to insure effective federal protection of civil rights in every state."[15]

Beyond agreeing on a platform, the conference attendees contemplated the more daunting task of building an organizational structure to represent all constituencies and effectively challenge the conservative dominance of Congress and the White House. "The most powerful and sinister political party in America," White told the gathering, was the party of "reactionary Southern Democrats and reactionary Republicans . . . joined in a coalition of death to progress and enlightenment." Patton came closest to advocating a third party when he claimed that the conference proposals could not be addressed "within the framework of the existing political organizations." But there was little evident support for a third-party movement. Pepper argued that the only way progressives could gain control was through the Democratic Party. White also dismissed the idea of a third party as unworkable given the fact that state laws inhibited the possibility of getting on the ballot. But he warned that the black vote, a potential balance of power in seventeen states, was increasingly independent and not beholden to either major party. "The Negro shares none of the tired liberalism of many of his white fellow Americans," White said. "We are looking forward, not backward, . . . and are determined to use our growing political power to end lynching, the poll tax, unequal education . . . and every form of discrimination that afflicts America generally."[16]

Conferees celebrated the advances made during the 1946 primaries in the South as offering the most promising sign that serious realignment within the Democratic Party was within reach. "Our successful work in the southern primaries," boasted CIO-PAC Director Jack Kroll, "was striking evidence . . . that the reactionaries that have traded so long on the one-party system in that region can be defeated in their own strongholds." The number of registered black voters—600,000—was evidence of growing interest among "the Negro people . . . in political action." For the first time in its history, Kroll noted, the NAACP had set up machinery for political action. White emphasized the importance of the white primary decision in heightening voter participation among blacks and whites. In Georgia alone, White told the gathering, 100,000 blacks had voted in the primary for the first time, and the number of white voters far exceeded that in previous primary turnouts. Kroll predicted that in 1948 one million black voters would be eligible to vote in the South, "even under present poll tax restrictions, due to the work now being carried out in the South." He added, "If the drive to root out the poll tax succeeds, and we intend to intensify our efforts, then the progressive cause will be even further advanced."[17]

The conference emphasis on political action and the election of a liberal Congress in November provided a fragile basis for unity in the midst of deepening factionalism within the CIO and the growing significance of anticommunism as a measure of political legitimacy. The largely unpopular strike wave of 1945–46 and the CIO's high-profile involvement in electoral politics left it more exposed to charges that the organization was a vehicle for the Communists. During 1946, the three largest unions—the United Auto Workers, the Steel Workers Union, and the United Electrical Workers—became fierce battlegrounds between those who wanted to purge Communist Party members from their ranks and those who resisted. For most of 1946, Murray publicly maintained a neutral position and continued his support of the nonexclusionary CIO-PAC movement. Meanwhile the UDA laid the groundwork for an alternative liberal-labor organization based on the ideology of anticommunism.[18]

Liberal anticommunism had roots in the factional struggles that developed among labor unions and within the Left during the 1930s. Its appeal broadened in the wake of the 1939 Nazi-Soviet Pact, when the American Civil Liberties Union (ACLU) and several union locals purged Communist Party members from their ranks. In 1941 a group of disaffected Socialists led by Reinhold Niebuhr and James Loeb organized the UDA. Unlike most other New Deal–inspired organizations, the UDA barred Communists from membership. UDA members became known as the "hang back boys" during the war. They remained isolated from the broad consensus of Popular Front politics that was rejuvenated when the Soviets and the Allies joined to defeat fascism. But with the rapid deterioration of U.S.-Soviet relations at the end of the war, the UDA expanded its effort to create a viable alternative to the Popular Front politics that had long dominated the New Deal coalition, settling on anticommunism as "the central rational for its existence."[19]

The UDA differed from progressive groups like the CIO-PAC and the SCHW in two basic ways. Most obvious was its policy banning Communists from its ranks. Equally significant was that the UDA was not a political action group and did not aspire to build a non-Communist "Popular Front." Its appeal was to northern, white, college-educated individuals, a relatively cohesive group of intellectuals, labor leaders, and aspiring politicians. In the political battles that ensued, the UDA had the advantage of an ideological consistency and certainty that more readily accommodated the cold war era at the expense of the eclectic views and organizations that composed the Popular Front. The indiscriminate reach of the UDA attack, and its timing, suggest that political pragmatism rather than fear of Communist subversion was the most potent force behind the UDA's postwar revival.

The UDA was "at the end of its rope" in the spring of 1946 when its national board decided to undertake an aggressive expansion effort. Churchill's speech, and the subsequent convening of a "Win the Peace" rally, provided the opening. The rally's roster of 250 sponsors included well-known independent liberals and several members of Congress, including Senator Pepper and Congresswoman Helen Gahagan Douglas, along with reputed fellow travelers and a few avowed Communists, including New York City councilman Ben Davis. In a series of resolutions, the conference opposed the militaristic, anti-Soviet course advanced by Churchill and called for a foreign policy that sought to maintain the Big Three alliance and was committed to ending colonialism, destroying the remnants of fascism, and securing international control of atomic energy.

James Loeb, the UDA national director, launched the campaign to revive the organization with a letter to the *New Republic* on 13 May 1946. Echoing Churchill's call to vigilance, Loeb attacked the "Win the Peace" rally as hopelessly pro-Soviet. It was time for the liberal-progressive movement to reevaluate its goals in light of the new postwar order. Was economic security the sole objective, even if it meant compromising aspirations to human freedom? The choice, Loeb insisted, was implicitly clear. If progressives were not apologists for the Soviet Union, and if their commitment to human freedom was unwavering, then they had to act: "They must make a third strategic decision no less important than the first two: whether or not they can or should work within the same political organizations with those who have decided for the other alternatives, namely Communists." Communists were devious, subversive, and bound to dominate any organization they participated in, Loeb warned. "No united front will long remain united; it will only become a front." If the progressive movement was to survive and grow, it had to completely disassociate itself from Communists and their sympathizers.[20]

Loeb's letter drew numerous responses on both sides of the issue as he had defined it. Supporters, some citing personal experiences, endorsed Loeb's view that Communists followed orders from Moscow and wrecked whatever organizations they belonged to. Stanley Isaacs, a former Manhattan borough president and a prominent UDA member, argued that the behavior of individual Communist Party members should not be the defining issue for liberals in the postwar period. No matter how disagreeable Communists might be, they posed no threat "in this conservative country of ours." The democratic process was challenged, Isaacs observed, not by a small minority of Communists but by the growing obstructionism of the reactionary forces in the country—the Rankins and the Bilbos, the Hearst press, and other right-wing groups. In such a climate, liberal red-baiting, Isaacs explained, was a form of self-destruction. Clark Foreman agreed and warned, "If liberals in this country spend their time attacking each other rather than the Byrd's and the Bilbo's they will—whether they wish it or not—inevitably form a liberal front for reaction."[21]

Arthur Schlesinger Jr. expanded on Loeb's epistle in an article in the July issue of *Life* magazine. The heading announced: "The Communist Party: Small but tightly disciplined, it strives with fanatic zeal to promote the aims of Russia." Illustrated with photographs of dour-looking Communist Party officials and children at a Communist summer camp in Beacon, New York, Schlesinger's essay offered a caricature of the Communist Party of the United States as a cult-like group populated by lonely, frustrated people for whom the party offered "social, intellectual and even sexual fulfillment." It was not a "normal" political party. The party member's obsequiousness to Moscow compared to a devout Catholic's allegiance to Rome. Allowing for the fact that Communists across the country had "performed commendable acts against [racial] discrimination," Schlesinger discounted this by noting that "the Ninth Floor" of the party headquarters continued to view the race problem as a source of propaganda. Communists' pro-Russian sympathies, Schlesinger warned, were often cloaked under legitimate domestic issues. Communists were, in short, a corrupting force in the body politic, spreading "their infection of intrigue and deceit" wherever they went.[22]

Did the Communist Party of the United States, with its devotion to a foreign power that was fast becoming America's primary adversary, pose a fifth-column threat? Schlesinger could not say for sure; that was a matter best left to "the competent hands of the F.B.I." But it was imperative, he maintained, that liberals identify and isolate Communist Party members within their ranks. To aid in that endeavor, he offered a blueprint of the patterns of Communist infiltration. The trade unions were the primary field of "communist penetration." He listed the left-wing CIO unions that followed the party line with fidelity and warned that they were "even boring into" Philip Murray's Steel Workers Union. Second only to the unions was "the drive to organize Negroes." He ominously warned that the Communist Party was "sinking its tentacles into the NAACP." Third were groups of liberals, like the ICC-ASP, who, "because of the innocence, laziness or stupidity of most of the membership, [were] perfectly designed for control by an alert minority." Hollywood intellectuals had also been beguiled by the party, which offered them "a means for resolving their own frustrations and fears." According to Schlesinger, Washington too remained within the Communist Party's orbit. Party members were still well-placed in the Truman administration, and known sympathizers staffed some senatorial offices and congressional committees.[23]

It was the Communists, Schlesinger warned, who threatened to immobilize the left. The choice was clear. Liberals must insist "that Communists and fellow travellers . . . stand and be counted"; the left could not leave the job to the "witch-hunting" of the Dies Committee, which had only obscured the problem by smearing non-Communist liberals as well as Communists. He offered the UDA as "the one left wing group" that had "sought to combat the confusion and corruption coming inevitably in the wake of Communist penetration." It was prepared to lead in building a new liberal coalition, unblemished by foreign ideologies and sympathies.[24]

Arthur Schlesinger, James Wechsler, and Joseph Rauh served as the UDA's planning committee for a postelection conference to launch a new, UDA-sponsored organization. The success of a new liberal organization depended largely on the level of support it received from the CIO. Loeb and the planning committee assiduously courted the support of labor leaders and New Deal figures, such as Eleanor Roosevelt. They found important allies in Walter Reuther, president of the United Automobile Workers and leader of its anti-Communist faction, and CIO Secretary-Treasurer James Carey, who had waged an unsuccessful campaign to purge Communists from the United Electrical Workers. But officially the CIO remained noncommittal. Philip Murray remained publicly associated with the CIO and the NCPAC through the campaign season.[25]

The most immediate challenge facing Democrats of all persuasions was the upcoming election. During the months preceding the election, support for the Democrats dropped to 43 percent, its lowest level since 1928. With the unpopular Truman noticeably absent from the campaign trail, the party leadership recycled recordings of FDR's speeches, hardly reassuring to an electorate weary of strikes, meat shortages, and inflation. Polls showed that the high cost of living was the key issue among the majority of voters. "Had Enough?," asked the Republican campaign slogan. Republicans blamed Democrats for inflation, shortages, and controls, focusing on the meat shortages resulting from a standoff between meat producers and the government over price controls. "In a world charged with atomic energy," one reporter observed, "a national campaign has been fought in the shadow of a meatball."[26]

Smelling victory, the Republicans bore away at a Democratic Party on the defensive, using the worn issue of the left-wing proclivities of the New Deal to much greater effect. Circumstances invited an exploitation of the "red menace" to an extent unprecedented in American electoral politics. Just weeks after Churchill's address, the U.S. ambassador to the Soviet Union, W. Averall Harriman, publicly referred to "Commies in the CIO" in an address to the Business Advisory Council and drew enthusiastic applause. Attorney General Tom Clark and Federal Bureau of Investigation (FBI) Director J. Edgar Hoover, on separate occasions, warned that the Communist conspiracy threatened American institutions, and the liberal historian Arthur Schlesinger trumpeted an alert in the pages of Life magazine.[27]

As the fall campaign heated up, Republicans on the stump warned that left-wing support of Democratic candidates was evidence of the conspiracy at work. The CIO-PAC became a lightning rod. Republican candidates used "CIO," "PAC" and "Communist" interchangeably, breeding widespread mistrust of candidates supported by the CIO-PAC and the NCPAC. In many contests, a PAC endorsement was more likely to aid in mobilizing opposition to a candidate than to garner support. Such tactics were given an extra boost by an English-language broadcast from Moscow in mid-October that urged Americans to vote for CIO-PAC candidates on 5 November. Richard Nixon rode the PAC issue to his first electoral victory, successfully tarring his opponent, Jerry Voorhis, as a follower of "the PAC line," even after Voorhis had disavowed an NCPAC endorsement. Joseph McCarthy was also among the new faces in the Eightieth Congress, though he did not resort to red-baiting as a tactic to win the senatorial seat from Wisconsin in 1946.[28]

"Bow your heads folks, conservatism has hit America," announced *New Republic*'s "T.R.B." in the wake of the 1946 election. The Republicans swept both houses of Congress, enjoying majority status for the first time since 1930; the southern Democratic bloc remained firmly intact. The causes and consequences of this reversal in political fortunes invited much commentary, analysis, and speculation. The most striking defection was registered among northern urban black voters, who abandoned the Democratic Party in significant numbers. Democrats had suffered from a low voter turnout, with the vote falling eight million short of the forty-three million projected for a midterm election. To what extent was the 1946 election a referendum on Truman's failure to provide decisive leadership in advancing the Roosevelt program? Was the election a rejection of the party of the New Deal? Was it a vote for a return to "normalcy"? Analysts would have to await the outcome of the 1948 presidential election to plot the national trends. But in the short term, the CIO-PAC and the NCPAC had suffered a crushing defeat. Not only had the PACs failed to establish themselves as a force to be reckoned with, but their endorsement was widely perceived to be a liability.[29]

For Democrats close to the White House, the most obvious lessons of the 1946 election were quickly applied. DNC Chairman Robert Hannegan, along with his effort to coordinate Democratic Party strategies with the PACs, was sacked. Clark Clifford, who had served as an assistant naval aid to President Truman, emerged as the president's top adviser. A political pundit described Clifford as "the great white hope of Democrats of all faiths." With the looks of a movie star, he had a sharp, politically astute mind, unencumbered by any strong social philosophy or political convictions. His job was "to raise the gallup ratings of the irrepressible little Missourian." Truman emerged from the shadows of the election prepared to lead the struggle against communism abroad and at home. With the aid of the UDA and the CIO, the

Democrats constructed a new, post-Roosevelt consensus that accommodated conservatives and liberals while seeking to isolate Truman's critics on the left.[30]

In the months following the election, the national leadership of the CIO, the UDA, and the Truman administration collectively narrowed and revised the parameters of legitimate political activity. Philip Murray sought to shield labor from the emerging internecine battle over foreign policy and its domestic implications by restricting the political activity of CIO unions. At the national CIO convention late in November, the CIO constitution was amended to limit the political independence of its state and industrial union councils. Councils were told to "confine their activities and statements to issues of local concern and to matters of general policy" that had been "passed upon by the national CIO." John Brophy, director of councils, instructed officers of all CIO affiliates to refrain from contributing to or participating in any organization not included on a preapproved list issued by the national office. The Southern Conference for Human Welfare (SCHW) and Highlander Folk School were noticeably absent.[31]

The UDA was prepared to reap the fallout from the rout of 1946. With Murray's blessing, Loeb attended the CIO's November convention to recruit labor leaders for what would be the founding meeting of the Americans for Democratic Action (ADA). By November, Eleanor Roosevelt had emerged as an active supporter of the UDA, separating herself from organizations that had long enjoyed her trust and support. As early as 1945, she had expressed her doubts about the SCHW to SCHW board member Frank Graham, explaining that James Carey had advised her that SCHW Executive Secretary James Dombrowski was a Communist and that Clark Foreman was incapable of recognizing one. Late in December 1946, probably in response to an invitation to attend the founding meeting of the Progressive Citizens of America (PCA), Eleanor Roosevelt wrote Beanie Baldwin and expressed her concerns on this issue. It was of the utmost importance, she told him, that "the NCPAC, the CIO-PAC and the ICC-ASP make up their minds to remove from their membership all people affiliated with or supposed to have . . . leanings to the American Communist Party."[32]

Baldwin responded at length. He explained that such a resolution had been introduced at the recent NCPAC board meeting and had been defeated by a 35 to 2 vote. Baldwin explained that the nearly unanimous rejection of the proposal reflected a shared feeling that "to cater to loose charges of influence by the Communist Party in the work of our Committee" would weaken the organization and aid the campaign being waged by the reactionary press and political leaders in their effort to "hopelessly divide and then destroy the liberal movement." He reminded Roosevelt that the affiliated organizations of the newly established PCA had "worked hard and with considerable success during the past few years to build an effective organization" in spite of the ever-present opposition of those who "questioned our sincerity and our purposes." He hoped that the ADA would "refrain from using these methods because it might be disastrous." Trusting that there were "honest differences among sincere liberals on this issue," Baldwin concluded his letter by requesting an appointment to meet with Roosevelt. "There are honest differences," Eleanor Roosevelt wrote in reply. "One is the fear of expressing openly the feeling one has about the American Communists which I consider essential." There was no need for a meeting, she said.[33]

The PCA and the ADA both claimed the Roosevelt legacy and reflected an irrevocable split in the New Deal coalition. The PCA was established on 29 December 1946, and the ADA was founded less than a week later. The NCPAC, the ICC-ASP, and several smaller independent political organizations combined to form the PCA; three hundred delegates from twenty-one states attended. Its founding committee included Beanie Baldwin, Clark Foreman, Walter White, Philip Murray, Jack Kroll, Robert Kenney of the California chapter of the National Lawyers Guild, Mary McLeod Bethune, and Dr. Joseph L. Johnson, dean of Howard University Medical School. The PCA's "Program for Political Action" reiterated the platform put forward at the September conference of progressives. Its constitution prohibited discrimination within the organization because of political beliefs. Henry Wallace delivered the keynote address and emerged as the group's leading figure.

The PCA intended to continue building a broad political action movement that would neither allow attacks by the right to "stampede" members into "foolish red-baiting" nor permit those whose primary allegiance was to a foreign power to determine the PCA's course, Wallace said. He warned, "The people who get us into trouble [are] the lukewarm liberals"—those who tried "to sit on three chairs at a time." Wallace urged liberals not to divide over minor issues but to join forces in resisting the postwar reaction through a program of organized political action. He emphasized the importance of creating a genuine two-party system by expanding organizing efforts at the precinct level, providing voters with information about the issues, and getting people to register and vote.[34]

Early in January a striking array of New Dealers, journalists, labor leaders from the CIO and the American Federation of Labor (AFL), intellectuals, and rising young politicians attended the founding meeting of the ADA, the UDA's successor organization. Eleanor Roosevelt and Franklin Roosevelt Jr.

were prominent among them. Others included John Kenneth Galbraith, Joseph L. Rauh, Hubert H. Humphrey (then the mayor of Minneapolis), Walter Reuther, and Joseph and Stewart Alsop. Philip Murray attended as an observer. Several participants still hoped to leave open the possibility of working with non-Communist elements in the PCA. Chester Bowles was among those who attended the founding meeting but declined to join the new organization because it "concentrated too much of its time opposing communism and not enough on opposing Republicans." The ADA adopted six basic principles; four concerned foreign policy. There was no reference to the struggle for voting rights or racial justice in the South. But in announcing its aims, the ADA proclaimed, "The interests of the United States are the interests of free people everywhere." Americans must oppose communism and fascism because both were "hostile to the principles of freedom and democracy on which the Republic" had grown "great"; thus the ADA left little room for compromise with the PCA or any other Popular Front organization.[35]

When the Eightieth Congress convened in January 1947, the new Republican leadership set forth ambitious plans to purge Communists and their allies from major institutions in American life. The House Un-American Activities Committee (HUAC) announced a sweeping program of investigative hearings that would focus on unions, the motion picture industry, and educational institutions. But for HUAC, as for several other committees eager to mine the political capital of the 1946 campaign, the New Deal bureaucracy would be the primary target of their loyalty investigations. In his first speech as House Speaker, Joseph Martin warned, "There is no room in the government of the United States for any who prefer the communist system [or] who do not believe in the way of life which made this the greatest country in the world."[36]

Despite Republican initiatives, the partisan political advantages inherent in the red issue were steadily defused. The Truman administration joined congressional concerns with a bold program to investigate and weed out subversive employees. Early in 1947, the administration announced the convening of a federal grand jury in New York to review charges concerning Communist infiltration of the federal government, and it subpoenaed Whittaker Chambers and Elizabeth Bentley, the primary sources of these charges. The enactment of President Truman's "loyalty program" in March 1947, with its provisions for a sweeping investigation of all federal employees, preempted congressional plans to tar the Truman administration with the brush of New Deal radicalism, at least temporarily. Under Attorney General Tom Clark, the relationship between HUAC and the Justice Department—a relationship that was adversarial during the Roosevelt years—was reversed. Clark cultivated a cooperative and supportive relationship with HUAC.[37]

During 1947 the Truman administration led in fashioning a cold war consensus that joined concern about domestic communism to the crusade against Soviet expansionism abroad. The loyalty program was enacted less than two weeks after the president introduced the Truman Doctrine in a speech to Congress, requesting military aid to Greece and Turkey. Bernard Baruch remarked that Truman's speech was "tantamount to a declaration of ideological war" against the Soviet Union. Democratic strategists implemented a domestic cold war policy capable of serving multiple ends. In addition to defusing anticommunism as a Republican issue, it helped to unify public opinion behind the foreign policy initiatives of the Truman administration while marginalizing critics on the Left.[38]

The Truman Doctrine and the "loyalty order" accentuated the divisions among liberal Democrats around the issues of communism, civil liberties, and civil rights. Truman's cold war policies answered the ADA's stated concerns regarding Soviet expansionism and domestic subversion and underscored the ADA's compatibility with the administration's worldview and its politics. Although there was some internal wrangling concerning aid to military dictatorships, the majority of ADA members agreed that resistance to Soviet expansionism took precedence over the ADA's commitment to support democratic governments. The ADA endorsed the objectives of Truman's loyalty program while expressing reservations about the procedures established for its enactment.[39]

The loyalty order elevated the issue of domestic communism from the realm of partisan politics to the arena of national security. "No other event, no political trial or congressional hearing," wrote historian Ellen Schrecker, "was to shape the internal Cold War as decisively as the Truman Administration's loyalty-security program." The president's action legitimized the charge, long waged by Republicans and opponents of the New Deal, that Communist Party members and their sympathizers had infiltrated government agencies and that the threat posed by their presence was serious enough to warrant an investigation of all employees.[40]

The order not only affirmed that the Communist Party was primarily an agent of a foreign power but also implied that anyone associated with the party was a security risk. Such associations were liberally defined to include "membership in, affiliation with, or sympathetic association with any foreign or domestic organization, association, group or combination of persons, designated by the Attorney General as totalitarian, fascist, Communist or subversive." Here was, said historian Henry Steele Commager, "guilt by association with a vengeance." Guilt was no longer personal or dependent on overt acts but was "an infectious thing to be achieved by sympathetic association with others presumed to be guilty or movements presumed to be subversive."[41]

In the months following the enactment of the Truman administration's cold war policies, critics sought ways to counter a policy that made the act of opposition itself suspect. *Nation* editor Freda Kirchwey feared that the country was slipping into a period reminiscent of the post–World War I "red scare," when "a legal reign of terror broke the strength of the progressive forces for a grim ten year stretch." Liberal unity was essential in resisting such an assault, yet, Kirchwey reported, an "alarming percentage of liberals" were "either taking cover or digging up reasons to believe that the Truman purge order, the inquisition now going on before the House Un-American Activities Committee, and the rash of repressive legislation before Congress [were] merely signs of healthy resistance to communism." She observed, "Fear of Russia has become an obsession with groups which a generation ago had a more solid faith in the country's capacity to remain both democratic and free."[42]

Clifford J. Durr, a member of the Federal Communications Commission (FCC), was one of the few government officials to publicly oppose the Truman loyalty program. Durr wrote a carefully reasoned critique of the order, its interpretation and implementation, and its likely consequences. He argued that the provisions of the loyalty program tended to undermine confidence in the democratic process and impair the national security that it was devised to safeguard. By focusing on attitudes and associations rather than wrongful behavior, by relying on nameless accusers, and by giving the FBI power over government employees, the loyalty program was fraught with "potentialities of injustice, oppression and cruelty." It was most likely to breed alienation and impair employee morale, to confuse conformity with loyalty. At a time when "new and unorthodox ideas were desperately needed to cope with new and unorthodox problems," the federal loyalty program tended to force all social, economic, and political thinking into orthodox patterns. At a time when confidence in government was of vital importance, the order tended to destroy confidence by implying that the government could not be trusted because there were subversives within its ranks. Whatever good the loyalty program was intended to advance was far outweighed by the evils inherent in its conception.[43]

The anti-Communist orthodoxy promoted by the federal loyalty program had a particular resonance for political activists familiar with the South. Charges of communism routinely met the efforts of labor to organize and of blacks to vote. Moreover, Communist Party members had played a catalytic role in the southern labor movement and were often conspicuous among the thinly populated vanguard in the fight for racial justice. In refusing to endorse a 1943 ACLU resolution condemning the Communist Party, Charles Houston explained that the Communists were working in many fields that interested him: "anti-lynching, anti-poll tax, anti-segregation, integration of the Negroes in the labor movement, etc." One did not have to agree with the party's ideological assumptions or economic analysis to acknowledge that their work was bringing about "a broader base of democratic participation by the common people." And to Houston's mind, this was no small achievement.[44]

The federal loyalty program, Houston believed, was a form of tub-thumping to divert attention from the government's lack of a program. Without demonstrating that the country was in imminent danger of attack by the Soviet Union, the Truman administration was willing to sacrifice one of democracy's most sacred rights, the right to disagree. Houston contrasted the government's aggressive and legally dubious effort to root out Communists and their sympathizers with its feeble response to the revival of the Ku Klux Klan in the South and the acceleration of racial violence and terror aimed at individuals seeking to vote. The loudly proclaimed crusade "to lead the world to democracy" apparently did not extend below the Mason-Dixon Line. Houston said that he might be reassured if the government "would use 50 percent of the G-men" it was using to chase Communists "as Task Force No. 2 against the native fascists in Georgia and Mississippi." But he had little confidence that this would happen. Indeed, if Communists wanted to seek cover in the South, Houston advised that they "put on white night shirts and wave the American flag."[45]

Southerners who had participated in efforts to expand political and civil rights since the 1930s were wary of the likely consequences of the loyalty program, which had the support of many liberals and major segments of the labor movement. The majority of SCHW board members continued to oppose an exclusionary policy based solely on political beliefs and affiliations as self-defeating, particularly for an organization striving to build confidence in the democratic process. Virginia Durr, cochair of the SCHW's Virginia committee, voiced a sentiment common among SCHW officials when she explained: "My position on the Communists is as it has always been— that they represent the extreme left of the political circuit, and I often disagree with their program and methods, but I see so clearly that when one group of people are made untouchable the liberties of all suffer, and our Democracy is on the way to ruin. I see and feel so clearly how it has crippled the lives and hopes of both the Negro and white people of the South."[46]

The SCHW remained part of a shrinking coalition dedicated to sustaining an independent movement within the Democratic Party, free to challenge and debate Truman's cold war policies. At the same time, the national CIO and the ADA sought to purge Communists and their sympathizers from political life, claiming a leading role for labor and liberals in fashioning a cold war consensus. This internal struggle to define postwar liberalism, waged among major components of the old New Deal coalition, had a southern variation. It was played out around the ADA's attempt to establish a southern base, and it underscores the gulf between cold war liberalism and the emergent movement for racial justice and voting rights in the South.

Following preliminary work by Frank McAllister and the UDA, the ADA opened a southern office in Memphis early in 1947. Under the directorship of Barney Taylor, formerly on the staff of the NFU, the ADA promoted itself as the liberal, non-Communist alternative to the SCHW. One primary factor distinguished the two organizations, Taylor explained: "The SCHW does not police its membership as we do." But the differences were more substantial. The ADA did not plan to engage in direct action or organized political struggle in the South or support groups that did. ADA organizers did not demonstrate any interest in the voter-registration drives of the mid-1940s, nor did they attempt to cultivate local or regional black leaders. The ADA's role, James Loeb explained, was not to build a mass organization but to serve "as the conscience of the community." ADA organizers proposed "to extend democracy into the South" by appealing to their southern counterparts—moderate, middle-class white people.[47]

The ADA aimed to establish a southern presence by winning the endorsement of prominent southern liberals. The organization's aggressive anticommunism appealed to author Lillian Smith, undoubtedly the ADA's most noted supporter in the region. When the ADA tried to obtain the endorsement of the nationally acclaimed Ellis Arnall, former governor of Georgia, Arnall declined. He doubted that the ADA was prepared to contribute to the liberal movement in the South, which, Arnall contended, could be built only from the grass roots. "The advance of liberalism in the South," Arnall explained, "can be more effectively directed by liberal southerners than by a national organization which is not too conversant with southern problems, attitudes, and reactions." Later Arnall learned that the ADA had gone ahead and listed his name among its supporters. He demanded and won a retraction. Stunned by Arnall's rebuff, a national official wondered "whether Dr. Clark Foreman's fine Italian hand" could "be discerned in the background."[48]

The ADA found support among textile union officials in North Carolina who had become disaffected with the SCHW's Committee for North Carolina (CNC). According to CNC Director Mary Price, late in 1946, officials of the Textile Workers Union of America (TWUA) began pressuring the CNC to restrict participation by blacks in the organization. The board tabled the proposal, which violated the founding principles of the SCHW. Several months later TWUA official William Smith enlisted the support of CNC board member Margaret Knight to organize a state chapter of the ADA. Price charged that Smith and Knight were waging "an out and out move against the CNC." She added, "They are obviously going after people . . . who have been participants in CNC and are trying to work in the same localities where we have been active."[49]

Price attempted to steer clear of the joint campaign by the TWUA and the ADA to discredit the CNC by maintaining the CNC's attention and resources on political action, education, and organizing. This proved increasingly difficult as the cold war climate intensified during 1947. Late that summer, Junius Scales, who had been a member of the SCHW since his college days at the University of North Carolina, decided to reveal that he had also been a longtime secret member of the Communist Party and was head of the party in Chapel Hill. He did so under pressure from the national office of the Communist Party of the United States. But Scales also rationalized that his revelation might help to put a human face on the party and thus defuse some of the anti-Communist hysteria. Scales came from a prominent North Carolina family, was well-known in Chapel Hill as a young protégé of University of North Carolina President Frank Graham's, had served in World War II, and was then enrolled as a graduate student in history at the university. At the risk of jeopardizing his academic career, Scales nevertheless looked forward to being able to speak openly and without the feeling of duplicity that nagged him whenever he concealed his party affiliation.

Before making a public statement, Scales attempted to prepare fellow CNC board members for the announcement and offer his explanations. He had anticipated denunciations by representatives of the anti-Communist TWUA. But he was unprepared for the widespread confusion and hostility among members of the CNC. "The hatred and fear of Communism, even in so liberal an organization, was far greater than I'd imagined," Scales recalled. "Some who had liked and respected me as a left-winger hated me as a Communist. . . . my candor caused more rage than reflection among my anti-Communist colleagues." Though Scales resigned from the executive committee, his statement led to an open split and hastened the departure of many liberals, many of whom joined the newly formed ADA chapter. But the ADA provided little more than a refuge for anti-Communist liberals. It never attempted to duplicate the work of the CNC by challenging the racial status quo in the South.[50]

Increasingly, the SCHW's efforts were diverted by charges that the organization had failed to purge its ranks of Communists and Communist sympathizers. Internal divisions over a nonexclusionary policy erupted in the SCHW Committee for Virginia in the spring of 1947 when its chairman, Henry Fowler, succeeded in passing a resolution, at a poorly attended board meeting, barring Communists from membership. Fowler had called the meeting to discuss financial problems; cochair Virginia Durr, having just given birth, was unable to attend. Durr issued a strong protest to the chairman, charging that his actions were "a denial of the very democratic procedures" that he professed to uphold. At Durr's insistence, the resolution was debated at a full meeting of the board. The board voted 12 to 5 to rescind it. Four of the five members who favored the ban, including Fowler, resigned from the committee.[51]

In May 1947, on the eve of a rally for Henry Wallace at the Watergate in Washington, D.C., HUAC issued a report charging that the SCHW was "perhaps the most deviously camouflaged communist-front organization," whose sole purpose was to serve the aims of the Soviet Union through the Communist Party of the United States. Distortions and inaccuracies filled the seventeen-page report, which failed to present any substantial evidence in support of its charges. The open-air meeting, sponsored by the Washington Committee of the SCHW, drew ten thousand people and raised more than twenty thousand dollars. In the short term, the publicity stirred by the HUAC report may have helped boost attendance. But the report provided more ammunition to SCHW critics in the South and caused potential supporters to avoid any association with the organization. In an effort to counter HUAC's smear, Clark Foreman tried, unsuccessfully, to persuade the ACLU to undertake an investigation of un-Americanism, beginning with the SCHW.[52]

From the spring through the fall of 1947 the SCHW and the PCA worked jointly to support a full and open discussion of domestic and foreign policy issues. Wallace toured the nation as a major spokesperson for this effort. Wallace's appearances also served to test his appeal as a potential presidential candidate. The defection of the national CIO from the PCA-sponsored coalition diminished the possibility of effectively challenging Truman for the Democratic nomination. But Wallace's strong reception in all parts of the country increased the likelihood of a third-party candidacy.

Clark Foreman led in coordinating Wallace's appearances in the South. Working with Virginia Durr, Mary Price, Palmer Weber, Senator Claude Pepper, and other SCHW supporters, Foreman aimed to secure the broadest audience possible without compromising the racial policy of the SCHW; local planning committees secured only those facilities that would allow non-segregated gatherings. During Wallace's first tour of the South, race did not become a contentious issue. Wallace himself focused on foreign policy, campaigning against Truman's cold war policies before enthusiastic audiences in Chapel Hill and Raleigh, North Carolina, Montgomery, Alabama, and Austin, Texas. Alabama Governor Jim Folsom introduced Wallace in Montgomery, and *Raleigh News and Observer* editor Josephus Daniels hosted Wallace in Raleigh at a dinner attended by University of North Carolina President Frank Graham. Daniels's newspaper, however, chastised the SCHW for "taking advantage" of Wallace by insisting on nonsegregated audiences and making race an issue.[53]

Wallace's experience in Austin, Texas, invited a more overt challenge to the segregation system. Speaking to a largely white group affiliated with the University of Texas, Wallace was surprised by the applause that greeted his endorsement of equality for all minority groups. Encouraged by the response, Wallace went on to describe an integrated reception that he had attended at Green Pastures Restaurant, the homestead of humorist John Henry Faulk. "This heresy, than which none could be greater," Foreman observed, "was also greeted with great applause." A university official told Foreman that Wallace should have placed more emphasis on racial equity because that was "the hot issue in Texas." Foreman discussed the possibility of another southern tour with Wallace, one that would promote a public challenge to segregation barriers.[54]

In November, Wallace returned for a more extensive tour of the region. Mary Price and Edmonia Grant, acting administrator of the SCHW national office, coordinated plans for Wallace's tour, organizing his appearances around a mass meeting and affording Wallace an opportunity to meet with local liberal politicians and SCHW members. The SCHW had never attempted to hold a succession of nonsegregated meetings on this scale, and Grant reported tremendous difficulty in securing facilities. Leading members of the SCHW's Committee for Arkansas opposed what they charged was the national office's insistence on calling attention to the nonsegregation policy, arguing that it was more important that people hear Wallace. When the national office refused to sponsor Wallace in the segregated municipal auditorium of Little Rock, plans for a visit to that city fizzled. Due to segregation restrictions and local unwillingness to consider black churches and other alternative gathering places, Greenville and Columbia, South Carolina, and Memphis, Nashville, Knoxville, and Chattanooga, Tennessee, were eliminated from the original agenda. When the final arrangements were completed, Wallace was scheduled to speak at fifteen meetings in six southern cities.[55]

Just weeks before Wallace's tour began, President Truman's Special Committee on Civil Rights issued its report, "To Secure These Rights." It recommended extensive reforms, including antilynching legislation, an end to segregation in the armed forces, legislation to prevent discrimination in voter registration, abolition of the poll tax, and other antidiscriminatory measures. Foreman hailed the report and was pleased with its timing. It offered an ideal platform for Wallace and the program of nonsegregated meetings arranged around his tour. Foreman urged that at least one of Wallace's speeches in the South be based on the president's report and that Wallace challenge the Democrats and the Republicans to follow through with action.[56]

Wallace opened his tour in Baton Rouge on 26 November and continued on to New Orleans, Macon, Atlanta, Louisville, and Norfolk. The meetings were peaceful, despite threats from the Klan in Atlanta, and well attended. Wallace spoke out against Truman's cold war policies abroad and at home and placed greater emphasis on civil rights than he had before. He repeatedly called for an end to racial discrimination and segregation and endorsed the report of the Special Committee on Civil Rights, calling it "the one bright spot" in the Truman administration. In a speech to students at Morehouse College, Wallace focused almost exclusively on southern economic and political problems and on the recommendations of "To Secure These Rights."[57]

Clark Foreman and other SCHW sponsors anticipated that this tour would "set the stage for demanding that all national political figures make speeches in the South on a nonsegregated basis." At the Colonial Auditorium in New Orleans, Wallace's audience was composed of roughly equal numbers of blacks and whites. In Atlanta he addressed an overflow audience of more than three thousand people at Rev. William Holmes Borders's Wheat Street Baptist Church. The *Atlanta Journal* reported that this was "one of the largest nonsegregated gatherings in Atlanta's history." Approximately 60 percent of the audience was black. The crowd of sixteen hundred who heard Wallace at the Louisville Armory made up the largest nonsegregated meeting ever held in that city, according to press reports.[58]

Wallace and the SCHW won their most notable victory over segregation in Norfolk, Virginia, the last stop on Wallace's tour. Virginia had the only state law prohibiting nonsegregated public meetings. Three thousand people crowded into the auditorium to hear Wallace and did not cooperate with attempts by the police to usher them into segregated seating areas. The director of the auditorium barred Virginia Durr from the stage, declaring that the meeting would not begin until segregation was observed.[59]

Undeterred, Foreman climbed from the orchestra pit onto the stage and addressed the audience. He explained what the police were trying to do and declared that the SCHW did not recognize the constitutionality of the state law prohibiting nonsegregated meetings. If the police tried to enforce the edict, the SCHW would challenge the law in court. He then invited Durr to the stage to start the meeting. Anticipating Wallace's imminent arrival, Foreman was confident that the police would not break up the meeting if Wallace was there. Durr and Foreman held the police at bay while they led the audience in several rounds of "The Star-Spangled Banner." With Wallace nowhere in sight, Durr invited a preacher to join them on the stage and lead the crowd in prayer. "We prayed on and on," Durr recalled. Just as the preacher was about to run out of breath and the police seemed ready to start making arrests, Wallace entered the auditorium. He was greeted by a three-minute standing ovation as he came down the aisle. The next day, Virginia newspapers announced that the Wallace meeting had killed the state law prohibiting nonsegregated meetings. That, Foreman later recalled, was worth the whole tour.[60]

Reaction to Wallace was generally positive throughout the region. An estimated twenty-five thousand people attended the mass meetings, and countless others heard Wallace over the radio. Some newspapers dismissed Wallace as, in the words of the *Memphis Commercial Appeal*, "an agent of discord for the Southern Conference for Human Welfare." *Atlanta Constitution* editor Ralph McGill vented his deep hostility toward the SCHW, charging that its primary motive for bringing Wallace to Atlanta was to provoke violence. A longtime critic of the SCHW, McGill blasted the organization as a "communist infiltrated group" and called its officials "Ku-Klux minded" and "discredited professional phonies." Since McGill had asserted that individuals who were not Communists were affiliated with the party, the SCHW prepared to sue the *Constitution* for libel. The paper, ironically, was managed by Clark Howell Jr., Foreman's cousin. McGill printed a retraction.[61]

Wallace's tour was hailed as a great success by SCHW officials and supporters. SCHW membership increased by nearly fifteen hundred as a result of the tour, which also succeeded in raising five thousand dollars to support the work of the conference. The most significant accomplishment of the entire exercise, according to Foreman, was being able to complete the tour "without submitting to segregation and without provoking violence." An important precedent had been set, for this was the first time in the twentieth century that a "presidential possibility" had gone to the South and addressed southerners as equals. Foreman praised Wallace for his "wonderful job" in linking the SCHW to the fight for democracy in the South.[62]

The success of Henry Wallace's tour of the South and his enthusiastic welcome in other parts of the country pointed toward the possibilities of creating a national platform that offered an alternative to the politics and policies of the cold war. By the end of 1947, it was clear that such a campaign could not be effectively mounted within the Democratic Party. Beanie Baldwin and Clark Foreman were among those who urged Wallace to continue his challenge on an independent ticket. On 27 December 1947, Henry Wallace declared his candidacy for the presidency at the head of a new party. The Progressive Party incorporated the PCA, much of the SCHW, and a host of union members, civil rights activists, and independent liberals; it did not disavow Communist support.

Nationally, the Progressive Party could not escape the parameters established by the cold war. The 1948 campaign completed the rout of the Left from American political life and secured the ascendancy of a cold war consensus that embraced the entire spectrum of liberal political activity. But in the South, beyond the realm of mainstream politics, the Wallace campaign provided an electoral structure outside of the Democratic Party, one that tapped into the movement that had taken root during the previous decade. Drawing on remnants of the New Deal's southern coalitions, it allowed black and white southerners to rehearse the strategies and tactics that would ultimately overturn the legal and political foundations of Jim Crow.

The form of our resistance to segregation may be slow in materializing. It will vary from time to time and from place to place.
But the spiritual climate has been formed. Underground in Mississippi or out in the open in New York Wallace has forced the fight.

CHARLES HOUSTON, *Baltimore Afro-American,*

11 September 1948

I had waited all my life to hear a white man say what he [Henry
Wallace] said.

DAISY BATES, Little Rock, Arkansas

Epilogue: 1948

On 28 August 1948, Henry Wallace embarked on a
week-long tour of the South as Progressive Party candidate for president.
Wallace and a small entourage of campaign workers and reporters traveled
alternately by bus, train, and car motorcade from Virginia to Mississippi in
the dog days of summer. The itinerary included more than thirty campaign
appearances in seven southern states. It embraced a broad spectrum of
southern life in the shadow of war-induced change.

Opening his southern tour in Virginia, Wallace reminded a Richmond
audience of *The Report on the Economic Conditions of the South* and its
continuing relevance. A decade had passed since the report focused national
attention on the region's poverty and underdevelopment. In the interim, the

wartime infusion of defense dollars had ignited an industrial boom that accelerated the pace of urbanization and ensured the region's economic modernization. Yet wartime prosperity was unevenly distributed and did little to alter the racial and political foundation of the region's economic development. The antiunion, segregationist politics of the one-party South remained deeply entrenched. According to statistics on average income, literacy, incidence of disease, and infant mortality, the South was still the nation's poorest region.

Wallace proposed a dual strategy for addressing the economic inequities and disadvantages that continued to plague the South. He outlined a four-year, four-billion-dollar program of federal aid—aid targeted specifically for schools, hospitals, home loans, and wider social security, as well as for agricultural and industrial development. But the success of this or any other program of assistance depended on fundamental social and political change. Such change, Wallace maintained, required a continuing assault on the "twin pillars of segregation and poll taxes" supporting the wall of privilege that retarded the region's development.[1]

During the months preceding Wallace's southern tour, Progressive Party organizations sprouted up across the region. A loose affiliation with the national campaign office was established early in the year when board members of the Southern Conference for Human Welfare (SCHW) met with Beanie Baldwin, chairman of the national Progressive Party, to discuss plans for mounting Wallace's campaign in the South. Participants acknowledged that a volatile political terrain made it difficult to anticipate the short-term consequences of such an effort. Myles Horton of Highlander Folk School and Lou Burnham of the Southern Negro Youth Congress (SNYC) warned that labor "was on a hot spot"; the Congress of Industrial Organizations (CIO) national policy barring any official endorsements of the Wallace candidacy would inhibit unions that might be inclined to support Wallace. Mojeska Simkins of South Carolina explained that black people in her state were still caught up in the fight to vote in the Democratic Party primary. In January 1948 a U.S. Court of Appeals dealt the final blow to South Carolina's all-white primary. But Simkins predicted that after the summer primary election, "thousands" would "turn to Wallace."[2]

While the Democratic Party and the national CIO sought to limit progressive political activity, the Wallace campaign offered an electoral arena for expanding on the developments of the previous decade. Clark Foreman resigned as president of the SCHW to work full-time for the Wallace campaign as treasurer of the national party. State committees of the SCHW disbanded and, in many instances, provided a base for state offices of the

Progressive Party. Union participation came from the National Maritime Union, the Mine, Mill and Smelter Workers, the Food and Tobacco Workers Union, and other left-wing CIO affiliates. The national Communist Party's endorsement of the Progressive Party brought the energetic support of its sparse band of southern activists.

World War II veteran Randolph Blackwell, an active member of the National Association for the Advancement of Colored People (NAACP) branch and of the SCHW chapter in Greensboro, North Carolina, remembered the Progressive Party effort as a new departure that set the stage for integrated political activities. Although the national NAACP maintained its allegiance to Truman and the Democratic Party, the Progressive Party attracted the support of black southerners like Blackwell who had been working to expand black participation in the electoral process. Among them were people like Lulu White, a leading organizer of the NAACP branch in Houston, Texas, Heman Sweatt, plaintiff in the NAACP's *Sweatt v. Painter* case, Rev. D. V. Kyle, NAACP leader in Memphis, and Mojeska Simkins, longtime NAACP official in Columbia, South Carolina. Black newspaper publishers Louis Austin in Durham, North Carolina, Larkin Marshall in Macon, Georgia, and Daisy and C. L. Bates in Little Rock, Arkansas, were among those who organized for the Progressive Party. Rev. Maynard Jackson Sr., founder of the National Progressive Voters League, took part in the Wallace effort in Atlanta. Floyd McKissick, who had joined the NAACP at the age of twelve, served as president of the Progressive Party chapter at Atlanta University.[3]

Palmer Weber joined the Progressive Party as codirector of the southern campaign in May 1948 after resigning his position with the CIO Political Action Committee (CIO-PAC). In his letter of resignation to CIO-PAC Chairman Jack Kroll, he wrote, "I feel as though I were tearing up deep buried roots—almost as though I were paddling into an ocean storm in a small rowboat." But efforts on the part of the CIO's national executive committee to squash independent political action among industrial union councils and enforce loyalty to Truman administration policies had, in Weber's words, pushed him over the line. Weber strongly believed that the fight was on both the economic and the political fronts and that CIO President Phil Murray had surrendered to "that lousy White House mob," which knew that the CIO had "nowhere to go." He thanked Kroll for his support of the southern CIO-PAC operation and urged him not to write it off. "At least every penny and every effort made on that front is to the good."[4]

The Wallace campaign, Weber recalled, afforded an opportunity "to make one last fling at civil rights and civil liberties." He agreed to take responsibility for the Progressive Party's southern campaign under two conditions:

that Louis Burnham serve with him as codirector, and that they have the freedom to run the campaign in the South as "a head on attack against the segregation system."[5]

Burnham and Weber, both veterans of the student movement of the 1930s, enlisted student volunteers as the backbone of the southern campaign. With barely enough money to cover the most basic expenses, they coordinated a network of college students, many of whom were veterans, to help organize southern supporters, get petitions signed, and register voters. Northern students came to the South during the summer months to aid with voter registration and petition drives to get Wallace on the ballot.

The "eager young volunteers from up north [sometimes] created more problems than results," recalled William Moody, publicity director for the southern campaign. Moody recounted an incident in Macon, Georgia, a center of Klan activity. The northern volunteers, determined to defy southern ways, "staged mixed white and black dancing in the streets. It became a struggle to get them out alive . . . then make them aware, without dimming their enthusiasm, that southern segregation was not something to be defiant about if one were going to undermine one of its main pillars—disenfranchising the black vote, which was what they were there to do." Weber was infuriated by the incident, which had senselessly risked the lives of the student volunteers. Weber later recalled his reaction when he found out who the instigator was: "I threatened to kill him with my bare hands if I caught him near the students again."[6]

Burnham and Weber worked hard at turning students into effective, knowledgeable volunteers. They established a clearly defined protocol for setting up voter-registration projects and for dealing with local law enforcement officials and the press. Contact between the volunteers and the Atlanta office of the Progressive Party was to be maintained on a daily basis. They were instructed to immediately contact the nearest office of the Federal Bureau of Investigation (FBI) and the press when they experienced or uncovered civil rights violations.

Moody, a white volunteer who accompanied Louis Burnham in establishing voter-registration drives in various cities, recalled how they manipulated southern racial etiquette.

> The procedure, as Lou carefully explained it, was we first went to the chief of police. I would be the leader of the group, each of whom I would introduce, while Lou would be last. The introduction of Lou was offered in a cavalier, casual manner as "Oh that boy is Lou." An intelligent, committed progressive like Lou being introduced like something the cat

dragged in made me gag. Lou assured me they were aware of him and his role. . . . Lou knew his south and he was right, as the conversation sooner or later gravitated to Lou and the chief of police talking about the details and conduct of the operation in that town. But, first, the protocol was necessary to properly get Lou established to play his role. . . . And so it went from town to town as we set up the voter registration teams.

In setting up voter-registration drives and organizing rallies and meetings around the South, Louis Burnham relied upon an extensive network of black community leaders. Moody recounted a tense situation that occurred in Savannah, Georgia, where he assisted Burnham with preparations for Paul Robeson's appearance at a campaign rally in the city's largest auditorium. A group of local black leaders accompanied Burnham and Moody to meet with the chief of police. The chief promised to provide a large contingent of officers to "preserve the peace" at the auditorium and enforce racially segregated seating. On the evening of the meeting, the auditorium was surrounded by white police officers and by uniformed black men known locally as Colonel Gray's troops. When efforts by the police to enforce segregation failed, they ordered the crowd to disperse. Colonel Gray's troops distributed leaflets to people as they left, announcing that the Robeson meeting had been transferred to Colonel Gray's church. Moody recalled: "The meeting at minister Gray's church turned out to be a sensational, nonsegregated meeting in the black section of town where no white policemen put in an appearance."[7]

Palmer Weber's frequent visits to white and black college campuses to mobilize Wallace's young supporters and keep the campaign "moving" became legendary. Some former Chapel Hill students jokingly remembered what they called "the Palmer raids." Randolph Blackwell had a vivid memory of Weber's meetings with students at North Carolina A&T and of how Weber talked at length about "what this nation could be . . . if we ever made it over the hurdle of racial discrimination." Blackwell explained, "That had a great deal of influence in causing those of us whose lives he touched to . . . dedicate ourselves to the task of ridding the society of racial discrimination—in terms of what it would mean as it related to the development of this nation and this society. . . . I don't think I ever heard Palmer Weber say anything I would interpret as negative, only in terms of what was possible."[8]

Wallace supporters organized state parties, held conventions, nominated candidates, and elected delegations to attend the national Progressive Party convention. Blacks and women participated in all phases of the campaign. In Virginia, Jerry Gilliam, a postal worker and NAACP activist, ran for the U.S.

Virginia Durr, chair of the Progressive Party of Virginia, with Paul Robeson and Palmer Weber at the founding convention of the state party. (Photograph from the *Richmond Times-Dispatch*, 28 June 1948)

Progressive Party supporters in Georgia circulate petitions to gain a place on the ballot for presidential candidate Henry Wallace and his running mate, Glen Taylor. They collected more than 80,000 signatures. (Photograph courtesy of Branson Price)

Top. More than six hundred people crowded into Mount Olive Baptist Church in Knoxville, Tennessee, and hundreds more spilled over into the basement and outside the church for the final gathering of Wallace's southern tour. In his address, Wallace described his tour through the South as "the most memorable week of my life." (Photograph courtesy of Kenneth and Nona Clarke)

Bottom. Pete Seeger leads the Mount Olive Baptist Church in song. Louis Burnham, codirector of the southern campaign, is the second person to Seeger's right. (Photograph courtesy of Kenneth and Nona Clarke)

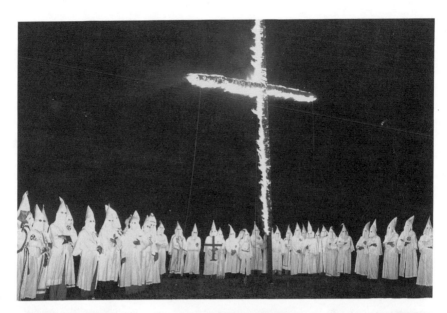

Top. The Ku Klux Klan planned an initiation ceremony in a field outside Knoxville to coincide with Wallace's last scheduled appearance. (Photograph courtesy of Kenneth and Nona Clarke)

Bottom. In mid-1948, Judge J. Waties Waring struck the final blow to South Carolina's relentless efforts to bar blacks from the state Democratic primary. Blacks lined up outside the polling station in Columbia, South Carolina, were among some 30,000 African Americans who voted in the primary elections on that day. (Photograph courtesy of the South Caroliniana Library, University of South Carolina)

Congress from Norfolk; Virginia Durr challenged Harry Byrd for his seat in the U.S. Senate. Larkin Marshall, editor of the *Macon Daily World,* ran for the U.S. Senate in Georgia, and James Barfoot, a University of Georgia professor, ran for governor. Rev. D. V. Kyle, pastor of the African Methodist Episcopal (AME) Church in Memphis, was the Progressive Party congressional candidate for Tennessee's tenth district. North Carolina Progressives nominated Mary Price to run for governor of that state, and Emily Blanchard ran for governor on the Progressive ticket in Louisiana.

The Progressive Party aimed to get on the ballot in every southern state, a goal that proved especially challenging in North Carolina and Georgia. North Carolina required the signatures of ten thousand registered voters in order for a group to qualify as a new party and ten cents per name to cover the costs of processing the petitions. In Georgia, fifty-five thousand signatures were needed. Students mounted joint petition and voter-registration drives in both states and were joined by young northern volunteers who came to the South during the qualifying period. North Carolina organizer Marge Frantz recalled the tensions and cultural clashes that accompanied this brave experiment and remembered feeling empathy for her Mississippi counterparts in 1964. But in both states, the students collected even more than the requisite number of signatures. And canvassers in North Carolina were instrumental in opening the registration books to black citizens in at least six counties in which a black person had not voted in fifty years.

A contemporary observed that the effort in Georgia seemed more like "guerilla warfare" than a political campaign. In the face of escalating terror, student canvassers demonstrated courage and a youthful invincibility, approaching their task with the "zeal of crusaders." Nearly one hundred of them covered the state, concentrating mainly in urban areas. They sought signatures in white as well as black areas and treaded on known Klan strongholds. Vigilante groups ran them out of Columbus and threatened to lynch the volunteers before running them out of Augusta. In other places, the canvassers were routinely harassed by the police and arrested on loitering charges. Nevertheless, they collected more than eighty thousand signatures, most of them from registered black voters. Three hours before the deadline, however, a special session of the state legislature amended the law regulating the qualifications for listing new parties on the ballot. It was impossible for the Progressive Party to meet the new requirement and list its full slate of candidates. However, Wallace and his running mate, Glen Taylor, were able to secure a place on the Georgia ballot due to a special provision designed to accommodate the States' Rights Party presidential ticket of Strom Thurmond and Fielding Wright.[9]

Such southern-based challenges to the dominion of Jim Crow exposed the hollow rhetoric of freedom and democracy that hallmarked America's cold war policy. Civil rights attorney Charles Houston questioned the sincerity of those who wielded the blunt instrument of anticommunism against Wallace and his supporters. "Certainly there are Communists in the Wallace movement. So what?," Houston wrote in February 1948. "There are Fascists in the Democratic Party, such as Ellender, Eastland, Rankin and the whole crew of southern poll taxers and I do not see anybody trying to excommunicate them." Those who insisted on smearing Wallace were, said Houston, essentially dishonest. What they really feared was not communism but Wallace's demonstrated commitment to "a democracy which works and embraces all people."[10]

Wallace's clear attack on segregation contrasted with the Democratic Party's halting efforts to frame civil rights as a national issue. Following a campaign strategy crafted by Clark Clifford, Harry Truman sought to strike a balance between northern black voters and southern Democratic Party stalwarts, both groups considered critical to his victory in November. Early in 1948, the president met Wallace's third-party challenge with a State of the Union message that included a ringing endorsement of the recommendations of his Special Committee on Civil Rights. Several days later, Truman sent a special message to Congress urging the enactment of omnibus civil rights legislation that included provisions for abolition of the poll tax and desegregation of the armed forces. Leading southern Democrats served notice that the president was courting a revolt. Senator J. Howard McGrath, chairman of the Democratic National Committee, tried to convince his southern colleagues that the president had no intention of tampering with the segregationist system, but he had no success.[11]

In March, when a delegation of black leaders met with the president to discuss the desegregation of the armed forces, he was in retreat. Group spokesman A. Philip Randolph urged Truman to act swiftly, particularly since the enactment of legislation providing for universal military training was imminent. He reminded Truman that racial segregation in the military contradicted America's claim as the world's leading democracy and offered a potent issue for Soviet propagandists. In response, Truman noted that his civil rights message to Congress had helped to defuse Soviet propaganda. The delegates explained to the president, according to Charles Houston's report, that "neither Russia nor the colored people here would be fooled by civil rights messages which float off in thin air and are not backed up by action." Randolph warned that black soldiers would no longer fight in a segregated army. Truman remained noncommittal. Congress, he said, was responsible for ending segregation in the armed forces and any universal military training program. Houston concluded that Truman was afraid to take any firm initiatives.[12]

By the time the Democratic national convention met in Philadelphia in mid-July, increasing black demands for presidential action, along with the Progressive Party's steady assault on racial discrimination, forced the show-down that Truman had so assiduously avoided. On 26 June Randolph prom-ised a massive campaign of civil disobedience unless an executive order desegregating the armed forces was issued before the enactment of the new draft law in August. Meanwhile, Americans for Democratic Action (ADA) liberals, who had failed in their efforts to draft Dwight Eisenhower for the Democratic nomination, feared that Truman's retreat on civil rights would spell defeat in key northern races in November. Their concerns were shared by urban bosses who could not afford to lose black voters to Wallace. After an impassioned speech by Hubert Humphrey, U.S. Senate candidate from Missouri, the national Democratic convention voted to adopt a civil rights plank based on the provisions advanced by Truman in his February message to Congress. Southern delegates bolted the convention, reconvened in Bir-mingham, and established the States' Rights Party. On 26 July Truman issued an executive order providing for the desegregation of the armed forces.[13]

The 1948 Democratic Party convention was a defining moment. It was testimony to the power of the northern black vote and acknowledged that civil rights was a political issue of national consequence. The historic floor fight for a civil rights plank, culminating as it did with the walkout of southern delegates, was a decisive factor in securing Truman's upset win over New York Governor Thomas Dewey. By finally standing up to south-ern threats, Truman had, as a contemporary observed, "stopped the swing of many toward the Progressives, because now thousands of colored and liberal white voters can vote the Democratic ticket without apology."[14]

Gains for civil rights in Philadelphia and Washington, however, barely played at the edges of the movement unfolding in the South. When Wallace campaigned across the region at the end of the summer, the nation glimpsed a place where white supremacy reigned defiantly. Wallace's established pol-icy of speaking only before nonsegregated audiences met with even greater opposition than it had in the past. From North Carolina onward, threatening mobs and rigidly enforced segregation laws captured front-page news as Wallace and his caravan pushed deeper into the South. For seven days,

Wallace's unyielding opposition to segregation's grip engaged the loose infrastructure of organized resistance, legal struggle, and community activism that had developed during the previous decade.

Louis Burnham, Palmer Weber, and Clark Foreman accompanied Wallace and worked with local Progressive Party supporters in coordinating the southern tour. Wallace's entourage also included Lew Frank, a close confidant and aid, Pete Seeger, the balladeer of the Progressive Party, Edith Roberts, a young black woman who worked as Wallace's secretary, and Mabel Cooney, a former University of Iowa student who had been an assistant to Wallace for nearly a decade. Journalists for several major newspapers and magazines covered the southern tour. They included John Popham of the *New York Times*, Douglass Hall of the *Baltimore Afro-American*, and James Wechsler of the *New York Post*, who happened to be a founding member of the ADA. The interracial band of Progressives and reporters picnicked together at roadsides across the South and slept on trains and busses when traveling overnight, avoiding segregated situations whenever possible.[15]

After a peaceful day of campaigning in Virginia, few were prepared for the reception that greeted Wallace in North Carolina, reputedly the region's most liberal and tolerant state. Near-riot conditions prevailed at an evening meeting in Durham. Hundreds had gathered outside the city auditorium, waving picket signs and Confederate flags and jeering at Wallace supporters as they entered. More than fifteen hundred people filled the city auditorium to capacity. Shortly before Wallace arrived, a crowd of anti-Wallace protesters broke through the back entrance wielding sticks and picket signs in an attempt to break up the meeting. A hastily convened "security" force of University of North Carolina students blocked the intruders from getting to the stage. While fighting and scuffling rocked the back of the auditorium, the rest of the audience remained calm and sang Progressive Party campaign songs. Douglass Hall reported that the black members of the audience, who composed about half, "seemed to be contented in sitting back and letting 'the white folks fight it out among themselves.'" After a student was stabbed, a National Guardsman used the butt of his rifle to eject the protesters from the hall and bolted the door.[16]

Wallace finally arrived and entered through a side door, accompanied by a National Guardsman with a drawn pistol. Hecklers, clustered throughout the hall, greeted the former vice-president with rebel yells and chants of "We Want Thurmond" while picketers, locked outside, banged on the door. Wallace discarded his prepared speech, a sober discourse on the southern economy, and attempted to speak directly to the situation in the hall. But the din made it nearly impossible for him to be heard. Pointing to a crowd of hecklers gathered in a back corner, Wallace shouted, "I can stand here as long as you can yell."[17]

The organizers of the meeting became increasingly concerned for Wallace's physical safety. Several loud bangs, sounding like gunshots, punctuated the air, releasing screams of terror from the audience. Mike Ross, an experienced labor organizer, recalled: "The police were not handling the ugliness in the crowd. We didn't know if we could get him [Wallace] out alive. It was that bad." The organizers managed to disband the meeting without further incident, and Wallace retired to the home of George Logan, a black businessman. Logan had offered to provide accommodations after an abrupt tightening of the racial policy at the major hotel in Durham caused local arrangers to cancel Wallace's reservation there.[18]

Early the next morning, Wallace went alone to meet with nearly two hundred students outside of the post office in Chapel Hill. Then a small motorcade of North Carolina supporters joined the Wallace entourage and a busful of reporters for a two-day tour through the state, starting with the mill town of Burlington. Marge Frantz, organizer of North Carolina students for Wallace, drove a large touring car plastered with Wallace posters and stickers and carrying Pete Seeger, Lou Burnham, Edith Roberts, and Mabel Cooney. James Wechsler reflected the uneasiness shared by others in the press van. "In the aftermath of a riotous assault on his first major southern rally," he wrote, "Wallace advanced deeper into Dixieland . . . flaunting his opposition to the segregation tenets of the white supremacy bloc . . . amid ominous forecasts." As they approached Burlington, Burnham advised passengers in his car to roll up the windows.[19]

A crowd of more than twenty-five hundred waited for Wallace in Burlington and piled into the streets as the motorcade approached the town square. While police worked to clear a path, young men rocked the cars and climbed onto the hoods. Others banged the cars with sticks. Wallace's appearance in Burlington, Popham recalled, aroused the kind of violent ill will that went beyond mere protest. And the police were not controlling it. Wallace and Clark Foreman emerged into the tumult and attempted to speak. They were greeted by a barrage of eggs and tomatoes; Wallace "had the stuff pouring down his face." Each time he started to speak, the crowd shouted him down. But he remained physically fearless as he stood in a sea of "angry, screaming textile workers," any one of whom, Palmer Weber recalled, "could have pulled a knife out and slit his gut open." In a momentary burst of anger, Wallace grabbed one of the protesters and shook him, asking: "Are you an American? Don't you believe in free speech? Why won't you let me speak?" Just as quickly, the anger left his face. With a composed, almost messianic gesture, Wallace waved to the mob. "Goodbye my friends. I'll see you again."[20]

Angry crowds greeted Wallace at open-air meetings in Greensboro and High Point. There was increased police protection, and student supporters milled anonymously among the hecklers, bumping against pockets bulging with rotten eggs. Standing on the courthouse steps in Greensboro, Wallace told the crowd that althoug he did not mind some good-natured throwing of eggs and tomatoes, he would prefer that the food be used to feed children. Jeers and taunts defeated Wallace's efforts to speak in Greensboro and again in High Point. But Pete Seeger remembered a small victory in High Point. When a young Thurmond supporter bet Seeger that he could not sing "Dixie," Seeger invited the young man to sing along. Seeger proceeded to sing every stanza of "Dixie," including ones that few people had ever heard, leaving the Thurmond booster speechless.

That evening, Wallace supporters packed the Southside Baseball Park in Winston-Salem for a rally organized by black tobacco workers of Local 22 of the Food, Tobacco, Agricultural and Allied Workers Union of America (FTA). A steady rain was falling when Foreman opened the meeting. Foreman castigated "the Dukes, the Reynolds and the Cannons," who had "robbed the labor of whites and Negroes in this state for fifty years." Remembering that moment, Burnham recalled a "marvelous speech." Foreman, Burnham said, demonstrated "the kind of anger only a Southerner could have." He told the small cluster of hecklers in the audience: "We will not be frightened. You can call us black, you can call us red. But you can't call us yellow." Pete Seeger followed, leading the crowd in an old gospel hymn, "Farther Along the Way We'll Know All about It," but changing the words to ". . . They'll Know All about It," singing heartily at the hecklers. "With the black trade unionists roused in song," Seeger recalled, "you should have heard the harmony roll."[21]

The heckling reached a roaring crescendo when Mary Price attempted to introduce Wallace. Standing in the rain, Wallace began to shout his message; cheers of "We Want Wallace" eclipsed the boos. Though forced to pause frequently, he managed to deliver most of his speech, focusing on the need for massive federal aid to the South. Wallace ended the day encouraged by the receptive temper of the ballpark rally. Governor R. Gregg Cherry sent word to the Wallace group promising increased police protection during the next day's trip across the state.

With a state police car leading the way, the motorcade stopped in Charlotte, Hickory, and Asheville. Nearly three thousand people had assembled outside of the Mecklenburg County Courthouse in Charlotte. A mob atmosphere prevailed. Screaming protesters banged on the cars with baseball bats and pulled and tugged on Wallace as he emerged from the car. Wallace's attempt to speak on the Mecklenburg Declaration of Independence was, once again, eclipsed by boos and a barrage of eggs and tomatoes. This time the food seemed to hit everyone except Wallace.

The crowd waiting in the small manufacturing town of Hickory was among the most menacing. Mary Price recalled that it was the only time she had ever experienced such bone-chilling fear. People pressed their faces against the car windows, shouting obscenities and threats. Police officers surrounded Wallace's car, enabling him to make his way to a small portable microphone set up on the sidewalk. He grabbed it with both hands and asked for a chance to speak. Suddenly it was quiet. Wallace began by telling about his initiatives as secretary of commerce to aid black businessmen, explaining that black businesses were entitled to the same opportunities as white businesses. The crowd broke into shouts of "Communist" and "nigger lover!" Someone asked, "Did Stalin tell you to say that?" Protesters hurled a barrage of overripe tomatoes and eggs. Exasperated, Wallace ended his talk abruptly, paraphrasing a biblical passage: "As Jesus Christ told his disciples, when you enter a town that will not hear you willingly, then shake the dust of that town from your feet and go elsewhere."[22]

Mairi Foreman greeted her husband and the rest of the Wallace tour with a fresh supply of shirts when they arrived in Asheville. The egg-and-tomato-splattered group bore "shocking evidence of bad receptions," she later recalled. For the first time in two days, Wallace spoke without interruption when he addressed the crowd assembled in Asheville's courthouse square. Most of this speech focused on foreign policy issues. At its conclusion, he smiled and thanked his listeners "for this wonderful opportunity to democratically express" his views. He thanked "all the fine people" who had turned out to see him throughout the state. Later that evening, the Wallace party boarded an all-night train heading to Alabama.[23]

The mob atmosphere that prevailed during Wallace's two-day trip through North Carolina commanded front-page notice in the nation's major newspapers and invited much commentary within the state. Expressing disdain for the rabble-rousers who had tarnished the Tarheel State's good image, editorialists nevertheless blamed Wallace for inciting such behavior. The *Winston-Salem Journal* chided Wallace for "his sensational overplaying of the jim crow issue" and for his bad manners. He had failed in his "obligation to defer to the traditional social customs of his host." The *Raleigh News and Observer* lectured those citizens who had denied Wallace his right to speak, but it simultaneously appealed to the prejudices used to justify such behavior. Wallace, the paper said, was "the stooge if not the spearhead of those who talk[ed] much about democracy as a cloak for their own disloyalty"; his entourage was "an insignificant and contemptible crew."[24]

For Douglass Hall, events in North Carolina served as a healthy corrective to the myth of North Carolina's exceptionalism. It was time to "stop listening to white people praise themselves" and time to "weigh them by their actions," he advised his readers. The uniformly hostile reception that had greeted Wallace illustrated that, like white southerners in other states, white North Carolinians hated "anyone, white or black," who advocated "better conditions for brown Americans." If nothing else, Hall hoped that Wallace's visit had demonstrated to black Carolinians that their situation was not different from that of blacks anywhere else in the South. "They were good colored folk" who paid the price of segregation and economic slavery for peace and "good [race] relations." Hall urged his readers to choose to be "full-blooded American citizens" and to act accordingly. "If we have to pull ourselves up by our bootstraps, WE WILL DO IT."[25]

While journalists digested the events in North Carolina, Wallace and his aids debated whether they should continue on to Alabama. Lew Frank expressed fear for Wallace's personal safety and advised that the rest of the trip be canceled. Almost everyone else admitted to a state of nervous exhaustion and supported Frank's recommendation. Clark Foreman and Henry Wallace were the exceptions. To turn back, Foreman said, would be a concession to hoodlumism. Wallace, who remained outwardly unshaken, agreed and insisted on going forward.

Contemplating the journey ahead, James Wechsler predicted that two days in Alabama and Mississippi "would restore North Carolina's prestige as a health resort and center of enlightenment." For Wechsler and most of the other reporters on the tour, it was as if they had entered a foreign land. Press badges offered no shield from the mobs in Burlington and Hickory, nor did the "I'm for Thurmond" button sported by a reporter from *Life* magazine. Weber remembered how in Burlington, a terrorized reporter ran into a phone booth seeking protection. "They were looking at something completely incomprehensible. They were frightened stiff." He added wryly, "It was very educational for these reporters." Several reporters described a feeling of incipient danger and terror that persisted throughout the journey, and they expressed their disgust with the indignities and brutality inherent in the segregation system. Douglass Hall remembered his satisfaction in seeing his white colleagues taste what black people lived with constantly.[26]

As they traveled deeper into the South, Burnham and Weber strategized in advance with local contacts and organizers along their route, trying to minimize the danger awaiting the Wallace tour in Alabama and beyond. Their efforts were aided, if grudgingly, by state officials anxious to avoid the kind of publicity that North Carolina had attracted. Expanded police patrols, however, hardly guaranteed safety, particularly in the sprawling industrial centers of Gadsden and Birmingham, both rife with Klan activity.

J. P. Mooney, Charles Wilson, and Asbury Howard, organizers of the Mine, Mill and Smelter Workers, escorted the Wallace group in Alabama. Wallace addressed three outdoor meetings during a quick tour of northern Alabama and then headed to Gadsden. Having been informed that steelworkers there were planning a major anti-Wallace demonstration, Weber instructed everyone to keep their car windows closed after they arrived in Gadsden. A heavy rope and markers designating "colored" and "white" segregated the courthouse lawn where Wallace was scheduled to speak. As the motorcade approached the square, men wielding baseball bats and iron pipes surrounded the cars and hollered, "Kill Wallace!" Weber was convinced that if they had gotten out of the cars, they would have been killed "right there."[27]

Mooney, armed with a concealed pistol, emerged from Wallace's car. Reading a brief statement over a portable public address system, he recited the Progressive Party's policy of not participating in meetings that violated the constitutional guarantees of free assembly and free speech. The police "just stood there and watched," Mooney recalled, while people threw rocks and banged on the cars. Remarkably, there was only one minor casualty. It occurred when a reporter, ignoring Weber's advice, rolled down his car window to interview some of the demonstrators. His inquiries brought a hefty punch in the side of his head, leaving a bump "the size of a goose egg."[28]

From Gadsden, Wallace's entourage headed to Birmingham for a late-afternoon meeting. Police Commissioner Eugene "Bull" Connor eagerly awaited their arrival. Connor had won much acclaim earlier in the year when he had arrested Wallace's running mate, Senator Glen Taylor, for violating a segregation ordinance. A local columnist wrote that Connor hoped that events surrounding Wallace's visit would secure his place "as a Horatius at the bridge of Alabama's states rights with a governorship . . . as a possible reward." Connor positioned himself prominently on the rear plaza of the Jefferson County Courthouse, with a loudspeaker system to aid in managing the crowd. Sixty uniformed policemen milled among the boisterous crowd of more than two thousand whites who had gathered. Even though there were no laws prohibiting nonsegregated meetings outdoors, a barrier of heavy rope and sawhorses separated an estimated four hundred black people who had turned out to hear Wallace.[29]

John Popham described how Wallace and Connor "each directed the movements of their followers like opposing generals in battle." Before entering the city, Wallace and his advisers carefully instructed the reporters on the procedure that they would follow in Birmingham. Using a walkie-talkie, Connor monitored Wallace's entry into the city block by block. As the motorcade neared the courthouse square, he addressed the crowd: "Help me see that he has a respectful hearing of whatever he has to say. Birmingham must not injure her good name by being unkind to any visitor within her gates." Canisters of tear gas were on hand to enforce Connor's admonitions, if necessary.[30]

When the motorcade reached the front of the courthouse, Mooney and Foreman emerged from Wallace's car. Mooney read a statement similar to the one he had read in Gadsden. The crowd booed and jeered: "Where is Henry? Why doesn't he show up?" Popham recalled that it was the most hostile crowd yet. After Mooney and Foreman returned to the car, a crowd gathered around Wallace's car and pressed their faces against the window. "Look at that guy, he can't even afford a hair cut," one sneered. "Send him out and we'll take him to Harlem and get him a hair cut." They began to rock the car and nearly turned it over before the police cleared a path for the motorcade. The Wallace entourage continued on to De Bardelaben Park in neighboring Bessmer, where police-enforced segregation required Mooney to read his statement a third time to the three hundred people gathered there.[31]

Wallace ended his day in Alabama in the quiet of a Birmingham radio station. For the first time in three days, he addressed the people of the South without interruptions, without threats of violent assault, without racial definition. He began by asking listeners to join him in the Lord's Prayer. Then followed one of the most impassioned speeches of Wallace's political career. Deeply moved by what he had seen and experienced in North Carolina and Alabama, he expanded on a text drafted by Weber and Frank. He framed his comments with liberal references to the beliefs and values fundamental to Christianity and to the democratic principles to which America had aspired since its founding: brotherhood and equality.

"God hath made of one blood all the nations to dwell upon the face of the earth," Wallace intoned, in one of several biblical references. By attacking segregation, the Progressive Party was acting on the simple Christian truth "that all men are brothers." Those who divide the people, Wallace declared, "sin against man and God." In seeking to secure equal rights and equal opportunity for all men, Wallace and his supporters sought to realize the promise of democracy embedded in the Declaration of Independence and the Constitution. Why, Wallace asked, did the Progressive Party's espousal of "fundamental Christian and democratic principles" draw such violent opposition in the South? Wallace pointed to the giants of wealth, the "Big Mules"—the men who owned Tennessee Coal and Iron, the textile industries of the South, and the large plantations—the individuals who had ruled the region for generations, keeping the vast majority of people "in economic poverty and political bondage." They were the people who fought the trade unions so bitterly; who kept wages in the South far below the national average so that an Alabama family had only half the income of a family in New York; who, through the promotion of falsehoods and ignorance, kept "the people divided—section against section, race against race, farmers against workers." Thus, they opposed the Progressive Party and all it stood for. "They hate us and lie about us when they hear us say that social injustice is sin and that segregation is sin. They wish to silence us when we speak the simple Christian truth that all men are brothers."[32]

Wallace remained hopeful, for these powerful interests were not representative of the South. "One of the most beautiful sections" of the country, the South was also one of the areas "offering the greatest potential in human talent and natural resources." Wallace outlined his proposed four-year, federally assisted plan to develop these resources and to raise the income of southern families. There was a political awakening under way that could loosen the grip of those who had retarded the development of the South for so long. Wallace closed with one final appeal, asking his audience to join him in the spirit of their shared Christian and democratic tradition. "Truly we are all members, one of another. We shall prosper together in love and understanding, or perish in hatred and ignorance."[33]

After the radio address, the Wallace group traveled by overnight train to Mississippi, relieved to have made it through Alabama physically unscathed. Bull Connor had demonstrated that white leadership could effectively assert itself and keep an explosive situation from getting completely out of hand. Mississippi Governor Fielding Wright was equally determined to maintain order while Wallace visited the stronghold of the Dixiecrat movement. In fact, the governor provided the best police protection that the entourage had had during its southern journey. Wright, who was the vice-presidential candidate for the States' Rights Party, urged the people of his state to extend Wallace the same courtesies to which any visitor to the state was entitled and avoid giving "our enemies" the kind of ammunition they loved to use to besmirch the good name of Mississippi.

Wallace's visit to Mississippi opened with a breakfast meeting at the Southern Christian Institute, a black community college in Edwards, followed by a radio address from the college. Afterward, Wallace accompanied Mississippi members of the Progressive Party to the secretary of state's office in Jackson to present a slate of nine electors. Denied a permit to speak from the steps of the state capitol, Wallace did not deliver a speech in Jackson. He made his only public address in Mississippi on the lawn of the Warren County Courthouse in Vicksburg to an integrated but mostly white crowd of three hundred. Mississippi reaped praise for its restrained reception. The *Arkansas Gazette* noted the stark contrast between the calm in Mississippi and the violence in North Carolina, a state that had "a way of looking down its nose at the Deep South."[34]

Two state police cars met the Wallace tour at the Louisiana state line and escorted them to Monroe, where the entire police force was on alert. Wallace gave a short address on the grounds of Central Grammar School to an enthusiastic crowd of nearly one thousand. Black supporters crowded around Wallace afterward to shake his hand and offer their encouragement. A friendly crowd of two hundred received Wallace in Ruston. But aids canceled plans for an open-air evening meeting in Shreveport when local officials advised that there would be no police protection. Wallace, however, did deliver an address from the radio station in Shreveport. He was accompanied by several burly members of the National Maritime Union, who served as bodyguards. Afterward, a car carried Wallace to the home of another supporter, dodging through alleys and back roads to avoid being followed. At midnight the group boarded a plane to Little Rock.

When Wallace's local hosts were unable to obtain a hall in Little Rock, J. N. Heiskell, publisher of the *Arkansas Gazette*, volunteered free radio time. Heiskell offered it as a public service, explaining that, as a candidate for the presidency, Wallace had a right to be heard and that the people of Little Rock had a right to hear him. *Gazette* editor Harry Ashmore hosted Wallace on the radio and provided an open and relaxed forum. He framed the discussion around general points of Wallace's platform that Ashmore believed to be of most interest to southerners: his views on Russia and the American Communist Party; his economic program for the South; and his position on segregation.

The Wallace-Ashmore exchange regarding racial segregation was particularly revealing and facilitated one of the most probing discussions of Wallace's thoughts on the subject. Ashmore was a rising figure among the region's cadre of white liberal journalists, which included figures like Ralph McGill and Hodding Carter. Up until the mid-1950s, these so-called racial moderates protested the excesses of segregation but defended the institution. As Ashmore explained to Wallace, "Most of us believe in the separation of the races, and we also believe that this can be done, and in most cases is being done, without any injustice to the Negro." He asked if Wallace believed it was possible to eliminate segregation by the kind of head-on assault launched by the Progressive Party.[35]

"It is not only desirable to break down segregation," Wallace responded, "it is absolutely necessary. We must meet this issue head on." The South had moral and practical reasons for doing so. Wallace cited the huge cost of segregation and commended a recent action by the state of Arkansas admitting the first black medical students to the University of Arkansas. It was "an admirable and sensible action," Wallace observed, one that struck at the very heart of the segregation problem. Clearly, "The state could not afford separate facilities, when its facilities for white students were already less than they should be." Without "the discord of segregation," Wallace maintained, the region would have long since pulled itself up to the national levels of economic growth and prosperity.[36]

Ashmore queried Wallace with many of the arguments used to defend the racial status quo. Did Wallace think it was possible to change attitudes by passage of a law? The candidate agreed that it was not possible to legislate love, but he added, "We must legislate against hate." Shouldn't individuals be free to associate with whom they pleased? Yes, Wallace said, and this basic civil right was abridged by legally mandated segregation. Wallace dismissed Ashmore's suggestion that the Fair Practices Employment Committee (FEPC) was an invasion of the private relationship between employer and employee, calling this a specious argument. Whereas he agreed that the South had made progress in the field of race relations, Wallace maintained that it was "in spite of segregation."[37]

The Wallace tour concluded in Tennessee with appearances in Memphis, Nashville, and Knoxville. With the cooperation of Ed Crump, the political boss of Memphis, the Progressive Party sponsored what was believed to be the first nonsegregated mass political meeting in the city since Reconstruction. A sympathetic crowd of more than twenty-five hundred blacks and whites mingled peacefully at the Bellevue Baseball Park. In a speech, delivered without interruption, Wallace talked about New Deal initiatives that had aided the South, particularly the Tennessee Valley Authority (TVA), and urged the renewal and expansion of such government-sponsored programs. Commenting on the new challenges facing America in the postwar world, Wallace invited his audience to consider the national security dimension of the race question. "If the United States is to be secure in a world largely populated by men of color, then the end of segregation must come to pass." To ignore the issue was to jeopardize America's position in the world.[38]

Wallace's last day in the South opened in Nashville. A local newspaper described the crowd of fifteen hundred that had assembled near the steps of the War Memorial Building. "The two races rubbed shoulders to get a glimpse of the candidate and hear him talk." As Wallace began to speak from the steps, cheers and loud applause drowned out the boos. He recalled for his audience that day in 1944 when he had "looked at the Texas delegation to the Democratic convention in the eye and told them 'Jim Crow must go.'" Everything he had experienced since then, Wallace attested, confirmed his view. "I say now as I did then, Jim Crow must go."[39]

Mt. Olive Baptist Church in Knoxville hosted Wallace's last appearance. Just days before, the Ku Klux Klan had announced that it would hold an initiation ceremony on a field just outside of the city at roughly the same time as the Wallace gathering. Local Progressive Party organizers rescheduled their meeting to begin two hours earlier than planned. Six hundred people, mostly black, crowded into the church, and hundreds more gathered in the basement and outside, where the meeting was carried over a loudspeaker system. Wallace looked drawn and tired in his rumpled gray suit as he entered the church. The audience stood and welcomed him with the national anthem, followed by warm and enthusiastic greetings and applause. Dr. O. B. Taylor, a local black physician, introduced Clark Foreman, and Foreman introduced Wallace. Repeating some of the major points he had made during the previous week, Wallace described his time in the South as "the most memorable week" of his life. On the trip back to New York, he told a reporter that his tour had left him firm in the conviction that "the race problem" was "the South's and the nation's number one problem."[40]

Henry Wallace's southern campaign tour seemed oddly remote from the 1948 presidential contest. The stories that made front-page news fed popular images of the region as a place of violence and Ku Kluxery—H. L. Mencken revisited. *Life* magazine introduced its three-page photographic spread with a quote from Hodding Carter of Mississippi: "The South is still a violent land . . . largely frontier in spirit. Its folkways unduly emphasize an exaggerated sense of personal honor which requires physical vengeance for an affront." Wallace, said *Life*, was like a man "who deliberately picks a fight in a waterfront saloon." Even more than his views on Russia, Wallace's "desire to use the force of the federal government to end segregation" was guaranteed to stir up a hornet's nest in the South, as the accompanying photographs illustrated. The magazine's implication was that Wallace got what he asked for.[41]

James Wechsler's experience on the southern tour caused him to moderate his initial assessment of Wallace's candidacy. Like his fellow ADA organizers, Wechsler had portrayed Wallace as, at best, an unwitting tool of the Communist Party, going south merely to stump for votes in the North. But seven days on the road shook that assumption. Wechsler noted, "The kind of ideological distinctions I talked about didn't seem to loom as large [in the South]." He sensed that he was witnessing an extraordinary event. Assessing Wallace's campaign after the election, Wechsler gave special notice to the southern tour, suggesting that there, for a moment, Wallace broke free from his "ghost writers." In the face of constant physical danger, he preached the Sermon on the Mount "and established in at least a dozen southern places that unsegregated meetings could be held without civil war." In "violent street scenes" from North Carolina to Louisiana, Wallace was "a genuinely distinguished figure."[42]

For seasoned activists, Wallace's historic challenge invited reflection on the nature of the movement that was unfolding in the South. In separate commentaries, Palmer Weber and Charles Houston challenged the persistent image of a static, unchanging South. Each had witnessed and participated in the formation of a loosely organized movement for racial democracy in the South, easily measured by gains in the courts, by the remarkable growth of black voter participation, and by the slow development of interracial alliances. This movement made Wallace's tour possible and offered a context for measuring its significance.

Palmer Weber highlighted the southern tour in a letter to Thurgood Marshall and reported on the general situation in the region. Reciting the places where Wallace was able to speak, Weber wrote, "We established to our satisfaction and I think everybody else's that unsegregated meetings are both proper and peaceful under any and all circumstances anywhere in the South." Wallace, displaying physical and moral courage, "pulled no punches" and told folks everywhere "that segregation is sin and that was that." Weber noted, "The various Negro communities were electrified and tremendously heartened to see one white man with guts who was willing to take it standing up." Weber implored Marshall to pass on his advice to Walter White: "See to it that Harry S. [Truman] comes South and slugs. He can't lose a thing by doing so, and he would enormously help himself nationally, and I believe the whole Negro liberation struggle, both here and elsewhere."[43]

"By and large," Weber reported, "I find the Negro leadership fighting for the ballot as never before." If only the NAACP could concentrate field staff in the South for the next couple of months, he noted, there was much to be gained. Money was also necessary. In Birmingham, Arthur Shores needed five hundred dollars to test a city ordinance, but Weber's coffers were dry. "Honest to John, nothing but money, rather its absence, is keeping us from tearing the South apart this year." Ending on a humorous note, Weber teased, "Be a good guy and send us $25,000 from anywhere, will you Thurgood?" He added, "I think every day of the NAACP's wonderful work, and pray for it to keep going."[44]

Charles Houston contemplated the meaning of Wallace's journey in his column for the *Baltimore Afro-American*. The violent reception that had greeted Wallace was not surprising. What was important was that Wallace had made the trip and, in doing so, "stirred thousands of white people and hundreds of thousands of colored people to greater resistance to segregation." Houston wrote, "He pioneers a movement toward freedom that has implications far more significant than the ballot count in the coming election."[45]

Wallace's campaign defied routine political reporting and analysis. Personally, Wallace "may have committed political suicide in hurling a personal challenge at segregation while . . . standing on southern soil." Houston doubted that Wallace picked up any votes in the South. "He cemented the Dixiecrats in the north against him [and lost] the fuzzy 'good willers' who want a little reform but never too much at any one time." Indeed, Wallace had "gone so far out in front" that he had "almost fractured the possibilities of building a polygot heterogeneous political movement around himself."[46]

That the real significance of Wallace's journey escaped national attention was understandable. Great social movements, Houston explained, mature almost imperceptibly. "The form of our resistance to segregation may be slow in materializing . . . but the spiritual climate has been formed. Underground in Mississippi or out in the open in New York Wallace has forced the fight." Houston urged confidence and continuous struggle. "The more violent the repression of a growing movement, the more dynamic and revolutionary the movement becomes when it gets headway." Houston reminded his readers, "Let us never forget how eternal slavery looked at the time John Brown was hanged, and how soon afterwards Union soldiers were on the march."[47]

In the aftermath of Wallace's trip, the Truman campaign concluded that there was little to gain by going south and much to lose. Truman stayed away. As the election approached, even those sympathetic to Wallace had to consider the prospect that a vote for Wallace would be Truman's loss and

Thurmond's gain. In Ward 6 of Columbia, South Carolina, local Truman supporters tried to ensure that this did not happen. According to a poll watcher for the Democratic Party, Wallace registered 125 votes in that ward on election day. But the official returns listed "zero" votes for Wallace; Truman's tally increased by 125. Still, the Dixiecrats carried South Carolina, as well as Mississippi, Alabama, and Louisiana.[48]

In the short term, the Wallace campaign registered few tangible gains. The rapid escalation of the cold war during 1948 made it impossible for the Progressive Party to establish an identity in the public arena apart from its Communist Party supporters. Popular preoccupation with the specter of internal subversion heightened during the summer: the House Un-American Activities Committee (HUAC) began its public investigation of former New Dealer Alger Hiss, and the Justice Department indicted the American Communist Party's top officials. Support for the Progressive Party withered. Wallace won barely one million votes on election day, far below the six million that political analysts had projected at the start of the 1948 campaign.

Palmer Weber had frequently emphasized that the southern campaign was part of a broad, ongoing effort to open up the electoral process to blacks in the South, one that was essential "to truly realizing democracy and bringing about progressive change." In a sober assessment of the election returns, he cautioned against defeatism and isolation, reminding young volunteers that their efforts had not been realistic in terms of electing Wallace. He urged Wallace's supporters to return to the Democratic Party and work in the primary elections and with the NAACP. On a seemingly barren political landscape, these remained vital sites in the effort to liberate the South from the racist, antidemocratic politics that had long dominated the region and held inordinate power in the national political arena.[49]

Others shared Weber's confidence that the southern movement would endure, but the form it would take was decidedly unclear. There was an abiding sense that an era had ended. "We may have to stop and start over again," Charles Houston wrote not long before his death in 1950, "[or] leave it to those who come after us."[50] Clark Foreman named the period that ended in 1948 "the decade of hope." For a time, southerners had reached across racial boundaries to advance political and economic democracy in the region, with the support of the federal government and a strong national labor movement. The significance lay less in the successes, which were fleeting, than in the struggle waged and the lessons learned. The central lesson was the power of segregation to undermine all efforts to establish a healthy democracy in the region. If progressives in the South were to be a force for change, they required the moral, political, and financial support of democratically minded people throughout the nation.[51]

Yet the hopes and strategies born at the high tide of the New Deal could not survive the repression and political sterility of the cold war era. After the November election, the Southern Conference for Human Welfare and the Southern Negro Youth Congress disbanded. The national CIO expelled its left-wing unions. Highlander Folk School and the Southern Conference Educational Fund, an SCHW affiliate, endured as embattled remnants of the Popular Front in the South, marshaling scarce resources in behalf of desegregation efforts. Northern foundations inclined to support civil rights efforts, such as Ford and Rockefeller, steered clear of groups tainted by any association with the Progressive Party. The Ford Foundation established the Fund for the Republic specifically to undermine alleged communist influence on blacks. In the South, the largely nonpolitical Southern Regional Council was the primary beneficiary of the fund's support.[52]

The defense of civil liberties, on a personal and organizational level, absorbed much of the energy that had been devoted to opening the political process in the South. The National Emergency Civil Liberties Committee (NECLC) and the Committee to Defend Negro Leadership, both established in the early 1950s, were, in the words of former Southern Negro Youth Congress leader Esther Jackson, "like fingers in the dike." Palmer Weber was a founding member of the NECLC, and Clark Foreman became the executive director of the New York–based organization. Borrowing from the NAACP's model, the NECLC's legal counsel, Leonard Boudin, selected test cases in an effort to build a systematic legal defense against the assault on individuals who had participated in progressive politics during the 1930s and 1940s. Defendants ranged from public school teachers who had been fired by local school districts to Paul Robeson and others whose passports had been confiscated by the U.S. State Department because of their political views and affiliations.[53]

During the 1950s, the southern black freedom struggle remained isolated from main currents of American social and political development. The steady migration of black southerners to northern cities and the postwar transformations of American society heightened and extended patterns of racial segregation and exclusion. Suburbanization, the explosion of consumer culture, and the growth of the middle class expanded the reach of the "racial dream world," a white world devoid of racial tensions or concerns. After 1948 the national Democratic Party placated its conservative southern wing while its civil rights agenda floundered. Leaders in both major parties shrank from the mandate of the 1954 *Brown* decision.

The foundation of the civil rights movement remained anchored in the cumulative gains of the NAACP legal campaign and its extensive network of branches. Southern NAACP leaders and activists, however, were increasingly confronted with an emboldened defense of the racial status quo. The Christmas Day assassination of Florida NAACP leader Harry T. Moore and his wife in 1951 inaugurated a decade of white terrorism and state-sponsored repression that heightened in the aftermath of the *Brown* decision. The Montgomery bus boycott and the determined efforts of Daisy Bates and the nine students who desegregated Central High School in Little Rock captured national attention but failed to engage sustained national support for the struggle to dismantle Jim Crow. Virginia Durr, who had returned to Alabama earlier in the decade, wrote despairingly from Montgomery in 1958: "We have such a feeling here that we have been abandoned by the rest of the country and by the government and left to the tender mercies of the Ku Klux Klan and the White Citizens Council."[54]

In the aftermath of the student sit-ins of 1960, direct action campaigns and mass protests brought national and international attention to the South, a critical lever in the final assault on the segregation system. The civil rights movement of the sixties defied the racial and political boundaries of cold war America and inspired a renaissance of social protest, political action, and cultural creativity. The dismantling of legalized segregation in the South also exposed the centuries-old patterns of racial exclusion and discrimination woven into the fabric of national life. The 1968 Kerner Commission report described a nation "moving towards two societies, one black, one white—separate and unequal."[55]

The modern movement for racial justice in the United States was born during an extraordinary era of economic transformation mediated by government expansion and social innovation. Although little, if any, memory of the New Deal years informed the civil rights movement of the 1960s, the activists of the earlier decades tilled the ground for future change. They created legal precedents, experimented with new political forms, and organized around issues of social and economic justice. Such eclectic and improvisational efforts collectively expanded the possibilities of democracy in a racially fractured civic landscape. By all measures, this was a pivotal stage in the complex trajectory of modern American politics—both in terms of the opportunities that were lost and the hopes that endured.

Notes

ABBREVIATIONS

ADA   Americans for Democratic Action
AP   Associated Press
COHC   Columbia Oral History Collection
ER   Eleanor Roosevelt
FDR   Franklin Delano Roosevelt
NAACP   National Association for the Advancement of Colored People
NPC   National Policy Committee
NYT   *New York Times*
OF   Official Files
PPC   Progressive Party Collection
SCHW   Southern Conference for Human Welfare

INTRODUCTION

1. Lord, *The Wallaces of Iowa*, p. 460.

2. Ibid., pp. 460–62; Raper, *Preface to Peasantry*, p. 4.

3. Raper, *Preface to Peasantry*, p. 5; Wright, *Old South, New South*.

4. Shulman, *From Cotton Belt to Sun Belt*, p. 10.

5. Lowitt and Beasley, *One Third of a Nation*, p. 185.

6. Ibid., p. 182.

7. *Washington Post*, 16 August 1938; "Address of the President at Barnesville, Georgia," 11 August 1938, Lowell Mellett Papers, box 5.

8. Raper interview with author.

9. *New York Herald Tribune*, 6 September 1938.

CHAPTER ONE

1. McElvaine, *The Great Depression*, pp. 78–79.

2. Simpson, "Colored People in Virginia," p. 373.

3. Bond, "A Negro Looks at His South," p. 98.

4. Ibid.

5. Perman, *The Road to Redemption*, pp. 57–86; Ayers, *The Promise of the New South*, pp. 249–310; Daniels quoted by Kousser, *The Shaping of Southern Politics*, p. 76.

6. Ayers, *The Promise of the New South*, pp. 328–33; W. E. B. Du Bois's *Black Reconstruction in America, 1860–1880*, published in 1935, was the first full-scale study of the role of blacks in the political, economic, and social Reconstruction of the South. In 1929 Du Bois withdrew his article "The Negro in the United States," written for the fourteenth edition of the *Encyclopedia Britannica*, after refusing to

eliminate his assertions that blacks had played a crucial and positive role in Reconstruction. See Du Bois, *The Souls of Black Folks*, p. 208.

7. Perman, *The Road to Redemption*, pp. 237–77; Wright, *Old South, New South*, pp. 156–77. In discussing the South's lag in industrial development and modernization, Wright considers the argument that U.S. Steel deliberately suppressed "incipient industrial expansion" of Tennessee Coal and Iron in Birmingham after its purchase of the company in 1907 through the freight rate differential and other policies. He argues that such an explanation is insufficient. The absence of an indigenous regional technical community, the isolation of the southern labor market, and the fact that the major growth industries using steel were located in the North and the Midwest, Wright suggests, were the primary factors inhibiting the growth of the steel industry in Birmingham.

8. Brown, "Negotiating and Transforming the Public Sphere," pp. 107–27; Ayers, *The Promise of the New South*, pp. 290–300.

9. Higginbotham, *Righteous Discontent*, pp. 1–18.

10. Meier and Rudwick, "The Boycott Movement against Jim Crow Streetcars"; Meier, *Negro Thought in America*.

11. William Cohen, *At Freedom's Edge*; Meier, *Negro Thought in America*, pp. 59–68; Grossman, *Land of Hope*, chs. 3–4; Wright, *Old South, New South*, pp. 201–7.

12. Grossman, *Land of Hope*, part 2; Meier, *Negro Thought in America*, pp. 256–78.

13. Wright, *Old South, New South*, pp. 177–97, 224–25. Wright provides compelling evidence of the development and gradual institutionalization of this trend through the 1950s. He notes for instance, "A 1941 survey found that 95% of new job openings in Georgia were reserved for whites." Robert J. Norrell cites Birmingham as an exception in terms of rigid job classification. The number of semiskilled jobs in Alabama's steel industry more than quadrupled between 1910 and 1930, and as of 1930, whites held 65 percent of the new positions. But Norrell wrote, "TCI [Tennessee Coal and Iron] also gave blacks new opportunities by blurring the sharp division between skilled and unskilled workers as a way to maintain competition between black and white workers, and thereby mitigate against any sense of unity among the workers." Norrell, "Caste in Steel," pp. 671–72.

14. Tindall, *Emergence of the New South*, pp. 318–53.

15. Wolters, *Negroes and the Great Depression*, pp. 113–17; Raper and Reid, *Sharecroppers All*, pp. 124–27; Raper, *Preface to Peasantry*, pp. 183–200; Douglas Smith, "The New Deal and the Urban South," pp. 38–40, 50–53.

16. Fite, *Cotton Fields No More*, pp. 120–26; Douglas Smith, "The New Deal and the Urban South," pp. 27–49, 71–72.

17. McElvaine, *The Great Depression*, pp. 48–94; Badger, *The New Deal*, pp. 29–32, 48–50.

18. Badger, *The New Deal*, pp. 54–57; Douglas Smith, "The New Deal and the Urban South," pp. 54–80 (James Patterson quoted on p. 80).

19. Aubrey Williams, "A Southern Rebel Speaks," sketches, drafts, Aubrey Williams Papers, FDR Library, Hyde Park, New York, box 44; Maverick, *Maverick American*, pp. 150–66; Douglas Smith, "The New Deal and the Urban South," pp. 90–91.

20. Fite, *Cotton Fields No More*, pp. 126–28.

21. Williams, "A Southern Rebel Speaks"; *The New Dealers*, p. 25.

22. Burns, *Roosevelt*, pp. 148–55, 171–73; *The New Dealers*, pp. 3–27.

23. Garson, *The Democratic Party*, pp. 2–3.

24. Wallace, *Democracy Reborn*, p. 62.

25. Alexander interview, COHC, pp. 369–70.

26. Ibid., 370–72.

27. Foreman, "First Eighteen Years," unpublished memoir, Clark Howell Foreman Papers.

28. Ibid.

29. Clark Foreman to Robert and Effie Foreman, 18 February 1921, Clark Howell Foreman Papers.

30. *Atlanta Constitution*, 17 February 1921, p. 1, 18 February 1921, editorial; Clark Foreman to Robert and Effie Foreman, 20 February 1921, and Foreman, "Intellectual Awakening," unpublished memoir, Clark Howell Foreman Papers; Foreman interview, November 1974, Southern Oral History Program.

31. He was unable to enroll in a master's program because he lacked the German requirement. Foreman, "Intellectual Awakening."

32. Ibid.

33. Wells, *The Outline of History*, pp. 1086–101.

34. Foreman, "First Trip to Europe," unpublished memoir, Clark Howell Foreman Papers.

35. Ibid.

36. Ibid.

37. Ibid.

38. Ibid.

39. Alexander interview, COHC, pp. 290, 369–70; Foreman, "Interracial Commission," unpublished memoir, Clark Howell Foreman Papers; Kirby, *Black Americans in the Roosevelt Era*, pp. 10–11.

40. Foreman, "Interracial Commission."

41. Ibid.

42. Ibid.; Dykeman and Stokely, *Seeds of Southern Change*, pp. 158–59; Raper interview with author.

43. Foreman, "Interracial Commission."

44. Ibid.

45. Foreman, "Rosenwald Fund," unpublished memoir, Clark Howell Foreman Papers; Embree and Waxman, *Investment in People*, pp. 28–36, 60–67; Edwin Embree to Clark Foreman, 17 October, 23 October 1928, Clark Howell Foreman Papers.

46. Foreman, "Rosenwald Fund."

47. Foreman, *Environmental Factors*, p. 40.

48. Foreman, "Rosenwald Fund."

49. Utley, *The Dream We Lost*, pp. 99–100.

50. Foreman, "Romance and Russia," unpublished memoir, Clark Howell Foreman Papers. Langston Hughes describes his experiences as a black man in the Soviet Union in "Going South in Russia," *Crisis* 41 (1934): 162–63.

51. Foreman, "Romance and Russia."

52. Ibid.; Foreman, "The End of Internationalism," 334–35.

CHAPTER TWO

1. Kenneth Crawford, quoted in Louchheim, *The Making of the New Deal*, p. 16.

2. Paul A. Freund, quoted in ibid., p. 103.

3. Alger Hiss, quoted in ibid., p. 237.

4. Paul A. Freund, quoted in ibid., p. 104.

5. Badger, *The New Deal*, pp. 116–17; Shulman, *From Cotton Belt to Sun Belt*, pp. 16–31; Cobb, "Somebody Done Nailed Us on the Cross," pp. 912–15.

6. Associated Negro Press release, 1 September 1933; Grubbs, *Cry from the Cotton*, pp. 17–29; Lewis D. Redding, *Opportunity* 12 (1934): 211; Clark Foreman, excerpts from speech before Eleventh Annual Conference of Presidents of Land-Grant Colleges, *Chicago Defender*, 18 November 1933.

7. *New Republic*, 6 September 1933, p. 87.

8. Lorena Hickock's field reports to Harry Hopkins during the first four months of 1934 document the widespread support the New Deal enjoyed in the South, coupled with a growing uneasiness among planters and businesspeople about the effect of relief and government jobs on the region's traditionally dependent labor force. Said one worried cotton grower, "The CWA [Civil Works Administration] wage is buzzing in our niggers head." Lowett and Beasley, *One Third of a Nation*, pp. 143–229.

9. Clark Foreman, *NYT*, 15 April 1934; Ira DeA. Reid, "Black Wages for Black Men," *Opportunity* 12 (1934): 73.

10. Reid, "Black Wages for Black Men," p. 73. See Wolters, *Negroes and the Great Depression*, pp. 98–106, on code hearings and procedures.

11. Clark Foreman to Harold Ickes, 13 December 1933, New Deal Agencies and Black Americans, papers, microfilm, reel 14; Wolters, *Negroes and the Great Depression*, pp. 107–8.

12. W. E. B. Du Bois, letter of resignation, *Crisis* 41 (1934): 245.

13. Weaver, "Blending Scholarship with Public Service," p. 6.

14. Weaver interview with author, 13 January 1992; Charles Edward Russell, "Report of the Interracial Committee of the District of Columbia," (Twenty-Third Annual Conference of the NAACP, 20 May 1932), NAACP, microfilm, reel 9.

15. Weaver interview with author, 13 January 1992; Ware, *William Hastie*, pp. 6–11; McNeil, *Groundwork*, pp. 28–30.

16. Weaver interview with author, 13 January 1992.

17. Ibid.

18. Lester Granger, "Step Children of the Depression," *Opportunity* 12 (1934): 219; Lester B. Granger, "Leaders Wanted—1934 Model," *Opportunity* 12 (1934): 310–11.

19. Weaver interview with author, 13 January 1992.

20. Wolters, *Negroes and the Great Depression*, pp. 111–13; Weaver interview with author, 13 January 1992; John P. Davis, "NRA Codifies Wage Slavery," *Crisis* 41 (1934): 298–99, 304; Robert C. Weaver, "A Wage Differential Based on Race," *Crisis* 41 (1934): 236–38.

21. "New Deal Has Not Aided Negro Workers," press release, NAACP, 28 June 1934, NAACP, microfilm, reel 9; John P. Davis, "The Maid-Well Garment Case," *Crisis* 41 (1934): 356–57. The widespread violation of codes affected white as well as black workers. See Cayton and Mitchell, *Black Workers and the New Unions*, pp. 323, 341.

22. Wolters, *Negroes and the Great Depression* (on Southland case), pp. 120–22.

23. Ibid., p. 122; Statement by Clark Foreman, "Hearing before Industrial Appeal Board, National Recovery Administration," 9 October 1934, New Deal Agencies and Black Americans, papers, microfilm, reel 14.

24. Reid, "Black Wages for Black Men," p. 73; Davis quoted by Wolters, *Negroes and the Great Depression*, p. 111; Weaver interview with author, 13 January 1992. In the end, black job displacement under the NIRA codes was not widespread. Weaver believes southern employers used the threat in an effort to intimidate blacks into supporting the racial differential.

25. Weaver, *Negro Labor*, p. 14; Will Alexander, "A Strategy for Negro Labor," *Opportunity* 12 (1934): 102–3; Kirby, *Black Americans in the Roosevelt Era*, pp. 36–37. Federal policy, though providing for escape clauses like regional differentials, did overrule racial wage differentials in this instance, initiating a trend toward the weakening of all race-based wages.

26. Ware, *William Hastie*, pp. 55–65, 81–82; Weaver interview with author, 23 December 1980; Clark Foreman, "The New Deal," unpublished memoir, Clark Howell Foreman Papers.

27. Weaver interview with author, 23 December 1980; Weaver, "Blending Scholarship with Public Service," p. 6.

28. Motz, "The Black Cabinet," pp. 12–13, 88–89; Foreman, "The New Deal"; Kirby, *Black Americans in the Roosevlt Era*, pp. 24–25. Arthur Goldschmidt and Elizabeth Wickenden worked with Harry Hopkins in the Federal Emergency Relief Administration and agreed with Foreman's assessment (Interview, 9 Nov. 1991). By 1935, however, Hopkins acted more deliberately in behalf of a no-discrimination policy in the administration of the Works Progress Administration (WPA). He was probably influenced by the racially progressive Aubrey Williams, who served as deputy administrator. And Eleanor Roosevelt constantly pressured Hopkins and Williams for a racially fair policy in the administration of relief. Mrs. Roosevelt referred Mary McLeod Bethune to Hopkins and Williams, who joined the WPA's National Youth Administration (NYA) to direct its Office of Negro Affairs. Under Williams and Bethune, the NYA would be at "the forefront of New Deal efforts to insure fair treatment for blacks." Badger, *The New Deal*, pp. 207–8. See also Kirby, *Black Americans in the Roosevelt Era*, pp. 110–21.

29. Foreman, "The New Deal"; Clark Foreman to Harold Ickes, 8 September, 7 November, 9 November 1933, New Deal Agencies and Black Americans, papers, microfilm, reel 14.

30. Robert Weaver, "An Experiment in Negro Labor," *Opportunity* 14 (1936): 295–98.

31. Foreman, "The New Deal."

32. Ibid.; Robert Weaver, "The Negro and the Federal Government" (address delivered 30 June 1937 at the Twenty-Eighth Annual Conference of the NAACP, Detroit), NAACP, microfilm, reel 9.

33. "Address of the President at Barnesville, Georgia," 11 August 1938, Lowell Mellett Papers, box 5.

34. Louchheim, *The Making of the New Deal*, p. 237; Hiss interview with author; Abt interview with author; Grubbs, *Cry from the Cotton*, pp. 30–31.

35. Sidney Baldwin, *Poverty and Politics*, p. 54; Schlesinger, *The Coming of the New Deal*, p. 46; Wolters, *Negroes and the Great Depression*, pp. 40–45.

36. Gilbert and Howe, "Beyond 'State vs. Society,' " p. 212.

37. Ibid., pp. 212–14; Grubbs, *Cry from the Cotton*, pp. 30–61; Wallace interview, COHC, pp. 363–93.

38. Sidney Baldwin, *Poverty and Politics*, pp. 82, 93–103; *New York Post* cited in Gilbert and Howe, "Beyond 'State vs. Society,' " pp. 209, 214–15; Johnson, Embree, and Alexander, *The Collapse of Cotton Tenancy*. The terrorism directed against the efforts of the Southern Tenant Farmers Union (STFU) inspired the establishment of the La Follette Committee, which investigated management-financed terrorism against labor unions. But the La Follette Committee steered clear of the STFU, for fear that southern members of Congress would block the committee's appropriations. Grubbs, *Cry from the Cotton*, pp. 96–98.

39. Wolters, *Negroes and the Great Depression*, pp. 46–50; Sidney Baldwin, *Poverty and Politics*, pp. 117–20; Lord, *The Wallaces of Iowa*, pp. 460–62.

40. Roosevelt quoted in Burns, *Roosevelt*, p. 268.

41. Ibid., pp. 264–88; Badger, *The New Deal*, pp. 247–60.

42. Boylan, *The New Deal Coalition*, pp. 2–3; Burns, *Roosevelt*, pp. 283–88.

43. Burns, *Roosevelt*, pp. 291–93.

44. Badger, *The New Deal*, pp. 263–71; Burns, *Roosevelt*, pp. 293–315.

45. Badger, *The New Deal*, p. 269; Caro, *Years of Lyndon Johnson*, pp. 395–96, 405, 417, 445–46; Lucy Randolph Mason to ER, 11 February 1938, ER Papers, FDR Library, Hyde Park, New York, box 733; Weaver interview with author, 23 December 1980.

46. Franklin Roosevelt, *Public Papers and Addresses* 7:399; Clark Foreman, "Nation's No. 1 Economic Problem," unpublished memoir, Clark Howell Foreman Papers.

47. Miller, *Man from the Valley*, pp. 80–84; Southern Policy Committee, "Objectives of the Committee," NPC Papers, Library of Congress, Washington, D.C., box 4; Foreman, "Nation's No. 1 Economic Problem"; Hays interview with author, 3 June 1980.

48. Foreman, "Nation's No. 1 Economic Problem."

49. Ibid.; Arthur Goldschmidt interview with author, 6 July 1991. The report discussed the following topics: economic resources, soil, water, population, private and public income, education, health, housing, labor, women and children, ownership and use of land, credit, use of natural resources, industry, and purchasing power. National Emergency Council, *Report*.

50. Foreman, "Nation's No. 1 Economic Problem"; Southern Advisory Committee, Arthur "Tex" Goldschmidt Papers; Krueger, *And Promises to Keep*, pp. 13–14.

51. "Address of the President at Barnesville, Georgia," 11 August 1938, Lowell Mellett Papers, box 5.

52. *Washington Post*, 16 August 1938; *New York Herald Tribune*, 6 September 1938; Kneebone, *Southern Liberal Journalists*, pp. 165–67.

53. *Washington Daily News*, 25 August 1938.

54. *Washington Post*, 7 July 1938.

55. Durr interview with author, 3 May 1978; Lowell Mellett to President Roosevelt, 26 August 1938, Lowell Mellett Papers, box 5.

56. Lowell Mellett to Marvin McIntyre, Secretary to the President, 21 October 1938, Lowell Mellett Papers, box 5.

57. Frank Graham to Francis Pickens Miller, 19 February 1939, NPC Papers, box 4; Raper interview with author.

CHAPTER THREE

1. Weber, "The Negro Vote in the South," p. 6.

2. Unless otherwise noted, sources for the discussion of Palmer Weber's early life and later reflections include Weber interviews with author, 9 September 1978, 17 November 1980, 24 February 1984.

3. Dabney, Mr. Jefferson's University, p. 152.

4. Palmer Weber, "The Five Together: Locke, Rousseau, Smith, Jefferson, Paine," unpublished manuscript, 1950, p. 12 (in author's possession).

5. Robert Cohen, "Revolt of the Depression Generation," p. 76.

6. Ibid., pp. 71–93.

7. Ibid.; Rob Hall interview with author; Schrecker, No Ivory Tower, pp. 28, 65.

8. Robert Cohen, "Revolt of the Depression Generation," pp. 93–122.

9. Ibid., p. 120.

10. College Topics, 18 May, 22 May 1934, 26 November 1935; Robert Cohen, "Revolt of the Depression Generation," p. 385.

11. College Topics, 1 May 1934; Weber interview with author, 24 February 1984.

12. College Topics, 28 October 1938.

13. Ibid., 27 November 1937.

14. Robert Cohen, "Revolt of the Depression Generation," pp. 494–98; Richards, "The Southern Negro Youth Congress," p. 17; Sarah Alice Mayfield, "Southern White Students and Race Relations" (address before the Twenty-Fourth Annual Conference of the NAACP, Chicago, Illinois, 30 June 1933), NAACP, microfilm, reel 9; George Streator, "Negro College Radicals," Crisis 41 (1934): 47; Preston Valien, "I Attended the NSL Conference," Crisis 41 (1934): 67–8; Monroe Sweetland, "Negro Students Superior," Crisis 41 (1934): 68; Langston Hughes, "Cowards from College," Crisis 41 (1934): 226–28.

15. James Jackson, panel presentation on the Southern Negro Youth Congress, Harvard University, 12 July 1995.

16. College Topics, 21 September, 10 October, 22 October, 24 October 1935, 4 January, 18 February 1936; Frederick W. Scott, Rector, to Alice Jackson, 3 October 1935, Presidential Papers, University of Virginia, Charlottesville, box 18; Weber interview with author, 9 September 1978.

17. White interview with author; Randolph White, "F. Palmer Weber: A Giant," Charlottesville Albemarle Tribune, 28 August 1986.

18. Weber, "The Negro Vote in the South," p. 25.

19. Charles Houston to Walter White, 1 November 1934, NAACP, microfilm, reel 16. (Unless otherwise noted, references to Charles Houston's correspondence and speeches are from NAACP, microfilm, reel 16.)

20. McNeil, Groundwork, p. 32.

21. Ibid., p. 42; Charles Houston, "An Approach to Better Race Relations" (address

delivered to the Thirteenth national YWCA Convention, 5 November 1934), records file collection, YWCA of USA, National Board Archives, New York, microfilm, reel 32.

22. McNeil, *Groundwork*, pp. 52, 71, 84–85.

23. Houston, "An Approach to Better Race Relations."

24. "Address delivered by Charles H. Houston before the Twenty-fourth Annual Conference of the National Association for the Advancement of Colored People, Chicago, Illinois, 2 July 1933," p. 6, NAACP, microfilm, reel 9; McNeil, *Groundwork*, pp. 88–101. George Crawford was found guilty by an all-white jury and sentenced to life in prison.

25. Meier and Rudwick, "The Rise of the Black Secretariat"; Meier and Rudwick, "Attorneys Black and White"; "Memo from Mr. White re. long distance telephone conversation with CHH, 11 November 1933," NAACP, microfilm, reel 16; Charles Houston to Walter White, 21 May 1935.

26. Carter, *Scottsboro*, chs. 1–2.

27. Weaver interview with author, 16 April 1992; Houston, "An Approach to Better Race Relations."

28. Charles Houston to Executive Staff, "Memorandum re: Further Steps in Anti-Lynching Campaign, 2 March 1938," and Charles H. Houston, copy of speech delivered to ILD National Conference, Hamilton Hotel, Washington, D.C., 8 July 1939; Zangrando, *The NAACP Crusade against Lynching*, p. 140.

29. McNeil, *Groundwork*, p. 121.

30. Houston, "An Approach to Better Race Relations."

31. Ibid.; "Negro Should Unite with 'Poor Whites'—Houston," press release, NAACP Annual Convention, July 1934, Oklahoma City, NAACP, microfilm, reel 9; Roy Wilkins, "NAACP Meets in Oklahoma," *Crisis* 41 (1934): 229.

32. Charles Houston to Walter White, 2 November 1934, 4 November 1934, and Charles H. Houston to Edward P. Lovett, 14 November, 10 December 1934.

33. Charles Houston to Walter White, 5 November 1934.

34. Charles Houston to Roy Wilkins, 22 May 1935.

35. Ibid. ·

36. Carter interview with author; Charles Houston, "A Challenge to Negro College Youth," *Crisis* 45 (1938): 14–15; Meier and Rudwick, "Attorneys Black and White," p. 153; Charles Houston to Walter White, 21 May 1935.

37. Weaver interview with author, 16 April 1992; McNeil, *Groundwork*, p. 135; Franklin interview with author.

38. Houston, "An Approach to Better Race Relations"; Bunche, *Political Status of the Negro*, pp. 72, 87–88, chs. 12–15; Cochran, "Arthur Davis Shores," pp. 26–27; Shores interview with author.

39. Bunche, *Political Status of the Negro*, p. 429.

40. Palmer Weber, *College Topics*, 11 November 1936, 29 January 1937; Fraser, *Labor Will Rule*, pp. 356–72; Weiss, *Farewell to the Party of Lincoln*, p. 203.

41. Weiss, *Farewell to the Party of Lincoln*, pp. 189–208; Frank R. Kent, "The Great Game of Politics," *Baltimore Sun*, 12 November 1936, p. 1.

42. Smith quoted by Weiss, *Farewell to the Party of Lincoln*, p. 186.

43. *Chicago Defender*, 18 November 1933; Palmer Weber, *College Topics*, 8 February 1937; Fraser, *Labor Will Rule*, p. 349.

44. Johnson quoted in Cayton and Mitchell, *Black Workers and the New Unions*, pp. vii–viii.

45. Fraser, *Labor Will Rule*, pp. 373–406.

46. Ibid., pp. 378–88; Richards, "Southern Negro Youth Congress," pp. 42–3; Glenn, *Highlander*, pp. 44–46; Kelley, *Hammer and Hoe*, pp. 142–51.

47. Durr interview with author, 25 June 1992.

48. Salmond, *Miss Lucy of the CIO*, pp. 1–49.

49. Ibid., pp. 50–74.

50. Ibid., p. 79; Lucy Randolph Mason to ER, 1 February 1938, ER Papers; Fraser, *Labor Will Rule*, pp. 397–99.

51. Krueger, *And Promises to Keep*, pp. 3–6, 16; Auerbach, *Labor and Liberty*, pp. 94–97. Auerbach explained that the furor accompanying the Barton-Gelders hearings sparked a movement on Capitol Hill to block further appropriations for the La Follette Committee. "Consequently, the committee never again ventured South in its probe of civil liberties infractions."

52. Krueger, *And Promises to Keep*, p. 16; Rob Hall interview with author; Joseph Gelders telegram to Franklin Roosevelt, 10 July 1940, FDR Papers, FDR Library, Hyde Park, New York, PPF 5664; H. C. Nixon to Brooks Hays, 27 July 1938, NPC Papers, box 3.

53. H. C. Nixon to Brooks Hays, 27 July 1938, NPC Papers, box 3; Lucy Randolph Mason to ER, 28 July 1938, ER Papers; Rob Hall interview with author.

54. H. C. Nixon to Brooks Hays, 27 July 1938; H. C. Nixon to Francis P. Miller, 16 September 1938; H. C. Nixon to Francis P. Miller, 19 October 1938; all in NPC Papers, box 3. Shouse, *Hillbilly Realist*, p. 110.

55. Raper interview with author; Durr and Dombrowski interview with author; *New South*, January 1939, pp. 6–7.

56. *New South*, January 1939, pp. 6–7.

57. Rob Hall interview with author; Roosevelt, *This I Remember*, pp. 173–74; *Richmond Times Dispatch*, 23 November 1938; Murray, *Song in a Weary Throat*, p. 113.

58. Tindall, *Emergence of the New South*, p. 637; Krueger, *And Promises to Keep*, pp. 38–39.

59. Murray, *Song in a Weary Throat*, p. 115.

60. Charles Houston, Speech to ILD Conference, 8 July 1939; Weber, "The Negro Vote in the South," p. 6.

CHAPTER FOUR

1. Weber interviews with author, 9 September 1978, 17 November 1980..

2. Badger, *The New Deal*, pp. 268–71.

3. *Crisis* 48 (1941): 375; *Crisis* 49 (1942): 117.

4. Arthur Goldschmidt interview with author, 6 July 1991; Durr interview with author, 22 June 1992; Rob Hall, "What Tom Watson Taught the South," *New South*, June 1938, pp. 12–13; Rob Hall interview with author.

5. Bunche, *Political Status of the Negro*, pp. 328–31, 336–37; Arkansas State Policy Committee, "The Poll Tax and Suffrage," subcommittee report, April 1938, NPC Papers.

6. Bunche, *Political Status of the Negro*, pp. 328–83.

7. Krueger, *And Promises to Keep*, pp. 44–47; George Stoney interview with author; Norrell, "Labor at the Ballot Box," pp. 207–8. The Myrdal-Carnegie study refers to the project directed by Gunnar Myrdal and funded by the Carnegie Corporation; it culminated with the publication of Myrdal, *An American Dilemma*.

8. Krueger, *And Promises to Keep*, pp. 44–46; Stoney interview with author.

9. Biographical background on Virginia Durr is based on the series of oral history interviews conducted by the author with Durr and on Durr's memoir: *Outside the Magic Circle*.

10. Salmond, *Conscience of a Lawyer*, pp. 43–46.

11. Ibid., p. 49; Durr interviews with author.

12. Mitford, *A Fine Old Conflict*, pp. 23–24.

13. Joseph Gelders to Mrs. Franklin D. Roosevelt, 3 November 1938, ER Papers, box 2579.

14. Durr interview with author, 3 May 1978. Mary McLeod Bethune served as head of the "Negro section" of the National Youth Administration and chaired the informal gathering of black New Dealers known as the "Black Cabinet."

15. Carliner interview with author.

16. Lawson, *Black Ballots*, p. 61; Joe Gelders to FDR, 10 July 1940, Records of the SCHW, Hollis Burke Frissell Library, Tuskegee, Alabama, box 24; Virginia Durr to Curtis MacDougall, n.d., PPC, University of Iowa Libraries, Iowa City, box 33.

17. Virginia Durr to ER, 26 July 1941, ER Papers, box 1820; Virginia Durr to ER, 30 September 1941, and ER to Virginia Durr, 8 October 1941, ER Papers, box 1598; Virginia Durr to Curtis MacDougall, n.d., PPC, box 33.

18. Virginia Durr to ER, 14 July 1941; ER to Sidney Hillman, 21 July 1941; ER to David Dubinsky, 21 July 1941; ER to Daniel Tobin, 21 July 1941; Virginia Durr to ER, July 1941; all in ER Papers, box 1598.

19. Durr interviews with author; Cohen interview with author.

20. *NYT*, 6 September 1942, IV, p. 7.

21. *NYT*. 24 July 1942, p. 9; 25 August 1942, p. 13; 26 August 1942, p. 22; 9 September 1942, IV, p. 7; Lawson, *Black Ballots*, p. 66.

22. *NYT*. 25 October 1942, p. 31; 26 August 1942, p. 22; 6 September 1942, IV, p. 8; Lawson, *Black Ballots*, p. 66.

23. Weber interviews with author.

24. Colmer quoted in Lawson, *Black Ballots*, p. 67.

25. Lawson, *Black Ballots*, pp. 67–68; U.S. Congress, House, "Roll Call Vote on Bill H.R. 1024," 77th Cong., 2d sess., 13 October 1942, *Congressional Record* 88:8174. The vote broke down along sectional lines with the exception of nine southern congressmen who supported the bill and eleven northern representatives who sided with the opposition. The southern congressmen who supported the Geyer-Pepper anti-poll-tax bill were W. O. Burgin (Lexington, N.C.), Wirt Courtney (Franklin, Tenn.), Albert Gore (Carthage, Tenn.), Estes Kefauver (Memphis, Tenn.), John Hennings Jr. (Knoxville, Tenn.), Luther Patrick (Birmingham, Ala.), J. Percy Priest (Nashville, Tenn.), Albert Thomas (Houston, Tex.), and R. Ewing Thomason (El Paso, Tex.).

26. Quotes in the preceding paragraphs are drawn from U.S. Congress, Senate,

"Elimination of the Poll Tax in Election of Federal Officials, H.R. 1024," 77th Cong., 2d sess., 20, 21, 23 November 1942, *Congressional Record* 88:9029–31, 9048–49, 9063–64.

27. Ibid., 9005–6, 9015–22, 9052–63.

28. Schlesinger, *The Politics of Upheaval*, pp. 362–79; *NYT*. 10 April 1935, p. 5; 24 April 1935, p. 12; 1 September 1935, II, p. 2; 24 December 1935, p. 5; 18 April 1936, p. 2; 23 January 1936, p. 1; 15 December 1936, p. 11; 8 December 1937, p. 21; 4 January 1938, p. 1; Clark Foreman, "Power for the People," unpublished memoir, Clark Howell Foreman Papers.

29. Louis E. Martin, "The Truth about Sojourner Truth," *Crisis* 49 (1942): 112–13; Walter White, Mary McLeod Bethune, and Channing Tobias to FDR, 17 June 1942, FDR Papers, OF 4947; Meier and Rudwick, *Black Detroit*, pp. 176–81.

30. Clark Foreman to Drew Pearson, 19 December 1951, 3 January 1952, Foreman Papers; Lucy Randolph Mason to ER, 28 April 1942, ER Papers, box 841; White House Memo, 23 July 1942, FDR Papers, OF 4947. Hugo Black agreed that it was because of Foreman's opposition to the power companies that Boykin was against him. Foreman did have his southern supporters in Congress. In 1938 Lyndon Johnson told the president, "A group of southern members of the House would be very much gratified if Mr. Clark Foreman is appointed to the Power Commission" (White House Memo, 10 June 1938, FDR Papers OF 4947).

31. Foreman to Pearson, 3 January 1952, Foreman Papers.

32. Walter White, Mary McLeod Bethune, and Channing Tobias to FDR, 17 June 1942; Rev. D. V. Jemison to Walter White, 20 June 1942; Earl Dickerson to Walter White, 16 June 1942; Bishop W. J. Walls to Walter White, 15 June 1942; all in FDR Papers, OF 4947.

33. Senator George W. Norris to FDR, 7 May 1942, FDR Papers, OF 4947. The president tried to reassure Senator Norris that Foreman's dismissal was not part of a deliberate purge. According to FDR, Foreman's position was lost in the reorganization and consolidation that accompanied the creation of the National Housing Agency. He assured Norris that efforts were being made to see that Foreman's services were used to the best advantage in the government. FDR to Senator George Norris, 28 May 1942, FDR Papers, OF 4947. See also Lucy Randolph Mason to ER, 28 April 1942, ER Papers, box 841; Lucy Randolph Mason to ER, 7 May 1942, ER Papers, box 842; ER to FDR, 6 May 1942, FDR Papers, OF 4947.

34. ER to FDR, 30 April 1942, 6 May 1942, FDR Papers, OF 4947. FDR acted quickly on ER's suggestions. He sent copies of her memos, along with a personal note, to Paul McNutt, saying that he wanted to talk with McNutt about a job for Foreman. By late June, McNutt had not acted. FDR sent another memo to McNutt: "What can we do for Mr. Foreman? He's not as bad as you think" (26 June 1942). In late July the president received assurances from McNutt that he would take care of Foreman. By this time Foreman had taken a job with the Navy. ER to FDR, 30 April 1942, FDR to Paul McNutt, 26 June 1942, and Memo for the President, MHM (Marvin H. McIntyre), 13 July 1942, FDR Papers, OF 4947; ER to Lucy Randolph Mason, 11 May 1942, ER Papers, box 841; Clark Foreman to ER, 6 July 1942, ER Papers, box 1641.

35. Paul Conkin quoted in Gilbert and Howe, "Beyond 'State vs. Society,' " p. 217.

36. Alexander interview, COHC.

37. Ibid.; Baldwin interview with Doud; Abt interview with author.

38. Sidney Baldwin, *Poverty and Politics*, pp. 279–83; Key, *Southern Politics*, p. 645; Gilbert and Howe, "Beyond 'State vs. Society,' " pp. 215–16.

39. Baldwin interview with Doud; Sidney Baldwin, *Poverty and Politics*, p. 222.

40. Baldwin interview with Doud.

41. Gilbert and Howe, "Beyond 'State vs. Society,' " pp. 216–17.

42. Sidney Baldwin, *Poverty and Politics*, pp. 338–46, 54.

43. U.S. Congress, Senate, 77th Cong., 2d sess., 18 May 1942, *Congressional Record* 88:4283, 4286, 4288, 4289, 4312.

44. Baldwin interview with Doud; *NYT.* 24 January 1942, p. 1; 7 February 1942, p. 9; 14 February 1942, p. 1; Helen Fuller, "Who Speaks for the Farmer?," *New Republic*, 23 February 1942, pp. 267–68.

45. Baldwin interview with Doud; U.S. Congress, Senate, 77th Cong., 2d sess., 18 May 1942, *Congressional Record* 88:4283, 4288.

46. Gilbert and Howe, "Beyond 'State vs. Society,' " p. 217; Alexander interview, COHC, p. 483; Sidney Baldwin, *Poverty and Politics*, pp. 361–94.

47. Baldwin interview with Doud; Sidney Baldwin, *Poverty and Politics*, pp. 366, 395–98; Alexander interview, COHC, p. 483; *NYT.* 31 August 1943, p. 5; 5 September 1943, p. 5; 7 September 1943, p. 32.

48. Weber interviews with author.

49. Garson, *The Democratic Party*, pp. 44–53.

50. *NYT*, 4 December 1943.

51. Ibid., 10 December 1943.

52. Weber interview with author, 17 November 1980.

CHAPTER FIVE

1. Tindall, *Emergence of the New South*, pp. 694–701; Wright, *Old South, New South*, pp. 239–69.

2. Gates, *Colored People*, pp. 84–85.

3. *Baltimore Afro-American*, 8 May 1948; Merl Reed, *Seedtime for the Modern Civil Rights Movement*, pp. 11–13; Richard Dalfiume, "The Forgotten Years of the Negro Revolution," pp. 300–301; Burran, "Racial Violence in the South," p. 23 (Houston quote).

4. Weaver, *Negro Labor*, pp. 16–60; Richards, "The Southern Negro Youth Congress," p. 57; Merl Reed, *Seedtime for the Modern Civil Rights Movement*, pp. 179–85.

5. Merl Reed, *Seedtime for the Modern Civil Rights Movement*, 13–15; Dalfiume, "The Forgotten Years of the Negro Revolution," pp. 305–6.

6. Merl Reed, *Seedtime for the Modern Civil Rights Movement*, p. 15; Mary McLeod Bethune to FDR, 26 June 1941, FDR Papers, OF 93, box 4.

7. Burran, "Racial Violence in the South," pp. 43–79, 133–52.

8. Ibid., pp. 79, 153–57; James Baldwin, *Notes of a Native Son*, p. 101.

9. Burran, "Racial Violence in the South," pp. 152–57;

10. Ibid., pp. 32–36, 85–95; Merl Reed, *Seedtime for the Modern Civil Rights Movement*, p. 91; "Text Books in Mississippi," *Opportunity* 18 (1940): 99–100; Dabney, "Nearer and Nearer the Precipice," p. 95; *Birmingham World*, 25 June 1943.

11. *Palmetto News*, 17 May 1941; Madison Jones to Walter White, 21 July 1942, Papers of the NAACP, Library of Congress, Washington, D.C., II-A, box 77.

12. J. L. LeFlore, "The South Awakens," *Crisis* 47 (1940): 180; Membership figures, "Annual Reports, 1940–1946," Branch Department, Papers of the NAACP, II-C, box 253.

13. Hine, *Black Victory*, pp. 176–80; Clifford Kuhn, "Two Small Windows of Opportunity: Black Politics in Georgia during the 1940s" (paper delivered at the joint meeting of the Georgia Association of Historians and the Georgia Political Science Association, 29 February 1992), 14–16; McCray interview with author, 19 February 1985; Hoffman, "The Genesis of the Modern Movement," p. 194.

14. The two cases were *Missouri ex rel. Gaines v. Canada* (1938), which ruled that Missouri's failure to provide a law school for blacks constituted a denial of equal protection, and *Alston v. School Board* (1940), which held that a school board could not arbitrarily pay black teachers less than white teachers. The Court held that such action violated the due process and equal protection clause of the Fourteenth Amendment. Tushnet, *NAACP Legal Strategy*, pp. 44–48, 70–81.

15. For biographical background and discussion of Baker's years in Harlem and her work as southern field organizer for the NAACP, see Youngblood, "Testing the Current."

16. Ella Baker to Branch Presidents, 11 January 1946, Papers of the NAACP, I-A, 383.

17. Baker, "Developing Community Leadership," p. 347.

18. Simkins interview with author; "Negro Citizens Seize Opportunity to Vote," AP news feature, n.d., John H. McCray Papers, South Caroliniana Library, Columbia, box 2; Bunche, *Political Status of the Negro*, pp. 80–83; NYT, 23 August 1936, II, p. 6.

19. Bunche, *Political Status of the Negro*, pp. 319–22, 421–24; "Report of the Secretary for the February Meeting of the Board of Directors," February 1940, Papers of the NAACP, II-A, 131; Hoffman, "The Genesis of the Modern Movement," pp. 210–11.

20. Levi J. Byrd, Treasurer of the Cheraw, S.C. Branch, to William Pickens, 10 November 1939, and A. W. Wright to William Pickens, 12 November 1939, Papers of the NAACP, I-G, 196.

21. *Columbia Record*, 18 April 1942; *Columbia Morning Star*, 23 April 1942; James Hinton to Thurgood Marshall, 22 April 1942, and Mojeska Simkins to NAACP national office, 20 April 1942, Papers of the NAACP, II-B, 209.

22. "Negro Voting in Primaries Rejected Here," 4 May 1942, news clipping in Papers of the NAACP, II-B, 209; Bunche, *Political Status of the Negro*, p. 79.

23. James Hinton to Thurgood Marshall, 13 May, 20 May, 21 May, 18 June, 21 July 1942; NAACP News Release, 19 June 1942; Marshall to Hinton, 8 August 1942; Thurgood Marshall to Victor Rotnem, Justice Department, 11 September 1942; and Hinton to Marshall, 21 September 1942; all in Papers of the NAACP, II-B, 209.

24. For a history of the legal campaign against the white primary, see Hine, *Black Victory*.

25. Hine, *Black Victory*, p. 222; The two earlier cases were *Nixon v. Herndon* (1927) and *Nixon v. Condon* (1932); see Hine, *Black Victory*, pp. 202–7, 212–22.

26. Weber interview with author, 8 September 1978; Weber interview with El-

wood; Luther Porter Jackson, "The Negro Vote," n.d., Luther Porter Jackson Papers, Johnston Memorial Library, Petersburg, Virginia, box 74; press release, Hot Springs National Park, 18 April 1944, Records of the SCHW, box 35; Moon, *The Balance of Power*, p. 178.

27. Richards, "Southern Negro Youth Congress," pp. 27–33, 42–43, 49–72.

28. Ibid., pp. 77–108; Burnham interview with author; Davis interview with author.

29. Glenn, *Highlander*, pp. 47–107.

30. Ibid.

31. Ibid., pp. 90–91; Adams, *James A. Dombrowski*, pp. 128–33.

32. Glenn, *Highlander*, pp. 55–56.

33. Adams, *James A. Dombrowski*, pp. 4–56.

34. Ibid., pp. 136–37.

35. Ibid., pp. 138–46; Krueger, *And Promises to Keep*, pp. 96–106.

36. Krueger, *And Promises to Keep*, pp. 97 (Roosevelt quote), 98 (Graham quote).

37. Frank McAllister to Clark Foreman, 4 May 1942, and Roger Baldwin to Clark Foreman, 19 May 1942, Records of the SCHW, box 5; Walker, *In Defense of American Civil Liberties*, p. 131.

38. James A. Dombrowski to Roger Baldwin, 27 May 1942, Records of the SCHW, box 20.

39. Clark Foreman to Roger Baldwin, 19 May 1942, and Foreman to Baldwin, 26 May 1942, Records of the SCHW, box 20.

40. Clark Foreman to Frank McAllister, 12 May 1942, Records of the SCHW, box 20.

41. Thomas Sancton to W. A. White, 23 May 1943, Papers of the NAACP, II-A, 77.

42. Williamson, *The Crucible of Race*, pp. 475–82.

43. Johnson, *To Stem This Tide*, p. 65.

44. Ibid., pp. 62–67; Anderson, *Wild Man from Sugar Creek*, pp. 195–212; *Baltimore Afro-American*, 19 September 1942, p. 6; Clark Foreman, "Race Tensions in the South," *New Republic*, 21 September 1942, p. 341.

45. Merl Reed, *Seedtime for the Modern Civil Rights Movement*, pp. 66–76, 90–91; Norrell, "Labor at the Ballot Box," pp. 225–26; AP clipping (1943), Papers of the NAACP, II-B, 209.

46. Merl Reed, *Seedtime for the Modern Civil Rights Movement*, p. 71.

47. Norrell, "Labor at the Ballot Box," pp. 225–26; AP clipping (1943), Papers of the NAACP, II-B, 209.

48. Odum, *Race and Rumors of Race*, p. 7; Wallace interview, COHC, p. 3241; Thomas Sancton, "Race Fear Sweeps the South," *New Republic*, 18 January 1943, p. 83.

49. Lash, *Eleanor and Franklin*, p. 297; Patricia Sullivan, "Eleanor Roosevelt and the Mind of the South, 1933–1945" (paper delivered at the Eleanor Roosevelt Centennial Conference, Vassar College, 15 October 1984).

50. *Rosslyn (Virginia) Chronicle*, n.d. [1936], FDR Papers, OF 93, box 2; "Blunt Criticism," reprint of *Georgia Women's World* article in *Columbia Observer*, n.d. [1936], FDR Papers, OF 93, box 2; NYT, 30 January 1936; *Atlanta Constitution*, 2 February 1935; Anderson, *Wild Man from Sugar Creek*, pp. 136–40.

51. *Ladies' Home Journal*, September 1941, p. 21; Eleanor Roosevelt, "Race, Religion, and Prejudice," *New Republic*, 11 May 1942, p. 630.

52. Chester B. Collins to FDR, 26 May 1944, FDR Papers, OF 4952; ODUM, *Race and Rumors of Race*, pp. 73–89; NYT, 1 September 1942, 23 September 1942.

53. "Mrs. Roosevelt Sits in on Mixed Racial Dancing," news clipping, AP, 16 February 1944; Mary Malone et al. to FDR, 22 February 1944; and Mayor J. H. Bradford to FDR, 21 February 1944; all in FDR Papers, OF 93, box 6; Fred Oakley to ER, 5 March 1944, ER Papers, box 2962.

54. *Memphis Commercial Appeal*, 27 January, 29 January 1944.

55. Ibid., 30 January 1944.

56. Burran, "Racial Violence in the South," chs. 4–6.

57. Daniels interview, COHC, pp. 124–25; Washburn, *Question of Sedition*.

58. Kneebone, *Southern Liberal Journalists*, pp. 53, 95, 108–9, 156–74.

59. Raper interview with author; Kneebone, *Southern Liberal Journalists*, pp. 153–54, 167–74.

60. Dabney, "Nearer and Nearer the Precipice"; John Templeton Graves, "The Southern Negro and the War Crisis," *Virginia Quarterly Review* 18 (1942): 509; Kneebone, *Southern Liberal Journalists*, p. 201.

61. E. Franklin Frazier, "Race: An American Dilemma," *Crisis* 51 (1944): 105.

62. McDonough, "Clearinghouse for Change," pp. 186–96.

63. *Crisis* cited in ibid., pp. 196–218.

64. Ibid., pp. 221–27.

65. Sancton, "Southern View of the Race Question," pp. 198–99.

66. Ibid.; Louis E. Martin, "To Be or Not to Be a Liberal," *Crisis* 49 (1942): 285.

67. Sancton, "Southern View of the Race Question," p. 204.

68. Walter Jackson, *Gunnar Myrdal*, pp. 186–271.

69. Myrdal, *An American Dilemma*, p. xix.

CHAPTER SIX

1. John McCray, "The Need for Changing," McCray Papers, box 1.

2. McCray interviews with author; Clement interview with author; *Norfolk Journal and Guide*, 29 July 1944.

3. *Norfolk Journal and Guide*, 20 May 1944; *Columbia Record*, 27 May 1944.

4. *Columbia Record*, 13 July 1944; McCray interviews with author, 27 July, 23 September 1985; Clement interview with author.

5. *Columbia Record*, 18 July 1944; McCray interviews with author, 27 July, 23 September 1985.

6. Josephson, *Sidney Hillman*, p. 607; Fraser, *Labor Will Rule*, pp. 506–17; *Time*, 24 July 1944, pp. 18–20; *Chicago Defender*, 2 September 1944, p. 1.

7. NYT cited in MacDougall, *Gideon's Army* 1:53; Crown, "The Political Action Committee of the CIO," p. 19.

8. NYT, 8 November 1944, p. 2; Crown, "The Political Action Committee of the CIO," pp. 1–5; C. B. Baldwin to George Rettinger, 17 March 1944, C. B. Baldwin Papers, University of Iowa Libraries, Iowa City, box 15.

9. NYT, 5 May 1944, p. 13; 13 May 1944, pp. 1, 10; 20 May 1944, p. 10; Garson, *The*

Democratic Party, pp. 105–6; Crown, "The Political Action Committee of the CIO," pp. 108–15.

10. Fraser, *Labor Will Rule*, pp. 524–25.

11. Garson, *The Democratic Party*, pp. 94–113.

12. Ibid., pp. 114–16.

13. *Fortune*, October 1942, p. 144.

14. Lord, *Wallaces of Iowa*, p. 152.

15. Ibid., pp. 140–54, 184–88, 230–39; Schapsmeier and Schapsmeier, *Henry Wallace of Iowa*, pp. 21–28, 38–82.

16. Bean interview, COHC, p. 62; Wallace interview, COHC, pp. 117–45; Schapsmeier and Schapsmeier, *Henry Wallace of Iowa*, pp. 105–10.

17. Badger, *The New Deal*, pp. 150–52, 186–87; Gilbert and Howe, "Beyond 'State vs. Society,'" pp. 204–20; Judis, "Henry Wallace and the Common Man," pp. 55–59; Lord, *Wallaces of Iowa*, pp. 460–62; Wallace interview, COHC, p. 423.

18. Wallace, *Whose Constitution*, pp. 11, 92; Schapsmeier and Schapsmeier, *Henry Wallace of Iowa*, p. 221.

19. Sirevag, *Eclipse of the New Deal*, pp. 90–97, 106; Roosevelt, *This I Remember*, p. 217; Judis, "Henry Wallace and the Common Man," p. 47.

20. Wallace interview, COHC, pp. 1480–81; Reston quoted in Sirevag, *Eclipse of the New Deal*, pp. 443–47.

21. Wallace, "The Price of Free World Victory," *Democracy Reborn*, pp. 190–96.

22. *Fortune*, October 1942, p. 135; Blum, *The Price of Vision*, pp. 75–77, 84; Wallace interview, COHC, 3662, 4472–73. Wallace's alleged promise of "a quart of milk for every Hottentot" was attributed to this speech. Wallace never made such a statement, a fact that Roosevelt himself was surprised to learn. Sirevag, *Eclipse of the New Deal*, p. 419.

23. Wallace, "The Genetic Basis of Democracy," *Democracy Reborn*, pp. 152–58. Black spokesmen had been among the most vocal critics of the first Agricultural Adjustment Administration (AAA), particularly its widespread displacement of sharecroppers and tenant farmers. In 1937, Wallace met with twenty black newspaper editors to enlist their support and invite their criticism, and he maintained a working relationship with the black press from then on. The department increased the number of black people in professional positions, including James T. Davis, who worked as head fieldworker for the southern division of the AAA, and Thomas Roberts, special assistant to the director of personnel, who was responsible for promoting inclusive hiring practices. By the late 1930s, Wallace had won the confidence and support of the black press and vocal segments of the black community. See Bunche, *Political Status of the Negro*, pp. 76–77, 505–15; Bledsoe interview, COHC, pp. 130–38; "Wallace and the Negro," PPC, box 32.

24. *Norfolk Journal and Guide*, 25 March 1944.

25. *NYT*, 26 July 1943.

26. *NYT*, 26, 27, 29 July 1943, 1 August 1943; *Birmingham World*, 30 July 1943, 3 August 1943; Sirevag, *Eclipse of the New Deal*, pp. 247–49; Blum, *The Price of Vision*, p. 228.

27. C. B. Baldwin, "Report on the Democratic National Convention, 27 February 1951," Baldwin Papers; Williams interview with author; Helen Fuller, "Throwing

Wallace to the Wolves," *New Republic*, 31 July 1944, p. 122; Carleton, "The Conservative South," p. 191; *Time*, 31 July 1944; Tindall, *Emergence of the New South*, 728.

28. "Address of the Honorable Henry A. Wallace as Chairman of the Iowa Delegation, Seconding the Nomination of President Roosevelt, Democratic National Convention, Chicago, Illinois, 20 July 1944," Henry A. Wallace Papers; Lord, *Wallaces of Iowa*, pp. 532–38; *Norfolk Journal and Guide*, 29 July 1944.

29. *Time*, 31 July 1944; Baldwin, "Report on the Democratic National Convention."

30. Ibid.; Wallace interview, COHC, pp. 3434, 3394, 3413, 4564; Fuller, "Throwing Wallace to the Wolves," p. 122; Williams interview with author.

31. Pepper interview with author, 25 March 1980; *Time*, 31 July 1944.

32. Mooney interview with author; Wallace interview, COHC, p. 3519; Baldwin, "Report on the Democratic National Convention"; *Pittsburgh Courier*, 29 July 1944; Fraser, *Labor Will Rule*, 495–538.

33. Lord, *Wallaces of Iowa*, p. 536; Fuller, "Throwing Wallace to the Wolves," p. 122; Baldwin, "Report on the Democratic National Convention"; Pepper interview with author, 25 March 1980; *Chicago Defender*, 29 July 1944.

34. Mark Ethridge to Franklin D. Roosevelt, 25 July 1944, copy in Wallace interview, COHC, pp. 3398–400.

35. *Pittsburgh Courier*, 29 July 1944.

36. Ibid.; "Up for Sale: The Negro Vote," *Chicago Defender*, 15 July 1944; *Chicago Defender*, 29 July 1944, 5 August 1944; *Baltimore Afro-American*, 29 July 1944; Walter White to ER, 9 August 1944, ER Papers, box 1751.

37. *New Republic*, 31 July 1944, pp. 117–18; Walter White, *Chicago Defender*, 5 August 1944; *Chicago Defender*, 29 July 1944; *Pittsburgh Courier*, 29 July 1944; Sirevag, *Eclipse of the New Deal*, pp. 434–35.

38. Analysts predicted that voter turnout in 1944 would be well under forty-five million and perhaps a little more than forty million. Actual turnout exceeded forty-nine million. NYT, 8 November 1944; Louise Overacker, "Labor Rides the Political Waves," *Current History*, December 1944, pp. 472–73.

39. *Chicago Defender*, 2 September 1944.

40. Clark Foreman and James Dombrowski, Memo for the CIO Executive Board, 13 November 1944, Records of the SCHW, box 32.

41. Ibid.; Honey, *Southern Labor and Black Civil Rights*, pp. 214–15.

42. Clark Foreman and James Dombrowski, Memo for the CIO Executive Board, 13 November 1944, Records of the SCHW, box 32.

43. Krueger, *And Promises to Keep*, pp. 54, 137; Weber interview with author, 17 November 1980; James Dombrowski to ER, 26 November 1944, ER Papers, box 86; Dombrowski to Roosevelt, 7 December, 12 December 1944, ER Papers, box 1720; Roosevelt to Dombrowski, 12 December 1944, Records of the SCHW, box 51.

44. *Columbia Record*, 9 August 1944.

45. Osceola McKaine, "For Victory at the Ballot Box," monthly bulletin, Southern Negro Youth Congress, McCray Papers, box 2; John McCray to Luther P. Jackson, 10 October, 21 October 1947, Jackson Papers, box 84; Abraham interview with author.

46. John McCray to Thurgood Marshall, 9 November 1944, and Thurgood Marshall to John McCray, 13 November 1944, Papers of the NAACP, II-B, 209; John

McCray to Virgie Evans, 15 February 1945, McCray Papers, box 2; *The State* (Columbia, South Carolina), 4 January 1945.

47. McKaine, "For Victory at the Ballot Box," p. 3.

CHAPTER SEVEN

1. *PM*, 16 May 1946, p. 2.

2. St. Clair Drake, "An American Problem," *New Republic*, 2 December 1946, pp. 727; Carleton, "The Conservative South," pp. 179–92; Barnes, *Journey from Jim Crow*, pp. 44–51; *Norfolk Journal and Guide*, 13 April 1946, p. 1.

3. Durr interview with author, 25 June 1992; Moon, *Balance of Power*, pp. 178–79; Moon interview with author.

4. Ella Baker to Branch Presidents, 11 January 1946, Papers of the NAACP, I-A, 383; Lulu White to Ella Baker, 15 August 1945, Papers of the NAACP, II-C, 194; Youngblood, "Testing the Current," pp. 78–80.

5. Moon, *Balance of Power*, p. 194; Weber interview with author, 19 March 1982.

6. Moon, *Balance of Power*, p. 194; Weber interview with author, 12 July 1983; McCray interview with author, 19 February 1985. National Office of the League for Democracy, pamphlet; Major W. H. Loving to Director of Military Intelligence, 25 April 1919; Oseola McKaine to the Secretary of War, 24 May 1919; and Major W. H. Loving to Director, Military Intelligence, re. mass meeting of League for Democracy, 17 June 1919; all in League for Democracy file, Federal Surveillance of Afro-Americans, microfilm.

7. Abraham interview with author.

8. The biographical sketch of Osceola McKaine is based on the following: "The McKaine Story," Osceola McKaine file, South Caroliniana Library, Columbia; Abraham interview with author; McCray interview with author, 19 February 1985; Weber interview with author, 12 July 1983; *Palmetto News*, 3 May 1941.

9. James Dombrowski to George Buchanan, 27 April 1945, Records of the SCHW, box 1.

10. "Vets March in Ala., Seek Right to Vote They Fought for as GIs," *Norfolk Journal and Guide*, 2 February 1946, p. 1; Burnham interview with author.

11. James Dombrowski to George Mitchell, 11 June 1946, and McKaine, Memo to Executive Secretary, n.d., Records of the SCHW, box 2.

12. Osceola McKaine, Report, 31 January–20 February 1946, Records of the SCHW, box 2; S. H. Bell to James Dombrowski, 20 February 1946, and Dombrowski to Bell, 6 April 1946, Records of the SCHW, box 2; *Norfolk Journal and Guide*, 15 June 1946, p. 1.

13. Osceola McKaine, "The Third Revolution," July 1946, Jackson Papers, box 80.

14. Ibid.

15. Rebecca Stanfield to James Dombrowski, 24 October 1944, and John Hunt to Marge Frantz, 23 October 1944, Records of the SCHW, box 3; Gennie Seideman to James Dombrowski, 9 September 1944, Records of the SCHW, box 1; Osceola McKaine column, *Norfolk Journal and Guide*, 26 May 1945; Key, *Southern Politics*, p. 657; Krueger, *And Promises to Keep*, pp. 109, 128; *Southern Patriot*, May 1945, June 1946.

16. Krueger, *And Promises to Keep*, p. 136; Honey, *Southern Labor and Black Civil Rights*, p. 216; Dombrowski interview with author, 8 November 1980.

17. *Atlanta Constitution*: 1 February 1945, p. 7; 4 February 1945, p. 10c; 11 February 1945, p. 11c; Clark Foreman, "Georgia Kills the Poll Tax," *New Republic*, 26 February 1945, pp. 291–92; *Southern Patriot*, February 1945.

18. Kenneth Stewart, "Ellis Arnall: A Liberal Grows in Georgia," *PM*, 18 August 1946, pp. m7–m9; "Georgia's Arnall Opens All-Out Battle against the Klan," *PM*, 31 May 1946.

19. Krueger, *And Promises to Keep*, pp. 131–33; Margaret Fisher to ER, 12 October 1944, ER Papers, box 1722; Margaret Fisher to James Dombrowski, n.d. [ca. January 1945], Records of the SCHW, box 3; Salmond, *Miss Lucy of the CIO*, pp. 119–21; Crown, "The Political Action Committee of the CIO," p. 60.

20. Salmond, *Miss Lucy of the CIO*, p. 119; Committee for Georgia File, Glen Rainey Papers, Robert W. Woodruff Library, Atlanta, Georgia; Dan Powell, "PAC Field Report," February 1947, copy provided by Dan Powell.

21. Committee for Virginia file, Records of the SCHW, box 2; Committee for Virginia file, Jackson Papers, box 80; Key, *Southern Politics*, 28–29; Virginia Beecher to James Dombrowski, 25 June 1946, Records of the SCHW, box 2; Meier and Rudwick, *Black History*, pp. 85–89.

22. "Byrd Foes Meet in Dark," *PM*, 23 August 1946, p. 9.

23. "Byrd Challenged at Polls Today but He'll Probably Win Anyway," *PM*, 6 August 1946, p. 4.

24. Painter, *Narrative of Hosea Hudson*, pp. 257–68; Committee for Alabama file, Records of the SCHW, box 3; Arthur Shores to Thurgood Marshall, 13 September 1939, 3 June 1939, 15 February 1940, and Marshall to Shores, 15 February 1940, Papers of the NAACP, I-D, 48. Thurgood Marshall forwarded details on Shores's handling of registration cases to all of the other NAACP branches in Alabama as a model of how to proceed. Marshall to Alabama branches, 16 September 1939, Papers of the NAACP, I-D, 48. Norrell, *Reaping the Whirlwind*, pp. 61–69; *Norfolk Journal and Guide*, 2 February 1946; Kelley, *Hammer and Hoe*, pp. 223, 225.

25. Powell, "PAC Field Report"; Mary Price to Frank Graham, 18 September 1945, Frank Porter Graham Papers, Southern History Collection, Chapel Hill, North Carolina, box 1819; Adamson interview, Southern Oral History Program; Franklin interview with author; *Norfolk Journal and Guide*, 1 June 1946.

26. Franklin interview with author.

27. Marshall, *Labor in the South*, pp. 258–59.

28. Honey, *Southern Labor and Black Civil Rights*, pp. 177–216.

29. Ibid., pp. 214–44.

30. Weber, "The Negro Vote in the South"; *Norfolk Journal and Guide*, 15 June 1946; Weber interview with author, 21 December 1978; Weber interview with Meier, 20 October 1979; Secretary to Palmer Weber, 21 June 1946, Papers of the NAACP, II-A, 142. Bethune's tour included Nashville, Tennessee, Birmingham and Mobile, Alabama, Jacksonville, Florida, Savannah and Atlanta, Georgia, and Durham, Winston-Salem, and Greensboro, North Carolina. *Southern Patriot*, January 1946, p. 7, February 1946, p. 7.

31. McKaine quoted in Krueger, *And Promises to Keep*, p. 140.

32. Krueger, *And Promises to Keep*, pp. 139–43; *NYT*, 19 April 1946, p. 4.

33. Bacote, "The Negro in Atlanta Politics," p. 344.

34. Key, *Southern Politics*, p. 520; Spritzer, *Belle of Ashby Street*, pp. 64–74; Dan Powell, "PAC Report of February 1 through 21, 1946" and "Report on PAC in Georgia and Fifth Congressional District Special Election, February 12th," copies provided by Dan Powell; Hamilton interview with author.

35. *Atlanta Constitution*, 18 April 1946.

36. Ibid., 2 April, 18 April, 21 July 1946; Moon, *Balance of Power*, p. 194.

37. *Atlanta Constitution*, 7 April, 18 April 1946; *NYT*, 19 May 1946, p. 6.

38. "Atlanta All Citizen Registration Committee"; Ira DeA. Reid, "The White Primary," July 1946, Grace Townes Hamilton Papers, Trevor Arnett Library, Atlanta, Georgia, 15-B-3; Hamilton interview with author; Bacote, "The Negro in Atlanta Politics," pp. 346–48.

39. Anderson, *Wild Man from Sugar Creek*, p. 232.

40. *Atlanta Constitution*, 20 July 1946; "Talmadge Wins against Georgia's Will," *PM*, 19 July 1946, p. 5; Powell interview with author.

41. Bernd, "White Supremacy."

42. Moon, *Balance of Power*, p. 186; *NYT*, 4 August, 14 November 1946; *Nation* 169 (1952): 251.

43. Tom O'Connor, "Lynch Law Back in Georgia—4 Murdered," *PM*, 28 July 1946, p. 4; *PM*, 5 August 1946, p. 4; *NYT*, 4 August 1946.

44. Tom O'Connor, "Portrait of a Lynch Town," *PM*, 5 August 1946, pp. 2–4.

45. Reid, "The White Primary"; "Presentation of a Plan for an Adult Education Extension Service for the State of Georgia," presented to the Atlanta Urban League, September 1946, Hamilton Papers, 15-B-3; Hamilton interview with author.

46. Malcolm Dobbs to James Dombrowski, 7 May 1946, Records of the SCHW, box 3.

47. Malcolm Dobbs to Clark Foreman, 8 June 1946, Records of the SCHW, box 3.

48. Ibid.

49. Sims, *The Little Man's Big Friend*, pp. 27–37; Grafton and Permaloff, *Big Mules and Branchheads*, pp. 59–69; Key, *Southern Politics*, p. 42; Powell, "PAC Field Report"; Norrell, *Reaping the Whirlwind*, p. 74.

50. Palmer Weber, report on Homer Rainey campaign, August 1946, copy provided by Palmer Weber.

51. Ibid.

52. Ibid.

53. *NYT*, 27 July, 25 August 1946; Ben Ramey to James Dombrowski, 18 March 1946, Records of the SCHW, box 3; Palmer Weber, report on Homer Rainey campaign, August 1946.

54. *Nation* 163 (1946): 579; Clark Foreman, keynote speech, Southern Youth Legislature, Columbia, South Carolina, 19 October 1946, McCray Papers]; Flamming, *Creating the Modern South*, pp. 248–53; *PM*: 2 August 1946, p. 3; 4 August 1946, p. 5; 5 August 1946, p. 5; 6 August 1946, p. 5; 11 August 1946, p. 4; 13 August 1946, p. 4; 14 August 1946, p. 4.

55. Dittmer, *Local People*, pp. 1–9.

56. Carleton, "The Conservative South," pp. 188–90.

57. Beeler, "Race Riot in Columbia, Tennessee"; George McMillan, "Race Justice in Aiken," *Nation* 163 (1946): 579–80; *PM*: 17 July 1946, p. 10; 12 August 1946, p. 3; 16 August 1946, p. 4; 18 August 1946, p. 5; 22 August 1946, p. 4; 30 August 1946, p. 5; *Crisis* 53 (1946): 276.

58. *Southern Patriot*, December 1946; Frank Graham to Clark Foreman, November 1946, and Foreman to Graham, 4 December 1946, Graham Papers, box 1819.

CHAPTER EIGHT

1. Stone, *The Truman Era*, pp. xxi–xxiii; Blum, *The Price of Vision*, pp. 464–65; Wallace interview, COHC, p. 1442; Boylan, *The New Deal Coalition*, pp. 19, 25–28.

2. Polenberg, "The Good War?"; Lichtenstein, "The Making of the Postwar Working Class," p. 50.

3. Hooks, *Forging the Military-Industrial Complex*, pp. 120–22; Lipsitz, *Class and Culture in Cold War America*, pp. 37–55.

4. *Atlanta Constitution*, 8 April 1946.

5. *Crisis* 53 (1946): 9.

6. NYT, 24 September 1946; *Crisis* 53 (1946): 9; McNeil, *Groundwork*, pp. 170–75.

7. Murphy, *Fortas*, pp. 68–71; Alonzo Smith, "Afro-Americans and the Presidential Election of 1948," p. 102.

8. Harbutt, *The Iron Curtain*, pp. 183–208; Leffler, *Preponderance of Power*, pp. 100–140.

9. Boylan, *The New Deal Coalition*, p. 107; Weber interview with author, 17 November 1980.

10. Leffler, *Preponderance of Power*, p. 108.

11. Henry A. Wallace, "The Way to Peace," 12 September 1946, in Blum, *The Price of Vision*, pp. 661–69.

12. Boylan, *The New Deal Coalition*, pp. 108–10; NYT, 13 September 1946, p. 1.

13. *New Republic*, 30 September 1946, pp. 395–97; Freda Kirchwey, "The Challenge of Henry Wallace," *Nation* 163 (1946): 337–39; Wallace interview, COHC, pp. 4968, 4970, 4978; Boylan, *The New Deal Coalition*, pp. 108–12.

14. Hamby, *Beyond the New Deal*, p. 154; *New Republic*, 30 September 1946, p. 400; *New Republic*, 7 October 1946, p. 433; CIO News, 7 October 1946.

15. Emspak, "The Break-up of the Congress of Industrial Organizations," pp. 119–20.

16. "Address by Walter White, Conference of Progressives, Chicago, 28 September 1946," Papers of the NAACP, II-A, 467.

17. Jack Kroll, "The PAC Today," *Nation* 163 (1946): 510–11; transcript of Jack Kroll's speech, *Daily Worker*, 20 October 1946; *New York Post*, 16 October 1946.

18. Emspak, "The Break-up of the Congress of Industrial Organizations," pp. 52–100.

19. Gillon, *Politics and Vision*, pp. 6–12.

20. Ibid., pp. 11–22; Hamby, *Beyond the New Deal*, pp. 33–38; James Loeb to the Editors, *New Republic*, 13 May 1946, p. 699.

21. Responses to James Loeb's letter in *New Republic*: Stanley M. Isaacs, 20 May 1946, p. 733; Jackson Valtair and Clark Foreman, 10 June 1946, p. 837; Curtis MacDougall, 1 July 1946, p. 936.

22. Arthur Schlesinger Jr., "The U.S. Communist Party," *Life*, 29 July 1946, pp. 84–85, 87, 90.

23. Ibid., pp. 88, 90, 93.

24. Ibid., pp. 94, 96.

25. Gillon, *Politics and Vision*, pp. 12–24.

26. *Nation* 163 (1946): 489.

27. Boylan, *The New Deal Coalition*, pp. 132–44; *New Republic*, 21 October 1946, pp. 337–39.

28. Boylan, *The New Deal Coalition*, pp. 111–12, 135–43; *Los Angeles Times*, 21 October 1946, p. 1; Irving M. Engel, "Rankin and the Republicans," *Nation* 163 (1946): 465–66; Helen Fuller, "Smearing the PAC," *New Republic*, 22 July 1946, pp. 168–70.

29. Boylan, *The New Deal Coalition*, pp. 151–77; *New Republic*, 18 November 1946, p. 643.

30. Helen Fuller, "Democrats after the Deluge," *New Republic*, 2 December 1946, pp. 714–15; Tris Coffin, "Harry Truman's Bright Young Man," *New Republic*, 6 January 1947, pp. 14–17; Boylan, *The New Deal Coalition*, pp. 182–83.

31. Kampleman, *The Communist Party vs. the CIO*, pp. 64–65; Krueger, *And Promises to Keep*, pp. 142–43.

32. Joseph Lash to Jim Loeb, 21 November 1945, and Loeb to Lash, 24 October 1945, ADA, microfilm, reel 9; ER to C. B. Baldwin, 29 December 1946, Baldwin Papers, box 8.

33. C. B. Baldwin to ER, 13 January 1947, and Roosevelt to Baldwin, 16 January 1947, Baldwin Papers, box 8.

34. MacDougall, *Gideon's Army* 1:114–17.

35. Gillon, *Politics and Vision*, pp. 16–24.

36. Freeland, *The Truman Doctrine*, pp. 130–33.

37. Ibid., pp. 133–50; Patterson, *Meeting the Communist Threat*, chs. 5, 6.

38. Freeland, *The Truman Doctrine*, p. 101.

39. Gillon, *Politics and Vision*, pp. 26–29.

40. Schrecker, *No Ivory Tower*, pp. 4–6.

41. Henry Steele Commager, "Washington Witch-Hunt," *Nation* 164 (1947): 385–88.

42. Freda Kirchwey, "Liberals Beware!," *Nation* 164 (1947): 384.

43. "Dissenting Views of Commissioner Clifford J. Durr Re Proposed Rules Governing FCC-Loyalty Procedure," Virgina Foster Durr Papers, Arthur and Elizabeth Schlesinger Library, Cambridge Massachusetts.

44. Charles Houston, *Baltimore Afro-American*, [1943].

45. Charles Houston, *Baltimore Afro-American*, 12 April 1947, 3 May 1947.

46. Virginia Durr to Luther Porter Jackson, n.d., Jackson Papers, box 89; Aubrey Williams, "What Is Happening to Our Civil Rights?," 11 September 1947, Williams Papers, box 35.

47. Frank McAllister to James Loeb, 8 June 1945, and Loeb to McAllister, 14 June

1945, ADA, microfilm, reel 61; Barney Taylor correspondence, ADA, microfilm, reel 50; Notes on Atlanta ADA meeting, 19 February 1949, ADA, microfilm, reel 50.

48. McAllister to Loeb, 27 August 1946; Ellis Arnall to Reinhold Neibuhr, 1 December 1946; Loeb to Arnall, 2 December 1946; Tucker to McAllister, 3 December 1947; and Arnall to Wilson Wyatt, 3 January 1947; all in ADA, microfilm, reel 50.

49. Mary Price to William Poteat, 9 January 1947, SCHW Papers, box 36.

50. Scales, *Cause at Heart*, pp. 182–87; Mary Price to Clark Foreman, 19 October 1947, SCHW Papers, box 36.

51. Virginia Durr to Henry Fowler, 18 March 1947, and Minutes of the Executive Board Meeting of the Committee for Virginia, 12 April 1947, SCHW Papers, box 31.

52. U.S. Congress, House, Committee on Un-American Activities, *Report on the Southern Conference for Human Welfare*, 80th Congress, 1st sess., 1947, p. 17; Clark Foreman to Mojeska Simkins, 23 June 1947; Foreman to Arthur Garfield Hays, 14 June 1947; Hays to Foreman, 15 June 1947; and Roger Baldwin to Foreman, 15 June 1947; all in SCHW Papers, box 41; H. C. Nixon to Frank Graham, 11 August 1947, Graham Papers, box 1819. Walter Gellhorn, professor at Columbia University School of Law, wrote a critical analysis of HUAC's report on the SCHW. He concluded that the charges were groundless and raised serious questions about the committee's motivations and/or competence. Gellhorn, "Report on the Report of the Committee on UnAmerican Activities," pp. 1193–1234.

53. Sullivan, "Gideon's Southern Soldiers," pp. 222–25.

54. Clark Foreman to Lew Frank, 27 May 1947, SCHW Papers, box 41; Faulk interviews with author; Clark Foreman to Mary Price, 29 August 1947, SCHW Papers, box 36.

55. Edmonia Grant, "Memo to Chairman of State Committee Regarding Henry Wallace Meetings," 5 October 1947, SCHW Papers, box 41; Edmonia Grant to Clark Foreman, 30 September 1947, SCHW Papers, box 36; Edmonia Grant to Clark Foreman, 7 October 1947, SCHW Papers, box 41; Clark Foreman to Lew Frank, 6 November 1947, SCHW Papers, box 41. After Rev. William Holmes Borders agreed to host the Atlanta meeting at his Wheat Street Baptist Church, he began to receive threats from anonymous callers and others who identified themselves as Klan members. Rev. Borders responded by purchasing $100,000 in additional property insurance for his church. Curtis MacDougall to Rev. William Holmes Borders, 19 October 1954, and Borders to MacDougall, 25 October 1954, PPC, box 45; Borders interview with author.

56. Clark Foreman to Lew Frank, 4 November 1947, SCHW Papers, box 41.

57. *Atlanta Journal*, 20 November 1947, p. 46.

58. Ibid., 20 November 1947, p. 46, 21 November 1947, p. 16; Washington Committee of SCHW, Minutes of Executive Board Meeting, 22 October 1947, SCHW Papers, box 28; *New Orleans Times-Picayune*, 18 November 1947, p. 3; *Louisville Courier-Journal*, 22 November 1947, p. 16. Clark Foreman explained that a city ordinance had been passed in Atlanta during World War II requiring separate seating of the races. However, there was no attempt to enforce it at the meeting held for Wallace at the Wheat Street Baptist Church. Foreman to the Editor, *Washington Afro-American*, 9 December 1947, SCHW Papers, box 41.

59. A bill requiring racial segregation in public halls in Virginia became law on 22

March 1926 without the governor's signature. Charles Houston, *Baltimore Afro-American*, 6 December 1947.

60. Virginia Durr, "Profile of a Southern Patrician Freedom Fighter," *Voice*, n.d.; Clark Foreman to Editor, *PM*, 26 November 1947; *Norfolk Journal and Guide*, 29 November 1947, p. 1; Durr interview with author, 3 May 1978; Clark Foreman to Curtis MacDougall, 10 December 1952, PPC, box 32; Clark Foreman to Thomas Krueger, 19 December 1967, SCHW Papers, box 1.

61. Clark Foreman to Henry Wallace, 24 November 1947, SCHW Papers, box 41; Editorial, *Memphis Commercial Appeal*, 25 November 1947; *Atlanta Constitution*, 15 November 1947; *Atlanta Constitution*, 30 January 1947. A folder of correspondence concerning the impending lawsuit is contained in SCHW Papers, box 37; also see Clark Foreman to Curtis MacDougall, 11 November 1953, PPC, box 32.

62. Edmonia Grant to Clark Foreman, 24 November, 25 November 1947, SCHW Papers, box 36; Mary Price to Edmonia Grant, 24 November 1947, Foreman to Wallace, 24 November 1947, and Foreman to William Mitch, 28 November 1947, SCHW Papers, box 41; Foreman to Editor, *PM*, 26 November 1947.

EPILOGUE

1. Speech by Henry A. Wallace, Richmond, Virginia, 29 September 1948, Henry A. Wallace Papers, University of Iowa Libraries, Iowa City, box 78.

2. "Notes on a Meeting to Discuss the Third Party in the South," PPC, box 35.

3. Sullivan, "Gideon's Southern Soldiers," ch. 6; Gillette, "The NAACP in Texas," pp. 173–77; McKissick interview, Southern Oral History Program.

4. Palmer Weber to Jack Kroll, n.d. [May 1948], Jack Kroll Papers, box 1.

5. Weber interview with author, 19 March 1982.

6. William Moody to Patricia Sullivan, 17 July 1987; Weber interview with author, 19 March 1982.

7. Moody to Sullivan, 17 July 1987.

8. Friedlands interview with author; Saunders interview with author; Blackwell interview with author. After taking a law degree at Howard University, Randolph Blackwell went on to work with Martin Luther King Jr. in the Southern Christian Leadership Conference. In 1966 he founded Rural Action, a nonprofit corporation dedicated to helping small, poor, and mostly black communities in the South become self-reliant economically and politically. Faced with the difficulties of creating jobs and better housing in some of the country's most impoverished regions, Blackwell once said of Rural Action's work, "We are trying to make it impossible for anyone to argue that it can't be done by demonstrating that it can be done." *NYT*, 23 May 1981.

9. Price interview with author; Weber interview with author, 21 December 1978; *Atlanta Constitution*, 27 September, 1 October, 3 October 1948.

10. Charles Houston, *Baltimore Afro-American*, 7 February 1948.

11. Berman, *Politics of Civil Rights*, pp. 81–93.

12. Charles Houston, *Baltimore Afro-American*, 3 April 1948; Berman, *Politics of Civil Rights*, pp. 97–100.

13. Berman, *Politics of Civil Rights*, pp. 100–121; Gillon, *Politics and Vision*, pp. 39–50.

14. Charles Houston, *Baltimore Afro-American*, 31 July 1948.

15. Weber interview with author, 3 May 1980; Hall interview with author; Wechsler interview with author; Popham interview with author.

16. *Baltimore Afro-American*, 4 September 1948.

17. *New York Post*, 30 August 1948.

18. Ross interview with author, 5 August 1981.

19. *New York Post*, 30 August 1948.

20. Weber interview with author, 3 May 1980; MacDougall, *Gideon's Army* 3:712.

21. Burnham interview with MacDougall; Seeger interview with author.

22. *NYT*, 1 September 1948; *Washington Post*, 1 September 1948.

23. Mairi Fraser Foreman to Patricia Sullivan, 20 March 1979 (in author's possession); *NYT*, 1 September 1948.

24. *Winston-Salem Journal*, 1 September 1948; Daniels quoted in *Washington Post*, 1 September 1948.

25. Douglass Hall, "If You Ask Me," *Baltimore Afro-American*, 11 September 1948.

26. *New York Post*, 1 September 1948; Weber interview with author, 3 May 1980; Hall interview with author.

27. Weber interview with author, 3 May 1980; *NYT*, 2 September 1948; *Washington Post*, 2 September 1948.

28. Mooney interview with author; Weber interview with author, 3 May 1980.

29. *Knoxville News-Sentinel*, 1 September, 2 September 1948.

30. *NYT*, 2 September 1948.

31. Ibid.; Mooney interview with author.

32. "Broadcast by Henry A. Wallace," Birmingham, Alabama, 1 September 1948, Lew Frank Papers, box 1; Weber interview with author, 3 May 1980.

33. "Broadcast by Henry A. Wallace," Birmingham, Alabama, 1 September 1948, Lew Frank Papers, box 1.

34. *Jackson Daily News*, 31 August 1948; *Arkansas Gazette*, 3 September 1948; *Jackson Clarion Ledger*, 1 September, 3 September 1948.

35. *Arkansas Gazette*, 4 September 1948.

36. Ibid.

37. Ibid.

38. *Nashville Banner*, 4 September 1948; *Washington Post*, 4 September 1948; *New York Post*, 4 September 1948; *New York Star*, 4 September 1948.

39. *NYT*, 5 September 1948; *Washington Post*, 5 September 1948.

40. *New York Post*, 4 September 1948; *Washington Post*, 4 September 1948; *NYT*, 4 September 1948.

41. "The South Gets Rough with Wallace," *Life*, 13 September 1948, pp. 34–36.

42. Wechsler interview with author; James Wechsler, "My Ten Months with Wallace," *Progressive*, November 1948, p. 5.

43. Palmer Weber to Thurgood Marshall, 11 September 1948, Papers of the NAACP, II-A, 142.

44. Ibid.

45. Charles Houston, *Baltimore Afro-American*, 11 September 1948.

46. Ibid.

47. Ibid.

48. McCray interview with author, 23 September 1985.

49. Moody to Sullivan, 17 July 1987; Weber interview with author, 6 September 1980.

50. Charles Houston, *Baltimore Afro-American*, 11 September 1948.

51. Foreman, "Decade of Hope."

52. McDonough, "Clearinghouse for Change," p. 18.

53. Esther Jackson, panel presentation on the Southern Negro Youth Congress, Harvard University, 12 July 1995; Clark Foreman to Clifford Durr, 17 November 1954, Durr Papers.

54. Clark, "Civil Rights Leader Harry T. Moore"; Virginia Durr to Mildred Olmstead, June 1958, Durr Papers.

55. *Report of the National Advisory Commission on Civil Disorders, 1 March 1968* (Washington, D.C.: GPO, 1968), p. 1.

Bibliography

MANUSCRIPTS

Atlanta, Georgia
Trevor Arnett Library, Atlanta University
   Grace Townes Hamilton Papers
   Southern Conference for Human Welfare (SCHW) Papers
Robert W. Woodruff Library, Emory University
   Ralph McGill Papers
   Glen Rainey Papers

Cambridge, Massachusetts
Arthur and Elizabeth Schlesinger Library, Radcliffe College
   Virginia Foster Durr Papers

Chapel Hill, North Carolina
Southern Historical Collection, University of North Carolina
   Frank Porter Graham Papers

Charlottesville, Virginia
Manuscripts Division, Alderman Library, University of Virginia
   Presidential Papers, 1935–1936

Columbia, South Carolina
South Caroliniana Library, University of South Carolina
   John H. McCray Papers
   Osceola McKaine File

Hyde Park, New York
Franklin D. Roosevelt Library
   Lowell Mellett Papers
   Eleanor Roosevelt Papers
   Franklin D. Roosevelt Papers
   Aubrey Williams Papers

Iowa City, Iowa
University of Iowa Libraries
   C. B. Baldwin Papers
   Lew Frank Papers
   Progressive Party Collection (PPC)
   Henry A. Wallace Papers

Petersburg, Virginia
Johnston Memorial Library, Virginia State University
   Luther Porter Jackson Papers

Tuskegee, Alabama
Hollis Burke Frissell Library, Tuskegee University
  Records of the Southern Conference for Human Welfare (SCHW)

Washington, D.C.
Library of Congress
  Jack Kroll Papers
  Papers of the National Association for the Advancement of Colored People
    (NAACP)
  National Policy Committee (NPC) Papers

Manuscripts on Microfilm
Americans for Democratic Action (ADA)
Federal Surveillance of Afro-Americans
National Association for the Advancement of Colored People (NAACP)
New Deal Agencies and Black Americans
YWCA of USA, National Board Archives, New York

Private Collections
Clark Howell Foreman Papers, Adjuntas, Puerto Rico; Cambridge, Massachusetts
Arthur "Tex" Goldschmidt Papers, Haverford, Pennsylvania

INTERVIEWS AND ORAL HISTORIES

Interviews with Author

Ansley Abraham, 15 July 1985, telephone
John Abt, 17 December 1980, New York
Harry Ashmore, 27 March 1980, Washington, D.C.
Lillian Baldwin, 13 December 1980, Kent, Connecticut
Daisy Bates, 21 January 1982, Little Rock, Arkansas
Randolph Blackwell, 22 March 1979, Washington, D.C.
Rev. William Holmes Borders, 10 January 1979, Atlanta, Georgia
Dorothy Burnham, July 1994, Oak Bluffs, Massachusetts
David Carliner, 21 May 1980, Washington, D.C.
Robert C. Carter, 21 December 1984, 16 May 1985, New York
Kenneth and Nona Clarke, 23 December 1978, New York
Arthur Clement, 13 April 1985, Charleston, South Carolina
Aliene Austin Cohen, 3 September 1980, Baltimore, Maryland
Sallye Davis, August 1994, Oak Bluffs, Massachusetts
James Dombrowski, 7, 8 November 1980, New Orleans, Louisiana
Virginia Durr, 3 May 1978, Wetumpka, Alabama; 16, 25 January 1980, Montgom-
    ery, Alabama; 22–26 June 1992, Vineyard Haven, Massachusetts
Virginia Durr and James Dombrowski, 25 January 1980, Sarasota, Florida
John Henry Faulk, 17, 19 January 1982, Austin, Texas
Mairi Fraser Foreman, 29 June 1981, Atlanta, Georgia; 18 March 1986, Adjuntas,
    Puerto Rico

John Hope Franklin, 24 May 1985, Durham, North Carolina

Laurant Frantz, 4 February 1982, Palo Alto, California

Marge Frantz, 3 February 1982, Ben Lomond, California

Doris and Eli Friedland, 22 March 1982, Larchmont, New York

Arthur Goldschmidt, 6 July 1991, Durham, New York; 9 November 1991, Charlottesville, Virginia; 4 June 1992, Haverford, Pennsylvania

Elizabeth Wickenden Goldschmidt, 6 July 1991, Durham, New York; 4 June 1992,
Haverford, Pennsylvania; February 1994, Charlottesville, Virginia

Douglass Hall, 22 August 1980, Trenton, New Jersey

Rob Hall, 21 October 1991, Willsboro, New York

Grace Townes Hamilton, 22 February 1985, Atlanta, Georgia

Brooks Hays, 3 June, 6 September 1980, Washington, D.C.

Alger Hiss, 7 December 1984, New York

Floyd Hunter, 2 February 1982, Sonoma, California

Will Inman, 27 January 1982, Tucson, Arizona

Jack Lorenz, 23 November 1979, Sewanee, Tennessee

Curtis MacDougall, 22 June 1980, Evanston, Illinois

John McCray, 19 February 1985, 27 July, 23 September 1985, Talladega, Alabama

Henry Lee Moon, 10 September 1981, New York

J. P. Mooney, 28 January 1982, Phoenix, Arizona

Paul Moorhead, 1 April 1982, Philadelphia, Pennsylvania

Claude Pepper, 25 March, 4 June 1980, Washington, D.C.

John Popham, 24 November 1979, Chattanooga, Tennessee

Daniel A. Powell, 25–26 January 1982, Memphis, Tennessee

Branson Price, 16–19 January 1982, Austin, Texas; August 1985, London, England

Glen Rainey, 29 November 1979, Atlanta, Georgia

Arthur Raper, 3 January 1975, Oakton, Virginia

Mike Ross, 4–5 August 1981, Chapel Hill, North Carolina

Preston and Henry Saunders, 1 February 1982, Sacramento, California

Junius Scales, 29 March 1979, 18 March 1982, 3 December 1989, New York

Pete Seeger, 26 April 1980, Washington, D.C.

Sid Shanker, 15 March 1982, New York

Arthur Shores, 19 February 1985, Birmingham, Alabama

Mojeska Simkins, 24 February 1985, Columbia, South Carolina

I. F. Stone, September 1978, Washington, D.C.

George Stoney, 31 May 1990, New York

Studs Terkel, 3 July 1980, Chicago, Illinois

Strom Thurmond, 9 May 1980, Washington, D.C.

Robert C. Weaver, 23 December 1980, 13 January 1992, New York; 16 April 1992,
Charlottesville, Virginia

Palmer Weber, 8–9 September 1978, 24 February 1984, Charlottesville, Virginia;
21 December 1978, 3 May 1980, 6 September 1980, 17 November 1980, 19
March 1982, New York; 12 July 1983, Atlanta, Georgia

James Wechsler, 16 December 1982, New York

Randolph White, 13 February 1987, Charlottesville, Virginia

Osgood Williams, 13 October 1988, Atlanta, Georgia

Charles Wilson, 28 January 1982, Phoenix, Arizona
Herman Wright, 18 January 1982, Houston, Texas

Columbia Oral History Collection, Butler Memorial Library, Columbia University

Will W. Alexander, interview by Dean Albertson, 1952
C. B. Baldwin, interview by Dean Albertson, 1951
Louis Bean, interview by Dean Albertson, 1953
Samuel B. Bledsoe, interview by Dean Albertson, 1954
Jonathan Daniels, interview by Daniel Singal, 1972
Henry A. Wallace, interview by Kenneth Davis, 1952

Progressive Party Collection, University of Iowa Libraries

Louis Burnham, interview by Curtis MacDougall, 1 July 1953
Clark Foreman, interview by Curtis MacDougall, 8 September 1952
Lew Frank, interview by Curtis MacDougall, 18 October 1952
Marge Frantz, interview by Curtis MacDougall, 24 March 1953
Edith Roberts, interview by Curtis MacDougall, 14 July 1953

Southern Oral History Program, Southern Historical Collection, University of North Carolina

Mary Price Adamson, interview by Mary Frederickson, 19 April 1976
Clark Foreman, interview by Jacquelyn Hall, November 1974
Floyd McKissick, interview by Jack Bass, 6 December 1973

Miscellaneous Interviews and Oral Histories

Ella J. Baker, interview by John Brotton, 19 June 1968. The Civil Rights Documentary Project, Ralph J. Bunche Oral History Collection, Moorland-Spingarn Research Center, Howard University, Washington, D.C.
C. B. Baldwin, interview by Richard K. Doud, 24 February 1965, C. B. Baldwin Papers, University of Iowa Libraries, Iowa City
Jonathan Daniels, interview by Emily Williams Soapes, Eleanor Roosevelt Oral History Project, FDR Library
Palmer Weber, interview by August Meier, 20 October 1979, August Meier Papers, private collection

GOVERNMENT DOCUMENTS

U.S. Congress. House. Committee on Un-American Activities. *Report on the Southern Conference for Human Welfare.* 80th Cong., 1st sess., 1947.
U.S. Congress. Senate. Committee on Education and Labor. *Violations of Free Speech and the Rights of Labor: Hearings before a Subcommittee of the Committee on Education and Labor.* 75th Cong., 1st sess., 1953.

——. "Debate on Appropriations for the Farm Security Administration." *Congressional Record,* 77th Cong., 2d sess., 26 March–18 May 1942. Vol. 88.

——. "Elimination of the Poll Tax in Election of Federal Officials, HR 1024." *Congressional Record,* 77th Cong., 2d sess., 20, 21, 23 November 1942. Vol. 88.

U.S. Congress. Senate. Subcommittee of the Committee on the Judiciary. *Hearings on S1280.* 77th Cong., 2d sess., 19 July 1941, 12, 13, 14 March, 30 July, 22, 23 September 1942.

NEWSPAPERS AND PERIODICALS

Arkansas Gazette, 1948
Atlanta Constitution, 1921, 1935, 1945–47
Atlanta Daily World, 1947–48
Atlanta Journal, 1947–48
Baltimore Afro-American, 1942–48
Baltimore Sun, 1936, 1948
Birmingham World, 1943
Chicago Defender, 1933, 1944
College Topics, 1933–40
Columbia Morning Star, 1942
Columbia Record, 1942, 1944
Crisis, 1933–48
Daily Worker, 1944–48
Jackson Clarion Ledger, 1948
Jackson Daily News, 1948
Louisville Courier-Journal, 1947–48
Macon News, 1948
Macon World, 1948
Memphis Commercial Appeal, 1944, 1947–48
Nashville Banner, 1948
Nashville Tennessean, 1948
Nation, 1944–48, 1952
New Orleans Times-Picayune, 1947–48
New Republic, 1933, 1942–47
New South, 1938–39
New York Herald Tribune, 1938
New York Post, 1946, 1948
New York Star, 1948
New York Times (NYT), 1933–48
Norfolk Journal and Guide, 1944–48
Opportunity, 1933–34, 1936, 1940
Palmetto News, 1941
Pittsburgh Courier, 1944
PM, 1946–47
Raleigh News and Observer, 1947–48

Southern Patriot, 1945–46
Washington Daily News, 1938
Washington Evening Star, 1945, 1948
Washington Post, 1938
Winston-Salem Journal, 1948

BOOKS, ARTICLES, AND THESES

Adams, Frank T. *James A. Dombrowski: An American Heretic, 1897–1983*. Knoxville: University of Tennessee Press, 1992.

Anderson, William. *The Wild Man from Sugar Creek: The Political Career of Eugene Talmadge*. Baton Rouge: Louisiana State University Press, 1975.

Auerbach, Jerold S. *Labor and Liberty: The La Follette Committee and the New Deal*. Indianapolis: Bobbs-Merrill, 1966.

Ayers, Edward L. *The Promise of the New South: Life after Reconstruction*. New York: Oxford University Press, 1992.

Bacote, Clarence. "The Negro in Atlanta Politics." *Phylon* 16 (1955): 333–50.

Badger, Anthony J. *The New Deal: The Depression Years, 1933–1940*. New York: Noonday Press, 1989.

Baker, Ella. "Developing Community Leadership." In *Black Women in America*, edited by Gerda Lerner. New York: Vintage Books, 1973.

Baldwin, James. *Notes of a Native Son*. Boston: Beacon Hill Press, 1955.

Baldwin, Sidney. *Poverty and Politics: The Rise and Fall of the Farm Security Administration*. Chapel Hill: University of North Carolina Press, 1980.

Barnes, Catherine A. *Journey from Jim Crow: The Desegregation of Southern Transit*. New York: Columbia University Press, 1983.

Beeler, Dorothy. "Race Riot in Columbia, Tennessee, February 25–27, 1946." *Tennessee Historical Quarterly* 39 (Spring 1980): 49–61.

Berman, William C. *The Politics of Civil Rights in the Truman Administration*. Columbus: Ohio State University Press, 1970.

Bernd, Joseph L. "White Supremacy and the Disfranchisement of Blacks in Georgia, 1946." *Georgia Historical Quarterly* 66 (1982): 492–513.

Blum, John Morton, ed. *The Price of Vision: The Diary of Henry A. Wallace, 1942–1946*. Boston: Houghton-Mifflin Company, 1973.

Bond, Horace Mann. "A Negro Looks at His South." *Harper's*, June 1931, pp. 98–108.

Boylan, James. *The New Deal Coalition and the Election of 1946*. New York: Garland Publishing, 1981.

Brown, Elsa Barkley. "Negotiating and Transforming the Public Sphere: African American Life in the Transition from Slavery to Freedom." *Public Culture* 7 (1994): 107–27.

Bunche, Ralph. *The Political Status of the Negro in the Age of FDR*. Edited by Dewey W. Grantham. Chicago: University of Chicago Press, 1973.

Burns, James MacGregor. *Roosevelt: The Lion and the Fox*. New York: Harcourt, Brace, 1956.

Burran, James Albert. "Racial Violence in the South during World War II." Ph.D. diss., University of Tennessee, 1977.

Carleton, William G. "The Conservative South: A Political Myth." *Virginia Quarterly Review* 22 (Spring 1946): 179–92.

Caro, Robert A. *The Years of Lyndon Johnson: The Path to Power.* New York: Knopf, 1982.

Carter, Dan T. *Scottsboro: A Tragedy of the American South.* Baton Rouge: Louisiana State University Press, 1969.

Cayton, Horace R., and George S. Mitchell. *Black Workers and the New Unions.* College Park, Md.: McGrath Publishing Company, 1969.

Clark, James C. "Civil Rights Leader Harry T. Moore and the Ku Klux Klan in Florida." *Florida Historical Quarterly* 72 (October 1994): 166–83.

Cobb, James C. " 'Somebody Done Nailed Us on the Cross': Federal Farm and Welfare Policy and the Civil Rights Movement in the Mississippi Delta." *Journal of American History* 77 (1990): 912–36.

Cobb, James, and Michael Namorato, eds. *The New Deal and the South.* Oxford: University Press of Mississippi, 1984.

Cochran, Linda Dempsey. "Arthur Davis Shores: Advocate for Freedom." Master's thesis, Georgia Southern College, 1977.

Cohen, Robert. "Revolt of the Depression Generation: America's First Mass Student Protest Movement." Ph.D. diss., University of California, Berkeley, 1987.

Cohen, William. *At Freedom's Edge: Black Mobility and the Southern White Quest for Racial Control, 1861–1915.* Baton Rouge: Louisiana State University Press, 1991.

Crown, James. "The Political Action Committee of the CIO in the Southeast, 1944–1945." Master's thesis, University of Florida, 1950.

Dabney, Virginius. *Mr. Jefferson's University: A History.* Charlottesville: University Press of Virginia, 1950.

———. "Nearer and Nearer the Precipice." *Atlantic Monthly,* January 1943, pp. 94–100.

Dalfiume, Richard. "The Forgotten Years of the Negro Revolution." In *The Negro in Depression and War: Prelude to Revolution, 1930–1945,* edited by Bernard Sternsher, pp. 298–316. Chicago: Quadrangle Books, 1969.

Dittmer, John. *Local People: The Struggle for Civil Rights in Mississippi.* Urbana: University of Illinois Press, 1994.

Du Bois, W. E. B. *Black Reconstruction in America, 1860–1880.* New York: Harcourt, Brace and Company, 1935.

———. "Federal Action Programs and Community Action in the South." *Social Forces* 19 (1941): 375–80.

———. *The Souls of Black Folks.* New York: Vintage Books, 1990.

Durr, Virginia. *Outside the Magic Circle: The Autobiography of Virginia Foster Durr.* Edited by Hollinger Barnard. Tuscaloosa: University of Alabama Press, 1985.

Dykeman, Wilma, and James Stokely. *Seeds of Southern Change: The Life of Will W. Alexander.* Chicago: University of Chicago Press, 1962.

Embree, Edwin, and Julia Waxman. *Investment in People: The Story of the Julius Rosenwald Fund.* New York: Harper Brothers Publishers, 1949.

Emspak, Frank. "The Break-up of the Congress of Industrial Organizations, 1945–1950." Ph.D. diss., University of Wisconsin, 1972.

Fairclough, Adam. *Race and Democracy: The Civil Rights Struggle in Louisiana, 1915–1972*. Athens: University of Georgia Press, 1995.

Fite, Gilbert. *Cotton Fields No More: Southern Agriculture, 1865–1980*. Lexington: University of Kentucky Press, 1984.

Flamming, Douglas. *Creating the Modern South: Millhands and Managers in Dalton, Georgia, 1884–1984*. Chapel Hill: University of North Carolina Press, 1992.

Foreman, Clark. *Environmental Factors in Negro Elementary Education*. New York: W. W. Norton and Company, 1932.

———. "The Decade of Hope." *Phylon* 12 (1951): 137–50.

Fraser, Steven. *Labor Will Rule: Sidney Hillman and the Rise of American Labor*. New York: Free Press, 1991.

Freeland, Richard M. *The Truman Doctrine and the Origins of McCarthyism: Foreign Policy, Domestic Policy, and Internal Security, 1946–1948*. New York: Alfred A. Knopf, 1972.

Garson, Robert A. *The Democratic Party and the Politics of Sectionalism, 1941–1948*. Baton Rouge: Lousiana State University Press, 1974.

Gates, Henry Louis, Jr. *Colored People: A Memoir*. New York: Alfred A. Knopf, 1994.

Gellhorn, Walter. "Report on the Report of the Committee on UnAmerican Activities." *Harvard Law Review* 60 (1947): 1193–234.

Gilbert, Jess, and Carolyn Howe. "Beyond 'State vs. Society': Theories of the State and New Deal Agricultural Policies." *American Sociological Review* 56 (1991): 204-20.

Gillette, Michael Lowery. "The NAACP in Texas, 1937–1957." Ph.D. diss., University of Texas, 1984.

Gillon, Steven. *Politics and Vision: The ADA and American Liberalism, 1947–1985*. New York: Oxford University Press, 1988.

Glenn, John M. *Highlander: No Ordinary School, 1932–1962*. Lexington: University of Kentucky Press, 1988.

Grafton, Carl, and Anne Permaloff. *Big Mules and Branchheads: James E. Folsom and Political Power in Alabama*. Athens: University of Georgia Press, 1985.

Grant, Nancy. *The TVA and Black Americans: Planning for the Status Quo*. Philadelphia: Temple University Press, 1990.

Gray, Fred. *Bus Ride to Justice*. Montgomery, Ala.: Black Belt Press, 1995.

Griffith, Barbara S. *The Crisis of American Labor: Operation Dixie and the Defeat of the CIO*. Philadelphia: Temple University Press, 1988.

Grossman, James R. *Land of Hope: Chicago, Black Southerners, and the Great Migration*. Chicago: University of Chicago Press, 1989.

Grubbs, Donald H. *Cry from the Cotton: The Southern Tenant Farmers Union*. Chapel Hill: University of North Carolina Press, 1971.

Hamby, Alonzo. *Beyond the New Deal: Harry S. Truman and American Liberalism*. New York: Columbia University Press, 1973.

Harbutt, Fraser J. *The Iron Curtain: Churchill, America, and the Origins of the Cold War*. New York: Oxford University Press, 1986.

Higginbotham, Evelyn Brooks. *Righteous Discontent: The Women's Movement in* the *Black Baptist Church, 1880–1920*. Cambridge: Harvard University Press, 1993.

Hine, Darlene Clark. *Black Victory: The Rise and Fall of the White Primary in Texas*. Millwood, New York: KTO Press, 1979.

Hoffman, Edwin D. "The Genesis of the Modern Movement for Civil Rights in South Carolina." In *The Negro in Depression and War: Prelude to Revolution, 1930–1945*, edited by Bernard Sternsher, pp. 193–214. Chicago: Quadrangle Books, 1969.

Honey, Michael. *Southern Labor and Black Civil Rights: Organizing Memphis Workers*. Urbana: University of Illinois Press, 1993.

Hooks, Gregory. *Forging the Military-Industrial Complex: World War II's Battle of the Potomac*. Urbana: University of Illinois Press, 1991.

Jackson, Luther Porter. "Race and Suffrage in the South since 1940." *New South*, June–July 1948, pp. 1–26.

Jackson, Walter. *Gunnar Myrdal and America's Conscience: Social Engineering and Racial Liberalism, 1938–1987*. Chapel Hill: University of North Carolina Press, 1990.

Johnson, Charles. *To Stem This Tide: A Survey of Racial Tensions in the United States*. Boston: Pilgrim Press, 1943.

Johnson, Charles S., Edwin R. Embree, and W. W. Alexander. *The Collapse of Cotton Tenancy*. Chapel Hill: University of North Carolina Press, 1935.

Josephson, Matthew. *Sidney Hillman: Statesman of American Labor*. New York: Doubleday and Company, 1952.

Judis, John. "Henry Wallace and the Common Man." In *Grand Illusion: Critics and Champions of the American Century*. New York: Farrar, Straus, and Giroux, 1992.

Kampleman, Max M. *The Communist Party vs. the CIO*. New York: F. A. Praeger, 1957.

Kelley, Robin D. G. *Hammer and Hoe: Alabama Communists during the Great Depression*. Chapel Hill: University of North Carolina Press, 1990.

Key, V. O. *Southern Politics in State and Nation*. New York: Alfred A. Knopf, 1950.

Kirby, John B. *Black Americans in the Roosevelt Era: Liberalism and Race*. Knoxville: University of Tennessee Press, 1980.

Kneebone, John. *Southern Liberal Journalists and the Issue of Race, 1920–1944*. Chapel Hill: University of North Carolina Press, 1985.

Kousser, J. Morgan. "Separate but Not Equal: The Supreme Court's First Decision on Racial Discrimination in Schools." *Journal of Southern History* 46 (1980): 17–44.

——. *The Shaping of Southern Politics: Suffrage Restrictions and the Establishment of the One Party South, 1880–1910*. New Haven: Yale University Press, 1974.

Krueger, Thomas. *And Promises to Keep: The Southern Conference for Human Welfare, 1938–1948*. Nashville: Vanderbilt University Press, 1967.

Lash, Joseph. *Eleanor and Franklin*. New York: W. W. Norton and Company, 1971.

Lawson, Steven. *Black Ballots: Voting Rights in the South, 1944–1969*. New York: Columbia University Press, 1976.

Leffler, Melvyn. *A Preponderance of Power: National Security, The Truman Administration, and the Cold War*. Stanford, Calif.: Stanford University Press, 1992.

Lichenstein, Nelson. *Labor's War at Home: The CIO in World War II*. New York: Cambridge University Press, 1987.

———. "The Making of the Postwar Working Class: Cultural Pluralism and Social Structure in World War II." *Historian* 51 (1988): 42–64.

Lipsitz, George. *Class and Culture in Cold War America: A Rainbow at Midnight*. New York: Praeger, 1981.

Lord, Russell. *The Wallaces of Iowa*. Boston: Houghton Mifflin Company, 1947.

Louchheim, Katie. *The Making of the New Deal: The Insiders Speak*. Cambridge: Harvard University Press, 1983.

Lowitt, Richard, and Maurine Beasley, ed. *One Third of a Nation: Lorena Hickock Reports on the Great Depression*. Urbana: University of Illinois Press, 1983.

McAuliffe, Mary. *Crisis on the Left: Cold War Politics and American Liberals, 1947–1954*. Amherst: University of Massachusetts Press, 1978.

McDonough, Julia. "Clearinghouse for Change: The Southern Regional Council, 1944–1965." Ph.D. diss., University of Virginia, 1992.

MacDougall, Curtis. *Gideon's Army*. 3 vols. New York: Marzani and Munsell, 1965.

McElvaine, Robert S. *The Great Depression: America, 1929–1941*. New York: Times Books, 1984.

McNeil, Genna Rae. *Groundwork: Charles Hamilton and the Struggle for Civil Rights*. Philadelphia: University of Pennsylvania Press, 1983.

Marshall, F. Ray. *Labor in the South*. Cambridge: Harvard University Press, 1967.

Maverick, Maury. *Maverick American*. New York: Covici, Friede, 1937.

Meier, August. *Negro Thought in America, 1880–1915*. Ann Arbor: University of Michigan Press, 1063.

Meier, August, and Elliot Rudwick. "Attorneys Black and White: A Case Study of Race Relations within the NAACP." In *Along the Color Line: Explorations in the Black Experience*, edited by August Meier and Elliot Rudwick, pp. 128–73. Urbana: University of Illinois Press, 1976.

———. *Black Detroit and the Rise of the UAW*. New York: Oxford University Press, 1979.

———. *Black History and the Historical Profession*. Urbana: University of Illinois Press, 1986.

———. "The Boycott Movement against Jim Crow Streetcars, 1900–1906." In *Along the Color Line*, pp. 267–89.

———. "The Rise of the Black Secretariat in the NAACP, 1909–1935." In *Along the Color Line*, pp. 94–127.

Miller, Francis Pickens. *Man from the Valley: Memoirs of a Twentieth Century Virginian*. Chapel Hill: University of North Carolina Press, 1971.

Mitford, Jessica. *A Fine Old Conflict*. New York: Vintage Books, 1977.

Moon, Henry Lee. *The Balance of Power: The Negro Vote*. Garden City, N.Y.: Doubleday and Company, 1948.

Motz, Jane R. "The Black Cabinet: Negroes in the Administration of Franklin D. Roosevelt." Master's thesis, University of Delaware, 1964.

Murphy, Bruce. *Fortas: The Rise and Ruin of a Supreme Court Justice*. New York: William Morrow and Company, 1988.

Murray, Pauli. *Song in a Weary Throat*. New York: Harper Collins, 1987.

Myrdal, Gunnar. *An American Dilemma: The Negro Problem and Modern Democracy*. 2 vols. New York: Harper and Brothers, 1944.

National Emergency Council. *Report on the Economic Conditions of the South*. Washington, D.C.: Government Printing Office, 1938.

The New Dealers: By an Unoffical Observer. New York: Literary Guild, 1934.

Norrell, Robert J. "Caste in Steel: Jim Crow Careers in Birmingham Alabama." *Journal of American History* 73 (1986): 669–95.

——. "Labor at the Ballot Box: Politics from the New Deal to the Dixiecrat Movement." *Journal of Southern History* 57 (May 1991): 201–34.

——. *Reaping the Whirlwind: The Civil Rights Movement in Tuskegee*. New York: Alfred Knopf, 1986.

O'Connor, Tom. "Portrait of a Lynch Town." *PM*, 5 August 1946, pp. 2–5.

Odum, Howard. *Race and Rumors of Race*. Chapel Hill: University of North Carolina Press, 1943.

Painter, Nell I. *The Narrative of Hosea Hudson: His Life as a Negro Communist in the South*. Cambridge: Harvard University Press, 1979.

Patterson, Thomas G. *Meeting the Communist Threat: Truman to Reagan*. New York: Oxford University Press, 1988.

Perman, Michael. *The Road to Redemption: Southern Politics, 1869–1879*. Chapel Hill: University of North Carolina Press, 1984.

Polenberg, Richard. "The Good War?: A Reappraisal of How World War II Affected American Society." *Virginia Magazine of History and Biography* 100 (1992): 295–322.

Raper, Arthur. *Preface to Peasantry: A Tale of Two Black Belt Counties*. Chapel Hill: University of North Carolina Press, 1936.

Raper, Arthur, and Ira DeA. Reid. *Sharecroppers All*. Chapel Hill: University of North Carolina Press, 1941.

Reed, Linda A. *Simple Decency and Common Sense: The Southern Conference Movement, 1938–1963*. Bloomington: Indiana University Press, 1991.

Reed, Merl E. *Seedtime for the Modern Civil Rights Movement: The President's Committee on Fair Employment Practices, 1941–1946*. Baton Rouge: Louisiana State University Press, 1991.

Richards, Johnetta. "The Southern Negro Youth Congress: A History." Ph.D. diss., University of Cincinnati, 1987.

Roosevelt, Eleanor. *This I Remember*. New York: Harper and Brothers, 1949.

Roosevelt, Franklin D. *The Public Papers and Addresses of Franklin D. Roosevelt*. Edited by Samuel I. Rosenman. 13 vols. New York: Random House, 1941.

Salmond, John. *The Conscience of a Lawyer: Clifford J. Durr and American Civil Liberties, 1899–1975*. Tuscaloosa: University of Alabama Press, 1990.

——. *Miss Lucy of the CIO: The Life and Times of Lucy Randolph Mason, 1882–1959*. Athens: University of Georgia Press, 1988.

——. *A Southern Rebel: The Life and Times of Aubrey Willis Williams, 1890–1965*. Chapel Hill: University of North Carolina Press, 1983.

Sancton, Thomas. "A Southern View of the Race Question." *The Negro Quarterly* (January 1943): 197–206.

Scales, Junius, with Richard Nickson. *Cause at Heart: A Former Communist Remembers.* Athens: University of Georgia Press, 1987.

Schapsmeier, Edward L., and Frederick H. Schapsmeier. *Henry Wallace of Iowa: The Agrarian Years, 1910–1940.* Ames: University of Iowa Press, 1968.

Schlesinger, Arthur. *The Age of Roosevelt: The Coming of the New Deal.* Boston: Houghton Mifflin Company, 1959.

——. *The Age of Roosevelt: The Politics of Upheaval.* Boston: Houghton Mifflin Company, 1960.

Schrecker, Ellen W. *No Ivory Tower: McCarthyism and the Universities.* New York: Oxford University Press, 1986.

Shouse, Sarah Newman. *Hillbilly Realist: Herman Clarence Nixon of Possum Trot.* University: University of Alabama Press, 1986.

Shulman, Bruce J. *From Cotton Belt to Sun Belt: Federal Policy, Economic Development and the Transformation of the South, 1938-1980.* New York: Oxford University Press, 1991.

Sims, George E. *The Little Man's Big Friend: James E. Folsom in Alabama Politics, 1946–1958.* Tuscaloosa: University of Alabama Press, 1985.

Sirevag, Torbjorn. *The Eclipse of the New Deal and the Fall of Vice-President Henry Wallace.* New York: Garland Publishing, 1985.

Sitkoff, Harvard. *A New Deal for Blacks: The Emergence of Civil Rights as a National Issue.* New York: Oxford University Press, 1978.

Smith, Douglas L. "The New Deal and the Urban South: The Advancement of Southern Urban Consciousness during the Depression Decade." Ph.D. diss., University of Southern Mississippi, 1978.

Spritzer, Lorraine Nelson. *The Belle of Ashby Street: Helen Douglas Mankin.* Athens: University of Georgia Press, 1982.

Stone, I. F. *The Truman Era.* New York: Vintage Books, 1972.

Sullivan, Patricia. "Gideon's Southern Soldiers: New Deal Politics and Civil Rights Reform, 1933–1948." Ph.D. diss., Emory University, 1983.

Tindall, George. *The Emergence of the New South, 1913–1945.* Baton Rouge: Louisiana State University Press, 1967.

Tushnet, Mark. *The NAACP Legal Strategy against Segregated Education, 1925–1950.* Chapel Hill: University of North Carolina Press, 1984.

Utley, Freda. *The Dream We Lost: Soviet Russia Then and Now.* New York: John Day Company, 1940.

Walker, Samuel. *In Defense of American Civil Liberties: A History of the ACLU.* New York: Oxford University Press, 1990.

Wallace, Henry A. *Democracy Reborn.* New York: DeCapo Press, 1993.

——. *Whose Constitution: An Inquiry into the General Welfare.* Westport, Conn.: Greenwood Press, 1964.

Ware, Gilbert. *William Hastie: Grace under Pressure.* New York: Oxford University Press, 1984.

Washburn, Patrick S. *A Question of Sedition: The Federal Government's Surveillance of the Black Press during World War II.* New York: Oxford University Press, 1986.

Weaver, Robert C. "Blending Scholarship with Public Service." *SAGE: Race Relations Abstracts* 16 (November 1991): 6.

——. *Negro Labor: A National Problem.* New York: Harcourt, Brace and Company, 1946.

Weber, Palmer. "The Negro Vote in the South." *Virginia Spectator,* November 1938, pp. 6–7, 22, 25.

Weiss, Nancy J. *Farewell to the Party of Lincoln: Black Politics in the Age of FDR.* Princeton: Princeton University Press, 1983.

Wells, H. G. *The Outline of History: Being a Plain History of Life and Mankind.* 3d ed. New York: Macmillan Company, 1921.

Williamson, Joel. *The Crucible of Race: Black-White Relations in the American South since Emancipation.* New York: Oxford University Press, 1984.

Wolters, Raymond. *Negroes and the Great Depression: The Problem of Economic Recovery.* Westport, Conn.: Greenwood Publishing, 1970.

Woods, Barbara. "Black Woman Activist in Twentieth-Century South Carolina: Mojeska Montieth Simkins." Ph.D. diss., Emory University, 1978.

Woodward, C. Vann. *Tom Watson: Agrarian Rebel.* New York: Macmillan Company, 1938.

——. *Origins of the New South.* Baton Rouge: Louisiana State University Press, 1951.

Wright, Gavin. *Old South, New South: Revolutions in the Southern Economy since the Civil War.* New York: Basic Books, 1986.

Youngblood, Susan Bernice. "Testing the Current: The Formative Years of Ella J. Baker's Development as an Organizational Leader in the Modern Civil Rights Movement." Master's thesis, University of Virginia, 1989.

Zangrando, Robert L. *The NAACP Crusade against Lynching, 1909–1950.* Philadelphia: Temple University Press, 1980.

Index

Abt, John, 56, 125

Agee, James: *Let Us Now Praise Famous Men,* 1

Agricultural Adjustment Act, 3, 23, 43, 56–57, 59

Agricultural Adjustment Administration (AAA), 3, 27, 177–78; impact on tenant farmers, 57; "purge" of liberals from, 58; market-quota referendum, 177

Alabama: relief to blacks in, 54, 90; black efforts to vote in, 91, 92; poll tax in, 107; defense industries, racial discrimination in, 135, 158; racial violence in, during World War II, 136, 137, 162; primary election in, 1942, 173–74; SCHW committee for, 205–6; gubernatorial primary in, 1946, 215; Wallace campaign tour of, 265–67

Alabama Dry Dock and Shipbuilding Co., 162

Alabama Power, 121, 122

Alexander, Will W., 1, 42, 114, 163; and New Deal racial policies, 24–25, 52; heads Interracial Commission, 32, 33–34; mentor to Clark Foreman, 34–35; on Hopkins' presidential ambitions, 54; and Resettlement Administration, 58–59; on C. B. Baldwin, 124, 125; director of FSA, 124, 127; and Eleanor Roosevelt, 159; and SRC, 165

Alsop, Joseph, 237

Alsop, Stewart, 237

Alston v. School Board of City of Norfolk (1940), 142, 289 (n. 14)

Amalgamated Clothing Workers of America (ACWA), 94, 95

American Civil Liberties Union (ACLU), 153–54, 230, 240, 243

American Dilemma, An (Myrdal), 167, 168

American Farm Bureau Federation, 22, 57, 126–27, 128, 129

American Federation of Labor (AFL), 94, 115; and SNYC, 150; growth of southern membership during war years, 188, 194; postwar organizing drive, 194, 208, 209

Americans for Democratic Action (ADA), 235, 241, 260, 271; founding meeting of, 236–37; and Truman's cold war policies, 238, in the South, 241–43; and 1948 convention, 259

American Student Union (ASU), 79

Ames, Jesse Daniel, 165

Anderson, William, 145

Anticommunism, 120, 128; SCHW and, 153–55, 242–43; postwar liberalism and, 225, 231–33; and 1946 election, 233–34; and founding of ADA, 235, 236–37

Antilynching legislation: Charles Houston on, 86, 88, 90; SCHW endorses, 99

Appleby, Paul, 125

Arkansas: and STFU, 57–58; racial violence in, during World War II, 136; 1942 Democratic primary, race issue and, 156; SCHW committee for, 244–45; Wallace campaign tour of, 268–69

Arkansas Gazette, 268–70

Arnall, Ellis, 211; 1942 gubernatorial campaign, election, 156–57; supports Wallace in 1944, 174, 184, 185; A. T. Walden on, 203; repeals poll tax in Georgia, 203; attends SCHW New Orleans meeting, 220; and ADA, 241–42

Arnold, Thurman, 56

Wallace campaign in Birmingham, 265–66, 267
"Conservative Manifesto," 61
Cooney, Mabel, 260–61
Corcoran, Tom, 63, 117
Costello, Frank, 173
Cox, Eugene, 105
Crawford, George, 74–75, 86
Crisis, 106, 136, 165, 224
Crump, Ed, 269

Dabney, Virginius, 73, 164; defends racial status quo, 165–66
Daniels, Jonathan, 66–67; and black protest, World War II, 162
Daniels, Josephus, 13, 37, 244
Davis, Ben, 230
Davis, James T., 292 (n. 23)
Davis, John Preston: at Harvard, 46, 47–48; and Negro Industrial League, 46, 49, 53; heads Joint Committee on Economic Recovery, 49–50, 52, 57; investigates racial discrimination in New Deal programs, 50, 57; Conference on Economic Status of Negro, 90; and schw, 99, 153, 155
Dawson, William, 170–71; supports Wallace, 1944 convention, 175
Dean, William, 47
Democratic National Committee, Women's Division of, 112, 113, 114
Democratic Party: and black vote, 65–66, 93, 143, 170–71; New Deal coalition and, 92–93, 94
Democrats, southern: endorse FDR and early New Deal, 3, 11–12; "redeem" the South, 13–14; and nra codes, 45; "Conservative Manifesto," 61; FDR challenges, 62, 65, 66; and 1936 election, 93; lead opposition to the New Deal, 100, 104–5, 121; naacp's *Crisis* on, 103, 105–6; oppose Soldiers Vote bills, 116–17, 129–31; defeat poll tax legislation, 117–21; wartime ascendancy of, 127–31, 134; and 1944 Democratic convention, 174–75,

183, 186; on Truman civil rights program, 258; bolt 1948 Democratic convention, 259
Dewey, Thomas, 259
Dickerson, Earl: and fepc Birmingham hearings, 157, 158
Dies, Martin, 104, 105, 173, 188
Dirba, Charles, 87
Disfranchisement, 13–14, 48, 106–7, 118–19; and voter turnout in Georgia, 66, 105
Dixon, Frank, 158
Dixon, Thomas, 158
Dobbs, John Wesley, 149
Dobbs, Malcolm, 205, 206; on Folsom's campaign and election, 215–16
Dobbs, Pauline, 205
Dodd, William, Jr., 65
Dombrowski, James: and Highlander, 151; schw executive secretary, 151, 152–55, 235; biography of, 152; analysis of southern political situation, 1944, 187–89; and Osceola McKaine, 197, 201; on postwar possibilities, 203
Dorsey, George, 214
Dorsey, May, 214
"Double V" campaign, 118, 119, 135–36
Douglas, Helen Gahagan, 230
Drake, St. Clair, 194
Du Bois, W. E. B., 15, 28, 46, 277–78 (n. 6); on impact of New Deal, 69
Dunbar High School, 47, 84
Dunjee, Roscoe, 90, 149
Dunning, William A., 13
Durham Manifesto, 165
Durr, Clifford, 4, 42, 63, 108, 110, 111, 112, 113; and *Report on the Economic Conditions of the South*, 64; on early New Deal, 111; critique of loyalty order, 239
Durr, Clifford, Jr., 112
Durr, Virginia Foster, 4, 28; on *Report on the Economic Conditions of the South*, 66; and schw, 99; on Wash-

23–24; Virginia constitutional convention, quoted, 118–19; attacks FSA poll tax loans, 128

Goldschmidt, Arthur "Tex," 42; *Report on Economic Conditions of the South*, 64, 111, 281 (n. 28)

Goldschmidt, Elizabeth Wickenden, 92, 111, 281 (n. 28)

Gordon, Max, 78

Gore, Albert, Sr., 286 (n. 25)

Grady, Henry, 25

Graham, Frank, 64, 114–15; and SCHW, 67, 99, 153, 154, 206, 235, 242; and Wallace's 1947 visit to N.C., 244

Granger, Lester, 11, 12, 48–49

Grant, Edmonia, 244

Graves, John Templeton: defends racial status quo, 164, 166

Green, Ernest, 137

Green-Lucas bill (Soldiers Vote bill, 1943), 129–31

Griffith, D. W., 13

Grovey v. Townsend (1935), 148

Guffey, Joseph, 130–31, 184

Hackney, Lucy Durr, 112

Hall, Douglass: covers Wallace's southern campaign tour, 260, 261, 264; on race relations in N.C., 264

Hall, Felix, 136

Hall, Robert F. "Rob": and founding of NSL, 78–79; leads student expedition to Harlan Co., 79; on founding meeting of SCHW, 98, 100

Hamilton, Grace, 204, 214–15

Hancock, Gordon: and founding of SRC, 165–66

Hannegan, Robert, 170, 228, 234; and 1944 Democratic convention, 183, 184–85

Harlan County, 79, 112

Harriman, Averall, 233

Harris, Julia Collier, 37

Harris, Julian, 37

Harris, Roy, 202, 211

Harrison, Loy, 214

Harvard University, 28, 46, 47, 48, 85, 110

Hastie, William, 42, 113; at Harvard, 46, 47, 48; and New Deal, 53, 55; and black self-defense, 145

Hayes, Roland, 33

Hays, Brooks, 63

Haywood, Allen, 209

Heiskell, J. N., 268

Hickock, Lorena, 3, 280 (n. 8)

Higginbotham, Evelyn Brooks, 14

Highlander Folk School, 7, 95, 149, 150–51, 208, 250, 274; racial policies of, 151, 164; and Eleanor Roosevelt, 159; CIO ends support of, 235

Highlands Museum of Natural History, 35

Hill, Lister, 63, 64, 65, 100; opposes Soldiers Vote bill, 1942, 116; opposes Geyer-Pepper bill, 119–20; supports C. B. Baldwin, 128–29; and 1944 primary, 174

Hillman, Sidney: on CIO's southern campaign, 94–95; and CIO-PAC, 129, 131, 139, 172, 174; on defeat of Green-Lucas bill, 130

Hinton, James, 149; director, S.C. State Conference of NAACP branches, 145–46; and SCNCC, 147

Hiss, Alger, 56, 273

Hobhouse, L. T., 32

Holland, Spessard, 218

Hollins, W. H., 149

Hoover, Herbert, 21–22

Hoover, J. Edgar, 233

Hope, John, 33, 34

Hope, Lugenia Burns, 33

Hopkins, Harry, 42, 178, 280 (n. 8); and relief policies in Alabama and Louisiana, 54; racial policies of, 281 (n. 28)

Horton, Myles, 151, 152; on labor and 1948 campaign, 250

Howard, Asbury, 265

Howell, Clark, 25–26, 29–30

Howell, Evan P., 25

201–2; on racial policies of CIO, 209–10; and SCHW 1946 New Orleans meeting, 220

McKellar, Kenneth, 128, 130, 193, 218

McKenzie, Charles, 160

McKenzie, Douglas, 87

McKissick, Floyd, 251

McNeil, Genna Rae, 84

McNutt, Paul, 124, 287 (n. 34)

Macon, Ga., 159–60, 252

Maid-Well Garment Company, 50

Malcolm, Dorothy, 214

Malcolm, Roger, 214

Mance, Robert C., 146

Mankin, Helen, 210–11

"March on Washington" movement, 7, 135–36

Marshall, Larkin, 251

Marshall, Thurgood, 271–72; and NAACP legal campaign in South, 5, 91, 133, 142, 143, 295 (n. 24); on violence against black soldiers, 137; advises SCNNC, 147; on implementation of *Smith v. Allwright*, 148–49; reports on voting violations in S.C., 191

Martin, Joseph, 237

Martin, Louis, 166

Marx, Karl, 72, 73, 79

Mary Baldwin College, 83

Mason, George, 70, 96

Mason, Lucy Randolph, 65, 70; reports on southern political scene, 62, 97; and Eleanor Roosevelt, 62, 97, 98, 123, 159; and SCHW, 67, 98–99, 154, 189; opposes residential segregation in Richmond, 96; as CIO publicist in South, 96, 97; biography of, 96–97; on KKK and antilabor violence, 97; on Clark Foreman, 123; as vice-chair, SCHW Georgia committee, 203–4

Mason, Vivian Carter, 205

Matthews, J. B., 80

Maverick, Maury, 107

Maybank, Burnett, 170, 171

Mayer, Herbert, 51

Mays, Benjamin, 204

Mellett, Lowell, 64, 65, 66–67, 70

Memoirs of a Revolutionist (Kropotkin), 28

Memphis, Tenn., 22, 55, 269

Memphis Commercial Appeal, 161

Mencken, H. L., 3, 270

Migrant farm workers, 126

Miller, Francis Pickens, 63

Mills, Ogden, 55

Mississippi: poll tax in, 106; censors textbooks, 137; racial violence in, during World War II, 137; black troops rebel at Camp Van Dorn, 162; and 1944 Democratic convention, 174; and 1946 primary election, 218; Wallace campaign tour of, 267–68

Missouri ex rel. Gaines v. Canada, (1938), 100–101, 142, 289 (n. 14)

Mitch, William, 98, 153

Mitchell, George, 52; as southern regional director, CIO-PAC, 173, 174

Mitchell, H. L., 64

Mitchell, Margaret, 34

Mitchell, Samuel Chiles, 72

Mitford, Jessica, 112

Monroe, Ga.: lynching in. *See* Lynching: in Monroe, Ga.

Moody, William: on Wallace's southern campaign, 252–53

Moon, Henry Lee, 33, 173; as southern field organizer, CIO-PAC, 195, 209, 217; on Osceola McKaine, 195–96; on black vote in Georgia, 212–13

Mooney, J. P., 184–85, 215, 265–66

Moore, Harry T., 275

Moore, Richard B., 80

Morgan, Irene, 194

Morgan v. Virginia (1946), 194

Morris, William, 211

Moton, Robert R., 50

Mount Olive Baptist Church (Knoxville), 255, 270

Murray, Pauli: on *Gaines* ruling, 100–101

Murray, Philip, 189, 230, 232, 233,

235, 236, 237, 251; announces CIO's southern drive, 207

Myrdal, Gunnar, 167, 168

Myrdal-Carnegie study, 91–92, 107

Nashville Agrarians: *I'll Take My Stand*, 37

National Association for the Advancement of Colored People (NAACP), 5, 15, 45, 49, 70, 100, 131; and legal campaign for equal education, 82–83, 91, 100–101, 142; Charles Houston and, 84, 86–91; and Scottsboro, 87, 88; attacks poll tax, 105–6; and NCAPT, 115; and white primary, 133, 147–49; growth of southern membership during World War II, 141–42

—branch activity: in Washington, D.C., 47; in Texas, 141; in Georgia, 141–42; in South Carolina, 142, 144–46; Ella Baker and, 142–43, 150

National Citizens Political Action Committee (NCPAC), 172, 173, 187; and postwar liberalism, 225, 226, 228, 233, 235, 236; and 1946 election, 234

National Committee for the Defense of Political Prisoners, 97

National Committee to Abolish the Poll Tax (NCAPT), 6, 115

National Emergency Civil Liberties Committee (NECLC), 274

National Emergency Council (NEC), 64, 66, 70

National Farmers Union (NFU), 115, 228

National Industrial Recovery Act (NIRA), 23, 43, 59; implementation of, 44–45, 50, 281 (n. 24); Section 7a of, 93–94

National Labor Relations Act (Wagner Act), 59, 61, 94

National Labor Relations Board (NLRB), 94, 95, 104

National Maritime Union, 251, 268

National Negro Congress (NNC), 115, 137, 150, 152, 153

National Park Service, 54

National Policy Committee, 63

National Progressive Voters League, 149, 251

National Recovery Administration (NRA), 23; minimum wage codes, 44–45, 49–52

National Resource Planning Board, 127

National Student League (NSL), 73, 78–82

National Urban League, 45, 48, 49

National Women's Association for the Preservation of the White Race, 159

National Youth Administration (NYA), 127, 281 (n. 28)

Nazi-Soviet Pact, 225, 230

Negro Industrial League (NIL), 46, 49

Negro Labor: A National Problem (Weaver), 135

Newman, Frances, 34

New Orleans, 21, 22

Niebuhr, Reinhold, 230

Nixon, Edgar Daniel, 150, 195

Nixon, H. C., 98

Nixon, Richard, 234

Norcross, Hiram, 57

Norfolk, Va., 201, 246

Norrell, Robert J., 278 (n. 13)

Norris, George: supports Geyer-Pepper bill, 118–19, 120; on FDR's retreat from New Deal, 123, 287 (n. 33); on 1944 Democratic convention, 186

North Carolina: repeal of poll tax, 107; SCHW committee for, 206–7, 242–43; Progressive Party in, 251, 253, 257; Wallace campaign tour of, 260–64, 268

North Carolina College for Negroes, 207

Odum, Howard, 64, 67, 98, 158; on southern "siege" mentality, 158, 164; and founding of SRC, 163, 166

155; and Truman's civil rights policy, 258–59

Rankin, John, 116, 117, 137, 218

Ranson, Leon, 74–75

Raper, Arthur, 2, 59, 163; and SCHW, 6, 67, 99, 163; addresses Interracial Council, Greenville, S.C., 144; and Highlander, 151

Rauh, Joseph, 233, 237

Rayburn, Sam, 114

Reconstruction, 13, 277–78 (n. 6); and traditions of freedom and citizenship, 14; and black responses to New Deal, 47, 48; and debate over Soldiers Vote bill, 130; and FEPC, 136; and white liberal defense of racial status quo, 163; Gunnar Myrdal refers to, 168; Osceola McKaine refers to, 190, 191

Reconstruction Finance Corporation, 108

Reddick, Lawrence D., 41

Redding, J. Saunders: on SRC and segregation, 166

Reid, Ira DeA.: on NIRA, 44–45; on NRA minimum wage codes, 45, 51–52; on racial discrimination in defense industries, 153; testifies at FEPC hearing, Birmingham, 157

Reitman, Al, 216

Report on the Economic Conditions of the South, The, 5, 63–67, 98, 249, 282 (n. 49); Palmer Weber on, 69–70; and founding meeting of SCHW, 99

Republican Party: Robert Weaver on, 47–48; congressmen join southern Democrats to cut spending, 104; gains in 1938 midterm election, 104; gains in 1940, 1942, 131; lily-whitism of, 143; and 1946 midterm elections, 233–34; 80th Congress, 237

Resettlement Administration, 1, 4, 58–59, 178; Photographic Section of, 58–59

Reston, James, 179

Reuther, Walter, 233, 237

Richmond, Va., 82, 95, 96, 249

Rivers, E. D., 211, 212

Roberts, Edith, 260, 261

Roberts, Thomas, 292 (n. 23)

Robeson, Paul, 153, 154, 274; campaigns for Wallace in Savannah, 253; and Progressive Party convention in Virginia, 254

Robinson, Byron "Pat," 61

Robinson, D. W., 147

Robinson, J. M., 149

Robinson, Joseph, 58

Rockefeller Foundation, 58

Rosenwald, Julius, 35

Rosenwald Fund, 35–36, 38, 58

Roosevelt, Eleanor, 5–6, 62, 97, 113; and Joe Gelders, 98; and SCHW, 99–100, 133, 189, 235; on segregation, 100; supports anti-poll-tax bill, 114–15; and Clark Foreman, 123–24, 287 (n. 34), 235; support for FSA, 129; and Highlander, 152; white southern attitudes toward, 158–61; on racial equality, 160, 161, 281 (n. 28); Jonathan Daniels on, 162; and Henry Wallace, 178–79, 180; on Truman, 223; and postwar liberalism, 233, 235–36

Roosevelt, Franklin D., 3, 4, 5–6, 7–8, 9, 233, 287 (n. 34); approach to government, 23–24, 41–42, 59–60; and 1936 election, 59–60; southern support for, 60–61; Supreme Court reform plan, 61; Gainesville, Ga., speech, 1938, 62; seeks Clark Foreman's advice on 1938 primary, 63–64; calls South "nation's number one economic problem," 65; "purge" effort, 65–66, 70; appeals to labor and black voters, 92–93; urges end to poll tax, 98; refuses to comment on Geyer-Pepper bill, 120; defends FSA loans for poll-tax payment, 128; supports Green-Lucas bill, 130;